Kay's Triumph

A Woman's Journey from Abandonment and Poverty to Model Parent and Hall of Fame Teacher

A Memoir
by
Peter C. White

Dedication

To Catherine Regina McCoy White;
Mom; teacher, and inspiration.
She was always there for my brothers,
sister and me. May others benefit from
the life she lived.

Acknowledgments

I thank my sister, Jeanne Callahan, for sharing stories from childhood and young adult years, and her husband, Kevin Callahan, for his technical knowledge and experience and his tireless attention to the details involved in printing and duplicating this work.

I extend my sincerest thanks to my brother, Dennis, who has been with me every step of the way on this project, for being available and spending countless hours on the phone, reading excerpts, checking facts, making suggestions, and most importantly, sharing his young life with me when we were "Kay White's boys."

About the Covers

The front and back covers are photos of Mom as an employee at Maggi Seasoning Company in New York City, late 1930's. The signature "Kay" is Mom's actual signature, taken from a Christmas card.

TABLE OF CONTENTS

Kay's Triumph

INTRODUCTION

This is the story of suffering and struggle, strength and wisdom, success and triumph. It is the story of a remarkable and powerful journey, the life journey of my Mom, Catherine "Kay" White.

Mom on her wedding day, January 10, 1942, with mother-in-law Mary Tighe White (l), Maid of Honor Ellen McCoy, bridesmaid Katherine McCoy (r).

Catherine Regina McCoy White (1917 – 1975), my first and most influential teacher, was born in Clarksburg, West Virginia on July 12, 1917. Her father, John McCoy, was an itinerant Irish bricklayer and her mother, Jane Paulson Timmerman McCoy, a laundress from the Danish Virgin Islands. Jane died in 1919 when Mom was just two years old. Then, as her father moved from job to job, young Catherine traveled with him to many parts of the United States and the Caribbean including the Panama Canal Zone. John died July 11, 1922 the day before Mom's fifth birthday leaving her a young orphan. Her two wonderful and generous unmarried aunts, Ellen McCoy and Katherine McCoy, adopted and raised her in the upper Manhattan neighborhood of Washington Heights. Though records indicate she had at least five and as many as seven half siblings, of whom she knew little, she grew up as an only child. Of two of her half-brothers, Mom said, *"They were 18-20 years older than I. It wasn't until I was 18 years old that I first met them. They decided to locate me and we spent several visits together, but then I never heard from them again. It was hard meeting someone for the first time and trying to fit them into your life."* Mom graduated from the School of the Incarnation in Manhattan in 1931 and All Saints Academy high school in 1935. She` attended Mount St. Vincent College in Riverdale, Bronx for two years and received a two-year degree in 1937, a time when few women attended college. She married Robert A. White in January 1942, one month after the attack on Pearl Harbor, and had four children, Robert (b. 1943), Peter (b.1947), Dennis (b. 1949) and Jeanne (b.1951). By late 1951, abandoned by her troubled husband, she began raising her four children alone without the benefit of any child support. Instead, she survived on a meager welfare allowance of less than $200 a month. While her name was on the deed to her unimproved Levitt house at 55 Twig Lane, Levittown, she could never sell it because Nassau County placed a lien on it. After her death in 1975, her house was sold and Nassau County got back every penny she received during the nine years she was a welfare recipient. This amounted to less than $19000. She became a Catholic school first grade teacher in 1960, never earning more than $6000 a year. Despite the scarcity of money in her life, she made sure her four children grew up healthy, educated, and with the proper values to take them through life. Despite her lifelong economic struggle, she somehow always found the time and the means to provide substantial help for others when she possibly could. She lived for 25 years in Levittown, NY, and she died in Levittown, within a mile of her house, in a tragic auto accident on June 21, 1975. More than a thousand people attended her funeral including family, friends, colleagues and former students.

PURPOSE

I recall a great many experiences from my childhood and teen years with my Mom in Levittown during the 1950's and 1960's. We were original Levittown settlers, moving from New York City into our first new house in September1950. Many childhood events and valuable lessons from Mom remain with me and have guided me all my life. These lessons aren't the kind teachers teach in class or the kind one learns from a book. They are profound, first-hand, life-changing lessons that I learned by watching Mom live her life, witnessing her uphill struggles, and being at her side as she groped to endure life's pains and hardships by herself, all the while managing to succeed in doing so much good for so many others. As a single mom of four, deserted by her husband, eking out a living on welfare and then on a very low paying job, I saw her manage her way through life's ups and downs and was amazed at her ability to overcome all obstacles and adapt to every situation. I admired her strength as she stood up for what was right, no matter what the personal consequences. I learned from Mom the willingness to persevere, to be loyal, to value family and religion, to overcome fear, to trust in others, and to be a community-minded activist. Her strong character and her strict moral code guided me and my siblings back then, and have become a beacon for us ever since. Long before Spike Lee coined the phrase "Do the Right Thing," Mom provided us, her four children, with that important message. She taught us early to distinguish between right and wrong, and insisted that we do that which was right. She was our Mom, our only parent. Moreover, she was our teacher, our strength, and our guiding light out of the poverty and the loneliness we faced as a family. This book is

During the Depression, Mom worked at Maggi Seasoning Company.

not a straightforward, chronological biography of Catherine White, who was often referred to as Kay, but a sharing of stories and recollections from the 1950's to the early 1970's, the quarter century I knew her. These childhood and early adulthood stories provided me with an important and proper direction as I grew up; they're stories I've tried to pass on to my children, my students and future generations. It is my great hope that family members and others will be guided by the wisdom, strength and greatness of Kay White.

STRUGGLE: THE EARLY YEARS

The Stores

Every ten minutes or so on this gray, blustery January afternoon, I dash out of the house with no coat on and run across the front lawn to the lamppost by the street. I look all the way down Twig Lane to see if she is coming. No, not yet. Quickly, back inside. I have a job to do – watch six-year-old Dennis and four-year-old Jeanne. Ten minutes later, I run back outside to check. Nothing yet. Then back in. Then out. Every ten minutes, checking to see if Mom is coming. I am eight years old and 45 minutes is an eternity to me. Still no sign of her. After sprinting to the lamppost then back in to check on the kids, I worry. Mom had to go buy groceries. When she left she said, *"Peter, You'll be ok. I'll be as quick as I can. Don't worry."* In my little eight-year-old mind, it seems like hours ago that she said that. "Where was she? She wouldn't stay away this long. The store isn't so far away. Why isn't she home yet? Maybe something bad happened. Maybe she isn't coming back." I look for the fourth time but the block is still empty. Not a soul in sight. Tears well up in my eyes. Then, finally, on my fifth trip to the lamppost, I spot an image way down the block. It is a gray-looking figure walking alone against the cold wind. Mom has a dark coat. Maybe it is she. The figure approaches and grows larger and larger until, at last, it reveals itself - a bundled up woman wearing a kerchief over her head, coat swirling in the January wind, pulling a shopping cart behind her. When this figure is about ten houses away, I calm down. It's Mom. She's almost home. We'll be safe. This responsibility is lifted from me. Thank God.

As children, there were times when Mom had to leave us alone. She didn't leave us for long periods of time, but once in a while, out of necessity, she had to do things that required us to sit still and follow her instructions while she stepped out, even if it was just to run across the street to ask a neighbor a question or borrow something. I'm sure that day back in 1955 Mom gave me very specific instructions, emphatically telling me that she'd only be 45 minutes, then leaving me in charge as she made her way to the stores on foot. With no car, Mom walked everywhere. I probably didn't pay attention to her instructions, so the ensuing panic was really my fault. In today's world, leaving kids alone, even for a brief moment, might be criticized, maybe even result in someone making a 911 call. But the 1950's were a much different time, and our family's needs were drastically different from those of most other families, those with fathers, cars and money. We grew up a little differently from other neighborhood kids because we had to.

Mom got home with the groceries, tired, cold and relieved to see us all intact. And we were ever so glad to see her. She didn't know about my worry or panic, only that I'd accomplished the mission she'd given me. *"Peter, you did a good job minding the house and kids while I was out. I'm proud of you."* The story of this shopping trip has remained with me for 60 years now. Many times as a young boy I was given the opportunity to undertake an important job, and, despite sometimes being frightened, I completed it and was rewarded with the pat on the back that all kids need. Knowing that my Mom trusted me and was proud of me for being responsible caused me to become self-reliant and trustworthy, something that has made a huge difference throughout my life.

Painting the House

For many families, suburbia is a great place for kids to grow up, a place to feel safe and have few worries except for how to be kids, how to do a back flip in the family pool, or field a grounder on a Little League field. Our suburban experience involved much more.

As children, Mom had great trust in us. She had to. Surrounded by four kids, there were few shoulders upon which she could lean. Orphaned by the age of four and an only child, Mom had no parents, sisters or brothers to call on for help. Her two elderly aunts, her adopted parents, Aunt Katherine and Aunt Nellie, lived in Manhattan and were unable to assist with the day-to-day struggles of running a household. As a result, we sometimes were asked, or assigned, to do things that caused us to grow up a bit quicker than our Levittown peers. My older brother, Robert, was the man of the house until the summer of 1957. Encouraged by a priest, at the age of 14 he went to a prep seminary in West Haverstraw, NY, where he remained for the next three years, visiting home only two weeks each summer. After living away for three years at the Don Bosco Juniorate, he returned home in 1960 and completed his senior year at Chaminade HS in Mineola. In the summer of 1961 he left for college in Honolulu and has been there ever since, more than half a century now. His travels left me man of the house at an early age. I had just completed 4th grade and was not yet ten years old when Robert entered the seminary. Proud as she was of Robert for his dedication and success, Mom began to rely more on Dennis, Jeanne and me to do things around the house. We had normal everyday chores like helping with the dishes, taking out the garbage, mowing the lawn and doing yard work. But some of the jobs we were assigned went beyond those routine tasks. Throughout the 1950's, our Levitt house remained its original small size, a basic Levitt, with no extensions or upgrades. The original faded, gray-colored, asbestos shingles covered the outside. Since all the other families in the neighborhood had fathers with jobs, they could afford to paint their houses, or have them aluminum sided. Those with more money enclosed their open carports and made them into garages, squared off their kitchens by eliminating the small vestibule, making their kitchens much larger, and even added extensions on to their basic Levitt dwellings, giving their families much larger living rooms, dens and upstairs dormered bedrooms. Ours was still the original Levitt, with two small bedrooms downstairs, and an unfinished, unheated attic space we called the "cold room," which served as the bedroom for Dennis and me. By 1961 Mom wanted the house to be white with nicely painted trim and shutters. With no money to hire a professional painter, a job that would have cost hundreds of dollars in those days, we set out as a family to do it ourselves. *"Peter, I want you to go over and speak with Mr. Kaiser or Mr. Schley and find out how to get started."* Going to these men was not an unusual occurrence for me. Long before the television show "This Old House," Pete Kaiser and Charlie Schley were the Bob Vilas of the block. Whenever I needed advice or to borrow a tool, they were my first stop. "Hi Mr. Kaiser, I have a few questions. We're about to paint out house. What's primer? Should we use latex or oil based paint? Brushes or rollers? And oh, one more thing, can I borrow your ladder?" Mom was a great believer in letting others know, however subtly, when she needed help, then allowing them to offer it if they were so inclined, which these neighbors always were. Mr. Kaiser and Mr. Schley lived right across the street. Both of these go-to men knew and understood Mom's plight and were very kind. After being dispatched across the street to ask for helpful hints and tips on house painting and borrowing what I could, my brother Dennis, age 11, and I, 13, got started. It was fun at first, and Dennis and I had no problem putting on the paint. Mom was the supervisor who often reminded us, *"Just keep your brushes moving as fast as you move your mouths and you'll be done in no time."* I'm sure we talked and kidded around a lot while we worked. Mom's sense of humor sometimes contained a bit of sarcasm, but we took it well. As we made progress, neighbors would slow down as they drove by, observing two boys doing an adult's job. They'd roll down their window and shout, "Nice job Kay. The house looks great!" Dennis and I would swell up inside at such comments. They were an important pat on the back for us. We were proud to be Kay White's boys, doing man-of-the-house work at a young age and getting recognized for it. Beyond mere recognition, something else stirred within me whenever passersby honked their horns and shouted their praise. Though it was hard to put my finger on it at the time, up until early adolescence something had always been missing inside me. Being trusted by Mom to do important jobs, actually doing those jobs, and being recognized for doing them, filled a big part of what was missing. Other neighborhood kids would run home from play to greet their fathers as they returned from work. Some of those dads would say to their kids, "Come on. Get in the car. We're going bluefishing." Others would have a catch with their kids on the front lawn, or build a snow fort with their kids, or say, "Nice hit, son" after attending their boy's little league game. The absence of a man in our lives created an inner wound. But the process of healing that wound began with Mom's trust and faith in us. By giving us those adult jobs, Mom elevated us a few ranks, to a position that kids who could field a grounder better or reel in a fish might never know. Mom's trust and the sound of those honks went a long way toward that healing.

The actual job of putting on the paint was not really difficult for us. The real problem came when the painting task got over our heads, literally. When we could reach no higher, we'd stand on chairs to extend our reach. Then we'd add thick telephone books on top of the chairs to reach higher still. When we could reach no farther, it was time to employ Mr. Kaiser's ladder. I had no problem going up the first few steps, except for having to be extra careful not to spill the precious paint. But when I had to go to the top rungs of the ladder, near the peak of the house, things got shaky. Little by little we managed, grew into the task, and the house began to look pretty good. We'd paint row after row of shingles, developing a style that both of us have kept throughout our lives, … runs of paint straight across, or up and down, square boxes of paint that we'd fill in, boxes with a big X in the middle, always mindful of making the precious paint spread as far as possible because…the almighty dollar was almighty and there could be no waste. When I got within two feet of the peak, I didn't think I could reach the very highest shingles. Either the ladder wasn't tall enough, or I was too short. Standing only a few rungs from the top, in what seemed to be the stratosphere, I told myself, "Don't look down." It was a long way. Mom stood at the bottom, holding the ladder, watching carefully as I reached from one of the highest rungs. But I still couldn't reach those top two feet. Then she said, *"Peter, you can do it. Just one more step up and you'll be there."* Trembling a little, I slowly took that one more step, made the reach, got the white paint to cover those top two gray shingles, and the job was done.

For most dads in the neighborhood, painting a Levitt house was not much more than a household chore, something on a to-do list. But to boys 11 and 13, it was an enormous job. With only limited painting experience, without any Home Depot or internet to log onto, and without any fatherly guidance, we made our house look as good as or better than most of the other houses in the neighborhood. Of course we weren't paid for our efforts. We never received an allowance or any quid pro quo for our work. Our reward came in other ways. We learned lessons that have lasted us a lifetime, that we were capable of performing big jobs, jobs that caused us to exude a newfound sense of confidence. And we got something that was even more important: a smile and pat on the back from Mom and the neighbors. We didn't do work around the house because we felt sorry for Mom. We worked because we were part of a whole, surviving, keeping our family's head above water. As kids, we knew that there were certain things Mom could do, and that there were other things that would not get done unless we did them.

I remember so often hearing neighborhood kids say, "I got to get home now. The men are coming. The men are coming." They'd get so excited whenever something was happening to their house or property, and "the men" were doing it. Suburbia had its constant parade of men. There were pool men, lawn men, carpet men, oil burner men, TV repairmen, all sorts of men. For the most part we, the sons of Kay White, were the men.

Freshly painted 55 Twig Lane.

Big jobs like painting the house never seemed like work to us. We wanted those jobs, those opportunities to come up big, especially in Mom's eyes, and in the eyes of passers-by. I don't know whether or not it was part of her plan, but it worked. After painting the house, building a fence, or doing any of the other adult jobs required of us, we gained something few suburban schools and teams could teach: a powerful sense of self-confidence and self-reliance and the ability to adapt and overcome most obstacles.

The New White Family

As a three-year-old in September 1950 I sat on the ground outside our new Levitt house, watching the big road graders level the dirt that would soon be Twig Lane. I watched the cement sidewalks and curbs being added too. A black 1940's sedan, with cushiony seats, a big round steering wheel and running boards under the doors stood parked out front on the still-dirt street. It was our family car, for a while. By the end of our first year in Levittown, America's first huge, mass-produced suburban community, that car no longer existed. My father, Robert A. White, intoxicated and with insufficient insurance, had a collision with it, leaving him to continue making payments on a car he no longer had.

Mom was furious. In addition to Robert A. White's drinking, he had some serious emotional and psychological problems, causing him to do unpredictable, even radical things. Mom, who never spoke ill of Robert A. White, told us years later that he once left home for nearly a week, stayed in an expensive hotel, ordered room service for himself, drank excessively, didn't show up for his job, then finally came home in a taxicab. As bad as not knowing his whereabouts for a week, the big surprise came the next morning when Mom saw the cab still parked in front of the house. The driver had sold it to Robert A. White for $200 in cash and taken off with the money. Of course the cab had to go back to the taxicab company, and Mom and the family were out $200. Events like this, and worse, like falling down the stairs with a child in his arms, or leaving Robert at a cub scout meeting and forgetting to pick him up, caused Mom to come to an important decision, one that she deemed necessary even though it would alter our lives forever. After several unsuccessful attempts to get him to change his behavior, and after speaking with her parish pastor, Mom decided that there was too much risk having him around four young children. He either had to make substantial changes, or he could no longer live with us. Robert A. White steamed off, never to be seen again. My brother Robert was eight years old; I was four, Dennis 2, and Jeanne just six months. This was a terrible time for Mom, a strict Catholic woman having to decide the fate of her family. But after a great deal of consultation, reflection, and prayer, she decided that a broken family was better than one in danger. Robert A. White had thrown objects, fallen down stairs, lost job after job, not woken up for days on end, and worse. Today a man like that might be guided, or ordered by a judge, into counseling, be prescribed medication, and have other avenues of help available. But in the early 1950's, that wasn't the case. With divorce reform legislation in New York more than a decade away, people basically took their spouses for better or worse, and most often stayed married despite separation. For Mom the issue was not so much whether she should stay married to Robert A. White, but whether, given his conduct, he could continue living with her and four small children.

As result of these circumstances, in January 1952, we were fatherless. Too young to know what was really going on, or what our future would hold, we kids eventually came to realize a few important things from all this: Mom stuck by us, worked tirelessly for us, fought for us, and gave us her best effort. Neither Robert A. White nor any members of his family did any of those things. We never saw him or any members of his family throughout our entire childhoods. None of us ever received a birthday card, Christmas card, letter, phone call, or gift of any sort from Robert A. White, his brothers, sister or mother. Broke and without any means of support, Mom took the bold step of going it alone. Her solo journey was made all the more difficult because we were the only family in our neighborhood, a place with little dependable, reliable mass transportation, without a car. Mom had no means to get herself or the four of us anywhere.

The Transportation Struggle

Life for the five of us was sometimes pretty hard, especially for Mom. With no man and no money, everything was a struggle. Besides the absence of any income, the most difficult part of this struggle was our complete and total lack of any means of transportation. Whatever we had to do, we did without a car from 1951 until 1965, when Mom finally got her first used car, a gift from her generous and kind Aunt Katherine. No matter what task, job, errand, chore or undertaking, big or small, from grocery shopping, doctors, dentists, church, emergencies, meetings, appointments, sports, jobs, paper routes, everything, for those fifteen years we had two basic struggles: figuring out where we had to go, then figuring out how we were going to get there. It was as if each of us had a giant iron ball chained to his leg, impeding our ability to get most anywhere and adding hours to the simplest of tasks. Yet, by watching Mom's perseverance, determination, willpower and grit, we learned to be self-reliant and find our way.

Mineola

In January 1952, the new, five-member White Family was jobless, penniless and car-less. And we couldn't have been poorer. When you have nothing, how could you be? A Nassau County Family Court judge ordered Robert A. White to pay a modest child support sum of $35 a week. Whether he was unable to pay, or unwilling, I don't know, but Mom received nothing from him after the first few months of separation. When Robert A. White failed to show for several court appearances, the judge urged Mom to seek help from the county's Department of Social Services (DSS), or welfare, for whatever type of assistance might be available. Mom faced a very difficult challenge: providing us with the basics like food, clothing, shelter and health care with no money and no other adult to help her or even consult with. On top of that, she faced the problem of carrying out that heavy task with absolutely no means of transportation other than her own two legs. Following the judge's advice, Mom decided to apply for whatever type of assistance might be available. She had to meet with welfare workers in Mineola, five miles east of our house. This brought about other problems: how was she going to get to Mineola with four kids, no funds for a babysitter, no real knowledge or experience with Long Island's towns and roadways, and no car?

Mom, who mastered the art of adapting to every situation, managed to get herself to important DSS appointments in Mineola. To do so, she either had eight-year-old Robert watch us while she ventured out to these appointments, or asked a neighborhood mom to look in on us every once in a while. Once she felt secure knowing we would be ok and exactly where in Mineola the DSS offices were located, she'd use whatever money she had for taxicab fare. When she didn't have cab fare, she'd walk the half mile from our house to the bus stop on Newbridge Road, wait for the bus, pay the 15 cent fare and take the bus north to Hicksville where she'd wait again for another bus west to Mineola. Once in Mineola, she'd walk from the downtown bus stop, past all the courthouses and other government office buildings, before finally reaching DSS headquarters. After enduring this rigmarole for weeks, she finally succeeded in obtaining from DSS the modest monthly sum of $180 a month. This sum, called aid to families with dependent children, was her only benefit. She did not receive food stamps. They weren't available until 1964, four years after she began working. Ninety dollars of this AFDC sum was due to the Bowery Savings Bank each month to pay the mortgage, and another portion had to be saved for the real estate taxes due on the house every six months. This left her less than

$60 a month to feed and clothe the five of us, to purchase the things necessary to run a house, like heating oil, groceries, shoes and doctors.

The Beach

Transportation to anywhere for us during those first few years, when we were so very young, usually involved a lot of walking, taking occasional taxicab rides, or being picked up by a neighbor from time to time when they'd see us walking, especially when it was raining. But there were certain trips that were absolutely out of the question, like going to Jones Beach State Park, only ten miles south of our house. Robert Moses had built his magnificent system of New York State Parks, all connected by curvaceous, tree-lined parkways, with the automobile almost exclusively in mind. The Powerbroker, a comprehensive biography of Robert Moses, describes in detail how fascinated he was by the newly mass-produced automobile, so much so that he built his great parks like Sunken Meadow, Jones Beach, and dozens of others, to be accessible only by car. He constructed seven state parks along the Taconic State Parkway from New York City all the way to Albany, so that only car-owning urban families could be carried out of New York City to enjoy them. For car-owning families in the new and growing Long Island suburbs, he built Jones Beach and other parks. For the mostly non-white urban masses, Moses built dozens of large swimming pools, for those poorer people confined to the city. Jones Beach was only 15 minutes from our house, yet it may as well have been a thousand miles away because it was totally unavailable to us. At times it was more than a little saddening, and it did create little clouds of inferiority within us when we'd see neighboring kids readying themselves for a trip to Jones Beach. From my upstairs window I'd sometimes see them help their parents load up their family cars with beach chairs, toys, suntan lotion and picnic baskets, while I sat by and watched. Once in a while an unthinking or unkind child would say something snotty like, "We're going to the beach, and you can't come." Of course kids do say things like that sometimes, but we became toughened by such remarks and survived being excluded from those beach outings in our own way. With a lawn sprinkler to run under, we found ways to cool off long before air-conditioning came along. And Levittown's builder, William Levitt, provided nine large swimming pools for the children of his new suburban experiment. Though every family in the neighborhood could be issued a "pool tag" every summer, for us there was a barrier. In order to get into the Levittown pool, a child had to be at least ten years old unless accompanied by an adult. Until we turned ten, a visit to the pool could only happen if Mom took the long hot walk to the West Village Green pool, across Newbridge Road, lugging bags with towels, lunch and other things. She did this when she could, but otherwise we stayed home and figured out our own ways to beat the July and August heat, until we turned ten that is. Mom was aware that other kids had more opportunities than we, but she always tried to get us to see the bright side of things. We'd find great joy in running through the cool oscillating waves of the sprinkler, or sitting in the shade of our breezy, slate and dirt floor carport playing games like initial tag and running bases.

I recall one exception to the general rule that Jones Beach was unavailable to us. When I was a little boy one of my playmates was Louise Schwartz. She lived across the street. Her parents, Stanley and Dinah Schwartz, were very nice people. The day before I was to start first grade, Labor Day 1953, Mr. Schwartz called Mom and said, "We're taking the kids to the beach. Would Peter like to come along?" I needed no coaxing. I was six years old and had never been to Jones Beach before. The Schwartz's had an early 1950's light blue car. It was plenty roomy and Louise's parents, sister Barbara, Louise and I all fit fine. We headed up Twig Lane, then turned south on Newbridge Road toward Hempstead Turnpike and the Wantagh State Parkway. No more than a mile from Twig Lane, Newbridge crosses over the Wantagh. As we drove over the parkway below, I looked out the window, stretching my neck as far as I could to see what was below, but I saw nothing. I was too short. I thought that maybe the ocean was beneath us, that we were at the beach already. Little did I know then that 22 years later, at that particular spot, an event would take place that would alter my life forever. I had a glorious day at the beach, playing in the sand and the waves, sharing their picnic lunch, feeling free. I came home exhausted and, especially since I was beginning first grade the next day, went to bed early with only thoughts of the beach on my mind. I had such a happy time. That night I dreamt about my great day at the beach with the Schwartz's, the sun, the waves, the ocean's roar, the freedom I felt there. It must have been a vivid dream because next morning when Mom woke me up, I thought I was still there. I couldn't believe I had to put on my St. Ignatius uniform for the first time and go to school. But I'd had my first and most memorable Jones Beach experience thanks to the kindness of our neighbors, the Schwartz's.

Biking

Once we were old enough to ride a two-wheel bike, we became the White Family transportation system. As a young child I was given the job of finding out where certain destinations were, which were the easiest and safest routes to get there, and which means of transportation, walking, bus, hitchhiking or biking, was best. Since the family had to eat, grocery shopping was always an important errand. As a six or seven year old kid, Mom would give me a short shopping list and a small sum of money, $3 or so, and dispatch me to the supermarket on foot. Until 1954 or so, we shopped at the Sunrise Supermarket, about three quarters of a mile away, and across busy Newbridge Road. When Mom couldn't perform the shopping task, Robert, as oldest, did so. By the time I was old enough to join the shopping force, a new supermarket opened called the Grand Union, which was only 4/10th of a mile away, and it was on our side of Newbridge Road, making it a much safer errand. At first, I took this as a huge responsibility, like a young man on an important mission. As the years went by and we were able to ride two-wheel bikes, the shopping task became quicker, but still a huge chore. Kids in the neighborhood rode bikes for fun. We biked because we had to. Consequently, biking became less and less fun, especially when riding in winter against the wind.

The shopping list Mom provided contained items that could be carried the nearly half-mile by one of us. Each of us had this job growing up. Robert had a nice green Schwinn, something he was very proud of since he saved up for it with money he'd earned from the sweat of his own brow, the proceeds from his Long Island Press paper route. When I was eight years old, I was the beneficiary of a red bike from Santa. "Santa" was undoubtedly Aunt Katherine. I'm certain that there was a great deal of contemplation and discussion between Mom and Aunt Katherine over this gift, wrestling with the question, *"How can we get Peter a bike and not the others?"* Since Robert was older, had a paper route and earned enough to get his own bike, they decided that I was next oldest, so it was my turn. Once things changed, Robert would move on, I'd inherit his green Schwinn, Dennis would fall heir to my red bike, and Jeanne would wait. The system of hand-me-downs was alive and well and at work in the White Family. We understood it, and we learned to patiently wait our turn. I really wanted Robert's 26-inch green Schwinn, the one that had two gears. I finally received it when he became a seminarian and rode it everywhere until more than half way through high school when it got stolen. Well, maybe I carelessly left it out one night and someone seized the opportunity. I heard about that mistake for years, and learned an important lesson the hard way.

Whether we walked or rode a bike, it didn't matter. We became the shopping force in the family and actually enjoyed it to some extent. Like painting the house, we were children doing the things that adults usually did. Long before unit pricing came into the economy, we were trained to look at prices and figure out whether the larger family size box of cereal was a better buy than two of the smaller sizes. We had to know which items were in which aisles. We had to handle money, check the change, get receipts, bag things properly, then lug everything home. When we'd return, there would be a review of some type. Mom would look over the groceries and check them against the list. She required us to buy the cheaper, generic Grand Union brand items, Freshpack, rather than the more expensive name brands. Every penny counted. If the grocery receipt totaled $2.97 and Mom had given me $3, she'd ask, *"Where's the 3 cents?"* With our family on an impossibly tight budget, there was little leeway for spending her 3 cents change on a piece of candy or bubble gum.

Sometimes we'd make a mistake while on these grocery shopping missions. Usually they were innocent and not very serious, and they often led to some good family laughter. When Dennis was old enough to be part of the family shopping team, he was called on by Mom to go to the Grand Union. It would be his first shopping trip alone and he was to buy one item, a box of detergent. Mom gave him a few dollars and a see-through nylon shopping bag and sent him on his way. He looked quite happy as he biked down Twig Lane with the bag strapped to the handlebars. Seven-year-old Dennis entered Grand Union supermarket, made his way right to the soap aisle, found the right detergent, and exited the store. En route home from his very first solo shopping trip, he beamed as he rode down Twig Lane with his precious cargo. We watched as he proudly handed Mom the bag through which we could all see the big letters "Tide," and…all the money she had sent him with. Mom questioned why he still had all the money. Dennis explained how he found the Tide, put it into the nylon bag, then walked out the door and biked home. Evidently neither Mom nor anyone else ever told Dennis that he had to pay for things before leaving. After a good family laugh, Mom immediately sent Dennis back to the store with the money to square things away with our friendly, hard-working neighbor, grocery clerk Mrs. Dianne Frazetta. Surveys show that a majority of Americans who obtain an item they didn't pay for usually just keep the item and forget the matter. Penniless as she was, honest Kay White immediately sent her young son back to the store to make sure the right thing was done.

Walking or biking to and from the stores wasn't too bad, except for the wind. As every kid who has ever had to ride a bike any distance on a cold winter day knows, riding against the wind is the worst. A cold wind seemed to make a short trip take forever, like we'd never get home with our bundle, or our 3 cents. But when we finally got home with our mission accomplished, we were always praised and rewarded with a positive comment from Mom. *"Good job. I knew you could do it."*

The School Bus

Walking and biking became a way of life for us. All the kids in Levittown back then did a substantial amount of both, but there was a difference. The other kids walked and biked for play, we did so out of necessity. When it was time to run errands or do most anything away from the house, there was no other choice. There were certain places we struggled to get to on a regular basis, like church and school for example. School was usually easy since we had school bus service from our neighborhood in Levittown to St. Ignatius School, two miles away. But even with bus transportation, problems arose. There were times when one of us missed the bus. When that happened, we knew how to take the municipal bus up Newbridge Road into Hicksville and find the school from there. One time I missed the bus and it was my fault. I "dillydallied," according to Mom, and took too long getting ready. I thought I might get fifteen cents bus fare from Mom, but no. Instead she was quite clear, *"Peter, just put one foot in front of the other, then the next, and so forth, repeating that until you get there."* Two miles later, I arrived at school tired, late and the beneficiary of a valuable lesson learned.

As a teacher for 38 years, from 1970-2008, I've seen many things change in the way kids are transported to and from school. In our day, suburban kids walked or took school buses; city kids walked or took subways. They had to learn some level of self-reliance, how to be on time, how to read a bus schedule or a subway map. At the very least, they had to know which bus or subway to even take. Today I see parents drive their children to the bus stop, even though it may be only one or two blocks from their house, or they simply avoid the bus completely and drive their children all the way to school, especially if the weather is the slightest bit inclement. I believe we learned a great deal just from the way we had to get to and from school back then. Today kids learn very little from being so umbilically attached to their parent's shuttle service. They don't have to make many decisions; their parents do that for them. They don't have to develop a sense of direction, or figure out an approach to problems, like how to deal with encountering strangers, or what to do when a road is closed, or how to adapt when their subway line is not running. Many kids today, at least suburban kids, figure it's better to take the ride to school in their mom's fully equipped SUV, than it is to walk to the corner, sometimes in the rain, or snow or cold, wait for the bus, then take the ride with the other children, schlepping all over the neighborhoods until the bus reaches the school. Perhaps there are bullies on the bus, who make the ride that much more uncomfortable. There were several on my bus. Perhaps there are cliques, kids who choose their favorite friends to sit with, leaving others out. Many kids today take the easy way out and avoid these problems by getting driven to school. Sadly, these Navigator Children miss the opportunity to learn some simple but essential lessons by having to figure things out for themselves. They don't have to face the consequences that result from missing a bus, or fending for themselves when facing a bully, or when cliquish kids exclude them. They aren't given the opportunity to learn important lessons from enduring bad weather, or garnering lessons in patience when a bus is late or breaks down. In certain communities, especially if a child is a special education student, the school district requires even less self-reliance. If a child misses the bus, the school sends another one. With so many hardships removed from kids, it seems more and more difficult to provide them opportunities to build character and self-confidence and grow their self-esteem. It was quite different for us in the 1950's and 1960's. During my 38 year teaching career I frequently heard kids phone home with that famous suburban cry, "Mom, pick me up." That was never an option for us in Kay White's car-less family.

One final point that can be learned from the transportation struggles described here is worth mention. As a teacher I have seen the following happen thousands of times: A child is late for school, not because he's sick or there is an extraordinary circumstance. He is late to school because he stayed up late, not doing homework, but spending excessive amounts of after-hours time on his cell phone, texting with friends, face-booking, plugged into his IPOD, watching the TV in his room, and playing his videogames. When morning rolls around, he simply can't get up because he's only had half a night's sleep. So he misses the bus and gets to school several hours late via his mom's shuttle service. Of course, the school undoubtedly has some type of standard for admitting a child to school late, a parental note at the very least. The child's mom or dad knows they can't tell the truth. They can't say, "Please excuse Johnny for being three hours late to school, he stayed up far too late playing games." So instead they write the school attendance office something different, like "Please excuse Johnny for being three hours late, he had a headache and I decided it was best if he rested a bit longer." Of course such a note is a complete fiction, a lie. It goes without saying, no such notes were ever written by Kay White. If we were late, we had the task of telling the school officials the truth, and, whether a reprimand or a detention was issued, we learned that there were consequences to our conduct. There were no freebies, no fabricated stories and no lies in our White House. Just learning important life lessons from our own conduct.

CYO Day Camp

During the summer of 1954, right after I completed first grade and Robert the fifth grade, Mom found a way to send the two of us to CYO Day Camp in Wyandanch, NY. I was six years old and Robert eleven. I don't know how Mom was able to enroll us, as there must have been some fees involved. Perhaps we were scholarship campers, or some type of benefactor was involved. The camp was not a sleep-away camp, but a day camp. Mom thought this would be a good experience for us, and with Robert and me out of the house, it would also leave her with only two small children to tend to for a few weeks, Dennis, age four, and Jeanne, age two. As with every other activity that took place outside the house, getting us there was always a problem. But Mom devised ways of dealing with this. The bus to CYO Day Camp left from the brand new Holy Family Church early every morning. Mom had to trust that we two young boys could complete the one mile ride each way every day, leaving at a very early hour. Then there was the problem of what to do with our bikes while we were in faraway Wyandanch all day long. She made arrangements with a woman who lived across the street from the church to store our bikes in her back yard while we took the daily, seemingly never-ending bus ride to distant Suffolk County. I was in the youngest group, the Apaches. Robert was with a group of older kids, the Cherokees. The Apaches did simple things like play tag and do arts and crafts. The Cherokees got to go out more and do better things. I remember being given what appeared to be warm Kool Aid, which many of the kids referred to as "bug juice." Maybe that's because the colorful liquid was poured into cups and allowed to sit out for some time, attracting bugs, before it was served to us. I did learn a few other things at that camp, partly because the bus picked up other campers who came from many different neighborhoods south and east of Levittown, all the way to Wyandanch. This was my first multi-cultural, multi-racial experience in life. Perhaps Mom wanted that for us too. I can't say that this CYO Day Camp experience, to such a distant place, which involved so much effort to get to, and left us so hot and exhausted every day, was fun, but Robert and I did appreciate the fact that Mom tried her best to get us to a camp, just like other kids.

Altar Boys

We were a Catholic family, and religion was a very important part of our lives. Beginning in 1952, when Mom first became a single parent of four with no income, she was quite troubled by just how she was going to succeed. After consulting with her parish priests and being guided by their counsel, Mom and the pastor decided on a special ceremony, to be performed at the church whereby we, her four children, were dedicated to the Blessed Mother, Mary. With no money, no spouse, no brother, sister, parent or other adult to help her, Mom sought aid from heavenly hands, then worked hard and hoped for the best. She had us all attend Catholic elementary schools, and of course attend mass on Sundays and Holy Days of obligation. Some of those days, like All Saints Day on November 1, were easy to understand. After all we were honoring all the saints. There were other holy days, like December 8, the Feast of the Immaculate Conception, and January 1, the Feast of the Circumcision, which we didn't really know too much about. We went to church anyway because we had to. When Robert became of sufficient age, he became an altar boy. A few years later, I became one too. Mom was quite proud to see us on the altar on Sundays, serving mass, ringing the bells, assisting the priest, and looking angelic in our black and white cassocks. But it wasn't all show for us. There were demands placed on us, like altar boy meetings every Saturday, run by the brilliant but strict Father Buckley, head of the altar boy society. One dare not behave out of line at an altar boy meeting, or complain about the schedule of masses for the week, including funeral masses, weekday masses, and other intrusions into the lives of kids with paper routes and homework. We were altar boys and we did what we were told. The last thing we possibly could have wanted was to have Father Buckley call Mom and tell her that we misbehaved. Mass in those days was conducted in Latin, so we did a lot of memorizing, struggling to remember the words to the "Confiteor Deo Omnipotenti" ("I confess to Almighty God...") and the "Suscipiat" ("May the Lord accept this sacrifice..."). Years later I learned that memorization was the lowest level of learning. Consequently, we didn't learn much from the Latin mass, but we did memorize and act in a way that was pleasing to Father Buckley, Mom, and God, who, we were taught, was always watching.

There was one part of being an altar boy that had little to do with the church or mass, but was very important: the grueling and tiring task of getting to Holy Family Church when we had to. In February 1959, while a sixth grader, I was assigned by Father Buckley to serve the 6:30 a.m. mass, all week, Monday through Saturday. That meant waking up at 5:30 a.m., getting ready quickly, bundling up, and riding my bike the mile or so to the church in the dark. Since Newbridge was a busy road, Mom required me to take the long way, walking my bike across Newbridge at the light at Levittown Parkway, weaving my way around a large potato field, now Holy Trinity High School, through several suburban side streets, turning the usual one mile journey into a 1.5 mile, frozen, Zhivago-like expedition. Often the streets would be icy, and the winds relentless. But I got there, frozen and, figuratively speaking, made to feel the sting of Father Buckley's lash on those occasions when I was late. One stern look from Father was enough to let me know when he wasn't pleased. Not only did we learn lessons in self-reliance and overcoming what seemed to an infinite number of problems from those altar boy experiences, we learned early lessons in injustice. While I had to make the trek alone by bike over the streets of Levittown and Hicksville, most other altar boys had their moms or dads drive them to the back of the church, right to the sacristy door. They'd get up later than I and get driven in their heated cars, while I biked my way. They'd arrive earlier than I, in time to prepare the cruets with the wine and water, and perform other priest-pleasing tasks, and not have to deal with the darkness, the cold or the danger. They'd get a pat on the back from the good father, while I'd be the recipient of a sullen, nasty stare. I stayed with the altar boys for three years and by the end of seventh grade I stepped down. Enough was enough. Most of my memories of being an altar boy are ones of struggle, anxiety and dread, but there were two positive things I'll never forget. I always felt good serving Sunday mass. The church was always crowded, Mom was in attendance, and she and our neighbors could see me participating as a young boy, serving God, church and family. The other benefit that came from being an altar boy was the annual altar boy outing to Playland, an amusement park in Rye Beach, NY. That was something I would never have been able to do were it not for the altar boys, have a day of fun on the rides. Those three trips to Rye Beach, where I rode the roller coaster and the Wild Mouse, were the only days during my career on the altar that I smiled.

Haverstraw

The word Haverstraw conjures up several notions within me: family, religion, high school boys in black suits, Hudson River views, farm animals, ice skating, picnics, anxiety and fatigue, just to name a few. Triple that for Kay White. As a ninth grader in 1957 my older brother Robert entered a prep seminary in West Haverstraw, New York. He'd been encouraged to seek a vocation in the priesthood by a Salesian Father who visited our elementary school, St. Ignatius Loyola in Hicksville. But for two weeks each summer to visit the family back home, Robert spent three years at the Don Bosco Juniorate in West Haverstraw, NY, from the summer of 1957 to the summer of 1960. After three years of dedication and hard work, he decided against the priesthood and returned home. While he was a seminarian, Mom and the three of us children visited Robert in West Haverstraw as frequently as we could. For families with a car, the trip from Long Island to West Haverstraw was a pleasant 90-minute drive, a getaway across the Tappan Zee Bridge, through the hills and mountains of Rockland County to reach the majestic Hudson River vistas north of the city. For our car-less family, getting to see Robert on visiting Sundays was an adventure, almost always accompanied by some level of struggle. Sometimes the trip worked out without a hitch. Other times it was as if Mercury was in retrograde, and whatever possibly could go wrong did. Preparation for the trip began on Saturday with shopping and packing up several bundles of things we'd need for a picnic up there. On Sunday morning we rise early and get dressed, usually in what we'd call our "good clothes," and Mom would call a cab. Taking a taxi was an expensive and rare option for us, but every now and then it was necessary to get to the Hicksville train station on time to catch the Long Island Rail Road to Penn Station. Cab drivers were sometimes late in picking us up, putting even more stress on our hectic schedule. If we missed the train due to a late taxi, then all aspects of the visit would be delayed, including missing mass at the Catholic church next to Penn Station, an absolute no-no for Mom. Mom would sometimes have to stand up to cab drivers who, after picking up the four of us, got orders from their dispatcher to pick up other passengers along the way. Mom would say, "We have to be on that 7:30 train, you've got to take us there now." We'd watch nervously as she'd argue about such issues. The most frequent clashes she'd have with cab drivers were about price. Money was always a major concern and every cent counted. Once a cab driver picked up his walkie-talkie and said to his dispatcher, to Mom's displeasure, "I got two longs and two shorts from Levittown to Hicksville train station." meaning two adults and two children. The driver was including me, a nine-year-old, as an adult for pricing the cab ride. Mom fired back *That's one long and three shorts,"* for a slightly cheaper fare. We'd watch silently as "Mom versus the cab driver" played out. Mom usually won.

Once we got to Penn Station, the dash was on. Across W. 31st Street we'd traipse, bundles and all, to mass at St. John's Church. Upon hearing the words, "Ita missa est," or "The mass is ended," we'd sprint to the 8th Avenue subway at 34th Street and take the A train to 175th Street. A subway ride in 1957 for children older than five was fifteen cents. To save that precious sum, I sometimes ducked under the turnstile to save Mom a token. We'd take the A-train beneath Manhattan's west side and Harlem and arrive at the Port Authority Bus Terminal at 178th St., then board a bus to Haverstraw in Rockland County. Once there, we'd take another cab to the seminary in West Haverstraw, always from Anderson's Cab Company. Mr. Anderson, the sole proprietor, was a friendly man who reminded me of the actor Ward Bond. He seemed to like taking us to the seminary. Mom would smile nicely at him and thank him over and over. Mr. Anderson would smile back and usually modify the price downward. It was always good to see Mom get a break.

 Upon arriving at the Don Bosco Juniorate we'd see the families of all the other seminarians. They'd get up later than we, cruise in their cars directly up to the seminary, and arrive earlier. Such was life for a car-less family from suburbia that had to get somewhere far away. Once at the seminary we really did enjoy our time, especially seeing Robert, whom we missed greatly. We also liked seeing Mom smile and laugh with the other parents. A day at Haverstraw was like a day in the country for Mom, with beautiful woods in the warmer months and colorful foliage in fall. During winter visits, we sometimes skated or played on the frozen pond on the seminary grounds. Of course that meant lugging ice skates, another burden. On every visit, we'd walk as a family about a mile or so, from the school and dormitory areas, to a working farm area where there was a barn with cows and horses. We three young suburban children actually got to have an interesting agricultural experience, complete with petting animals and riding a horse. While at the seminary area, we loved having Robert show us around his dormitory. Even though he was still only a high school teenager himself, we saw ourselves as kids and Robert as a young man. He had his own locker with his personal belongings, including a razor and other things men have. His fellow seminarians, guys like Ray Xifo and Bob McCready, whom Robert seemed to laugh and get along well with, were young men in our eyes as well. Maybe it was the dark suits and ties they all had to wear as part of their strict dress code that made them look older. Robert introduced us to some of his instructors, priests like Father Cappaletti, better known as "Father Capp." As a young man without a dad, Robert had someone to call "Father." We attended elementary schools with all-female staff members, mostly nuns. So meeting men like Father Capp was very important for us too. In fact, Dennis and I used to stare whenever any man came into our lives. Up until we went to public high school, with its many male teachers and coaches, we were awed by certain men, like Butch the TV repairman, with his knowledge of electronics, and our oil burner repairman with his muscular, hairy forearms.

One good thing about our monthly Haverstraw visits was picnic time. In nice weather, visitors would gather in a shady picnic table area and be joined by their seminarian for some family time. Mom would prepare some type of lunch to share with the other families, and they'd share with us. This was a special time for Mom, to be doing things with the other seminarian families. She was very personable and had a terrific smile. She made friends with a number of the other parents, especially the ones who lived on Long Island and sometimes offered us a ride back home. Sometimes humorous things happened on these Haverstraw visits. Once, as Mom was getting Dennis and Jeanne into the cab, she yelled back to me, *"Peter, grab the bag in the kitchen and hurry up."* I yelled back, "Which bag?" She said, *"The black plastic bag on the counter. You can't miss it."* Ten years old and trying my best to follow orders, I grabbed the only black bag I saw, the one I thought she was talking about, and brought it all the way to Haverstraw, carefully safeguarding it, never letting it out of my hands. Hours later, when picnic time came, to her surprise, shock and chagrin, in front of all the other picnicking families, she opened the bag to see, not the luncheon goods she purchased and prepared, but the garbage. I mistakenly brought the kitchen garbage bag all the way there, and left her precious bag of lunch in the kitchen. Mom was mortified, but no more than I at my blunder.

When visiting Sunday was over and it was time to go back to Long Island, Mom had three tired kids on her hands, some of whom probably still had homework to do. Our teachers at St. Ignatius were not always the understanding, forgiving kind. The trek back home was the same as the one there, maybe worse. Besides the darkness, there are fewer trains from Penn Station to Hicksville at night, and no buses from Hicksville to our Levittown neighborhood. So getting home was often colder, longer and more complicated than getting there. Thank God for the Pitchell family from Hicksville. Their son Joe was a seminarian with Robert. Joe Pitchell, Sr. had a station wagon that comfortably fit his family and all the things they brought up to the Don Bosco Juniorate. When it was time to leave, there was often extra room. Joe was an understanding and kind man and on a number of these trips he'd ask Mom if she needed a lift back home. Though she was a proud woman, Mom knew a good deal when she saw one, and politely accepted a kindness whenever it was extended. Through her struggles over the years, Mom had learned how to overcome obstacles and adapt. She was not a beggar, but grateful and humble enough to accept help when she needed it.

When we all piled in, the Pitchell car was a tightly packed one. The ride back to Long Island with them took a fraction of the time it did for us to get there via bus, railroad, subway and taxi. We'd come over the Whitestone Bridge, and admire the month to month advancements being made on the nearby Throgs Neck Bridge, which was under construction throughout the late 1950's. Joe Pitchell reminded me of the actor Robert Young who played Jim Anderson in "Father Knows Best." He took the time to point things out to me on the ride back to Long Island, like where the Rockefeller estate was in Westchester, and where the actor Sal Mineo lived in the Bronx. He also engaged all of us in conversation. I remember thinking how lucky the Pitchell kids were to have such nice and knowledgeable man as a dad, and fantasizing about how it would be to have such a person in our family. The attention of a nice, caring male was important to me, and Joe helped us out many times. We lost touch with him after those Haverstraw days, but if I could I'd love to be able to thank him and let him know something I probably took for granted back in the 1950's: how much his kindness and willingness to share meant to Mom and all of us.

More Transportation Struggles: Washington Heights

The Haverstraw adventure wasn't the only time as kids that we struggled with transportation and had to schlep far, haul luggage, take taxis, and dash like commuters. Every time we as a family wanted to go to New York City to visit Mom's wonderful aunts, Nellie and Katherine, her adopted parents, we had to traipse by bus to the Hicksville LIRR station to take the train to Penn Station, then the A train to 181st St./Ft. Washington Ave. in Washington Heights. As with the taxi companies, when I began exceeding the age for a children's price ticket, I must confess to shrinking myself down in my LIRR seat somewhat so as to still be considered a child in the railroad's eyes. Most conductors were empathetic and pretty good about it, but once in a while a conductor would demand adult fare from Mom for me. When she discovered that the railroad fare for a child from Hicksville to Penn Station was eighty cents, and the fare from Hicksville to Jamaica only fifty cents, Mom devised a rather cumbersome plan to save the difference. She would purchase adult off-peak tickets for herself, and children's off-peak tickets for us from Hicksville to Jamaica, then we'd walk with our luggage from the LIRR station in Jamaica all the way up to the subway at Sutphin Boulevard, nearly a mile away. Past the big, white Queens County Courthouse, we'd trek uphill to the station, take the E train to the 42nd St./Eighth Ave. station in Manhattan, then change for the uptown A to Washington Heights. The subway ride for Mom and Robert was fifteen cents, and the rest of us would scoot under the turnstile. With this railroad-to-subway approach, there'd be a savings of sixty cents, each way! When dealing with a household economy where literally every penny counted, this was how we traveled to the city. As kids, we didn't understand the reason for the ordeal, and we dreaded dragging suitcases and bundles all the way up the hill to Sutphin Boulevard. But such was life for White Family. We all wanted to see Aunt Nellie and Aunt Katherine, two very special, kind, and loving elderly women, and this was the cheapest way to do it

St. Hugh's School

In 1960, after having been on welfare for nine years, Mom accepted a job as a first grade school teacher at St. Hugh's School in Huntington Station NY, some 15 miles from Levittown. She'd been encouraged to take the job by a friend of hers, Mrs. Mildred Sannosian, of Hicksville. Mrs. Sannosian had been my third grade teacher at St. Ignatius School in 1955. Her son Gary was a classmate of Robert's who went on to become a star pitcher for Hicksville High School and a professional player for the Kansas City Athletics. The job at St. Hugh's didn't pay Mom very much, only a tiny bit more than she'd been receiving from welfare. However she had the requisite two years of college and some classroom experience, having taught religion in Harlem as a young woman. She also had several years of experience as a volunteer class mother at St. Ignatius. Whenever called on to do so, Mom would get herself to Hicksville by public bus and take over whatever classes she was needed in. St. Hugh's, a growing school in western Suffolk County, needed a teacher and Mom was available and willing. She needed little encouragement and wanted very much to undertake this challenge. A neighbor whom Mom confided in from time to time discouraged her from taking the job since it paid only $2800 a year, and she was receiving nearly $2400 a year from welfare. In a conversation I overheard between Mom and this neighbor, she made her position quite clear. "Catherine, why would you take on a difficult, full time job, with 50 children in your class, and travel all the way to Huntington Station every day for only a few hundred dollars more a year than you're receiving now from the county?" Mom knew the math pretty well. She spent hours each week paying bills, figuring out all the pluses and minuses and making sure everything worked out. Sometimes they didn't, but she was patient and always found a way. She knew that during summer months welfare provided about $180 a month, and during winter months, when fuel oil was necessary, she'd receive up to $200 a month. So in 1960 she was managing on about $2000 a year. She knew that by working and having to contribute some of her wages to Social Security and taxes, she'd make only a tad bit more than by staying home and remaining on public assistance. But proud, right-thinking, honest Kay White needed little time to reflect. Mom paused briefly, then said to her friend, *"Thanks for your suggestion, but I'm not taking this job because it's easy, or because I'll make a lot more money. I'm taking it because it's the right thing to do."* That was it. In a low-key, matter-of-fact way, Mom was quite emphatic. Her decision back then, more than half a century ago, is illustrative of the manner in which she faced all of life's choices. She always did the right thing, and she expected us to do the same. It is what she always taught us: Do the right thing, even when it may seem to be the more difficult path. Never despair. Never shy away from what is right. She was the model for us, the poster-parent for good parenting. Of all the struggles she encountered and decisions she had to make, this one led her to become an excellent teacher, one who improved and changed the lives of hundreds of children, and one who became a solid, respected leader in the community. Long before the movie, Mom embodied the notion of "Do the Right Thing." She began her career as a teacher at the age of 43, making less than one fourth of what public school teachers earned at that time, and only a few hundred dollars more than if she'd remained on welfare. But she wanted to become independent of the county and make a contribution to young people, her family, her community and her God. She found a way to do all this by becoming a teacher at St. Hugh's School in Huntington Station, NY.

As Mom's only source of transportation help, Mrs. Sannosian drove every work day from her home in Hicksville to our house in Levittown, picked Mom up, drove to St. Hugh's, about half an hour northeast of us, then back each afternoon. If it were not for Mrs. Sannosian, Mom would not have been able to take this, her first job since she was a working girl in the 1930's. As with Joe Pitchell, I wish I could go back and thank Mrs. Sannosian for her encouragement and thoughtfulness, for helping Mom establish herself as a teacher, and for her extraordinary effort in being her transportation system every day for a year.

Holy Family School

Happily, our local parish, Holy Family Church in Hicksville, built a brand new school in 1961. The pastor, Rev. Martin O'Dea, knowing Mom from parish activities and of her struggle raising four kids, asked her if she'd like to teach in the new school. She gladly accepted, and in September 1961 she began what became a stellar 15-year career as a first grade teacher at Holy Family. Even though this new school was only one mile from our house, transportation once again presented a problem. When the school year began Mom walked to work every day. It took her 30 minutes to get there, and another 30 minutes to walk back home after work. Not bad in terms of time, but she was in her mid-40's and often had to carry books, kids' schoolwork, and all sorts of things necessary for teaching 50 first graders. On rainy days, her apparently never-ending struggle to get to and from anywhere was compounded. Once in a while, a neighbor would stop and ask, "Hey Kay, Do you need a lift?" Mom would gladly accept. Jeanne was a third grader at Holy Family when Mom began teaching there. She recalled, "Since Mom did not drive or own a car, she would often ride on the school bus with me." It was true. There were times when the school bus driver, perhaps turning a blind eye to the rules, would allow Mom to take the school bus with the children, a favor she gladly accepted. Some might have considered riding a big yellow school bus filled with young children to be humiliating. But to Kay White, it was better than walking, left her feet less tired, her body less fatigued and more ready to go about her strenuous day. It also saved a lot of precious time. It was just one of the many things Mom had to do in order to get by without a car. She was a proud woman who never begged, but she did believe in accepting kindnesses, whether from a passing neighbor, or a cooperating school bus driver. We learned valuable lessons in humility, perseverance and survival from the way Mom got herself to work and dealt with such struggles.

For Mom and all of us, this transportation struggle ended in 1965 when Aunt Katherine gave Mom $600 to purchase a small used Ford. It was a black car with a red interior and had a three speed manual transmission, on the column. Not knowing how to drive, Mom began taking lessons from cousin Bill Fowkes, who had moved from Queens to a house down the block, 18 Twig Lane. It was quite a sight, seeing Mom behind the wheel of a car. We had several reactions as we witnessed the dawn of her career as a driver. Sometimes we laughed at the sight of this little black Ford bucking like a bronco, up and down Twig Lane, as Mom groped with learning how to shift the gears. But as with most new things, in groping there is learning and Mom eventually mastered the clutch and the ride got much smoother. Mostly we were proud that she was brave enough to try something new and never before done in our family, something that would greatly change all of our lives. Mobile for the first time in her life, she no longer worried about how she was going to get places. At the age of 49, she was finally free from the drudgery of having to walk everywhere, and from suffering the disappointment of having to forbear going places.

Doctors and Dentists

The transportation dilemma wasn't limited to grocery shopping, visiting relatives in the city, Robert at the seminary, or Mom getting to her job. Every time any of us had to travel any place, wherever it may have been, the same type of planning, extraordinary waste of time, and overall pain in the neck was involved. Until she got her first car in 1965, travel to any simple, everyday place was an ordeal. Going to a movie, for example, a twenty-five cent treat back then, meant walking to the distant Meadowbrook Movie Theater and back. Doctor visits required walking too, sometimes when we were not feeling very well. Thank God Doctor Scrafani, and later Doctor Juan Wilson, our friendly, family doctors, made house calls when one of us was really sick. Dentist visits were a different story. We had to use Dr. Schoen because he accepted welfare families. His office was not nearby, but two miles east, across Newbridge Road, then all the way down Orchid Road to Jerusalem Avenue on the Hicksville-Levittown border. As a child, I visited him a number of times, always by bike, and always alone. After riding that long way, I'd sit in the waiting room listening to the shrill sound of his drill, knowing I was next. I'm sure a big part of my present day white-coat fear stems from my time spent in Dr. Schoen's waiting room 60 years ago. He wasn't a particularly friendly man, and sitting alone in the dark, drab waiting room to be the stern-faced dentist's next patient made the visit all the more difficult. Maybe Dr. Schoen resented having to take welfare children because he'd have to bill less, or wait some time to be paid by the county. Perhaps to save money and cut a corner, he often drilled our teeth without the use of Novocain. That's the truth. But he was our dentist, and we'll always remember biking that distance as kids, unescorted and frightened by what was in store when we'd arrive.

Paper Routes

As young boys, Robert, Dennis and I all had paper routes. Robert had two routes, the Catholic paper, The Brooklyn Tablet, and the daily paper, the Long Island Press. Dennis and I were Tablet boys. The L.I. Press was dropped off at a nearby location for Robert to pick up, organize, and deliver. However, a Tablet route was different. It required a bike trip to Holy Family early every Saturday morning where we Tablet boys would count out, pay for, and pick up our papers, then ride back to our neighborhood and begin delivering them. This took all day and really didn't pay much, but it was a job. We paid eight cents a paper and customers paid us a dime plus tip, usually five cents. So we were guaranteed at least two cents a paper. Some customers, like Mr. Werther of Arbor Lane, Hicksville, were very generous. Mr. Werther always allowed me in to warm up on cold days. Good smells filled their kitchen as Mrs. Werther was always cooking something. Mr. Werther would smile and say something friendly to me, then reach into his pocket and pull out a handful of change. First he'd give me ten cents for the paper, then sift through his change and add an additional 25 cents for a tip. I couldn't believe that, a tip that was five times the average tip, from just one man! I thought he was a millionaire. Robert was the most industrious among us, with two routes at the same time. He kept accurate books on all his customers, always knowing when they were paid up, or falling behind. He also made himself a shoeshine kit and tried shining shoes to make some income. With the few dollars we earned each week from delivering papers, we felt more empowered than the other kids who received allowances from their parents. Those few bucks gave us the tiny bit of economic freedom that comes from having the ability to purchase things with our own, hard-earned money. It also freed Mom up, as she no longer had to hear us beg, mostly unsuccessfully, for a few cents here and there from her. We really liked the taste of financial independence our paper routes provided.

Hitchhiking

During my high school years, 1961-1965, I ended my job as a paperboy and began a four-year career as a caddy at the very exclusive Deepdale Golf Club in Manhasset, New York. Still a very private club for New York's elite, Deepdale is 15 miles northwest of Levittown, so walking or biking there weren't reasonable options. Once in a while, with my three caddying buddies, Drew, Gary, and Bob, I got rides to Deepdale from neighbors who commuted to the city on the brand new Long Island Expressway. When no rides were available, we hitchhiked. Getting a hitch was a very common form or transportation for young people back in those pre-crack days. While there were risks taking rides from strangers, we saw it as a fundamentally American thing to do. When a pioneer's wheel broke on his covered wagon, he undoubtedly was helped by the next wagon to come along. We viewed hitching as neighbor helping neighbor. We'd stand on a busy road, stick out our thumb, and wait to see what kind of ride we could get. Sometimes rides came quickly, and other times seemed to take forever. They also came from many kinds of people: young people looking to show off their hot cars to us teens, commuters who felt sorry for us, and some genuine kooks. Religious zealots tried to convert us to their cause, speeders wanted to show us how fast their cars could go, and even a few offered us money to stop at a motel with them. We handled the oddities of hitchhiking rather easily and were mostly interested in getting to our jobs and back home with our day's pay. The caddying job at Deepdale was drudgerous but fascinating since there were so many interesting stories and learning experiences that arose while working there. We made anywhere from zero dollars, on those days when there were too few golfers and we got "shut out," up to $20, on those days when we'd carry two bags or go around twice. Usually, we earned $6 - $10 a day. Caddies at other Long Island country clubs back then got $5 for carrying a bag for 18 holes. Most members of Deepdale paid $6, so we thought we had a good job. There were also the so-called "big hitters," men of very great wealth and prestige who usually paid $10. During my four years at Deepdale I caddied for such big hitters as Richard Nixon, the Duke of Windsor, the only "king" I ever spent the day with, Dan Topping, who owned the New York Yankees before George Steinbrenner, and Golf Hall of Fame's Craig Wood, who won both the Masters Tournament and U.S. Open in 1941. It was a special treat for me, a future history major, to have an actual chat with former Vice President Nixon about the two national political conventions that were taking place in the summer of 1964. Throughout the entire round, Mr. Nixon was a gentleman who uttered not one word of profanity during the five hours on the golf course. Ten years later, the Watergate tapes revealed a much different Nixon, with pages and pages of obscenities and other expletives.

There were times when we'd be hitching back home after a long, hot day of working for the rich, and find it difficult to get a ride. Sometimes it would take us hours to get home, and we'd grow hungry and thirsty by the time we reached Hicksville. Knowing we were only a few miles from home, we'd spend some of our hard earned money on donuts and soda and our big payday of $6 would shrink quickly. Sometimes we'd show up home with only half our earnings, or less. With hitchhiking to our caddying job and elsewhere, we learned some pretty important life skills in self-reliance, direction-finding, and being able to recognize safe people from unsafe people. Such things weren't taught in schools, so we learned them on our own. I don't recall Mom or any of the other boys' moms having any problems with our hitchhiking. They understood it to be a reasonable method of transportation when necessary.

Blue Stamps

Mom was an avid collector of stamps. Not U.S. or international postage stamps, but trading stamps. To entice shoppers back then, many stores offered Blue Stamps, Green Stamps, Plaid Stamps and some other kinds too. Depending on how much money a shopper spent on her groceries, she would receive a certain number of stamps for each dollar spent. A few dozen stamps filled a page, and several dozen pages filled a book. Once a shopper filled a few books, she would be eligible for a prize from the catalog provided by the store. Our supermarket, the Grand Union, offered Blue Stamps, and prizes could be picked up at redemption centers located throughout Long Island. The nearest Blue Stamp redemption center to our house was in Hempstead, about five miles west of Levittown. Mom diligently saved Blue Stamps for months and was overjoyed after filling three books, enough for a desk lamp, something she wanted very much. With no money to buy such a lamp, this was important to her because it was like getting something for free. The very thought of getting a free lamp was enough to put a big smile on Mom's face. But there was one big problem. With young children at home, she couldn't get to Hempstead herself to pick up her treasure. So she called on me, her ten-year-old son, to do so. I'd never been to Hempstead before but had a general sense of direction and felt quite grown up at being chosen for such a mission. I took this assignment as an opportunity to do something that usually was done by adults: be given a real life problem, asked to figure out all the details, then trusted to go out and solve it. My first step in this adventurous undertaking was to get directions. As with many things, my journey began with a visit to Mr. Kaiser, my very helpful neighbor, to borrow a map of Nassau County. Mr. Kaiser seemed to have everything we needed and did not have. Next, Mom and I located Hempstead on the map and figured out the best route to get there from Levittown. It looked pretty straightforward. *"Peter, just walk down Twig Lane to Newbridge Road, then get a hitch to Hempstead Turnpike, then make a right and get another hitch into Hempstead, and find this address. I'm sure it's on a main road. Everyone there will know where it is."* I confess to being a little afraid at first, but also quite excited, especially when Mom said so confidently, *"Peter, you can do this. I know you can."* Finding Hempstead on a map and figuring out how to get there was one thing – getting there was another. Mom then said, *"Here are three books of Blue Stamps. I worked hard to save them, so be very careful. And make sure you get the right lamp."* She then placed the valuable books into my hands and I was on my way. Like Jack of "Beanstalk" lore, I was a small boy being sent on a big errand. But there would be no magic beans, golden eggs or giants for me. Worried at first, my big errand actually turned out to be easier than I thought. Within minutes I got a ride down Newbridge Road to the Hempstead Turnpike, then another ride all the way into downtown Hempstead. As I sat in the front seat of a stranger's car, I passed through parts of East Meadow and Uniondale, then past Hofstra University, a place I'd never seen, into downtown Hempstead. Hempstead looked like the city to me, with more buses and cars, taller buildings, larger stores, and a more diverse, population. Levittown was all white; Hempstead was not. It reminded me of parts of New York City, with its many black and Spanish-speaking people. Having visited my great aunts in Washington Heights many times, I was used to riding the subway and seeing people of all races and nationalities getting on and off. So the changes I saw in Hempstead didn't affect me much. I minded my own business, stayed focused on my task, smiled at people, and made my way. Just as Mom predicted, I found the redemption center pretty quickly by asking a few safe-looking people like shopkeepers where it was. I entered the redemption center and decided to watch what went on for a while so I could learn the ropes. I needed a little time to figure out how to exchange Mom's treasured stamp books for the lamp without messing up the deal. The building wasn't too inviting, mainly a big, dull, boring-looking, musty-smelling room with nowhere to sit. So I just stood there checking things out for a while, constantly patting my pockets to make sure I still had the priceless books. Everyone at the redemption center was an adult. I was the only kid. I got on line and when it was my turn I handed the catalog to the clerk, showed her the picture of the lamp Mom had circled and said, "Do you have this?" The clerk said, "Let me check," and disappeared. A few minutes later she came back with a large brown box which she placed on the counter. I presented the stamp books to the woman who checked them carefully, page by page. Fortunately, everything passed the woman's scrutiny. She smiled and shoved the box toward me, then said loudly, "Next" as she called the person behind me on line. I stepped away with that big box, hoping it contained the exact lamp Mom was waiting for. Just to make sure, I decided to open the box right there in the redemption center. The last thing I wanted was to go all that way and come home with the wrong lamp, or a broken lamp. I opened the box, spread the tissue paper apart, and there it was, all intact, the right lamp. Thank God. There'd be no going back to Hempstead for me. Knowing Mom's rule against what she called dilly-dallying, I left for home right away, precious cargo in hand. Though the box was pretty big, it was light and I was easily able to carry it through the streets of Hempstead to "the Turnpike," as we called the main thoroughfare that ran from the Queens line out past Farmingdale. I quickly got a ride back toward Levittown. Sitting in the front seat of another stranger's car with that big brown box on my lap, I felt nothing but pride. Mission accomplished. I got another ride from the Turnpike, this time in a pickup truck, up Newbridge to Twig Lane, then proudly carried that box the rest of the way home. It was a great day for me. As I walked in the door, I was rewarded by the reaction on Mom's face after successfully completing this adult undertaking. Trusted by her to carry it out, and given the responsibility to safeguard and present her dear Blue Stamp books in exchange for the lamp she wanted, I had done so. I had gotten myself several miles away and back safely, without error or complication. I was as on top of the world as a ten-year-old boy could be. I was no longer a little boy reliant on his mommy, but a young man who thereafter believed he could accomplish anything.

Phones and Friends

A telephone did exist in our house, barely. That is, for as long as I can remember we had one, but we got to use it only infrequently. If I wanted to see a friend and he lived close by, that was easy enough. All I had to do is go over his house, knock on the door, and call for him. We didn't need appointments to see our friends in those days; and we didn't have play dates set up by our parents. We just knocked on the door and called for our friends. They either came out to play, or they didn't. When I wanted to visit a friend who lived farther away, like some of my St. Ignatius friends who lived in Hicksville, Westbury or other towns, I'd need to map things out and do some type of planning. Sometimes I'd get all the way to a school friend's house in Hicksville and find no one home. It would have been wise to call first, to let him know I'd be calling for him. That meant asking Mom to use the phone. Our phone number was Wells 1-5251. Later, for some reason, the phone company changed it to GE 3-5250. Welfare recipients live on a very tight budget, and if Mom's budget limited her to a $6 monthly telephone plan, she had to live within that limitation. Therefore she decided that the phone had to be for emergency purposes only, and only she determined what was and what was not an emergency. There could be no extra charges. In other words, Mom's bill could not soar to $6.10. There could be no frivolous use of the phone by kids, no unimportant personal calls, no chitchat with friends. I could use the phone if I received an incoming call, but outgoing calls were rare. One very rainy day I wanted to speak with my friends, Bobby and Freddy Hoffman. Most days I'd walk to see them, as they lived only six houses away. But this day it was raining very hard so I asked Mom, "Could I please use the phone to call Bobby and Freddy?" Without hesitation, she said, *"No. Just take a walk over like you always do."* I said, "But Mom, it's pouring. Look." She said, *"That's ok Peter. Just run between the drops. You'll be fine."* I believed her and went ahead. Mom didn't kid around too much with us, so I didn't always know when she was being serious and when she was not. I listened to her, as I usually did, and ran quickly down the block, zigzagging my way, thinking I actually could run between the drops. Soaked after my brief run, I learned that I could not run between the drops, that Mom had a sense of humor, and that it was ok to get wet. She had other expressions when it came to us kids asking for things she either couldn't say yes to, or didn't want to say yes to. On another rainy occasion, when I complained about having to go out, she said, *"Don't worry about the rain. It'll make you grow."* Again I believed her, went out, got as wet as could be, absolutely believing that I'd grow an additional inch or two by nightfall.

Aunt Katherine and Her Free Phone?

In 1960, after Mom's Aunt Nellie passed away, Aunt Katherine lived alone in her upper Manhattan apartment at 106 Pinehurst Avenue. Retired from the New York Telephone Company, she finally decided to give up her lovely, rent-controlled apartment and move to Levittown to live with us, permanently. I couldn't contain myself when I learned Aunt Katherine was coming, not just to visit, but to stay. I loved Aunt Katherine dearly. In addition to all she did to help Mom, beginning with adopting her as a child, she gave all of us something Mom couldn't always give, the time of day. In addition to her furniture and parakeet, "Pretty Boy," Aunt Katherine also brought with her something we thought would change our lives: free phone service. Sadly, that was not to be the case.

Aunt Katherine was the breadwinner in her NYC household. She was the youngest of 11 children of Irish immigrants Cornelius and Mary McCoy. Born in 1890, Aunt Katherine worked most of her life for the phone company, achieving the rank of chief operator, a boss. She often spoke to us about the problems she was having with some of the "goils" in her office. Aunt Katherine never married and took it upon herself to care for her many brothers and sisters as they grew in age and developed various handicaps and illnesses. She cared for her disabled, arthritic brother, Cornelius, whom we called Uncle Connie, until she could no longer do so. In his last few years, Connie lived at the Veteran's Administration Hospital in the Bronx where he died of severe burns caused when an attendant accidentally tossed a lit match into his pajama pants cuff. She cared for her sister, Ellen, whom we called Aunt Nellie, until the late 1950's when severe cognitive impairment set in and she had to go to a state psychiatric facility in Rockland County where she died in 1960. As kids, we remember Aunt Nellie as an elderly woman who had serious mental difficulties and memory loss. She would walk out of the apartment during the middle of the night in freezing weather wearing only her bedclothes. Aunt Katherine was getting older and could no longer care for Nellie, so, out of necessity, she had her placed in the state facility. This was very difficult for Aunt Katherine, and Mom, to do. On those occasions when they visited Nellie, they witnessed the horrible conditions she had to endure: rooms secured like cages, encased with metal bars, patients screaming, suffering alone. Fortunately, this dreadful but unavoidable situation didn't last too long. On October 22, 1960, Ellen McCoy, the woman we called Aunt Nellie and Mom called "Mother," passed away at the age of 73. Most of all, Aunt Katherine cared for Mom when she was a young girl, adopting her with Aunt Nellie, seeing her through high school and two years of college, and providing whatever help she could after we were born and Robert A. White left. I'll never forget the sight the day she arrived. A large moving van came down Twig Lane with Aunt Katherine sitting in the front seat next to the driver. On her lap, she held a birdcage containing her companion, the parakeet Pretty Boy. I loved Aunt Katherine so, and was ecstatic to have her become part of our family. She stayed from the summer of 1960 until she passed away in September 1966. Those were very special years for us, having another very loving adult in the family, one who would be home with us when Mom was just beginning her teaching career. Aunt Katherine was my "cookie person," the "yes" person I could go to, the adult who'd give me what Mom may not have been able to. Aunt Katherine went out of her way for me, as she did for all of us, whenever she could. A few times during the summers leading up to Aunt Katherine's move, Mom allowed me to go to the City by train, alone, to spend time with her. Aunt Katherine made me sandwiches, devoted time to me, and made me feel very special. She lived in upper Manhattan, not a long bus ride from Yankee Stadium. While there she took me to the Indian Museum at 155th Street, Grant's Tomb on 120th St., and my first Yankee game. At 70 years of age and suffering from an irritating and painful blood disease called macro globulin anemia, Aunt Katherine willingly took me by bus from Manhattan to the Stadium in the Bronx. It was a torridly hot and humid day, and not at all easy for Aunt Katherine to get around, in and out of buses, up and down stairs, to the Stadium's gates. When we entered, I looked up and was awed by the sheer size of "The House That Ruth Built." I couldn't believe the height of the upper deck, with its green copper façade seemingly extending into infinity. Aunt Katherine bought general admission seats, which meant that we could go as high up as we wanted in the grandstands. When she asked me where I wanted to sit, I pointed up, way up. I wanted to see that great stadium from the highest point possible. Of course this was totally selfish of me, but I didn't know, nor as an unthinking seventh grader, did I consider how sick Aunt Katherine really was at that time. There were no ramps or elevators to accommodate handicapped persons or the elderly back then, so Aunt Katherine slowly began the steep climb upwards, step after step, while I scampered up, row after row, waiting from time to time for her to catch up. My excitement increased as I climbed each flight, so much so that I didn't see Aunt Katherine sweating, her face reddening, and her breath growing short. As my exhilaration grew, Aunt Katherine became more and more exhausted. When it finally dawned on me that she was suffering, I realized that I'd been obtuse, blind and selfish by placing my wants ahead of her needs. I'd thought only of myself and not her. Pulling myself together only a few rows from the dizzying heights near the top of the upper deck, I said, "This is high enough Aunt Katherine. Let's stop here." Huffing and puffing, Aunt Katherine at last was able to sit and rest. We were the only two people in the entire upper section as we watched the Yank's Whitey Ford strike out slugger Rocky Colavito and several other Detroit Tigers, one after the other. By the end of the game, Aunt Katherine's maddening itch returned and she was in pain. The trip had been too much for her. I ran into the men's room and got a few damp paper towels and tried putting out the fire that overspread her wrists and arms. I felt more and more guilty for failing to consider my wonderful great aunt's age and health. But my thinking had been clouded by my first visit to the Stadium, my first major league ballgame, my first trip to heaven. Even though I asked her for far more than I should have, I'm glad I had that moment of happiness with her. To this day, whenever I think of Aunt Katherine, the New York Yankees, or that great old Stadium, I remember that special day more than half a century ago and how much love my great aunt Katherine McCoy showed. She did everything to please me, her 12-year-old grandnephew. Just being in that place, at that moment, with a loved one such as she, gave me the feeling that life could never get any better.

Aunt Katherine liked the Yanks, maybe because I did. I envied her because the Stadium was only a stone's throw across the Harlem River from her apartment in Washington Heights. After she moved in with us, she'd watch games while I was at school so she could tell me what I missed when I got home. Those were the days before videotape. Not only did we watch all of our favorite Yanks that day, like Mickey Mantle, Roger Maris, Yogi Berra and Bobby Richardson, but she also bought me three hot dogs, something that simply could not have happened on a Kay White outing with four kids. When we got back to her apartment later that evening, she asked me what I wanted for dinner and I said, "Hot Dogs." Apparently I hadn't had my fill. She made a whole pack of them and I ate five. It's hard to believe, but I ate eight hot dogs in one day. I often wondered what would have happened if someone like Aunt Katherine, nice as she was to me, were my parent. How much different my life would have been, and how big I'd have grown, from side to side that is. When Aunt Katherine moved in with us in 1960, we became more aware of her physical problem, and simply called it "the itch," as in, "Mom, Aunt Katherine has the itch again." Whenever any of us saw the flaming red itch begin to appear on her frail skin, we helped by getting her wet towels to douse the inferno.

Aunt Katherine McCoy, New York Telephone Co. photo.

As a phone company retiree, one benefit Aunt Katherine received was free telephone service, including long distance. With Robert moving to Hawaii in 1961 to attend college, we thought this would be a nice thing to have: the ability to call him regularly, making it seem like he was much closer to home. Hawaii is 5600 miles away, and we didn't see him for years at a time. We also thought that we would be able to make the local calls we'd been prevented from making all through childhood, and maybe even some long distance ones too. But we were wrong. I don't know whether it was Mom's decision, or Aunt Katherine's, but they viewed this phone company benefit as something special, something not to be overused, exploited or jeopardized. Aunt Katherine was a loyal phone company employee, one who believed the company had been good to her, and she didn't want to create the appearance of doing anything improper. Consequently, she rarely, if ever, took advantage of her phone company benefit in the manner we wished. When a long distance call absolutely had to be made, like an emergency call to Robert in Hawaii, that was viewed as something special. Such an emergency call would be made only by an adult, and only for important, never frivolous or trivial reasons. And never could a child make a long distance call. In other words, we had absolutely free phone service, including long distance, but we weren't allowed to use it.

Frank's Alibi

In 1955 I was an eight-year-old member of the Cub Scouts, Den 3, Pack 91. Mom wanted all of us to be involved in scouting, and all of us were. Robert, Dennis and I were Cubs and Jeanne was in Brownies and Girl Scouts. Robert was the only one who went on to Boy Scouts, even going on a two-week camping trip to far away Camp Wauwepex in Wading River. The center of my scouting life was Hicksville where my weekly den meetings and monthly pack meeting took place. Of course, I had the same problem as with everything else I wanted to do, or Mom wanted me to do. How was I, as a young kid, going to get to these weekly meetings when they were held some distance from our house in Levittown? And how would I possibly get to the larger pack meetings, where hundreds of cubs from dozens of dens gathered monthly with scout leaders to put on skits, show off their scout projects, and receive their merit badges, when they were held at St. Ignatius School at night? Mostly, these families came to the nighttime pack meetings by car. I usually took the bus, sometimes with Mom, sometimes alone. Since St. Ignatius was two miles away, Mom would sometimes call a friendly, cooperative parent to see if he might be kind enough to drive to our house and give me a ride. Mom didn't want to look like a beggar, so she only did this once in a while. In addition to the monthly pack meetings, there were also weekly den meetings, usually held on weekends or after school at the houses of den mothers, volunteer moms who tried their best to keep the young cubs interested and focused on accomplishing things from the scout handbook. I rode my bike to den meetings, regardless of where they were held. For a few years, Mom was a den mother, with her own uniform. During those years, getting to den meetings wasn't a problem. But having a houseful of active boys come every week took its toll on Mom and she had to resign. I was too young back then to appreciate the great effort she made to allow us the experience of scouting.

When I was a young cub, Mom wanted me to attend Pack 91's annual "Father-Son Mass and Communion Breakfast." The mass was at St. Ignatius Church, and the breakfast was held at a few nearby Hicksville eateries. One of them was a diner called Frank's Alibi. I'm not sure whether I really wanted to go to this mass and breakfast, but Mom really wanted me to go, perhaps so I could participate in what the other boys were experiencing, or so I could have breakfast in a nice place, or just because I was a scout and that was what they were doing that particular month. *"Peter, This will be good for you. You'll be with boys your own age, and get to eat a nice meal out. You'll see."* I was given permission by Mom to go, or told to go, I'm not sure which, and I went. As with getting to the dentist and so many other places that were not right around the corner, I had to either bike or walk there. In this case I walked the two miles from our house in Levittown to St. Ignatius for mass. This wasn't that big a problem for me because I was used to it.

The walk north on Newbridge Road to Hicksville took more than an hour, during which time I did what I always did when I had to spend substantial periods of time alone, I thought about things that were on my mind, talked to myself, and even sang and whistled a few tunes I knew from television shows and commercials. I was ok on this journey, content to use my imagination to help make the time pass. As a child, I spent many private moments this way, overcoming loneliness by just thinking about things. Years later, I learned that I wasn't the only one to talk or sing to himself during unavoidable periods of solitude, times when I was alone with no other person around. On my many visits to the campos of Nicaragua I've seen peasant farmers toiling long, hot hours in the fields, clearing and cultivating the land by hand with their prehistoric-looking tools, all alone. I've seen children manually pulling water from deep wells, bucket after bucket of green water contaminated with arsenic, cholera and parasites, hour after hour, day after day, then carrying it on top of their heads to their houses some distance away. This is the water they are forced to drink, the water that will cook their rice, provide their bath and nourish their few chickens. I've seen women walking several kilometers to wooded areas to gather precious sticks and logs, the only fuel they know, then dragging them back to cook tortillas inside their smoke-filled, dirt floor shacks. So what do the men, women and children who toil alone in these primitive places do to pass the time? How do two thirds of the world's people overcome boredom and loneliness when all they have is the hot dusty earth below them and the scorching sky above? I learned the answer while spending several days in the fields of Nicaragua with a friend of mine, Acencion Poveda. After hours of hard work I asked him about the monotony and boredom of working day after day with no one else around. Pointing toward the land and the heavens, he responded in the most eloquent manner, "Pedro, here we have no radios, nothing to pass the time but our work, ourselves and our words. Here we think, we speak out loud and we sing, sometimes to God, sometimes to ourselves. We sing at night until our wives fall asleep in our arms. Our children smile and sing as they pull water. Here we have few things, but we do have our words." When I heard that it reminded me of how I so often spent my time as a child, thinking, talking and singing to myself to pass the time and overcome being alone.

Many songs and thoughts later, I reached St. Ignatius Church and entered through the large, wooden gothic-style doors at the front entrance on Broadway. It was jam-packed, mostly with Cub Scouts wearing their blue uniforms and gold bandannas. It was quite a colorful sight, pew after pew, an endless sea of blue and gold. I thought to myself, "This is good for me. I can sit anywhere I want in this large crowd of cubs and their fathers, and I'll blend in. No one will know I'm alone." I made my way down the main aisle of the church, spotted a space in one of the rows, and sat down. Minutes later, Father Bitterman, the pastor, began to say mass. Father was a German immigrant with a really thick accent, very hard to understand, even when he spoke English. His mixture of German and Latin made it really difficult to follow. As an altar boy, I knew all the Latin from the mass, but didn't know what most of it meant. I did know the part from the Confiteor where they said, "Mea culpa, mea culpa, mea maxima culpa," "Through my fault, through my fault, through my most grievous fault." Even though I knew the translation, at the age of eight I wasn't at all sure why I had to contemplate being at fault three times in a row when I rarely did anything wrong. I tried my best to follow along with the mass, especially in case one of the nuns from my school was there and saw me not paying attention. Just the thought of being given a stern look from Sister Rose Dominic, a.k.a. Rosey, or Sister Mildred, a.k.a. Machine Gun Millie, was enough to keep me sitting up straight while following the mass in my missal.

This Father-Son mass took longer than most masses, maybe because of the size of the crowd for communion. Everyone went to communion because it was a Father – Son Communion event. Several priests were on the altar assisting Father Bitterman, so it was like a high mass. They used incense and even sang some portions of the mass, making it take much longer than normal Sunday masses. For more than an hour I kept a watchful eye on others, especially the fathers, so I'd know when to stand up, when to sit down, when to kneel, when to get back up, then down again, what page the hymns were on, and when to get on line for communion. Communion time was important for religious reasons – the body and blood of Christ. It also signified that the mass was ending soon. The whole thing seemed to take forever. Today, since mass is said in English, Catholics know when the mass is over. The priest says, "Go in peace, the mass is ended," then leaves the altar and everyone files out after him. Back then, we had to wait for the Latin words, "Ita missa est," "the mass is ended." Sitting on the altar for a few minutes after communion, Father Bitterman said a few more words in Latin, then finally "Ita missa est," to which the altar boys responded "Deo gracias," "Thank God," and the huge crowd left for breakfast. Since there were so many cubs with their dads, there were a few places to go for breakfast. I was on foot, so I went to the closest one, Frank's Alibi, a diner a few blocks from the church. I arrived there a few minutes later and, as I peered through the front door glass, all I could see were dozens and dozens of blue shirts and gold bandanas. Frank's was filled with scouts and their dads. I stood in the doorway and contemplated what to do next. I didn't know if I should just sit down at any table with people I didn't know, or maybe wait to see if someone would ask me to join them. I also thought of leaving. The diner was pretty noisy, mostly from the busy waitresses setting all the tables with plates, knives and forks, and the loud chatter and laughter from the scouts and their dads. They all seemed to know one another and to be having a good time. I knew a few of the boys from school, but their tables were full. Standing in the doorway not knowing what to do, I thought, "What was I doing at a father-son event anyway? How am I to fit in when I don't?" It's like when you're feeling depressed and someone notices it and says, "Cheer up." It's a nice thought, but it doesn't really change the way you feel. Having come this far, I didn't want to be a quitter. "Mom wanted me to go to this scout breakfast, so I'm doing it." I continued waiting patiently by the door, not crying, and not bailing out. My patience paid off because within a few minutes a waitress noticed me and asked nicely, "Who are you with young man?" I said, "Oh, I'm by myself." I'm sure she got the picture because she immediately smiled and said, "Come with me." This take-charge waitress brought me to a table that looked full and said, "C'mon everyone. Move down. There's always room for one more." I soon found myself sitting with some nice kids and their dads, and, for the very first time in my life, ordering breakfast from a menu and having that nice waitress bring me a plate full of food. I even laughed and joked along with the other scouts. After the event, the scouts and their dads made their way home in their cars. I made my way back to Newbridge Road and began the trip back home the old fashioned way, one foot at a time. On the way, I really didn't think too much about loneliness, but focused more on the fact that I just had a real restaurant experience, that I accomplished something pretty substantial by myself, the completion of another mission Mom set out for me. After an hour's walk and many more private thoughts and songs later, I arrived home and Mom was happy to see me. As usual, she gave me the verbal pat on the back I needed for successfully making my way to and from church and attending the breakfast. I believe Mom did her best trying to balance a few things by sending me to things like that communion breakfast. Weighing the sadness I might suffer by going alone against that which I might suffer by being the only scout not going at all, Mom came down on the side of getting me out there, affording me opportunities to have such experiences. As I grew older, whenever little twinges of loneliness would creep within me, I usually managed to subdue them, especially as I became aware of how much emotional and personal pain Mom herself must have been in. Now, nearly 60 years later, whenever I drive by that area of Hicksville, I think of how tough some of those boyhood situations were and how I was able to make it through them because of the model I had to follow, my shield against loneliness and fear. I think of those experiences as things that toughened and shaped me into one who, like Mom, believed he could adapt to almost any situation.

The Homemade Stool

"I, Peter White, promise to do my best, to do my duty to God and my country, to help other people, and to obey the law of the Pack." I made that promise in 1954 when I was seven and first joined Den 3, Pack 91 of the Cub Scouts of America. When a boy first joins the cub scouts, he starts at the bottom and has to work his way up the ranks from cub, to bear, to wolf scout by meeting certain requirements. In addition to attending weekly den meetings and monthly pack meetings, I had to do various projects that were assigned. I liked the pack meetings best because they were held at St. Ignatius School on Friday nights. Being in school at night, especially on a Friday night, was very different from being there in the daytime. There were no nuns to be afraid of. The meetings were held in the auditorium, and afterwards my friends and I were allowed to have fun running around and playing in the school basement. I was always afraid in school as a child, afraid of being yelled at or punished, afraid of being laughed at, afraid of failure. At the monthly pack meetings, I could be in school without being afraid. Pack meetings were also where we got our merit badges and promotions.

In order to be promoted from cub to bear scout, I had to complete a project from the scout handbook. Such a promotion would mean I'd get a small, square felt insignia with a bear on it to sew onto the front of my uniform. I really wanted to move up from cub to bear and have a uniform with a lot of badges, tangible, visible signs that I was doing my best. I looked through the handbook and picked out a project I thought I could make pretty easily, a small wooden stool. The handbook had written instructions to follow, and a few simple illustrations showing each step. I thought, "This looks easy enough. I'll just follow the pictures and make something with four legs and a top. Then I'll be a bear."

First I needed some wood. This I had to find myself. With no car in our family, a trip to a lumberyard to buy anything was out of the question, so I was on my own to find some suitable wood. Lucky for me, our street, Twig Lane, bordered a 28-acre farm that had been sold to a housing developer. Our Levitt houses were built in 1950, these new split-level houses were being built in 1954, so we called this "the new section." My friends and I were sad to see the farm go. We liked playing in the fields, riding the tractor with the owners, Dominic and Freddy DeMonaco, picking beets and having dirt bomb fights with the clumps of plowed earth. But there was a good side to the new section being built. We played every sort of game possible in the foundations and wooden frameworks as the houses went up, games like hide and go seek and war, imitating what we'd seen on TV newsreels from Korea. We watched the workmen, with their bare, muscular backs, shoulders and arms, hammering and sawing away for months. We also got to play with the scraps of wood that were leftover after each day's work. Duels and swordfights took place daily. One day, after the workmen had gone home, I went by myself to the new section and picked through a pile of leftover lumber until I found a nice size piece of 2 by 10. I thought, "This will be perfect, a great top for my stool." Next I grabbed a leftover section of 2 by 4, which I thought would make fine legs. Nails were no problem, they were scattered everywhere. I brought the wood and nails home with me, laid them out carefully on the dirt and slate floor of our carport and, after a quick look back at the scout handbook, I began making my project. We didn't have many tools at our house, only a hammer, a screwdriver, a bent saw and a chisel. They had been Robert A. White's and he had left them behind. I tried going step by step, following the images in the handbook, measuring each leg, then sawing it, then trying to fasten it all together with the nails. I found making the stool to be a little more difficult than I'd originally thought. For some reason, the legs weren't all the same size, maybe because some of the cuts I'd made weren't all even. When I was done it was clear that not only did my stool wobble, it didn't really look like the stool in the handbook. Instead it was a crooked, dilapidated thing, with a few bent nails sticking out here and there. What am I going to do? The pack meeting is coming and I've no time to start over." Panicked, I showed my stool to Mom and she said calmly, *"You'll be alright. You tried. There's nothing you can do about it now. Come in and get your uniform on."* With my stool in hand, Mom and I walked the half-mile to the Newbridge Road bus, took it to downtown Hicksville, and made our way to the school. On the bus a few thoughts swirled through my head. What if my project isn't good enough? What if I get laughed at? What if everyone gets to becomes a bear scout and I don't? Did I follow the scout motto? Did I really do my best?

I was completely mindful that all the other scouts had dads with some technical know-how who owned tools. Some even had a workshop in their garage. I was a young boy with no dad, no tools, no workshop, and no carpentry experience at all. I knew my stool was really rough looking, with nails sticking out and four legs that didn't line up too well. But I also knew that it was mine, the work product of an eight-year-old. At this well-attended pack meeting, the other scouts got up one by one to show off stools, coffee tables, even desks and chairs, most of which gave the appearance of store-bought furniture. Some were painted, others were varnished, glossy, perfect in every way. The moms and dads in the audience beamed as scout after scout got up to present their merit badge projects. It was obvious to me, even at my young age, that though my stool was no match for their slick-looking tables and chairs, my stool was mine, the work of a boy. The work being shown by the other scouts was not theirs but their dad's. Despite the obvious unfairness, the other scouts received thunderous applause for their shiny looking furniture. When I finished presenting my homespun stool, no one clapped. I wasn't sure what that meant. Would I not be getting my merit badge? I sat down next to Mom, who looked upon me with a smile as if to say, *"Good job, Peter. I'm proud of you."* I didn't cry, but inside I felt like it. Mom could tell. She quickly eased my pain, *"Don't worry, Peter. Those boys didn't make those tables. You made yours by yourself. You'll be fine."*

Mom's words did make me feel better. Apparently she was happy knowing that at the very least, I'd made an effort. Quality notwithstanding, I had tried and succeeded in creating something completely on my own. She insisted that we do our best, and that we should be proud of ourselves if we gave things our best effort, regardless of the outcome. Thanks to some right-thinking scout leaders, I became a bear scout that night, and felt then, as I do to this day, that my badge, the one I received for that shaky looking stool, was earned. I don't know what ever happened to that dilapidated, crooked thing. Maybe it got burned up in our fireplace along with some other scrap wood from the new section. Maybe it got put out with garbage. But I'd love to see it again, if only as a reminder of that painful and yet wonderful time in my life when such simple experiences were capable of teaching such important and powerful lessons. I received far more than a merit badge that night. I learned that life isn't always fair, that injustice can be found anywhere, and that honest, supportive parents are very important.

TEEN YEARS WITH MOM

Summer Camp Joy, Tears of Reality

In the spring of 1960, when I was 12 years old and about to finish seventh grade, Mom learned of an opportunity for me to have a weeklong summer camp experience in Ellenville, NY with the Catholic Salesian Fathers and Brothers, the same order that ran the seminary Robert was attending in West Haverstraw. In part, I had mixed feelings about going. I liked playing with my friends in the neighborhood during the summer, wouldn't know any of the kids at this far-away camp, and I had commitments with my paper route, altar boys and baseball. Mom strongly encouraged me to go. Perhaps she wanted me to be surrounded by priests and nice Catholic boys who didn't curse, or so she thought. Perhaps she just wanted me to have an opportunity to do something different, to grow up a little away from home. Rather than fight Mom on this, I reluctantly went along with the idea. In mid-July I packed a few things into a small suitcase and made my way on the Long Island Rail Road to Penn Station, something I'd done by myself a few times before when I visited my Aunt Katherine in the city. From Penn Station, I walked eight blocks up Eighth Avenue to the Port Authority Bus Terminal where I found the group of boys waiting to board the bus to the Catskills. I was the only Long Islander, the rest were Catholic school boys from the city. Most of them were white kids from Queens who seemed to know one another. A few were nonwhite. Not knowing anyone and not really wanting to go at all, I boarded the bus and sat by myself. Even though I knew Mom was trying hard to do something good for me, I felt like I was being sent away. As the bus crossed the George Washington Bridge, I looked to my left, down the rapidly moving waters of the Hudson River at the skyline of Midtown and lower Manhattan, a sight I was familiar with. I stared and stared until all the buildings of the city disappeared from view. I turned my head and looked straight at the Jersey side of the bridge. To my left was Palisades Amusement Park, where I'd gone several times with Mom, and even a few times with Robert. I'd have given anything to get off that bus right then and there, to ride the roller coaster at Palisades, then go back home. Not long after, the hills of northern Jersey and Rockland County appeared, then finally the mighty Catskill Mountains. I was assigned a bunk in a large, open-air room. The beds were lined up, like barracks I'd seen in Army movies. This is where'd I'd sleep for the next week. I was also assigned to a table in the cafeteria where I'd eat my meals. Three boys from Queens were assigned to the same table. Joe, Jack and Johnny, three J's. That would make it easy for me to remember their names. At our first meal that evening they made fun of me, mostly about small things. I knew that adolescents could be pretty cruel to one another, and I usually stood up to bullies when they taunted others or me. I really didn't like their teasing and bullying, but then I saw them making fun of everyone, including themselves, so I took it all in stride. At bedtime, when the counselors thought we were all asleep, one very tall black fellow named Ben got up and sang. Someone shined a flashlight on him and it looked like he was on stage in the spotlight. Ben didn't sing in the traditional way, but in a way that was much different from anything I'd ever heard. Long before the advent of modern day rap music, Ben made up his own tunes and created humorous, rhyming words as he went along, all spontaneously. Nothing was rehearsed. Ben sang most nights and everyone laughed and laughed. Even I laughed. His words were mostly about each of us, and what we did that day. No matter what activity we did at camp, the thing we all looked forward the most to was Ben's nighttime show. During the day, we took hikes, swam in a nearby lake, played ball, and visited a dark, cold and dangerous place called the Ice Caves, where we explored natural wonders like stalactites and stalagmites and underground streams. At night, after a few doses of Catholic retreat activities like prayers and meditation, and a religious lecture before bedtime, we listened to Ben. Joe, Jack and Johnny were good friends, all from the same neighborhood in Queens and, as the days went by, I became quite close with them. They got to know me pretty well, and I could tell that they soon began to like and respect me more. Part of the reason for this was swimming. One afternoon, the camp directors, who were mostly priests and brothers, held swimming races on a nearby lake. In groups, we'd race across the lake and back, probably a few hundred yards. After winning a few heats, I made it into the finals. Joe, Jack and Johnny weren't very good swimmers, so they got behind me, wished me good luck and cheered me on to build up my confidence. When the finals came, I began swimming across that lake as fast as I could. Out of the corner of my eye I noticed that no one was on either side of me. All the other swimmers were far behind. I won easily and was awarded the blue ribbon for my victory. I'd never won anything by myself before that, so this victory was like winning an Olympic medal to me. Not only did I feel pretty good about being the best swimmer in the entire camp, I got quite a boost in self-esteem from my win. All the other kids knew of me after that. I'd overhear some say, "There's that guy Pete from Long Island, the swimmer." In addition to the outdoor activities, meals, laughter and songs, the best part of this camp for me was meeting Father Joe. He was not like other priests I knew. He never wore priestly garb, no cassocks, no vestments, and no collar around his neck. Instead, he wore hiking boots, shorts and tee shirts all week. Father Joe was a very smart and handsome man with a sense of humor and a great attitude. Every one of the kids at the camp liked him. He led us on many of the activities including a long and treacherous hike to the Ice Caves. Following Father Joe's lead, we climbed up and down steep, rocky trails, around a few sheer drops, and took in magnificent Catskill vistas on our way to the cool, dark, wet, hazardous caves. On our way back, fresh from our daring walk, we were filled with the kind of confidence boys our age needed. We had all accomplished something very risky, a major challenge, one I'm sure most of our parents wouldn't have permitted. But we had Father Joe to pilot us and assure our success. On the long walk back to the camp, it grew dark and the sounds of night birds and little critters could be heard coming from the woods. As these nighttime sounds grew into a cacophony, Father Joe began telling us the first of several vivid, frightening stories, "Who Stole the Golden Arm." His scary tale included sound effects and some shrill screams. I shook. I really enjoyed this camp, and, as disinclined as I was to go at the outset, I've always remembered it as one of the best weeks of my life.

Back at Port Authority I said goodbye to Joe, Jack, Johnny and my other new friends and made my way on the uptown A train to 181st. Street and Ft. Washington Avenue, to Aunt Katherine's apartment. Before going to camp, I asked Mom and Aunt Katherine if I could visit for a few days by myself and they agreed. I always loved spending time with my elderly great aunt, Mom's adopted mother. She treated me with the utmost kindness, prepared meals to my liking and took me around upper Manhattan and to my very first Yankee game. After three carefree, glorious days at Aunt Katherine's, where I was treated like an only child, I waved goodbye to Aunt Katherine, took the subway to Penn Station, the Long Island Rail Road to Hicksville, then the bus to Levittown and arrived home. At first Mom was glad to see me, but for some reason the joy of being reunited didn't last too long. I couldn't wait to tell her everything that happened during those ten wonderful days. We sat in the living room and I yapped away about camp, and my visit to Aunt Katherine's. I went on and on about by new buddies Joe, Jack, and Johnny, our nighttime barracks singer Ben, our meals, our activities, and the great Father Joe. I described the hikes, the risks and dangers we'd overcome, my blue ribbon swimming success, the trust that had been placed in me, the new found sense of confidence I gained as a 12-year-old by getting to the city, then the Catskills, then to Aunt Katherine's and back by myself, the freedom I felt being away, and how much I'd grown up as result of these experiences. Mom sat, smiled, and listened for as long as she could. I'm sure, as I went on and on, she may have wanted to get a word in edgewise, but I left her very little opportunity. Before I was able to wrap up my story, Mom abruptly said, *"It sounds like you had a nice time, I'm glad it worked out for you. But now you're back. Dennis has been doing his jobs and yours too while you've been away. We have things to do, so let's get moving."* For reasons I didn't understand then, upon hearing Mom's words "now you're back," and the tone of her voice, I burst into tears. Her words cut my feeling of joy to sadness. For a short while I'd been effervescent, as happy as I'd ever been. Yet with this one brief expression from Mom, I found myself bawling like a baby. She looked at me and said, *"Why are you crying? You just had a wonderful week. What's wrong with you?"* In part I was crying because I did have a wonderful week, one I didn't expect to have, one that was a rarity in my childhood, and it was over. I was wounded by Mom's three words, spoken so matter-of-factly, "now you're back." I missed my new friends Joe, Jack and Johnny, Father Joe – the first man in my life who liked and cared about me, the Catskills and the freedom, fun and success I just had. In my 12-year-old mind, all Mom seemed to care about was doing jobs and getting back to normal. I'd been happy for a week. Now I was back.

Thirty years later, something happened that caused me to reflect on that time. While leading my first of more than 60 humanitarian delegations to Nicaragua, I found myself riding in a jeep with three missionary nuns who were driving from Poneloya to Leon. About 15 kilometers from the city, we passed a woman carrying a child in her left arm and a large sack in her right, and at the same time balancing a huge bundle on her head. She was walking toward Leon, along the side of the dangerous and dusty road in near 100-degree heat. The driver, Sister Rachel, stopped and asked, "La podemos llevar?" ("Can I take you there?" "Do you want a ride?") The woman smiled and answered enthusiastically, "Si, si." I got out and assisted the grateful woman and her child into the jeep, then lifted, or should I say tried to lift, her bundles. As I grabbed the sack she carried in her right arm, which weighed at least 50 pounds, and swung it into the jeep, I was in disbelief that this woman could carry such a heavy load. Then I tried tackling the bundle she carried on top of her head, and I could barely lift it. It had to weigh 80 pounds or more. The woman and the three nuns had a good laugh watching me struggle. We zoomed into Leon, and the woman, with her child and heavy bundles, rode with us the whole way. We dropped her off on the outskirts of the city in a place that I could only describe as nowheresville. I watched in awe as she once again mounted her heaviest bundle atop her head, picked up her child in one arm and her heavy sack in the other, and strode off. That night, I couldn't get the image of that woman out of my mind. Thoughts of her struggle in that intense heat and dust kept me from sleeping. I thought of how far she had to go, and her willingness to walk that whole way had we not picked her up. For a brief moment I thought of how lucky the woman was that we came along for her. That notion quickly left me as I realized that long, hot walk was just a small part of that poor woman's normal, daily life. Yes, she'd gotten a small break, a ride in a hot, cramped jeep from a passerby. But she wasn't the lucky one. We, the nuns and me, were the lucky ones. We were the North Americans fortunate enough to have a jeep. We were the lucky ones who didn't have to suffer and struggle as that young mom did. I thought of how obtuse most of us in the first world are, and of our inability to comprehend or even be aware of the plight of the poor. Then I thought of my own Mom, and how, like this poor Nicaraguan woman, she so often struggled with things that were so easy for others to accomplish, those with husbands, cars and money. I thought of how at times I was one of those obtuse ones, unmindful of the pressures and complications Mom faced every day. For the past 25 years now, the thought of that woman carrying her baby and bundles on the road to Leon continues to serve as an important metaphor for me, one that helps ground me, one that makes me think of my good fortune, and serves as a constant reminder of the great struggle of the poor and the struggles of my own Mom.

Just as the woman on the road to Leon, bearing her child and heavy load, had to move on, so did Mom. She couldn't wait forever listening to my tales of swimming medals and hikes, or sit too long watching me cry because my fun was over. In hindsight, while I learned many lessons at camp during the summer of 1960, my real learning began when I got home.

Shoes, Shirts, Hats and Other Things

Several years ago, while organizing his two daughters' rooms, a friend of mine noticed scores of shoes in their closets. He lined them all up, pair after pair, then he counted them. Forty one pairs in all! He was shocked. He had no idea that his daughters had that many shoes, nor why. When he mentioned this to me, I laughed at first and said, "I wonder, after the first 40, who decided to buy the 41st pair." He didn't think the situation was humorous at all. And of course, it led us to a discussion of how we grew up, of wants versus needs, of deprivation and patience. Mom was at the helm of our family and was always on a tight budget that didn't include such excesses. I had two pairs of shoes growing up, my good shoes, the ones I wore to church, on holidays or when company was coming, and my play shoes. We didn't own sneakers until we were teenagers, able to buy them with our own money. Sneakers would have meant each of us having a third pair. Mom believed that shoes were important for safety, warmth and most of all, economy, and that sneakers were cheaply made and not good for us. As with all struggling families, we followed the hand-me-down rule: once Robert outgrew his shoes, I fell heir to them, and so on down the line. It was that way with most everything, unless something became so worn out it had no further utility. Only then was it thrown out. We were made to take pretty good care of our belongings, including our shoes. If a heel got worn down, or a sole came loose and began to flap with each step we took, we'd take it to the shoemaker for repair rather than buy a new pair. We were also made to shine our shoes. Using an old wooden milk box, Robert crafted a sturdy shoeshine kit, complete with brushes, polish, rags, and even a metal form screwed to the top so a shoe could be held stationary while he polished away. He loved achieving a spit shine, the really high glossy look. Mom liked it when we looked good going out the door, and a pair of shiny shoes was part of that look.

Whenever it was time for new shoes, we'd take a bus trip to downtown Hicksville where, on the west side of Broadway not far from St. Ignatius School, C. Zucker's Shoe Store was located. Mr. Zucker must have known something of Mom's circumstances because he always smiled when Mom came in, always served her politely, and his prices were affordable so Mom never had to quibble. Mr. Zucker was more than a mere shoe salesman. Like a podiatrist, he would measure our feet carefully with his Brannock Device, the standard foot-measuring tool in the world, to ensure a correct fit. Then he'd select a proper shoe and press the end to see how far up our toe was, and decide on a size that we wouldn't outgrow too quickly. He worked with Mom to get her a good shoe, one that would last and for a good price. I miss merchants like C. Zucker, fair, friendly businessmen who put people's needs ahead of the almighty dollar. His store was right next to Goldman Brothers, a clothing and sporting goods store. In addition to selling baseball gloves, bats, balls and other sporting goods, Goldman's also sold the blue pants that were part of the St. Ignatius School uniform. As growing boys, we found ourselves at Goldman's every few years. When we entered, out attention was immediately drawn to the expensive baseball mitts and bats. The smell of the new leather caused us to wonder what it would be like to leave the store with one of those. We didn't have too long to contemplate such questions because Mom would quickly usher us to the school uniform section in the basement. She was glad St. Ignatius required uniforms; it meant we didn't need too much of a wardrobe. So long as we had our blue pants and a clean white shirt, and of course our blue knit tie with the letters STIL, for St. Ignatius Loyola, emblazoned on it, we were set for the week. By the time I reached eighth grade, pants styles changed a bit, and kids began wearing tighter, higher cut pants without cuffs. Made to cling to my baggy, blue, cuffed pants long after styles changed, I'd have to listen to the taunts of some who'd say, "Hey, Where'd you get those parachute looking pants with the dust-catcher cuffs?" Mom wasn't able to focus too much on new fads or trends. Utility came first. We got what we needed based on what she could afford, regardless of what was in vogue or who made sport of us. Speaking of sport, when he was an eighth grader Dennis begged Mom for a pair of sneakers. He pleaded and argued the best he could. "Mom, Please. All the other kids have sneakers. Please." Mom held him off as long as possible, then one day she came home with a box containing Dennis' first pair of sneakers. To her surprise and confusion, Dennis refused to wear them. Didn't Dennis really want sneakers? Didn't he beg for them? Though Mom didn't comprehend Dennis' refusal at the time, there was a reason that any normal adolescent would understand. While trying her best to please her son, Mom shopped around and was able to pick up a bargain pair of sneakers for Dennis, something within her means. But the logo on the side of each sneaker bore the face of TV puppet Howdy Doody. Howdy was a great TV icon when Dennis was a five year old, but his picture on the side of a sneaker was not something that would win him any popularity points with "the guys" in the eighth grade. Sometimes things didn't work out, but no one could say Mom didn't try. Dennis proudly wore his first pair of sneakers, …but only after he'd spent a long time removing the Howdy logo from each sneaker.

The Double-Breasted Shirt

In the spring of 1961 I was an eighth grader at St. Ignatius School in Hicksville. Graduation was coming and that meant I'd be saying goodbye to all my Catholic school friends, kids with whom I'd spent every day for eight years. It was a very exciting time since we were finally moving on with our young lives. But it was sad at the same time because it crossed my mind that I might never see any of these kids again. During the last week of school, the nuns allowed us to break rank and wear regular clothing instead of our school uniforms. We also had a class trip to Playland, an amusement park at Rye Beach in Westchester. For an entire week, we dressed like we were public school kids, able to wear different clothes each day. This was a very big treat, since we'd been required to wear the same blue pants, white shirt and blue tie every day for eight years. Some of the more outgoing, popular guys, like Vincent Giansante and Billy Schneider, wore the latest styles to school that week, including colorful double-breasted shirts, the rage in teenage male attire in June of 1961. I had no fancy clothing, nothing new to wear, only white uniform shirts and whatever hand me downs were in my drawer. The cool guys stood out, I did not. Understandably, I really wanted to fit in, to go to school and Playland like one of the guys. I'd saved a few dollars from my paper route and decided that for the upcoming class trip, I'd buy myself a new double-breasted shirt, just like the other boys had. I didn't ask Mom, or even tell her, for fear she'd tell me what I didn't want to hear like, *"Don't bother, Peter. You'll be wasting your money. Styles come and go. You'll be fine with what you have."* I also thought, "If she said no, then my plan of fitting in with the guys will be halted in its tracks," for there was no disobeying Mom. The weekend before the trip, I took the bus to Hicksville's Mid-Island Plaza mall and headed straight to National Shirt Shop, a men's clothing store that had everything imaginable. I checked my pocket to make sure I had my $5, no small sum back then, and began to do something I'd never done before, shop for myself. Within minutes, I found exactly what I wanted, an orange double-breasted shirt, size medium. Without hesitation, and without even trying it on, I brought it to the clerk and proudly paid for it, then made my way back on the bus to Levittown. When I arrived home, I smiled as I got my colorful cotton treasure upstairs without being seen. It was important not to be seen, for I had crossed what I believed would have been Mom's unwritten, unspoken, but clearly understood, rule. I'd also hidden it to prevent the other kids from making fun of me, and Mom from being upset for spending my money frivolously. I rationalized, thinking, "Buying this shirt is my business. I'm behaving like a normal adolescent. I'm simply exercising a bit of independence, a mild version of teenage rebellion. I work hard for my money, so why can't I spend it the way I want?" The sad fact was that even though I was bold enough to buy the shirt, I was afraid to make my rebellion public. With the tags still on it, I carefully placed my brand new orange prize underneath some other clothing in my drawer and smiled. Mission accomplished. I would look like the other boys. On the day of the Rye Beach trip I put on my new shirt, then wore a sweater over it so as to continue the secret nature of my purchase. My idea worked. I got out of the house fine, and then, upon arriving at school, removed my sweater to reveal my brand new, totally cool, orange double-breasted shirt. All the way on the bus ride to Rye Beach I sported this new shirt thinking it was my ticket to join the "in crowd." Truthfully, it was not, for little had changed. I sat on that long bus ride to Westchester with the same kids with whom I would have sat had I worn one of my old hand-me-down shirts. Neither the coolest guys, nor the prettiest girls, surrounded me. I was still eighth grader Peter White, but with a different shirt. When we arrived at Rye Beach, Vincent Giansante and Billy Schneider had no trouble asking girls to go on the rides with them, but I did. I faced the fact that they were more socially advanced and far less awkward than I, and what shirt I wore had absolutely nothing to do with anything. On the long bus ride home, I realized that I shouldn't have tried so hard to become someone I was not. I never wore that orange, double-breasted shirt again, partly because it reminded me of that sensitive and uncomfortable time in my life and partly because double-breasted shirts quickly went out of style, a fact that made me feel like an even bigger idiot. I kept that shirt in my drawer for several years after that, well hidden underneath my other clothing, where it served an important purpose, something Mom was undoubtedly aware of all along. It became my humility shirt, a constant reminder that I should be myself more and not delude myself by thinking life's external things are more important than what lies within.

No Varsity Jacket for Me

Following the personal embarrassment of the double-breasted shirt fiasco, I began putting the lesson I learned to work. I began using clothing, or rather my disregard for its importance, to make my own statement, to express my individuality. For example, in the mid to late 1950's singer Pat Boone and a few other celebrities sported white buck shoes and they quickly became a fad. By the early 60's, most stopped wearing them. I liked white as well as tan bucks for a few reasons: they were comfortable, they had thick soles that didn't wear out too quickly, and I thought they looked good on me. So I continued wearing them. At the school bus stop, I'd get teased. "Hey White, where'd you get those shoes? Don't you know they're out." I'd just smile. I never was in a position to worry about what was in or out, and increasingly I began to care less and less about what others thought of me, at least clothing wise. So in high school I decided not to be a lemming. I began wearing what I wanted to wear and not follow the crowd. I did my own thing, even when I was a minority of one. When I became a member of the W.T. Clarke High School football team, I was eligible to purchase a varsity jacket. Only athletes who played at the varsity level could buy them. The Clarke varsity jacket was made of a rather dull gray woolen fabric and it had the initials TC on front, for Tresper Clarke. The word VARSITY was printed on the back in large, bright red letters. Walking the halls of Clarke High School in a varsity jacket was a major status symbol for many self-esteem seeking males, a gray and red sign of respect. Younger kids actually made way for those wearing them. Guided by my own self-imposed anti-lemming rule, I never purchased a varsity jacket. For one thing, a leading player on the school's golf team had one, and he was a known cheat. I didn't want to be associated with him or others whom I didn't think were deserving of such a jacket. Also, varsity jackets weren't free. They cost $15, a sum hard to come by for me. So I played varsity ball, enjoyed it, learned a lot from it, and didn't bother at all with jackets, shoes, or most anything others expected of me. That became my identity, not following the crowd.

Booker T. Washington's Hat

In reflecting on this identity, which extended far beyond shirts, shoes and jackets, I am reminded of a passage from Up From Slavery, the autobiography of the great educator Booker T. Washington. In the mid 1860's, recently released slave Booker found himself attending his first school in West Virginia. Of his desire to fit in with the other school boys, most of whom were years ahead of him, Booker said,

> When I found myself at school for the first time, I also found myself confronted with (a difficulty). …All of the other children wore hats on their heads, and I had neither hat nor cap. In fact, I do not remember that up to the time of going to

school I had ever worn any kind of covering upon my head, nor do I recall that either I or anybody else had even thought anything about the need of a covering for my head. But, of course, when I saw how all the other boys were dressed, I began to feel quite uncomfortable. As usual, I put the case before my mother, and she explained to me that she had no money with which to buy a 'store hat,' which was a rather new institution at that time among the members of my race and was considered quite the thing for young and old to own, but that she would find a way to help me out of the difficulty. She accordingly got two pieces of 'homespun' (jeans) and sewed them together, and I was soon the proud possessor of my first cap.

The lesson that my mother taught me in this has always remained with me, and I have tried as best I could to teach it to others. I have always felt proud, whenever I think of the incident; that my mother had strength of character enough not to be led into the temptation of seeming to be that which she was not – of trying to impress my schoolmates and others with the fact that she was able to buy me a 'store hat' when she was not. I have always felt proud that she refused to go into debt for that which she did not have the money to pay for. Since that time I have owned many kinds of caps and hats, but never one of which I have felt so proud as the cap made of the two pieces of cloth sewed together by my mother. I have noted the fact, but without satisfaction, I need not add, that several of the boys who began their careers with 'store hats' and who were my schoolmates and used to join in the sport that was made of me because I had only a 'homespun' cap, have ended their careers in the penitentiary, while others are not able now to buy any kind of hat.

It seems that Booker's mom and my Mom shared some of the same values. Both were happy and proud to give their children all they could, however little that may have been. Both had the strength and character to refrain from trying to appear to be that which they were not. Both refused to fall into the trap so many parents are victims of today, entering into debt for something their children may "want" but not "need." And both were willing to do whatever it took, regardless of what others might have thought of them, to help their children through the most uncomfortable and difficult times of their youth.

Making It with Homespun Remedies

Young Booker T. Washington's mother showed a great deal of creativity with her homespun remedies, like the hat she made him a century and a half ago. Mom had to be creative too, and relied on similar remedies to see us through. When our socks developed holes, she didn't throw them out and buy us new ones. Instead she'd get out her small sewing kit, which contained a wooden sock form, and did what then was called darning. I haven't seen anyone darn socks in many years, but that's how she kept our feet covered. The same was true with shirts and pants. If one of our elbows or knees poked its way through a shirt or a pair of pants, the remedy wasn't to throw out the garment and head to the mall, but to get out her sewing kit and find a patch to match. I never minded this at all. I never felt like a patched-together hobo or considered myself ill-clothed. I was proud that Mom cared so much, that she took the time, and that she developed the sewing skills to keep our clothing going. Long before Earth Day or the national effort at recycling, Mom was mindful of not wasting things. With life skills honed growing up during the Depression, she was a master recycler. Today I see families go through whole sleeves of plastic cups in a day, only to throw them out after one use. Not Mom. She knew how to use things carefully, over and over, how to make them last longer than expected, and find alternate uses for them, to give them a second life. We've all made Mom's anti-waste, pro-recycling rules part of our lifelong behavior. There are other examples of Mom as Recycler-in-Chief. As elementary school kids at St. Ignatius School, we had to cover all our textbooks. The school sold colorful, shiny new book covers that had St. Ignatius information written all over them. They were fifteen cents each. We sat together the first night of school, as a family, and cut up used brown paper shopping bags from the supermarket, and even old copies of the Long Island Press, and made our own book covers. And even with that, we had to be careful not to waste the valuable brown paper by cutting it unevenly or too small. Every time we covered a book with a paper bag, fifteen cents was saved, the cost of a subway token or a gallon of heating oil back then.

Mom's anti-waste and recycling efforts weren't limited to book covers and patching up clothing. Cardboard boxes and shopping bags were used for every possible purpose including garbage and leaf collection, storage, even for sledding down a hill in winter. A piece of cardboard might even be inserted into a shoe with a hole peeking through until she could afford to head to the shoemaker for resoling. Plastic bags sometimes kept our feet and Mom's hair dry as we walked to church on rainy Sundays. Used nails from a nearby construction site were straightened and re-used, and scrap lumber was made into shelving or burned in the fireplace. While Mom was not a hoarder, she did hang on to things longer than most others, because, *"We might need that someday."* To this day I feel a slight sense of guilt whenever it comes to throwing something out, especially if someone else might find some utility in it. None of us remembers ever wearing a store-bought costume for Halloween. A few days before each Halloween, Mom took a look at what was around the house or yard, and got inventive. Through her efforts, we were transformed into authentic-looking hobos, pirates, farmers, soldiers, even Superman, sporting costumes made from old pajamas, drapes, and items from our own shed. We weren't the only family who made use of these homespun remedies. Every kid in the neighborhood knew that an old broom handle had a second life as a stickball bat, and the wheels from an old baby carriage were perfectly suitable for a push-mobile. With our creative, dollar-saving, recycling-conscious Mom, very little was wasted, and everything possible received a second life, unless she could find a way to give it a third or a fourth.

Sometimes the thriftiness with which we grew up was misunderstood. A few times each year the nuns at St. Ignatius required every student to bring in some type of snack food like Easter candy or cupcakes to share at class holiday parties. Running to the stores because we were assigned to buy something was not within Mom's welfare budget, but she complied the best she could. One Easter when we were assigned to bring in a snack, Mom purchased a package of six small marshmallow baby chick candies. Unable to buy two packages, one for me and one for Dennis, she opened the package and divided the chicks, wrapping up three in wax paper for me, and giving Dennis the other three in their original wrapper. When Dennis handed in his three marshmallow chicks, his teacher accused him of eating three of them. The circumstantial evidence, three missing chicks, seemed to point in that direction. I suppose the nun didn't realize, or couldn't imagine why a parent would divide candy like that, or even contemplate that there might be parents who had to. Dennis was punished for something he didn't do, breaking open a package and eating half the precious marshmallows. When he got home, he told Mom this baby chick story, which infuriated her. Next day she called the school and, in her direct and honest manner, told the nun what she did and why, emphasizing that Dennis had done nothing wrong at all. The nun was apologetic and learned an important lesson from Mom in being more cautious and less prejudicial when dealing with children and their families in the future.

Aside from holidays, the school did have a candy table where, after lunch, those with money could purchase licorice, pretzels and other snacks. Students ate lunch in their classrooms, but once they finished, those with candy money would line up and go downstairs to make their purchases. Kids without candy money had to stay in the classroom and watch. Robert, Dennis and I never got on that candy line. Asking for something we didn't need and couldn't afford was off limits.

The First Time I Realized We Were Poor
(***Note: For a poetic version of this story see Appendix C in the back of the book***)

One evening in mid-December 1954, Father Fagan, our parish priest stopped by. Father had an Irish brogue and I often found it difficult to understand him when he spoke. There was a pleasant, melodic quality to his voice, with tones rising upward and downward. It was hard to follow him during mass, as his Latin was laced with his thick brogue. Father knocked on the door and Mom greeted him with a big smile. He carried a large cardboard box that had fireplace brick crepe paper wrapped around it, as if to disguise it. Father placed the box on our kitchen table and he and Mom began to talk. Of course, with a man in the house, especially at night, we all gathered in the kitchen to watch as the two spoke. A man standing in our kitchen was a rare sight. The priests from the church helped Mom out once in a while, sometimes with food or clothing, and always with advice and friendship. We children were curious as to what was in the box, so we inched closer. Through a slight tear in the side of the box I could see what looked like the wing of a toy airplane. I wondered why Father Fagan would be bringing Mom a box decorated with Christmas-colored crepe paper and a toy inside. For a brief second, I got a pretty good look. It was a blue and gray metal toy plane. Mom noticed us peering a little too closely at the box and waved us all away. *"Children, go get ready for bed. Leave Father and me to talk."* We obeyed. But I was filled with curiosity. Why did he come at night? Whenever Father came to our house, it was usually daytime and most always to drop off or pick up some typing Mom volunteered to do for the Church. Why did Father bring this colorful box? And why was there a toy inside?

A few days later, on Christmas morning, I got the answers. Mom always made Christmas special, even when she was financially unable to do very much for us on her own. Jeanne remembered, "We would come down the stairs on Christmas morning and see presents under our beautifully decorated tree. There would be a big sheet covering up the presents.

I'd see a specific toy like a doll just under the end of the sheet and be so excited thinking Santa came." We weren't sure whether it was Santa or Mom who placed the sheet over the presents, but the sheet stayed until we all got home from Christmas morning mass. Then and only then would Mom allow the sheet to be removed so we could discover our treasures. There could be no peeking. When we removed the sheet, my eyes went straight to a small blue and gray metal plane, and it had a tag on it which said, "To Peter From Santa." It was the same plane I'd seen in Father Fagan's box. That didn't really matter at the moment. It had wheels on the bottom and as I pushed the plane forward along the floor,

Peter, Dennis and Jeanne, Christmas morning, 1952.

repeatedly, it made a noise and tiny sparks came flying out the back. That's all the toy plane did, make noise and produce a few sparks. It didn't fly. In fact, it had a slightly broken wing. But that didn't matter either. What mattered was that I was happy. I'd gotten something. After we opened our presents, we'd go out and play with our things. Our friends would be out also, showing off what they got for Christmas, all new things. While some of our gifts were new, thanks to the kindness of Mom's Aunt Katherine and her cousin, Florence Larkin, some were used. We knew that our small, simple toys could never match those which our friends received, but that's just how things were in our family. Some kids sported new bikes, and one girl from across the street, Sandra Chiffer, was the recipient of a brand new, gas powered go-kart. As she'd zoom up and down the street in her "new car," I wondered about a few things. Why would Santa give one kid something so big and new like that, and not us? Why did the other kids in the neighborhood get so much more? I never asked Mom these questions, nor did I ask her why Father Fagan brought us toys and not Santa. I never let on that I'd seen that blue and gray plane through a hole in the box. I didn't have to, partly because I was at an age when kids stopped believing in Santa. I was also old enough by then to know something of our family's plight and guessed, correctly, that Mom had to accept such donations from thoughtful, generous folks like Father Fagan in order to give us any type of Christmas at all. I'm sure I couldn't articulate it back then, but the story of Father Fagan and his crepe paper covered box with the plane inside caused me to realize something very important. It was then that I learned we were a poor family, the kind they spoke of at church and school that were "needy," the kind toward which others should be generous. It didn't make me angry to realize that we were poor. On the contrary, it toughened me and allowed me to learn that I would have to accomplish more on my own because things wouldn't easily be given to me in life. It also deepened my respect for Mom. Upon realizing these things, I felt nothing but pride about the things I did receive, whether they were new or used. When you don't have a lot, you tend to cherish that which you do have much more. Due to the circumstances under which we lived, my brothers, sister and I grew up a bit sooner than other kids and I believe we were all the better for it.

Christmas was a very happy time in our house, regardless of what we received or didn't receive, or whether it was new or used. To this day, more than 60 years later, Christmas remains a very special time for me, in great part because it reminds me of the happy times we had during our Levittown years.

Putting Things in Context: The Children of Nicaragua

So far, the focus of this writing has been on struggles of one kind or another, stories of life's difficulties without a dad, or a decent household income, or a family car. While all those struggles are true and so often complicated our lives, it is important to note that things weren't really that bad for us kids growing up in the 1950's, mostly because Mom shielded us from problems and gave us the time and room we needed to be kids, to join in what other kids were doing, so we could have safe, worthwhile, productive young lives.

There's another reason that things weren't really that bad for us. When I compare the conditions I experienced during my youth to those of children throughout so much of the world, I realize that I should have no complaints at all. For 36 years I was a teacher. I spent one of those years teaching in Ft. Greene, an inner-city neighborhood of Brooklyn, where many of my students were far poorer than I was as a kid. I spent my other 35 years as a teacher in suburbia, or "cupcake land" as one city teacher friend of mine dubbed school communities on Long Island's north shore. Throughout my years as a social studies teacher, I was lucky, privileged actually. I was permitted to dream big and then allowed to act on those dreams. From 1990 to 2008, my school board approved my applications to lead thousands of students to Central America 50 times or more, and even once to western Africa, where we gained first hand experiences in the poorest regions of the world. In Nicaragua, my students and I lived and worked side by side with the most impoverished people in our hemisphere, slept in their dirt floor shacks, used their primitive latrines, and ate their simple, meager diet of rice, beans and bread. On every visit I'd see children doing things that the vast majority of adults here would struggle to do, especially physical things. Almost everything in rural sections of Nicaragua is done manually, often in very primitive ways, whether by a muscular field hand with a machete, or a child manually pulling water from a deep well then carrying it, bucket by bucket to her distant, primitive schoolhouse. Everything is done by hand. There are no forklifts in the campos, no paved roads, and very few vehicles. When we began our work there in 1990, all the water was from contaminated open wells. There was no electricity, no ice cubes, no radios, no phones, no modern conveniences at all. Out of necessity, children in such places are a great part of the labor force. Five year olds tend to one year olds while both their parents toil in the fields for less than $2 a day. Children walk several kilometers to and from their schools each day on unpaved trails with dust a foot deep during the dry season and mud one foot deep during the rainy season. As they perform these tasks they don't complain but manage to smile instead. So being responsible for ourselves while Mom shopped, walking or biking wherever we had to go, while perhaps admirable and commendable by today's North American standards, is quite relative and needs to be placed in proper context. Compared with the jobs required of kids throughout the world, jobs that must be done in order for them to have the very means by which to live, we did only what Mom expected of us. As special and rewarding as our childhood jobs were, when looking at them from a global perspective, they really weren't that special. Regardless of how little we had growing up, kids throughout two thirds of the world, kids who walk barefoot everywhere on hot, dusty, rocky roads, hungry kids who eat only one mango a day, thirsty kids who drink contaminated water because it's all they've got, kids with only rags for clothing, have far less. Compared with them, we had it made.

W. T. Clarke High School

Toward the end of 8th grade I was pretty happy at St. Ignatius. I was a young teen with nice friends there, getting all ready for my next big step in life, high school. The teachers at St. Ignatius made a big deal of pushing all of us toward applying for acceptance into a Catholic high school. In order to be accepted I'd have to score well on a big test called the Cooperative Exam. My score on this exam, plus my elementary school record and teacher's recommendation were the criteria for getting in, or so I thought. I had my eye on the all-boys Chaminade High School for several reasons. Cousin Bill Fowkes lived nearby and he was an alumnus of Chaminade. Bill was ten years older than I and he married my second cousin, Joan Larkin, the daughter of Mom's first cousin, Florence Larkin. Bill had been an All-Catholic HS Football League champion when he went there in the mid 1950's. He also taught social studies and English at Chaminade at the time and urged me to apply. My brother Robert, who left the prep seminary after three years, was admitted to Chaminade in the fall of 1960, spent his senior year there, and graduated in June of 1961. Two months later he headed to Chaminade College of Honolulu. So while Chaminade was becoming a family tradition, the biggest reason I wanted to go to there was because most of my male classmates at St. Ignatius were applying. Getting accepted would be like making a who's who list. My second choice was St. Dominic's High School in Oyster Bay. All this became moot in the late spring of 1961 when I received a letter saying that I was not accepted into either Chaminade or St. Dominic's. I had to face the fact that I was not going to join my St. Ignatius friends in high school, and that I had basically failed to achieve my goal. I felt like I'd failed at high school before it had even begun. Instead I'd be going to the local public school, W. Tresper Clarke High School in Westbury NY, where my neighborhood friends went. That made my rejection feel a bit better. But the fact that I didn't get in to any of the Catholic schools while so many others from St. Ignatius did devastated me. My 90+ average at St. Ignatius, higher than some of the other kids who were accepted, and the medal I won at graduation seemed to count for nothing. My greatest problem with not getting into Chaminade or St. Dominic's was the plain fact that I'd fallen short of attaining a goal I deemed important. I was embarrassed when my St. Ignatius friends asked, "Which schools did you get into?" and I had to tell them that I didn't get in to any. The kids who'd done well on the Cooperative Exam and gotten accepted to the school of their choice were effervescent, with huge smiles on their faces as they held up their letters of acceptance. I felt terrible, a failure, and began to sink into a sort of teenage abyss. I cried the night I got the bad news.

As usual, and long before the Beatles sang "Let it Be," Mom came to me speaking words of wisdom. *"Peter, Don't worry about this. You're a good student, you'll do fine at Clarke. You'll be with your neighborhood friends, and you'll make new ones. You'll see."* I thought Mom was just saying that to cheer me up. How could she know about Clarke High School? How could she know how I felt? When I told her the names of some of my St. Ignatius classmates who did gain acceptance, she was more than miffed. She found out that some of the parents went directly to the principals of those Catholic schools and offered to donate money, something she neither could do, nor, if she had it, would she do, just to get her son in. Mom dealt above the table, not under it. She also learned that some very undeserving kids, troublemakers in fact, got in because they were big and tall and had promising athletic reputations. When Mom heard these stories, she called Chaminade to explain that I was worthy of acceptance, would do a good job, and become a strong and successful member of their student body. When her argument went nowhere, she came to the belief that if these schools did not want her son, then they were not good enough, and they couldn't have him. Besides, if Catholic education was so important, where was the charity and kindness from these institutions? St. Ignatius showed quite a bit of charity when it accepted a fraction of the tuition costs during Mom's welfare years. The Catholic high schools seemed to be less than charitable institutions. So it was off to Clarke High I went.

During the summer of 1961, on an extremely hot day, Mom and I walked the two miles to Clarke to meet with the principal's secretary, Mrs. Gray, and the guidance secretary, Ms. Fran Biasi. Mrs. Gray gave us all the papers we needed for me to become enrolled and then brought us to Ms. Biasi. Clarke was very different from St. Ignatius. It had many hallways that seemed to zigzag in all directions, and they were all painted in different colors. There was a large gym and auditorium, and lockers for students to put their things. It all looked so overwhelming. At St. Ignatius, I had a friend named Peter Biasi. He was a nice kid, quite smart. I asked Ms. Biasi if she had any relatives named Peter and she said," Yes, my nephew. He's your age and just finished St. Ignatius School." This made me feel so much better, that a smiling, helpful woman at Clarke was related to a good friend from my eight years at St. Ignatius. I felt closer to Clarke already, knowing that I had a person I could go to in the event I needed help. My schedule included the basics like Social Studies, English, Algebra, General Science, and a foreign language. Mom thought Latin would be a good choice, saying it'd be helpful throughout my life, so I went with that. We then walked back home in the hot, humid August heat.

Clarke Teachers and Coaches, My First Men

In September 1961, I became a member of the freshman class at Clarke High School. I had just come from eight years of having all women teachers. The only men I ever saw during my eight years at St. Ignatius were the non-English speaking school custodian, Steve, a bus driver named Vic, and a few priests who never once spoke with me. Prior to Clarke, women had guided every aspect of my life. Although she never said it to me, I think Mom was happy I was going to Clarke, where at least half the teaching staff was male. She knew the value of the guidance such men could provide me, especially since I'd had so little male influence thus far in life. Of my first classroom teachers at Clarke, two were men, my science teacher, Mr. Hugo DeCiutiis, a brilliant scholar and perhaps the most humorous man I ever met, and Mr. Harry Healy, a patient, knowledgeable and fair man. Mr. DeCiutiis was an excellent science teacher, one who kept the class attentive at all times, mostly because of his ability to explain complex science concepts in ways that made them easy to understand and appreciate. At St. Ignatius, we didn't have any science classes, so everything Mr. DeCiutiis taught was new and interesting to me. He opened my mind to things about which I had no awareness, like simple machines and physics, electricity, plants and animals, cell theory, the universe and so much more. Mr. DeCiutiis lived in Westbury and was very involved in civil rights and improving race relations. An officer of the NAACP, he stood for fairness in housing, employment and basic civil rights, and was often quoted in the newspapers. Having come from an environment that was almost completely man-less, spending a year with a genius like Mr. DeCiutiis was a powerful experience for me, as well as an extreme pleasure. My social studies teacher, Mr. Harry Healy, was a literal fountain of knowledge. His World Geography course was about more than mountains, rivers, plateaus and deserts, but about the whole world and its people. I looked forward to his class every day, tried my best on all the assignments he gave us, frequently raised my hand in class, and was so inspired by him that I became a history major in college and eventually a social studies teacher myself. Mr. Healy had a special way about him, so much so that I can still remember how he held the chalk, how he spoke, even some of his exact words when he called on me in his very manly voice. "Pete, please. Come on up to the map. Show us the British Isles and tell us what you learned from last night's homework." Not reluctantly but comfortable and enthusiastic, I'd find myself standing in front of the class uttering a few words about the British Isles or some other part of the world. It was in his class, six years before the Six Day War, that I first learned of the Arab-Israeli conflict and such names as Egypt's President Gamal Abdel Nasser, Israel's founder David Ben-Gurion, and the P.L.O. It was in Mr. Healy's class that I first learned of the horrors of apartheid in South Africa, world hunger, and sweatshops in Mexico and Central America. Mr. Healy's class opened up the whole world for me. After a few minutes of going it alone in front of the class, Mr. Healy would interrupt saying, "Pete. Great job. It's good to see a man who's prepared, unafraid to stand up and give it a try." He taught me how stand up in public, make eye contact with an audience, and take advantage of opportunities to come up big, all skills I'd use later on in life. More than that, he was the first man that ever told me I was doing a good job. He'd reward us when we were prepared, and treat us gently when we were not. I never felt afraid in his class, but instead free to learn. As my interest in the world grew, so did my respect for this wonderful teacher. I envied his children for having such a wise and kind man for a dad.

After I graduated from high school in 1965, I never saw Mr. Healy again. To my surprise, in late July 2013, I read in the newspaper that Harold J. Healy, a Navy Seabee during WWII, passed away at the age of 88. I was greatly saddened at first, and wished I'd known that he was actually a neighbor of mine for decades. His obituary said he lived on Lloyd Neck, only a few miles from me. His house abutted Caumsett State Park, a place I visit regularly to bike, jog and picnic. Then, despite my sadness, a smile came across my face as I realized that he lived to such an age, taught at Clarke until his retirement in1986, was an important member of the Lloyd Neck local government and a leading parishioner at his Huntington church. Harry Healy had lived a good and long life and helped thousands of young people. That's something to smile about. Despite the fact that five decades had lapsed, I decided to go to his wake in Huntington that night. Shortly before closing time, I entered the funeral home and met Mrs. Judy Healy, whom Harry so often affectionately referred to in class as "the wife." Mrs. Healy was surprised but very pleased that I, a student of her husband's from 52 years earlier, attended the service. She immediately called out to the 25 or so friends and family members in the room saying, "Can I have your attention everyone. Please listen. This man was Harry's student many years ago and he'd like to share some things with you." Being somewhat familiar with impromptu public speaking, I was happy to oblige and provided the group with a few stories about Mr. Healy, mostly about how important it was for me and so many other young kids to have had such a valuable and helpful role model as he when we were growing up, and how his knowledge of the world and its people was so inspirational. A number of emotions swirled within me as the friends and family of Harry Healy smiled and clapped at my remarks. It seemed so odd that I should be there, so many years later, and yet so good at the same time. I was saying goodbye to an old friend, and meeting his wife, or "the wife," of more than 50 years for the very first time. The situation was surreal. As I stood before this wonderful gentleman's casket and addressed his family and friends, the sound of his voice and the image of his smile came to me. Recollections of specific lessons came to me as well as I tried to bring some of Mr. Healy's wisdom and wit to those who mourned him.

Never having a dad caused me to be ever so impressed with and influenced by those first good men in my life. The back of the memorial card handed out that night states, "Grieve not…nor speak of me with tears…but laugh and talk of me as though I were beside you. I loved you so…'twas Heaven here with you." I'll always miss Harry Healy, one of my first and most important male role models.

There's a happy and important postscript to this story. At Christmastime 2013, five months after his passing, I received a beautiful handwritten letter from Mrs. Healy which said,

> Dear Peter,
>
> Your words about Harry at his wake have remained with me and your message continues to give me comfort. I would like to meet with you sometime in the New Year…. You mentioned a charitable group that you are involved with. Enclosed please find a check of $500 to support your efforts with the poor…. I know Harry would have responded.
>
> Love, Judy Healy

This letter and generous check did much more than bring a smile to my face. My heart was lifted in a manner that happens rarely in life. After more than 50 years I celebrated the life and career of one of my favorite teachers, began a friendship with his wife, and accepted, for the benefit of the poorest children in our hemisphere, a generous contribution from his family. Several months later, the Healy Family's generous donation was enough to complete the construction of a house for a homeless Nicaraguan family.

Clarke Football and Mr. Wong's

In early September 1961, I learned that a few of my neighborhood friends were going out for freshman football. Franklin Berger was a fast runner, Bobby Hoffman was knowledgeable about football, and Drew Keenan excelled in all sports. Except for swimming, I had no exceptional athletic skills or training but decided to join them and give it a try. After some initial running and calisthenics, the coaches divided up the large group, yelling, "Backs and ends over here, linemen over there!" I had absolutely no idea what they were talking about, so I stood on the field waiting to be told what to do. Coach Tony Lembo shouted, "Hey, what are you standing there for? Are you a lineman or a back?" Knowing little about football, I decided to put myself with the linemen and go with the flow. Not to sound like a sad sack here, but not having a father played a role in my ignorance of the game. With no one to throw the ball around with or give me a pointer or two, or even watch a game on TV with, I was at a loss. The other boys seemed to know what was going on, and many had played junior high football. I had not. But I learned by watching, tried hard and, happily for me, made the team. Coaches Jack MacDonald and Tony Lembo were pretty tough on us. They held rigorous practices every day after school, and Saturdays, and shared with us, publicly, verbally, and often quite loudly, how they felt, especially when we lost a game we could have won. No matter how fast the players would run in practice drills, Coach McDonald always let us know that his grandmother could run faster than we. Since I was new to football, I became a second string lineman on offense and defense. That meant I didn't play too much. Whenever I was put into a game, it was usually toward the end to give the first string players a rest. But I did my job, learned and, with the amount of running, calisthenics and hitting I found myself in pretty decent physical shape by the end of the season. Some of the first string players weren't much better at football than I, if at all, but they were known by the coaches and some had Jack McDonald as a classroom teacher. I was new, and not one of what we then called some of Mr. McDonald's closest students: "Jack's Pets." At the end of the season, I felt proud of myself, the first member of our family to have completed a high school sport. In November 1961, the coaches held the annual Freshman Football Father and Son Dinner at a Chinese restaurant called Mr. Wong's in Westbury. Mr. Wong's was on Old Country Road, two and a half miles from our house. I was so excited to be going to a restaurant, sitting with my new Clarke friends, ordering food from a menu, and having a waiter ask me what I wanted to eat that I forgot about the fact that I didn't have a ride, so I decided to walk. About 45 minutes before the dinner, on a chilly November night I set out for Mr. Wong's on foot. I didn't really mind the long walk in the dark. I took such things as challenges rather than uncomfortable burdens. Thinking I left myself enough time to get there I miscalculated my lengthy excursion by about 15 minutes and arrived at Mr. Wong's a little late. As I entered, I noticed all my teammates and their dads seated throughout the restaurant and Coach MacDonald making a speech. As with the father-son Cub Scout dinner at Frank's Alibi years earlier, I didn't know where to sit. But I was now 14 years old and less afraid, so I sat down at a table with a few of my teammates and their dads and tried to enjoy the evening. During the dinner Mr. McDonald presented all the players with their six-inch felt "C's," Clarke freshman letters for having completed the season. I beamed when my turn came and the coaches called me up, for I had accomplished something I couldn't envision a year earlier. When the dinner was over, the boys and their dads thanked the coaches and adjourned to their cars. I was among the last to leave, perhaps hoping that one dad might notice me and ask if I needed a ride. None did.

As I put my coat on, made my way to the door and prepared for the second leg of my trek, Mr. MacDonald, possibly having noticed that I attended the dinner by myself, asked, "Who's coming to pick you up?" "No one." He asked, "Why?" I usually had some type of answer prepared for folks who asked me things that I either didn't want to answer, or didn't know how to answer, so I just said, "No one can pick me up." Jack asked, "Where do you live?" I told him where and, as I was about to set forth on my moonlit walk, he offered me a ride. On the way, he probed in a sensitive, not a nosy way. Mr. McDonald was a special teacher, one who got involved with the lives and families of his students. When he learned our family circumstances, and that I had walked the long distance from Levittown to Mr. Wong's, he may have begun to see me, and hopefully some other students, in a different light, maybe as someone to watch over a bit more carefully. Mr. MacDonald politely came into my house and met Mom. Uncle Jack," as Mr. MacDonald was referred to by many of the kids, remained a friend of mine long after high school.

I continued to play football throughout my four years at Clarke, and by senior year I had worked my way to being a first string player on both offense and defense, serving as captain when one of our regular captains was not on the field. Mom was glad that I succeeded to some extent at high school football. She must have known how hard it was to begin something like high school sports with such a disadvantage, and how hard it was for me to attend things like father – son dinners, awards nights, and other events, alone. But she didn't want me, or my brothers or sister, to hibernate, or stay home and lick our wounds, or pine away. She encouraged us to join things and get involved, whether it was altar boys, paper routes, scouting or school sports. When I was on the freshman team, Mom came to one game. After teaching all day, she walked the two miles to the Clarke High School field to see a game that we probably lost and I was on the field for only a handful of plays. That was pretty embarrassing for me, to have Mom come that far and not see me play much. But by senior year, when I was on the varsity team, she proudly attended most every game, including some away games, and became a big fan. Once, when an opposing player accidentally thrust his fingers through my facemask and my eyes got poked pretty good, I went down in pain. Before the coaches got onto the field to check me out, Mom somehow made her way from the stands, right onto the field where she stood over me asking, *"Peter, are you ok? Can you see me? How many fingers am I holding up?"* How she got to that away game at Levittown MacArthur High School, four miles from our house, without a car, I don't know. But she was there, supporting me, caring, and worrying. I began to think that single parents have to care twice as much about their children than two-parent families do.

The Physical Fitness Test, Another Step Toward Manhood

Playing high school football raised my self-esteem a fair amount and taught me about self-confidence and the value of teamwork. But it was something else that really helped boost me into manhood: the school's annual physical fitness test. When I was in tenth grade, all the boys and girls were required to take a physical fitness test. The boys' test included five events, with points awarded for each. The first was pull-ups. To earn 100 points a boy had to do 18 regulation pull-ups where his chin had to be pulled all the way up above the bar. Another was sit-ups, where in one minute 60 good ones, with elbows coming all the way up to touch the knees, earned a perfect score. There was also the softball throw, squat thrusts, and a 300-yard run. Over the course of a few weeks, every boy in the school, more than 1000, completed all five events. The scores of the top 100 boys were posted on a large bulletin board right outside the gym door for all to see. Our school had many terrific athletes, including All Long Island Fullback Benny Benith, champion pole vaulter Jackie Carter, All County Catcher Skip Jutze, who later played five seasons of Major League Baseball, and champion wrestler Bryan Lambe. There were so many accomplished, big name athletes at Clarke, I didn't think I could compete with them on this test. I took the events one at a time, and, as was so clearly taught to me by Mom, gave each one my best effort. When the physical education staff totaled all the boys' scores, and the top 100 boys names were posted, dozens of students gathered to see who were the school's most fit young men. I stood in the back of a crowd of several dozen, mostly taller jocks, and tried to get a look. It came as a jolt to me when a top football player gave me with a jab of his elbow and said, "Hey White, Not bad. How'd you do that? You must have been holding out on us." I scanned the names on the board and there it was, my name, Peter White, number ten in the entire school. I was in a temporary state of disbelief, but more than happy, exhilarated in fact that I made that list. After that, my life changed. More kids in the school seemed to know me. I was no longer just the new kid from the Catholic school, but a respected high school athlete, capable of competing with the others. The coaches paid more attention to me, and even the school district's athletic director called me into his office, shook my hand, and congratulated me. Years later, as a graduate student, I took a course called Adolescent Psychology. One of the main points raised whenever we discussed teenagers was that they almost completely exist to have their self-esteem raised. That day, as a tenth grader, I easily could have been the poster boy for that course. No teenager's self-esteem could have been raised higher than mine was as I walked away from those gym doors that day. Mom always told me that she was proud of me, especially if I tried my best at things. *"Peter, if you try your best, don't worry about the results. They'll take care of themselves."* This time her advice paid off in a very special, life-changing way. That day in the fall of 1962 an important transition in life occurred. That was the day I went from feeling like a boy to feeling like a man.

Final Thoughts on Clarke High School

After I graduated from Clarke High School, my brother Dennis and sister Jeanne went there. Dennis excelled in football and lacrosse, and Mom, who by then had her first car, a small, used 1961 Ford Fairlane, attended his games and became his biggest fan. In hindsight, I'm glad I went to Clarke and didn't attend one of the costly, elite Catholic high schools. Mom was right, as she most always was. During my four years at Clarke, I met hundreds of wonderful kids, many of whom I continue to be close friends with to this day. I also learned a great deal from Clarke's co-ed, multi-religious environment. There were Catholics, Protestants and Jews. Most of the kids were from middle-income families. Some were upper-middle income, others from the lower-middle income strata. I'm not sure if I met anyone else who shared our family's circumstances, but as Mom predicted with such encouragement, I did fit in well at Clarke, and I did learn a lot from the many good teachers there. When I graduated from Clarke on a hot day in June 1965, I was incredibly sad to leave my coaches like Jack McDonald and Jack Boyle, my wonderful teachers, and my classmates. Mom and Aunt Katherine, who at that time had only one year to live, attended the graduation ceremony on that sweltering, sticky day and were proud of me.

Aunt Katherine with Peter on his high school graduation, 1965.

I had accomplished many things while there, including making lifelong friends, playing sports, earning a Regent's diploma, and taken a rather rigorous program that included a three-year sequence in Latin, as well as Advanced Algebra and some Calculus. And completely on my own, without any adult help, I applied to and was accepted into several good colleges.

University of Dayton, Getting in, Getting there, and Getting Through

While at Clarke High School, I didn't spend very much time with guidance counselors. There were only a few and I didn't find mine to be very helpful at all. I had a basic academic program and I followed it. When it came time to apply to college, I had absolutely no idea how to begin the process. The one time I visited my counselor was a waste of time. He wanted me to apply only to colleges with easy admission standards so he could boast of a high proportion of his counselees getting accepted. I didn't bother doing anything through him, and made my own college applications and decisions instead. I listened to what other kids were saying about their college plans, looked over a few brochures, and applied to three colleges. I was accepted into two of them, and placed on a waiting list for another. I decided to go to the University of Dayton in Ohio for a few reasons. I was a pretty strict Catholic then and Dayton was a mid-sized Catholic college.

It also had a football team and I thought, as many high school football players often do, that I had a good chance of playing college ball. In the spring of 1965, after I'd applied and been accepted to Dayton, two friends of mine planned to drive out to Illinois to visit the colleges to which they were accepted. They asked me to join them and share the costs. The plan was to drive out to Ohio where I'd get dropped off for a few days, make my way around the University of Dayton campus, see the different buildings, maybe make some appointments and do some planning, while they went on to Illinois to do the same at their colleges. I was curious to see what Dayton, a place I planned on spending the next four years of my life, looked like, so this seemed like a good opportunity for me. Excited about heading to the Midwest during our April school break, I shared my plan with Mom. She rejected it immediately. *"Peter, it sounds like a waste of money and time when you could be here working. You've seen the college in brochures so this trip won't change anything for you. Besides, you already sent in the $15 application fee, so you're going."* That was that. No spring break trip to Ohio. And once again I learned how the almighty dollar, or lack thereof, would have something to do with any plan I tried to make in life. While it may have looked at the time like Mom was just being contrary by not letting me go, the fact is that the two other boys' mothers wouldn't let them go either. Perhaps they saw three 17 year olds in a car going that far just to "check things out" as nonsense. So with no trip to the Midwest, we spent a few freezing days camping in the Catskills instead.

Happily, I found out I wasn't going to be alone at Dayton. A good friend of mine from Clarke, Frank Zeccola, whom we all called Zeke, decided to go there too. As we were both end-of-the-alphabet students, Zeke was in my homeroom and also a football teammate of mine, so we agreed to be roommates. My first challenge with going away to college was getting there. Dayton was a 16-hour drive and maybe an hour and a half plane ride from Long Island. With no car and no plane fare, I had to figure out how to get to southwestern Ohio somehow. My first thought was to hitchhike. It would be a cheap and adventurous way of getting to college, but it might also be quite risky and unreliable. Fortunately Zeke's sister knew of a guy from East Meadow who was heading to the Midwest during the third week of August. Lou, a football player at Purdue University in Indiana, would be passing about 20 miles north of Dayton on the interstate. He asked only that I chip in $10 for gas and share the driving, so I had a ride. In the days leading up to my departure, I packed a suitcase and said goodbye to friends and family. On a Friday night at 9 p.m. in late August 1965, Lou showed up at my house. As I was about to leave, a good friend if mine, Father Jack Murphy, a very popular priest from our church, came over to say goodbye to me. Father Jack, or as my friends and I called him, "Murph the Surf" because he was such an avid surfer, was my confraternity teacher in high school and a good friend. That night he told me he was leaving Holy Family parish and joining the Army as a chaplain. As a young man during World War II, Father Murphy had been an Army corporal. Now, 20 years later he decided he wanted to go back and minister to troops in Vietnam. We had become close, so the news of Father Murphy leaving was a shock. Another important male leaving my life. I was having such a good time with my family and Father Murphy I felt briefly that I didn't want to get into that car. I didn't really want to go to far away Dayton. But Lou was out front waiting, so after a few quick hugs and handshakes, in what seemed to take less than a minute's time,

I was gone. Lou took the first shift, driving throughout the night, getting us somewhere into the middle of Pennsylvania. I didn't know him so I mostly sat quietly by myself. When Lou got tired and needed to sleep, he gave me the wheel. I had a driver's license but not a lot of driving experience. Exhausted, I drove Lou's green 1957 Chevy through the rest of Pennsylvania during the night, through Wheeling, WV, and into Zanesville, Ohio by morning. Lou finally woke up and drove the rest of the way, dropping me off at an exit about 20 miles north of Dayton. On a hot August day in 1965, with suitcase in hand, I hitched my way into the Gem City, the Birthplace of Aviation, the sixth largest city in Ohio, my home for the next few years, Dayton.

Mom didn't want me to go to a large college. She cautioned, *"Those big colleges are like factories. You'll get lost in the shuffle."* I had been accepted to the much larger St. John's University, but followed Mom's advice and chose Dayton instead thinking it was a medium sized school and not factory-like. Once in downtown Dayton I walked south, toward the university. I couldn't help but notice a tremendously large building that looked just like a factory, with large smokestacks puffing huge plumes of smoke, and people hanging out windows to escape the heat. I thought, "Wow. Mom was right. Big colleges really do look like factories." For a brief moment I actually thought that I was looking at the University of Dayton. I asked around and was told that the large building was National Cash Register, the largest employer in the city of Dayton. I had arrived just around quitting time and thought NCR was UD. A worker pointed me about half a mile east where I finally came upon the university. There I encountered another problem: the dormitory I was supposed to live in wasn't open for another week. What was I going to do? Where would I sleep for the next week? I stood alone in the middle of the entirely empty campus with little to do and no one around. Just to hook an inexpensive ride with Lou, I'd come too early. Registration and classes didn't begin until after Labor Day so I walked around the campus and found a helpful dean named Ann Franklin who assisted me with course selection. After squaring some things away with Ms. Franklin and bored with moping around the campus, I still had to find a place to sleep. The thought crossed my mind that just as Mom faced many problems and had to find ways to solve them, I'd have to solve this one by myself. Small as my suitcase was, I had to drag it everywhere I went. I began knocking on the doors of what looked like college rental houses, seeking a place to stay. At most of the apartments, no one was in, but I kept trying anyway. I got frustrated after the first few guys said no to my request, which was understandable since I was a total stranger. A few tries later, a guy in one apartment, whom I woke up late in the afternoon, said yes, but with a condition. His roommates were coming in a week and they expected to sleep on the new beds that they had just received. The beds were still in boxes and I was welcome to sleep on top of them. This didn't matter to me; at least I had a place to stay. It rained most of the week, so I hung out in the college buildings, familiarizing myself with the campus, writing letters, waiting for college to start. On August 31, 1965, on a dreary, rainy day, I celebrated my 18th birthday by taking a bus into downtown Dayton and registering for the draft, something required of every 18-year-old then. The Vietnam War was just beginning to heat up.

After what seemed to be a never-ending, boring week with little to do, UD finally opened the dormitory and the students began to arrive. I felt totally out of place wearing sneakers and a tee shirt while these newly arriving kids got out of their parents' cars all dressed up. They wore neatly pressed clothes. Some looked like young businessmen, wearing winged-tip shoes and three piece suits. The parade of station wagons stretched for hundreds of yards from the dorm, Stuart Hall, down the long hill toward the main campus. The new students and their parents unloaded dozens of boxes containing everything their sons could possibly need. I looked at this migration of young men and their many boxes and compared it with my little suitcase. Why had I come to college with so little and they had so much? I didn't know anyone and didn't understand what was going on around me. I met kids in the dorm from Cleveland, Pittsburgh, Chicago, Toledo, and Indianapolis. Many were from Catholic high schools and seemed to know one another. They spoke what sounded like a different language than I was used to. Frank, a well-dressed young man from Indianapolis, asked me if I was a new student. Wearing a tee shirt, shorts and sneakers, I said yes. Frank looked at how I was dressed and said, "Hey, I didn't know we were allowed to wear shirts around here." I looked at my shirt and said, "What do you mean? What's wrong with wearing a shirt?" He pointed at my shorts and said, "No. Shirts." Evidently, in Indianapolis, the word "shorts" is pronounced more like the word "shirts" to the New York ear. With the differences in accents, I felt as if I was in a foreign country. Zeke arrived with his parents later that day. They had flown to Dayton.

After settling into the dorm with Zeke, I began classes the next day in sort of a fog. A few weeks went by and I didn't really know where I stood. I wasn't failing my tests and quizzes, but I wasn't doing very well either. I attributed this to being fearful of raising my hand in class, seeking extra help, and getting certain complex things clarified. I began to question whether or not I was prepared for the rigors of college. Dayton had a pretty strict method of determining grades. The grade inflation that is so rampant today hadn't begun yet. For example, if I received a 70 on an exam, it became a D on my report card. If I received a 79, it was still a D. I needed an 80 or better in order to get a C, and a 90 or better in order to receive a B. An A seemed completely out of reach, for that would have required a grade of 95 or better. My first midterms were alarmingly low. Afraid, embarrassed and without having any of the fun that is usually associated with a young person going away to college, I worried. I didn't drink alcohol at that time, so I wasn't going out with the guys when weekends came. Since this was decades before the advent of the cell phone or email, and a call from a phone booth was expensive, I was basically out of touch with home. Growing homesick and feeling very far away in my new state and my new life, I wrote to Mom. I'm sure I sounded like a spoiled whiner, but my letter was a chance for me to get a few things off my chest. This prompted a response from her that served to help and guide me. She answered in a manner that I very much needed to hear at that time. In late September 1965, after I'd been gone a little more than a month, Mom wrote,

Dear Peter,

Your nice letter arrived today and we all appreciated hearing from you. I'm glad you finally opened up because if you keep things to yourself too long, you can really explode. What you must realize is – everyone is bothered with

some type of a problem, but we can't let these problems get the best of us. When I was first left with four young children to rear my first act was to bring them to church and all of you were dedicated to Mary. This was a solemn ceremony performed by the priest. I thought she could help me and I don't think she has failed me. Then I said to myself, 'If God trusted me with so many children He must think me capable of the job.' So, I began this task. How? I didn't know – but begin I did. Each day brought many joys and ever so many problems, but I tried to overlook the latter for fear of faltering. I really and truly knew how, but I lacked the quality of leadership. I needed someone to 'tell' me what to do. Finally I began to get more confidence in myself and not to care about what people thought of me. And I lived through it and we managed.

I'm very glad to hear you turned to prayer for help and guidance because God will hear and answer our prayers – maybe not in the way we want but in His way. You know enough about God's will – If you look at things that way it is His answer. Not ours. We are all human and have human failings and must not expect to be perfect. Now you are a student at Dayton and you are there to do your best. That is all I ever asked of any of you. Frank's mother called me last night and said she was very pleased with the college. She told me you were worried about failing – You shouldn't waste your time worrying about something that hasn't begun yet. I know you will get very good grades and I want you to have much more confidence in yourself. Look how nicely you did in Clarke and that was very strange after a Catholic school. I think you were even sorry to leave Clarke. So you will cultivate the same feeling for Dayton when you are settled and used to the place.... Aunt Katherine is fine and asks you not to be too serious. She says get out and mingle with the fellows and girls and enjoy yourself. Don't bury yourself in the books. Nothing else is new. I'm getting all ready for my big "first" day in the classroom. That is really the hardest of them all. Today we had a mass at the cathedral in Rockville Centre and I volunteered to drive a few nuns. The car wouldn't start and I was stranded. I asked a neighbor and she took me up to the convent and the school nurse saved the day by driving all of us to the cathedral. So with no car, you see my problems are never ending. I'll have to take the school bus with the kids, but I'll manage. Peter, you are very capable and your schedule looks good. Take care of yourself.

Love from all,

Mom

This letter from Mom was exactly what I needed to allay my fears and set me on a straighter path. I was going awry, and her words of encouragement brought things into perspective and gave me a new direction. I was so worried about the possibility of failing at something that had only just begun, while Mom had to teach 50 five-year-olds and had no way of even transporting herself to her job. Her letter helped me see things more clearly and gave me the impetus to move on. She wasn't my only provider of confidence-building words. Around the same time her letter arrived, I ran into a friend at Dayton who I knew from Long Island named Charlie Newton. Charlie was two years older than I, and a very successful college student. He told me that he'd gotten all A's on his midterms. While my grades were passing, they were on the low side. I said, "Charlie, I read every night, do all my assignments, and I still struggle. What am I doing wrong?" In his laconic way, Charlie had a three-word answer, "You got books?" Then he walked away. I thought about what he said, and I concluded that, whatever amount of time I was putting in, it wasn't enough. I decided to work harder and seek help from peers who were doing better. These strategies helped, and by end of the first semester, I picked up my grades and stood on more solid academic ground.

I also received some moral support from my brother Robert during those first trying days away from home. In a letter dated September 29, 1965, Robert said,

Dear Peter,

I figured you would be depressed your first time away from home – this is only natural. I, too, felt the same way when I went to the seminary. The first day was great – I really involved myself with the life of the place. However, when I actually realized that I would not see home again for at least a year, the thought sunk deep. I was not homesick, I just realized I was in a strange place, doing something not many choose to do…. I was disappointed to hear you decided not to play football in college. I would like to see you play as it would make me very proud of my brother, but if your grades were to fall, I would be even more disappointed. Don't feel by any means that you are not good enough for anything; just try your best to do a good job – which I know you can….
I'm glad that Mom wrote to you and that now you fully realize the situation. This is one reason why I have had to do things the way I did…. Mom knows I've been working, but she doesn't know that I'm working full time as manager of a bar in downtown Honolulu, seven days a week. Since I began there one and a half years ago, I have had one day off. I work a total of about 50 hours a week, and for this I get the sum of about $275 a month, and take home about $225. This is all I have to pay tuition, rent, gas, telephone, electric, and loan…. I prefer it this way so that you will be able to get a good education. I want Mom to help you if possible and not me. She helped me for a while, but I must do it myself. Just bring home good grades. It'll please Mom. Life is hard and hectic, but that's the only way it can be done…. Right now the going is rough, but I'll stick it out as I have been doing…. I hope that by telling you this that you'll stick things out when the going gets rough. It will, believe me….

Love,

Robert

Robert's letter, combined with Charlie's advice and Mom's powerful words, got me back on track. They provided the recipe I needed to stay in school. Dennis, Jeanne and I always wondered why Robert came back to Long Island only one time during college, the summer of 1962, and now the answer was clear. He was being the best son he could be from afar, taking care of all his expenses himself, including tuition, school, and living expenses, and he lived in Hawaii, a brand new state, where the cost of living was higher than on the mainland. He was unburdening Mom and the rest of us and consequently had little money to spare. Coming back to New York to visit was an economic impossibility until much later on. His next visit to L.I. was ten years later, when he was married and had a young daughter, Ann Marie. Robert and Mom's letters sent me some strong messages: that I should get hold of myself, face things directly, and take life's obstacles as chances to grow and learn rather than mull over and become consumed by things. They challenged me to become a more independent, self-directed young man, reliant on myself and less of a burden on Mom and Aunt Katherine. When I first went to Dayton, I was able to pay my bills with money I'd saved from all the jobs I had. It was enough to pay for my entire first semester. When second semester rolled around, I was broke. At Christmastime, Aunt Katherine gave me a check for $500 and told me to go back to Dayton for the spring semester. "Peter, you have to stay in school," she said. I reluctantly took her check, not as a gift but as a loan, one that I would pay back in full. Thanks to her I finished my second semester owing no one but her. Eight months later Aunt Katherine died, but I didn't forget her kindness. By the spring of 1967 I paid the $500 back to Mom and, like Robert, I decided that I would rather work hard and live debt free than take loans and be obligated for years to come.

College tuition, room and board, especially at a private school, wasn't cheap. I knew nothing of the State University of New York, the SUNY system of more than 30 colleges, where costs were only half that of private colleges. Unfortunately, my high school counselor told me nothing of SUNY. In order to continue at Dayton, I needed to work. Reluctant to borrow, I found jobs that paid $1.50 an hour, the minimum wage back then. On weekends I worked as a hotel clerk at the no frills Hotel Holden in downtown Dayton, corner of Fifth and Wilkinson, near the old railroad station. Guests at the very inexpensive Hotel Holden, where room rents varied from $3 for windowless rooms next to the elevator, to $8.50 per night for corner rooms with two windows, were from a variety of backgrounds including truck drivers, people who couldn't afford more expensive hotels, and strippers and their "boyfriends" from the Mayfair Theater a few blocks away. I worked Saturdays and Sundays from 4:00 p.m. until midnight, usually walking the several miles back to the campus. Buses didn't run that late. My job was to run the hotel, since the manager, Jerry Thompson, was usually not there on weekends. I felt better when the bellman, Willie McCoy, was on duty, but that was rare. Willie was black and Jerry, who was from Cincinnati, just across the river from Kentucky, didn't want me to take black guests. The Civil Rights Act of 1965 had just been passed making it a violation of federal law to discriminate in places of public accommodation on the basis of race, religion or national origin. Jerry didn't care too much about the new law and told me to refuse black customers. I said, "Why? You posted the law right on the wall for all to see." He said, "I posted the new law because I have to. Just tell the black people we're full, we have no rooms left." Of course, this went against my beliefs and my entire upbringing, so Willie and I concocted ways to take in as many blacks as we could, especially families who couldn't afford or find lodging elsewhere. We'd give them rooms and have them leave early the next morning without even charging them. I learned a lot at the Hotel Holden. As an eighteen year old, I worked a busy desk, often alone, kept records, dealt with the public, solved problems, worked an old fashioned telephone switchboard, handled and kept track of money, and on occasion, dealt with emergencies like fires and stickups. Most importantly I learned to stand up for myself and make decisions I believed were right when I was expected and sometimes even ordered to make decisions that were wrong. When I'd return to the campus late on Saturday and Sunday nights, my friends would wait up to hear just what happened that night out in the real world, the world away from the dorm and the classroom.

The job at the Hotel Holden didn't pay enough for me to get by, much less save anything, so I found additional work. One night a week I became a banquet waiter at the Sheraton Hotel in downtown Dayton. As a banquet waiter I had two large tables of 12 people each, usually at some sort of testimonial dinner or large group event. I'd set 24 places, serve 24 salads, 24 dinners, 24 desserts, and 24 coffees, then bus both tables when the event was over. I was the only young man on the wait staff and the only white person. All of the other waiters were black and older than I. Many were Korean War veterans and as a history major I enjoyed listening to their stories of segregated America, the war, and their struggles. On Saturday mornings I had another job at Genuine Auto Parts on South Main Street. Coming from a car-less family, I was pretty unfamiliar with auto parts, but learned quickly on the job. In addition to organizing parts in the warehouse, and bagging old brake shoes, clutch plates and carburetors to be sent back to Borg-Warner in Chicago for rebuilding, I delivered parts to auto shops all over the city in their rickety pickup truck. I learned about more than auto parts while at Genuine. It was there that I that I first became acquainted with racial injustice. One afternoon, after bagging hundreds of dirty, greasy carburetors, my co-worker Jimmy, a black student from the nearby, mostly black Wright State Junior College, and I sat down to take a two minute break. Just then, the boss, Louie, stepped in and caught us in the act of what appeared to be loafing. He chastised us saying angrily, "Is this what I'm paying you for? To sit around? Now get back to work or get out!" After Louie left, I said to Jimmy, "I don't believe we have to take this crap for a lousy $1.80 an hour." In disbelief, Jimmy responded, "$1.80 an hour? They pay you that much?" I said, "Yes. What do they pay you?" Jimmy said, "I get $1.50 an hour." Learning that this young black man, who did the same work as I but much faster because he knew far more about auto parts, earned less than I, was shocking and upsetting to me. I said, "You should go right up to Louie and tell him to pay you what I get, or more. You know much more about this stuff than I do." Jimmy smiled, shook his head and said, "Pete, you don't understand. No matter where I go I'll never get more than $1.50."

While at Dayton, I have to admit to a bit of financial ignorance. This was probably due to the fact that I never had money. People without money usually know little about it. Whenever I ran absolutely broke and was hungry, which happened once in a while, I'd go to the student cafeteria and ask the ladies behind the counter for something to eat. I'd say, "I don't have any money right now, but if you give me a cheese sandwich, I promise I'll pay for it as soon as I can." Sometimes that worked, sometimes it didn't. When it didn't, when such a person was unwilling to advance me a forty-cent cheese sandwich for a day or two, I must confess to waiting patiently until she wasn't looking, and taking that sandwich. Only out of necessity of course. In the middle of my senior year, I had no money and was unable to register. One semester away from graduation and I'd finally found out there was a financial aid office. Like I said, people without money usually know little about it. I stopped in and asked to meet Mr. Hoover, who ran the office. Hoover also served as the university's baseball coach. Most of the people I saw coming in and going out were his players. He smiled and waved at each one. "Hey Tommy, Nice to see you. Don't worry. Everything's going to be alright." Tommy lived in my dorm freshman year and was Hoover's second baseman. After waiting a while, Hoover met briefly with me and allowed me to explain my situation, that I'd come from a single parent household of four children, that my Mom earned only a tiny salary, and that I would have to drop out if I didn't get some type of help. As a few more ball players waited outside his office with smiles on their faces, Hoover looked at me and matter-of-factly said, "There's nothing I can do for you, son." Dayton didn't offer scholarships for baseball players, but it was evident that Hoover made deals with them, that they were getting some kind of help, while guys like I were not. The more I saw what was going on, the angrier I grew. I wasn't there to mooch or beg. I was trying to get listened to, maybe eligible for a scant bit of help, a crumb, a $200 loan, anything just to be able to stay in school. Instead I got sent down the road. I've never forgotten Hoover's unwillingness to listen further, to even try finding a way to keep me in school. To this day I've never responded to any of the University of Dayton's fundraising appeals, never sent a dime, and never will. As with almost everything else in my life, I finished college on my own, paying my own way, one semester at a time until done. Since I had to work those three jobs to stay in school, my grade point average wasn't very high, but as Sinatra sang, "I Did It My Way." In the spring of 1969, when another tuition increase took effect, I didn't fold. So close to graduation and on the brink of dropping out, I knew I had to find some way to get through. It was then that Larry Sowa, a wonderful friend of mine from Chicago, rescued me. Larry was head resident of the largest dorm on campus. In addition to getting a salary, he also got free housing. Late one night, I visited him at his dorm office, thinking I might be saying goodbye. "Larry," I said, "I think I have to leave school. I can't pay for last semester." Without discussion, Larry looked seriously at me and said, "How much do you need?" "$500," I said. Larry opened his desk drawer, pulled out his checkbook and, without hesitation or reservation, wrote a check to me for $500. I didn't know what to say. From his own pocket, Larry had given me what this large university would not even loan me, enough to complete my last semester. Though I paid Larry back in full by the summer of 1969, I've never forgotten his kindness.

If Mom or I had known a fraction back then of what families today know about filling out financial aid forms, going to state schools or colleges that offer financial assistance, I'd have been able to go to college far more cheaply than I did, maybe even for free. Instead I paid for the whole thing myself, with no breaks, no reductions, no financial counseling, no aid at all

THE MISSING PARENT

Throughout my boyhood I increasingly became aware of the fact that other families were different from mine. They had mothers and fathers, while we had only Mom. I didn't really think too much of this as a young child, but the older I got the more curious I grew.

When we were very young, on occasion Mom would sit on the back yard grass with us and sing nursery rhymes. *"Clap hands, clap hands, till daddy comes home."* That little ditty caused me a slight glimmer of hope that someday my father would walk through our front door and stay. But that day never came. He never came back. As I got a little older, I didn't discuss our "missing parent" very much, but inside my questions remained. Was there such a person? Was he alive? Who was he? Where was he? What did he look like? What does he do? Does he know about us? Does he miss us? On the few occasions I recall asking Mom about my father, Robert A.

Peter, 3, wearing Robert A. White's Army hat.

White, she usually gave me brief answers, something that would suit me until the moment passed. "Mom, Where's daddy?" *"Chicago I think."* "When is daddy coming home?" *"Soon, maybe."* Satisfied with such answers, I'd go back out to play.

Levittown was located in central Nassau County, only a few miles from the Mitchel Field airbase. The early 1950's were the Korean War days. Air Force planes constantly flew overhead, disrupting our conversations and our play. I'd look up at the huge planes circling overhead, their loud propellers rocking the neighborhood, and ask Mom "Is daddy on one of those planes? Is that the one he's on? She'd answer, *"Maybe."* Of course the truth was he was not in Chicago, nor on one of those Air Force planes, nor was he coming home. I just didn't know that, and Mom may not have known how to deal with telling me. During my entire childhood, Robert A. White wasn't a real person, but more of a phantom, an image I conjured up in my head, perhaps from old photos. For the next decade or more, he continued to be someone I wondered about now and then, but of whom I knew very little.

Father Komescher

Years later, as a college student in early 1966, I took a mandatory course called the Theology of Christ. The teacher was the Theology Department chairperson, Father Matthew Komescher. On the first day of class Father Komescher required each student to fill out and submit a questionnaire that sought personal information. During the ensuing few weeks, he called each one into his office individually to chat and get better acquainted. Tall, bald, and firm when he spoke, Father Komescher was an imposing, no-nonsense man who commanded respect. Few would mess with him. Students dubbed him

"Yahweh," Hebrew for God. I wasn't used to being one-on-one with men, or having to answer personal questions posed by them, so when my turn came I was apprehensive. Wearing his long black cassock and Roman collar, he sat behind the large desk in his spacious office peering down at me. I looked up at him from my small chair. Referring to my responses to his questionnaire, Father began inquiring about my hometown, hobbies and family. These were safe questions, ones I could easily answer. A few minutes into the interview, I grew uncomfortable as he began asking personal questions about my family, including my father. I didn't want to answer some of them, mostly because I really didn't know the answers. Mom never spoke badly about Robert A. White. In fact, she never spoke of him at all unless one of us asked. Even then her answers were limited and vague. She had no recent awareness of

Robert A. White with Mom on their wedding day, January 10, 1942.

his whereabouts, his occupation, or anything at all, and neither did I. Up to this point in my life, I felt that certain things relating to my family were private matters. Whenever I was asked anything about Robert A. White, I'd always respond with one word, "deceased." This was my way of getting around those uncomfortable moments created whenever the topic of Robert A. White came up. One question on Father's list was "Father's Occupation." I suppose I could have responded, "I don't know," but that would have invited even more questions. "Deceased" was easier, a one-word answer that put the matter to rest in an instant. Though essentially I was lying, I felt this was my business and I didn't have to share it with anyone if I didn't want to, and that included "Yahweh" Komescher. When Father got to this question, he looked down at me through his bifocals, and in a serious, concerned way said, "How long has your dad been dead, son?" I paused briefly, then said, "It's a funny thing, Father. He's really not dead." Astonished at my answer, Father Komescher sat back, his face looking grim. I was confused and thought to myself, "What? Am I in trouble for lying about something that's totally my business? Why can't I have my own business?" On the other hand, I was not being truthful, and I was lying to Yahweh Komescher no less. Even though none of us knew much about Robert A. White, never had a visit from him, and never received as much as a birthday card, a phone call, or a cent from him, we all had our own way of dealing with our missing parent. I'd simply put thoughts of him aside and, respecting Mom, gone on with my life. But this was a different kind of moment, one I'd never experienced before. An uncompromising man of great influence was asking me direct questions about my father, and I didn't have any answers. Given the setting, it was impossible for me to do as I'd always done before: fabricate things just to end the inquiry. This insistent priest was demanding more of me than I'd demanded of myself. He was requiring me to consider questions I'd not asked, and Mom had never mentioned.

With a stern look on his face, Father Komescher continued. Leaning forward from his chair and across his big desk, he looked right into my face and said, "You wrote that your dad is dead and he isn't?" "Yes," I said sheepishly. As if to say, "What's wrong with you?" Father fired back, "Why would you do such a thing? Why would you lie about your own father?" Shaken, I told the truth. "It's the best answer I have, Father. I put that down because I really didn't know what to put. I don't know anything about him, and that's how I've always handled questions about him." I don't really know why Father Komescher probed so much, but he did. I don't remember every word he spoke, but one line remained etched in my memory, "Why would you say someone as important to you as your dad is dead when he very well may be alive?" I didn't argue with him, or try to exculpate myself, or lie any further. I didn't feel I had to. I just listened, said "Yes Father" a few times, and left his office far more puzzled than when I went in. Clouds of doubt entered my consciousness as I asked myself, "Was I was right to deny the existence of my father all these years? Father really believes I'm wrong about all this. Am I? And what of Mom? Why had she kept me in the dark for so long? Was there some secret from which she was shielding me?" For years I'd avoided asking Mom too much about Robert A. White, for asking her about him had always seemed tantamount to crossing her. But after this interview, for the first time in my life, I began to give serious consideration to the existence and whereabouts of Robert A. White. "I really do have a father. I wonder where he is and what he's like?" This curiosity remained until the semester ended in late April when I returned home and took a job as a swimming pool repairman. As I worked through early May on pool after pool, I continued to mull over these doubts, denials, and questions, until one day I decided to act. I made up my mind to locate Robert A. White.

Uncle Eddie

When we were growing up, almost all my friends had grandparents, uncles, aunts and cousins. I had none on Mom's side, as she was orphaned young and grew up as an only child. On my father's side there were a few relatives, but I knew nothing of my grandmother Mary White, whom we referred to as Nanny, nor uncles George and Edward, and aunt Peg. Throughout childhood I was always puzzled at the fact that none of them ever called, none sent a card or a gift, none visited, ever. Why? Why did they all stay away? If any had children, why were we deprived of knowing our cousins? Why did I never have anyone to call "uncle" or "aunt" or "grandma"? Those words were as foreign to me as the word "dad." Why did I know nothing of how these unseen, almost imaginary relatives spoke, laughed or behaved? Like Robert A. White, they were phantoms to me. In a baby book Mom kept of me there was a notation that my "Uncle" George White was my godfather when I was baptized in 1947. He accepted this responsibility by proxy, failed to attend my christening, then never once communicated with me.

The first step in my search for Robert A. White was to locate his older brother, Edward. From past conversations I'd had with Mom, I believed he lived in an apartment in Washington Heights, the Irish and Jewish neighborhood where Mom and Robert A. White grew up. With absolutely no personal knowledge of him, I hoped that Edward might be a decent man since he was a former Irish Christian brother and was reputed to have been good to his mother, my grandmother, Irish immigrant Mary Tighe White, of whom I had no knowledge. One night, in the spring of 1966, I made my way to the East Meadow Library to see if they had a Manhattan phone book. Lucky for me, they did. As I opened this thick directory, I became aware of the important transition that was taking place within me. Up until I'd met Father Komescher, out of convenience or fear, I'd always said that my father was dead, even though I knew he wasn't. Now I was in a library, running my fingers through the pages, up and down the many listings of Manhattanites named White, taking actual steps to find him. This was a major realization for me. By my actions, I was making Robert A. White, a man who'd always been an illusion, real. At first I thought my task was too monumental, as there were several pages of Whites, and even a few dozen Edwards. Then, Eureka! I found an Edward White with a Washington Heights address. Hoping that I had the right person, I copied the address down and left. A few days later, on a day off from my summer job, I made my way by train and subway to the Heights, where I quickly found the building I believed to be the residence of Edward White. Without a key to enter, I stood in the vestibule for about ten minutes until someone came along. A nice woman entered and opened the door. She smiled as I held the door for her, then let myself into the lobby. On the directory I found the name "E. White" listed with an apartment number next to it. After a quick elevator ride I stood alone outside the door of the man I hoped was my uncle. A bit timid but not terrified, I thought, "I've come this far. No sense in chickening out now," and knocked loudly. Nothing happened at first, but seconds later, I heard footsteps. What happened next was a little startling. Rather than see the door open or hear a voice call out, "Who's there?" the little round, three-inch-wide, latched peephole in the door opened and all I could see was an eyeball. At first the eyeball gazed left, then right, then straight ahead, looking right at me. An unidentified male voice said gruffly through the hole in the door, "Who are you?" I hadn't called first, so I was clearly taking this person by surprise. Not knowing whether the man behind the eyeball was in fact my uncle, I didn't say who I was. Instead, unrehearsed and on the spur of the moment, I made up a story. "I'm from Chicago. My parents are friends with the White's. They asked me to say hello if I could. Can you help me?" The yet-to-be identified man behind the door said nothing, slammed the latch shut and disappeared. I stood alone in the dark hallway, a little anxious – but not as nervous as I'd be a few days later. I wondered, "Am I done here? Am I at the right apartment? Is that man even my uncle? Is he coming back? Does he believe my story? Am I in trouble? What if this guy thinks I'm some type of trespasser? Should I get the hell out of here?" I decided to wait a minute to see what might unfold. Just then I heard a loud clanging sound from the door. It was the latch opening again. This time instead of an eyeball, two fingers holding a small piece of paper protruded through the round hole and the same raspy voice said, "Here." I took the piece of paper from the jutting fingers, then, clang, the latch shut for the final time. The paper contained a phone number. So ended the first and last encounter I'd ever have with "Uncle Eddie" White, the only uncle I'd ever meet.

Excited to finally have a lead on this wild goose chase, I quickly went to a phone booth on Broadway and 207th St. and called the 914 area code number. A receptionist politely answered, "New York State Hospital." I was calling a state psychiatric hospital in White Plains, NY, and Robert A. White lived there. With no means of getting from Washington

Heights to White Plains that day, I went back home.

For the next few days, my interest level remained high and I decided to get myself to White Plains somehow and continue my search. There was an undeniable sense of exhilaration to all this. I was an 18 year old boy on a secret mission, playing detective, finding clues in a phone book, a New York City apartment, and a psychiatric hospital that would lead me to solve the case of the missing parent. Intriguing as this all was, I knew very well that it wasn't a game. The stakes were real. Other people's lives and feelings were involved, not just mine. Everything I thought and did was behind Mom's back, partly because I didn't want to upset her, and partly because I didn't think she'd appreciate or even understand what this Father Komescher-driven curiosity was all about. I feared that if she knew of my conduct, she'd shut me down in an instant. In my mind I could hear her saying, *"You're not going up there to see him. Get that idea out of your head right now."* Guided by youth and immaturity, I was unmindful of the consequences that might follow if I found Robert A. White and he was not a good man, or my actions brought trouble to Mom or others. But I was at an age where I was developing my own sense of privacy, even from Mom, and felt entitled to have at least some of my own business.

New York State Hospital, White Plains, NY

There was no MapQuest or Google in 1966, but thanks to my Army R.O.T.C. training, I had pretty good map skills and was able to locate New York State Hospital quickly. Finding the hospital was one thing, getting there was another. With no idea of how to get from Long Island to White Plains by train, I needed a car. This caused me to do something I'd never done before, lie to Mom. Mom had only recently gotten her very first car, a small, used Ford Fairlane, as a gift from Aunt Katherine. Though it was several years old, this six-cylinder, stick-shift workhorse liberated Mom from the bondage of being homebound; easily carrying her to all the places she needed to go - work, church, errands, and even some fun-filled side trips. Her car became her lifeline, something not to be given to a teenage boy unless there was an emergency, like when Aunt Katherine was in the hospital. I completely understood and respected Mom's limits on the use of the car, and how difficult it must it must have been for her to turn the keys over to me, an inexperienced young driver. I also understood the distinction between an urgent matter and a frolic. Mom had waited until she was nearly 50 years old to own a car, so it was only rarely that I asked for permission to use it. I explained to Mom that it was important for me to visit a friend in Westchester. "Could I take your car? Please." I thought I'd get a quick *"No!"* for an answer, but surprisingly, she said yes, I could borrow the car for the day, *"...and be very careful, Peter."* As soon as I received Mom's permission, I immediately felt bad and overwhelmed with guilt. I don't recall ever having lied in my life, but I now knew firsthand the meaning of the old saying, "Oh what a tangled web we weave when first we practice to deceive." It was quite a burden. But I was on a priest-inspired mission. The next day, on my own, I went to see my father for the very first time.

Traveling through Nassau and Queens in Mom's car, I paid my first ever twenty-five cent toll on the Throg's Neck Bridge. Once on the Bronx side of the bridge, I quickly learned why someone wrote a book in 1970 called <u>Will They Ever Finish Bruckner Boulevard ?</u> After several miles of traffic snarls along the famed Cross Bronx Expressway, I exited onto a parkway and headed north, weaving my way to White Plains and the sprawling grounds of the New York State Hospital. Dozens of institutional-looking brick buildings stretched out as far as I could see. I followed signs to the administration building where I noticed the name, "Dr. McKillop, Director," above the door. "This is it. This man must know Robert A. White." In his office a polite secretary greeted me. "Hi. I'd like to see Dr. McKillop." "Do you have an appointment?" "No." "Well young man, what brings you here? Why do you want to see Dr. McKillop?" Sensing that my hunt to find my missing parent might seem trivial to a busy doctor, I didn't know what to say. Stupidly, I told this very nice lady the same story I told the man I believed to be my uncle a few days earlier, that I was a friend of the family from Chicago and my parents wanted me to give Mr. White their regards. She said, "Come with me," and escorted me into Dr. McKillop's office. The big room was poorly lit with an old fashioned, dark look to it. The only light came from the window. There were crammed bookshelves and file cabinets all over and a few antique-looking wooden chairs. Dr. McKillop introduced himself and said, "Have a seat. What's on your mind."? I introduced myself as Peter Pekar. That was the name of our landlord in Chicago when I was a young boy. The Pekars were friends of Mom's, and it was the only name I could think of at the moment. I began by telling Dr. McKillop the same story that I told his secretary, but perhaps less convincingly. Half way through, this wise doctor began probing me with a few targeted questions. I got a little tongue-tied with my answers and finally blurted out, "I'm sorry. I'm not really a friend of Robert A. White's. I'm his son and I thought he may be here." Dr. McKillop paused, then smiled and said, "I knew that the minute you walked in, son." Evidently, the doctor was smart enough to either see a likeness between Robert A. White and me right off the bat, or to see through the clumsiness of an 18 year old knocking on his door with such a bumbling excuse for being there. Fortunately Dr. McKillop didn't reprimand or intimidate me as Father Komescher had. Putting me at complete ease he said quietly, "Let's take a walk." We strolled slowly around the grounds, chatting as we walked. I'd never been to a mental hospital before, so this was a first. The images were sad. Nurses and caretakers were pushing grown men and women on swings like little children. I asked Dr. McKillopp, "Is my father a patient here? Is he mentally ill?" The doctor answered, "No, your dad isn't a patient. He works here." "What does he do?" "He has a simple job. We hired him mostly because of the condition he had when he came here a few years earlier: alcoholism and some other problems. So long as he's worked and lived on the hospital grounds, about seven years now, he hasn't had a drink."

It was on this brief walk, one that lasted only a few minutes, that the phantom nature of my father began to fade and the image of a real person began to appear. For the very first time in my life I finally had some actual facts about him, things Mom never told me or perhaps never knew herself. He had a job, although it was a menial one, answering phones and carrying out rather undemanding tasks. He was a troubled man, although I didn't know exactly what his troubles were. And at least for the past few years he was alcohol-free. Beyond these few facts, I still didn't know him, or how he sounded, or how he behaved or even what he looked like.

First Glimpse

After walking for a few minutes, Dr. McKillop stopped, gently placed one of his arms on my shoulder and pointed with his other arm to a group of men standing about thirty yards away. "Do you see those four men standing over there?" "Yes." "Do you see the man with the white shirt and blue tie?" "Yes." "Well Peter, that's your father."
I froze in place, trying to focus on his face. This first ever glimpse stunned me. Robert A. White was an average looking man about 5'10" tall and a bit overweight, but not terribly so. I didn't know what to think, or do, so I asked Dr, McKillop, "What should I do? Will you come over and introduce me?" He responded, "No. I'm going to leave you now. You can handle this on your own. If you want, go over and strike up a conversation and see if you think it's worth telling him who you are. Or go give him a hug and say, 'Dad. It's me, your son.' Or go punch him in the nose. It's up to you." The doctor left me standing there, mere yards from my father, and I didn't know what to do. The great pressure I'd been feeling increased as Dr. McKillop quietly walked away. I took a few steps toward these men to get a closer look, then stopped. Without waving hello or even saying a word to acknowledge him, I turned around, walked back to the car and headed to Long Island, mission only partially accomplished. On the way home, I felt both excitement and dread. Something I'd wondered about for years, the foggy notion that I had a father, was now more clear and within my grasp. But, confused and alone as I was, I'd chickened out, afraid to take a step across that threshold. For years I'd stopped asking Mom about him and long ago ceased singing "Clap hands, clap hands, til daddy comes home." After all the years of wondering I'd finally found my father, stood on the same ground as he, looked upon him with my own eyes and, out of fear, left.

Letting Dennis In

A few days passed and I continued to think about what I'd done. Still frightened I realized that I was not going to go any further trying to meet Robert A. White by myself. My continuing curiosity caused me to confide in my brother, Dennis. At that time Dennis was finishing tenth grade and was a happy high school student, very involved with sports and friends. He described his life back in those days:

> In high school during the mid to late 1960's, while my grades were average, I really didn't carry books around, usually just a towel and sports gear. My interests were mostly sports, friends, and fun. I didn't do so well with my studies because I was having too much fun. I loved the social aspects of high school, not the class work. I had success in playing football and lacrosse, and loved the friendships I made and the team unity. My big claim to fame in high school was becoming the captain of those teams. Success on the field gave me confidence and helped my leadership skills. I still look back on those days with a smile. I did have fun. My two brothers were different. They were good students. Unlike them, I always

struggled with the homework and tests. Peter was an independent thinker and not a follower of the crowd. He didn't try to stay with the crowd much at all. He had his own way of doing things and did not much care about what his peers thought he should be doing, but rather what he decided was best. I was different. I wanted to be one of the guys and joined a high school fraternity. Not Peter. He was always the individual thinker who guided me and tried to keep me in line. Peter was an important influence in my life. I admired him and respected him and his wise counsel. He had a unique way of explaining things when they seemed cloudy and confusing to me. He often would suggest things to me and influence me even when he wasn't trying to.

Dennis and I were close in age, only two years apart, whereas four years separated Jeanne and Robert from me. Dennis and I shared the cold room together as kids, and spent more years together at home than the others. We also both played high school sports and even shared some of the same friends. Dennis was an exuberant teenager, quite content with his life. He also had a very sensitive side, and cared deeply about Mom and things that concerned the family. He and I would often reflect on any number of topics, especially at night when we were in our beds. So after chickening out at my chance to meet Robert A. White, I thought that two heads might be better than one, and decided to let Dennis in on what I had been thinking and doing. In late May 1966, a few weeks after my abortive visit to the New York State Hospital, in a very private moment with Dennis, I discussed my curiosity about Robert A. White, how I felt, and what I thought. Dennis brought a humanitarian aspect to the conversation. "What if he's homeless, like guys you see in an alley? What if he needs help?" The religious principles we learned in school and at home dictated that we should care for the less fortunate. It was during this short chat that I finally revealed, "I know where he is."

Dennis got excited and was full of questions. "You do? Wow! Where is he? How did you find out?" No sooner had I explained my visit to Edward White's apartment and my stressful visit to the state hospital, in words that just seemed to leap from his mouth, Dennis said, "Let's go there! Let's see him!"

A Phone Call and Another Fib

Going back up to Westchester wouldn't be easy. It meant calling Robert A. White and actually speaking with him, then devising some sort of plan. The thought of such a call sent a shudder through me. A few nights later, charged with confidence by the addition of my younger brother to this venture, I found the nerve and told Dennis, "I'll make the call."

The next day I rode my bike several miles away to a pizza place in Westbury so I could use a public phone. There was no way I could use our home phone for this stressful and delicate call, and I needed complete privacy, especially from Mom. She wouldn't understand. I didn't want to call from a local pay phone and run the risk of being seen by someone who might overhear me and tell Mom. Still wavering about whether I should go through with this, I reached into my pocket, grabbed the handful of coins I'd brought and, from a pay phone on Post Avenue, dialed the hospital number. A switchboard operator answered, "New York State Hospital." I said, "I'd like to speak with a staff member named Robert A. White." She said, "Please hold." The next sound I heard was that of a man's voice, "Hello." I asked, "Is this Robert A. White?" The man said, "Yes it is." "This is Peter, your son." There was a brief pause, then Robert A. White said, "Oh Peter. You must be getting big now." I thought to myself, "What a dumb thing for him to say." But I realized that I was taking this 51-year-old man, who'd been absent for my entire life, by complete surprise. He had to be less prepared for a call from me than I was making one to him. I said, "Yes, I'm nearly 19 now." I explained the truth the best I could during our brief chat, that I was curious and found out where he lived, and decided to call him. He suggested we get together for lunch at a hotel in downtown New Rochelle. We picked a date and I said I'd be there. I left that phone booth in a topsy-turvy, emotional whirlwind. Greatly relieved that Dennis signed on as a joint venture, I was no longer alone on this journey. But I grew more worried and frightened than before because by making the call, I'd crossed the threshold. I was no longer playing detective; I'd actually spoken with Robert A. White and made a date to meet him. "What did I just do? Am I crazy? Too late now."

I had to find a way for Dennis and me to get to New Rochelle. This meant asking Mom to use her car again. And what? Another fib? Reluctantly, I convinced Mom to say yes once again. My tale didn't involve anything wild like Tevye's crazy dream. It was much more plausible, but a fable nevertheless. "It'll only take a few hours, Mom, and I won't be going too far away." In hindsight, I can't believe I did this, but at the time I felt I had little choice. I was going to visit a man of whom Mom was once afraid, a man who did nothing to support or even communicate with any of us. Worse than that, I was doing it behind Mom's back, using her car to do it, and lying about it. I rationalized my conduct by balancing this host of negatives against the scant few positives. Thoughts continued to swirl, "I'm not completely responsible for this mess, a respected priest set this whole thing in motion. Mom never told me anything, so why can't I get some answers myself? I'm not really acting alone. Dennis is with me on this." My entire inner conflict boiled down to my wish not to hurt Mom against my belief that I had at least some right to know about my father. This battle consumed me. Deep down I knew I was doing something wrong, but since I crossed the line with the phone call there was no longer a way out.

Hotel Meeting

On a hot, muggy day in late May 1966, I drove with Dennis to New Rochelle and found the hotel right away. It was an old building with a shabby, rundown look. In its heyday it may have been an important part of New Rochelle's skyline, but not anymore. We entered the dingy, bare-looking lobby and spotted the only place open, a small luncheonette. Everything else was closed. I wondered if this was the right hotel. I expected we'd be meeting at a normal looking place for lunch, not one that had a skid row look to it, like a movie set in the Great Depression. There were no young people around and Dennis and I stood out. We were athletic-looking young men, well-tanned from working in the open air. Before entering the hotel lobby, I'd been 50-50 about this whole thing. Now 99% of me was saying, "Get out of here." But I'd run away once before, so this time, despite the difficulty, I decided to finish what I started.

I didn't think it would be too hard to spot Robert A. White because I'd seen pictures of him. Even though the few photos I'd seen were from his wedding to Mom in 1942, I thought that he might look somewhat the same. Dennis seemed more excited than afraid. Older and more responsible for bringing things to this point, I trembled. What were we in for? What if he's nasty? This was all so confusing and awkward. From the doorway, we spotted a middle-aged man sitting alone at one of the tables. Since I had only one quick glimpse of Robert A. White from a distance at the hospital a week before, I really wasn't sure if this was he. Dressed in a white shirt and dark slacks, his grayish hair was combed straight back and he wore eyeglasses. An average looking, corpulent man, he didn't appear too physically fit. The thick orthopedic soles of his shoes, coupled with a bit of a waddle when he walked, were evidence of foot problems. Mom had said he was discharged from the Army in 1943 on account of his feet. The guessing game continued for a moment, then this lone patron looked up at us and we made eye contact. We paused a bit, and then advanced slowly saying only, "Hello." From his seat, the man responded, "Boys! It's good to see you." We may have shaken hands, but there was no hugging. "Sit down boys." How odd. How surreal. For as long as I could remember, I'd sung a little ditty, "Clap hands, clap hands, till daddy comes home." Now, for the first time in my life, I found myself sitting at a table with the man who never came home. I didn't bring anything with me, no photos, no notes, nothing. I hadn't rehearsed anything either. The moment seemed forced and artificial. The eeriness, even nuttiness of it all, to be finally sitting with him and not wanting to be sitting with him, thinking I should have some important things to say and having nothing to say. Robert A. White carried the initial moment with mostly small talk, corny chitchat about his former job at a fancy country club. He acted like a big shot, maybe to impress us. Snapping his fingers he called out to the waitress in a demanding way, "Miss, Miss, come here please." I felt sorry for the young waitress, and embarrassed for him. We shared a few things about ourselves, like school and sports, and about how the family was doing. But mostly, he chatted away about little. He talked a lot about his mother, our grandmother, a woman I'd never met, and of whom I knew nothing, and went on and on about rich and famous country club members I'd never heard of. He spoke not as if he worked for them, but as if he were one of them, rattling off name after name of so-called big shots. It became clear that we were in the presence of one who boasted of things imagined, a man easy to see through. Robert A. White had lost every decent job he'd ever had, and spent many years floating from workplace to workplace, doing menial work. It was sad to see him try so hard to convince us that he was important. I found it interesting that two years earlier, the summer of 1964, I caddied at Deepdale for some very important people like Richard Nixon and the Duke of Windsor. As a 16 year old, I knew that, just because I'd carried the golf bags of the rich and famous, didn't mean vice presidents and kings were my peers. "The old namedropper," a title he dubbed upon himself, tried so hard to show his sons, boys he did not know, that he was important, when he really was not.

To be fair, Robert A. White was quite successful earlier in life. Before World War II, he worked for several radio companies in sales and personnel. Radio was a huge industry before the advent of television. Mom said that he hired several people in radio who later went on to become major directors and producers in television. Sadly for him, and I suppose for all of us, the communications industry grew as television burst onto the American scene and he began to rely on his personality and drinking more than hard work. Younger, more educated professionals coming into the field passed him by. Unwilling or unable to handle these blows, he sank lower and lower, until he lost not only his jobs, but his family as well. What a different life he, Mom and all of us might have had had he been able to recognize, face and treat his problems.

He ordered a ginger ale and a sandwich and said a few nice things like "I always loved your mother." At one point, he excused himself to go to the men's room. That's when Dennis tapped me under the table and said, "He's full of shit." I agreed, but not too enthusiastically because I felt sad for him and didn't want to risk being caught talking about him." Throughout the lunch, the weight of my guilt grew. "What am I doing here? I wish I could get out of this?" After lunch he suggested that we take a swim at a nearby pool. Neither Dennis nor I wanted to hang out with him any longer, but we didn't want to be impolite. It was a hot day and we had bathing suits in the car, so we agreed. I picked up the bill for the lunch and the three of us got into Mom's car and made our way to a crowded public park in nearby Mamaroneck. We changed in a locker room and walked toward the pool together. Though I'd been a swimmer all my life, getting into the water with him was even more unpleasant than the luncheon. We really wanted to get on the road, to get this complicated and mortifying day over with. We didn't swim, as in laps or anything athletic or fun. Instead we more or less stood around in the water, listening to his graceless comments. "Did you boys go to Florida for spring break?" We didn't know what he was talking about. My existence consisted of working and scraping up enough money to help Mom and pay for college. Totally out of touch with the reality of our lives, and the values Mom taught us, he said, "You should go sometime. I hear there's a lot of making out going on down there." I looked at Dennis, who seemed stunned, then back at him, and said, "We've never been to Florida. We work." Maybe he thought by using the language of young people he was showing his sons that he could be cool. After this weird and thankfully brief dip in this pool, we returned to the car and he asked for a ride back to Manhattan. He never said where he wanted to go, only that he had to drop something off. I really wanted to take the Hutch from Mamaroneck to the Throgs Neck Bridge, then head straight home, but I felt sorry for this man. Confident I'd never see him again, I figured, "What the heck, what's one last favor," and obliged.

Our Grandmother

The three of us drove from Westchester through the Bronx into Manhattan. I grew increasingly nervous. It was a peculiar journey, my first and last ride in a car with my father. Growing up I'd wondered, "What did he look like? What was he like, the sound of his voice, his work, his life in general?" After this luncheon and swim, I got the answers to many of these questions, and I didn't like them. Ashamed, I wished that Father Komescher had not probed the way he did, and that I had never gotten involved. Mostly, I felt this way because I had betrayed Mom.

After so many surprises, beginning with my chilly reception at Edward White's apartment, my tongue-tied meeting with Dr. McKillop, and our uncomfortable luncheon and swim with Robert A. White, I didn't know what was going to happen next. As I drove him in Mom's car, down the Hutchinson River Parkway, past Co-op City, to the Cross Bronx Expressway, over the Harlem River and into Washington Heights, I agonized. I didn't know this man at all or what he was capable of. It was one thing to sit with him in a public place, like the hotel luncheonette or the crowded swimming pool. It was quite another to be in a car with this stranger from the psychiatric hospital sitting right next to me in the front seat. By his comments and exaggerations, he'd shown himself to be an odd man. But what if he was worse than odd? What if he was dangerous? Or suicidal? What if he grabs the steering wheel? Or touches me? "Oh God. Please let this day be over with." I was puzzled at first, then outraged when I discovered he had guided me right back to where all this began, the doorway of his brother Edward's apartment in Washington Heights. "What on earth are we doing here? Why didn't I ask more questions before I found myself back here?" I never wanted to go back to that apartment again, and now I was there and dreaded it.

Robert A. White never said exactly where he wanted us to take him in Manhattan, or why. Only that he had to drop something off. Instead of the surly Edward peeking with his eyeball through the opening in the door, something much different happened this time. Smiling and looking proud of himself, Robert A. White knocked on the door. Moments later the door opened slowly and a tiny, elderly Irish sounding lady appeared. I had absolutely no idea who this hunched over woman with the large, knobby-looking knuckles on her hands was. She gestured for Dennis and me to come in, then, using a cane, made her way through the small apartment, past the living room area into the kitchen. Before Robert A. White could introduce us, she looked up toward the ceiling and, in her Irish brogue, exclaimed, "Thank the Lord, I've finally seen them. I've finally seen my grandchildren." She repeated this phrase several times but we were too shocked to catch on right away. Robert A. White then said, "Boys, this is your grandmother, Nanny." Totally unprepared for this, Dennis and I stood speechless at this first and only meeting with our then 90-year-old grandmother. Mary Tighe White, or "Nanny," pointed with her cane to the couch where she slept in the apartment of her oldest son, Edward, and spoke briefly about how happy she was to have finally met two of her grandsons. I never knew this woman, and yet here I was, tricked into a surprise, unplanned visit with her and too stunned to speak. Perhaps "Nanny" was just as surprised to see us as we were to see her, because the only thing that came from any of our mouths was some very brief chitchat. Robert A. White puttered around the apartment for a few minutes and made himself a glass of ginger ale. Within minutes, we said goodbye to Mary White and left. As we were leaving we could hear her continuing to exclaim, "Thank the Lord. Thank the Lord." This entire episode happened so quickly that I don't remember much more than that. As we walked back to Mom's car, Robert A. White smiled and seemed proud as a peacock at what he'd done. He asked if I could drop him off in the Bronx. It was on our way home so I once again obliged. Over the Harlem River, as we approached the Jerome Ave. exit on the Cross Bronx Expressway he said, "This will be fine right here." I turned onto the exit ramp and stopped the car. In an instant, Robert A. White got out of the car and disappeared into the jam-packed Bronx streets. There was no handshake or hug with this farewell, or even any final words. He just melted into the crowd. That was the last time Dennis or I ever saw Robert A. White.

Over the years, we have spoken about that escapade and come to the belief that Robert A. White was more than the "old namedropper" he proclaimed himself to be. He was a conniver, one who willfully set us up to get his way. For us to meet his mother, and for her to meet us, he needed a reason. So he made up a story about needing to go to the city to drop something off as a pretext to get us there. He didn't drop anything off in the city. It's not that we wouldn't have wanted to meet our grandmother sometime, perhaps under honest and sincere circumstances. But the method he used to accomplish this was dishonest. Amazed as we were at seeing our very own grandmother, we did not enjoy being hoodwinked. We felt sorry for this 90-tear-old woman, forced to sleep on a couch in her son's apartment after a life of struggle, but there was little we could do about that.

Grandmother Mary Tighe White,
Early 1940's.

Mary Tighe White had a hard life. Born in Ireland in 1876, she married another Irish immigrant, John White, and had four children. Robert A. White, born June 13, 1915, was the youngest. Her husband John, whom she once described to Mom as "a quiet and good man," died in 1922. So, like Mom, Mary White had the task of raising four children alone, decades before welfare existed. She worked as a cafeteria helper in an insurance company in order to support her family. Of her mother-in-law Mary White, Mom once said, *"She was a deeply religious and extremely kind person…. I got along very well with her. I felt at home with her and she enjoyed visiting us."*

Grandmother Mary White seemed very nice, judging from our short, impromptu visit, though I was puzzled by one thing. If our only grandmother lived one hour away from Levittown, why hadn't she seen us before this? Postage stamps were only a few cents back then. Why hadn't she ever sent a birthday card, or a gift, or made a phone call? We'd done nothing wrong to Mary White. Why did she stay away? Something Mom wrote a few years later contains at least part of the answer:

> *When our marriage began to deteriorate, family visits from the White side of the family became less frequent. I recall telephoning Bob's brother, Ed White, on several occasions, begging him to try and help. I was getting desperate. I made the mistake of calling him at his office. His wife wrote me a very sarcastic letter telling me not to disturb him at work. I did not realize at the time that calling him at work wasn't the proper thing to do, but I needed help badly. Her letter went on to say that I should realize that marriage was for better or worse, that everyone*

has problems and no one is without them…. I never bothered with them after that. I kept my problems here in my own home and worked them out the best way I could alone.

Mom was a strong, religious person, willing to take on the task of raising the four of us alone, and sought God's and the Blessed Mother's help to do so. Desperate at first, she looked for support from Ed White, a request that was rejected for what appears to have been a trivial reason – Mom called him at his office. The rest is a big unknown. Maybe Grandmother Mary White really wanted to be part of our lives, but was pressured not to by Robert A. White or her other children. Maybe she believed Mom had our best interest in mind and any involvement on her part would only complicate things. For sure, she had no money, so she couldn't have provided any financial help. So while it might have been nice to have a real grandmother, we didn't really suffer by not having her in our lives. We had Mom and her aunts, Aunt Nellie and Aunt Katherine, instead, the best "grandmas" anyone could ever want.

The Bathing Suit

On the ride back from the Bronx, Dennis and I spoke about our day, how odd the whole thing felt, and how afraid we were of the possibility of having opened up an unmanageable can of worms. We agreed to keep the matter between us because we didn't want Mom hurt by our attempt to satisfy our curiosity. After all her years of struggle, she believed that the facts spoke for themselves: she had always been there for us, and the White family had not. What more was there to know? After our difficult and complicated experiences in Westchester and Manhattan, I hoped very much that Robert A. White would just take our visit as a one-day, youthful adventure, and nothing more. He didn't invite us back to Westchester, and we didn't invite him to Levittown. Considering the way he tricked us, and the way we parted, Dennis and I wanted the relationship to be short-lived and looked forward to having no further contact with him. On the way home Dennis said, "I hope we never see him again." Levittown looked pretty good to me when I arrived home later that afternoon. After the tense and exhausting whirlwind of meeting an uncle, a father and a grandmother who had all previously been nonexistent to me, I tried going about life as if this never happened. But I couldn't stop thinking that I was some type of criminal, my crime being that of deceiving and betraying Mom.

Dennis went back to his high school classes, and I to my summer job of working on the swimming pools of the rich. A few days passed and, to our surprise, nothing at all came from our visit. "So far, so good," I thought. "Maybe I'm going to survive this blunder after all." I wished with all my might that this misguided escapade would become nothing more than a mere secret between Dennis and me. But my wish was not to come true. One afternoon, about week after our jaunt to New Rochelle, Dennis and I walked into the house together and were met by Mom. She had a stern look on her face as she stood alone in the kitchen. In her hand she held a piece of clothing that I didn't recognize. Mom then reached out with her arm and demanded, *"What's this?"* We were unable to make out exactly what it was she was holding up to us, so we said nothing. She repeated, *"I said what's this?"* It didn't matter what the object was, her look and tone made it clear that she had somehow learned about our visit to Robert A. White. Mom was holding a man's bathing suit with the name "R. White" written on the label. Apparently, after our swim, Robert A. White had rolled up his wet bathing suit, tucked it under the back seat of Mom's car, and left it there. Whether he did so accidentally or on purpose, I don't know. Given his self-proclaimed title of the "old namedropper" and his connivance of the week before, I believe the latter, that he intentionally hid his bathing suit in the car. He wanted Mom to know we'd been there. Irate and with tears flowing, Mom insisted on answers, and she deserved them. For a few seconds I stood there in an unbearable silence, then stuttered and stammered a few words, trying to explain the situation. I brought up the involvement of Father Komescher, my natural curiosity as a fatherless boy, and even our humanitarian concern for our missing parent. These points went nowhere. Mom was hurt, and it was my fault. Whether she was more upset with me for taking such a step without discussing it with her, or because I lied about where I was taking her car, or because she feared the return of Robert White into her life, the reason really didn't matter. I had committed an unpardonable error in her eyes and I had to face that fact and live with the consequences.

Our kitchen was always a happy place. It was the first room one entered when coming through the front door, a bright place where we ate our meals, talked and laughed as a family. Suddenly, for the first time in my life, it had become a dark place, a place I didn't want to be. We stood in the kitchen before Mom, ashamed, caught red-handed for the betrayers we were. Fortunately, our sensible 76-year-old Aunt Katherine entered the room and witnessed the confrontation. As Mom thundered away at us, and we continued with our stumbling, bumbling responses, Aunt Katherine spoke up. Sick and with only three months to live, Aunt Katherine was direct and emphatic, "Catherine, stop it!" she shouted. "This was bound to happen! They're good boys. Leave them alone. They didn't mean to hurt you." Mom was definitely the head of our household, but in this instance she acquiesced and accepted the role of daughter, willingly listening and deferring to the counsel of her adopted mom, the wise old Aunt Katherine. The two of them discussed things briefly and, while Aunt Katherine's perception and understanding in no way got us off the hook, it enabled Mom to see the matter in a different light. She remained upset at our deception and lack of candor, however she eventually grasped how much youth and inexperience had influenced our thinking, that Dennis and I were just two curious boys that meant no harm. Half a decade later, Mom acknowledged what we'd done in a manner quite different from that uncomfortable kitchen confrontation. In her application to the Diocese for an annulment she said:

> *Just before my aunt died in 1966, my two middle sons decided on their own to visit their father. My son Peter had discussed his father with a priest at the University of Dayton. The priest told him to go ahead as an act of charity and also to settle his curiosity. The boys drove my car up to New York Hospital in White Plains, NY where their father was working. He was very surprised to see them and was not able to recognize them as they were so grown, ages 18 and 16 at the time. As they talked he asked them what I had told them about him and their honest answers were 'nothing' I never spoke unkindly of him to them, just*

explaining he was an alcoholic and that he had left. It was then that I filled them in on many of my financial struggles. From that short visit they had with him, they could see for themselves he was mostly interested in himself and not the family. They did not bother with him again.

A Few Checks

At our luncheon, Robert A. White spoke a few times about how much he loved Mom, and how he wished he could have been more help to the family over the years. He promised to do a better job and said he would send Mom $100 a month. When I visited him, I had absolutely no intentions of trying to obtain money or anything else from him. I was there purely out of curiosity and concern. After he made this unexpected promise, I thought there might be a silver lining to all this. If he did follow through on his promise to send Mom $100 a month, and if she did accept it, wouldn't her life and all of our lives be a bit better? He sent Mom $100 the first month after our visit, then $80 the second month. These two checks came with friendly but bizarre notes attached, then they stopped coming.

Letters from Robert A. White

Back at college months later, I received two letters from Robert A. White. One was written in January 1967, and the other in October 1967. In the first one he expressed his sorrow at learning of the passing of Aunt Katherine. He described her as "a sincere, lovable and generous lady, … his second love in the McCoy Family. Your mother has always been #1." I answered his letter and mentioned how Aunt Katherine's death was difficult for me as she was the first person that I ever loved and lost. Nine months later he wrote again saying he was sorry for my loss. Using the phrase, "Yo tu amo," he then said, "in any language, I loved her too," and that he'd be sending "under separate cover," a favorite phrase of his, a spiritual reminder to pray for her entrance into heaven. I didn't really know what that meant, but I never received it. This second letter included a check for $25, the only money he ever sent me, and said more would arrive in a few weeks. It did not. Finally, he mentioned that he'd been sending Mom $80 since August, or about six months, when in fact he'd only sent her the two checks. I concluded that while he really may have meant well, he was unable to follow through on his promises. In his second letter, he mostly spoke of how he resigned from his job at New York Hospital "under favorable circumstances" because of the "physical and mental stress involved in working with many young 17-22 year old wealthy Westchester type former narcotic and L.S.D. users." He took a job at the Sleepy Hollow Country Club, north of Tarrytown, NY as a switchboard operator and desk clerk. He described this job as "not big or important," and that he "got the job on his own, so didn't have to pay any fee." His letters were corny and rambling. They were also quite sad to read. At the time he wrote them, he was a 52-year-old underemployed, lonely man trying hard to make it look like he'd achieved some level of success in life. It was apparent from his letters that he wished his life had taken a different path, that he'd been able to make more of it. Of his decision to leave New York

Hospital he said, "I did not want to spend the rest of my life working in a mental hospital as an attendant. I'm sure none of my sons would take much pride in a career of this kind for their father." A year later, in late1968, when I was a senior at Dayton he wrote me again and told me that his mother had passed away at the age of 92. While I was saddened at the loss of this innocent elderly woman, my reaction was nothing like the one I had when Aunt Katherine passed away two years earlier. Mary White, or Nanny as he referred to her, as nice as she was the one and only time I met her, had not been part of my life, while Aunt Katherine meant everything to me. I never heard again from Robert A. White after that.

Dennis' Letter from Vietnam

In the fall of 1969, through an office of the U.S. Marine Corps, Robert A. White was made aware that Dennis was serving in Vietnam and wrote him a letter. Surprised to hear from him, Dennis responded. Commenting on this exchange of letters Dennis said:

Corporal Dennis White, Vietnam, 1969.

I was about four months into my tour when I received a letter from my father, Robert Anthony White. His letter wasn't long and didn't make much sense. It was a very "feel sorry' letter about how hurt he was at losing his mother, and how much she loved her grandchildren. At first I thought it would be best not to respond so I waited a few weeks. Then I received another rambling letter and decided that I should share my true feelings and clear the air, just in case I didn't come back from Vietnam. There was no email or cell phones then, just old-fashioned letter writing. So, I sent a two-page letter to let him know that it was now too late to establish a relationship. I shared how I felt about him and politely, but to the point, let him know I no longer would be responding to any other correspondence. I asked him to stop writing and let him know that I was a grown man and that I loved my Mom and brothers and sister and that they were my family and that they meant more than anything in the world. I continued that our mother struggled with four children all her life with no help from him or his family and that we never heard from him or our grandmother. I remember that night, after mailing my letter while lying on my poncho liner, reflecting back to my youth. When going to bed as a child, I would always say to Mom 'Goodnight Ma, I'll say a prayer for you and daddy.' Mom would always respond, *'Go to sleep.'* As a young boy I wanted my Mom to have a companion and to be with a man. I really wanted to see her happy. Even as a seven year old, I always wanted to make her happy and please her. If she was happy, I was. Even in Vietnam I was worried about her and her feelings. I suppose I was puzzled about how Robert A. White, a man I met only once, wrote to say how proud he was of me and calling me 'son,' and how bad I should feel about my grandmother's death. So I sent this final note to him and never looked back. I was never a revengeful person; I just think I was placing a shield up about my Mom's feelings, especially since I was reflecting on all this from so far away from home. I never heard from him again.

Jeanne's Curiosity

While Dennis and I took the bungling steps we did to satisfy our curiosity about Robert A. White, I'd long believed that my brother, Robert, did not share that curiosity. As an eight-year-old in early 1952, he undoubtedly experienced and remembered more than the other three of us had. In 1972, when Robert visited Long Island from Hawaii, I mentioned the word "daddy" to him in a conversation. He looked at me with a straight face and emphatically said, "Who?" It was obvious that he didn't want to speak about Robert A. White, almost denying his existence. I felt badly because I was not mindful of how difficult it may have been for Robert, as a more impressionable eight year old, than for the rest of us, who were really too young to remember much at all. I only have two recollections of Robert A. White from childhood. One was of him sitting in the dark on a green, fuzzy loveseat in the living room of our Levitt house, wearing a long overcoat and fedora hat, with a cigarette hanging out of his mouth. Mom was working in the kitchen. I thought he was a magician since he talked while holding the cigarette between his lips without having it fall. The other recollection I have is of him and Mom yelling at one another. In anger, he threw a cup across the kitchen, smashing it on the wall above the sink. He then stormed off, never to come back again. Robert went out the door chasing him down Twig Lane. I followed, but Mom halted me. She cried, so we cried too. We knew something was wrong, but we didn't know what. In later years, I learned that that argument was the last of several where Mom had grown weary of his leaving for days at a time and spending money they didn't have. She regularly urged him to get help and he either didn't know how, or refused to do so. Instead he continued with his unreliable, irresponsible and dangerous ways including drinking heavily, crashing cars, sometimes with one of us children in them, making gross errors, lying, losing jobs, borrowing money and not paying it back, leaving home for days and weeks at a time, and forgetting his children.

When Dennis and I visited Robert A. White in 1966, we decided not to tell Jeanne we were going, or even mention it to her upon our return. She was only 14 years old, and we felt we were protecting her in case he was odd or caused any trouble. Five years later, in the summer of 1971, Jeanne married Ernie Champagne, a correction officer at the Nassau County jail. Mom was against this marriage for a few reasons: Jeanne was only 19 years old, and Ernie was eight years older and a divorced man with a daughter. She thought Jeanne was too young and should date more and be a little more patient before accepting a marriage proposal. She also didn't know very much about Ernie, so she opposed the idea. There was tension between Mom and Jeanne about all this, and Dennis and I supported and advocated on Jeanne's behalf. We told Mom that this marriage may make

Jeanne happy and to think about this with a more charitable view in mind. Reluctantly, Mom went along with the marriage, gave her blessing, and in May 1971 hosted a back yard wedding reception at 55 Twig Lane. Jeanne and Ernie moved to an apartment in West Hempstead, NY. Two years later, perhaps for the very same reasons Dennis and I decided to locate and meet Robert A. White, Jeanne did too. On her own, she found out where he was living, made her own contact with him, and met with him at a diner in White Plains, NY. In the fall of 1973, Jeanne invited Robert A. White to Thanksgiving dinner at her East Rockaway apartment. He traveled to Long Island in a car. Jeanne was uncertain if it was his car, or a borrowed car. Oddly, he didn't park in front of her apartment, but farther down the block instead. He told Jeanne that he was unable to get the car into reverse gear, so he just left it where it was. As Jeanne prepared dinner, she realized that she'd forgotten cranberry sauce. Robert A. White volunteered to go to the store and Jeanne gave him the keys to Ernie's car for the errand. He returned with the cranberry sauce, but neglected to tell them that while pulling out he put a big dent in their car. Jeanne and Ernie didn't notice the damage until the next day. Upset, Jeanne called and confronted him about having crashed the front side of their car and not saying anything about it. Put on the spot, Robert A. White made up a story and said he'd pay for the dent. Though he said he was sorry, he came across to Jeanne as unrepentant. Jeanne saw through his tale and let him know that the dent wasn't really a problem for her, his lack of candor was. He never paid for the dent and Jeanne came to realize, as had Dennis and I seven years earlier, that going back in time to begin a relationship that was never there to begin with can be unpredictable and unpleasant. After that awkward Thanksgiving of 1973, Jeanne no longer heard from him.

Sweet Little Old Man

Years later, as a social worker in Albany, Jeanne met a sweet little old man who was alone and in need of help. He had no family or friends and only a few helping professionals, like Jeanne, in his life. She wanted very much to be of assistance, to make sure that he wasn't completely alone on this earth. I believe that Jeanne, Dennis and I sought out Robert A. White for similar reasons. Besides curiosity, I think we were concerned that, like Jeanne's "sweet little old man," perhaps our own father was such a person, a troubled man who became consumed by his many problems, and may have needed us. Dennis once asked, "What if he's a bum on the street? Shouldn't we do something about it?" Mom always taught us basic human kindness, to have a good heart, to place the needs of others ahead of our own. So although it was a natural instinct for us to demonstrate some level of care, sometimes you just can't, or shouldn't go back, especially when the lives and feelings of others are involved.

Robert A. White – The Final Years

In 1972 Mom confided something quite important to me. *"Peter, I'm afraid that, after 22 years of living here and struggling to keep this house, your father could end up with it someday. His name is still on the deed. I really think it should come off."* I agreed and made the first appointment I could get with a lawyer from Nassau County's Legal Department. Days later Mom and I met with the lawyer and explained the situation and asked what he might recommend. The lawyer took us into a small, plain-looking conference room equipped with only a metal desk and chairs. Right off the bat I predicted, "This doesn't look good. We're not going to be helped here." Though he couldn't have been a nicer man, he said he could not be of any help to us. "We can't force Robert A. White to remove his name from the deed. It's not our job. That's your business, not the county's." While there, we discussed another issue that weighed heavily on Mom, the fact that the Department of Social Services still had a lien on the property because of the ten years Mom accepted welfare benefits back in the 1950's. Under the law, welfare was entitled to be reimbursed in full for all the money it provided Mom over the years, if and when her house was ever sold. I argued the best I could on Mom's behalf saying to the DSS attorney, "Only a portion of the money Mom received went toward the mortgage. Most of it went to pay for food, heat, clothes, the basics." The lawyer countered, "It doesn't matter. You can't accept a benefit from welfare, use part of it to pay for your house, then profit from it years later." Frustrated with the outcome of this meeting, Mom consulted her cousin Lois Larkin Nicolosi's husband, prominent Queens attorney Vincent Nicolosi, who was able to locate Robert A. White in Westchester. Vinnie spoke with him about signing the house over to Mom. At first he argued, but Vinnie reminded him of his total failure to pay child support throughout the 1950's and 1960's and how signing the house over to Mom would be a wise and prudent thing to do. With that pressure, Robert A. White signed a new deed with only Mom's name on the title.

After that contact, no one heard from Robert A. White again. Decades later, through the miracle of the internet, Robert's daughter in Hawaii, Ann Marie, discovered that on August 13, 1999, Robert A. White passed away at the age of 84. Since he lived a mostly inactive life, I was surprised that he lived as long as he did. As the only next of kin living in the New York area, the Westchester County Administrator provided me with some interesting information. In 1983, at the age of 68, widower Robert A. White married a woman named Vivian Cuddehey. They lived briefly in Ryebrook, NY, not far from the Hutchinson River Parkway in Westchester. This was an eye opener for me, not that he decided to marry after Mom died, but that I actually had a stepmother and never knew it. Vivian had a son named Don, my stepbrother I suppose. I never knew that either. A few weeks later, while traveling upstate, I stopped in Ryebrook to see the final home of Robert A. White. It was a small, old, dilapidated house, apparently vacant. I knocked on the door and no one answered; then I peeked through the window and saw nothing inside, only emptiness. The County Administrator's records indicated that Robert A. White didn't follow through for long with this new marriage, nor did he stay long in Ryebrook. Within months of marrying Vivian, he checked himself into a nursing home in Elmsford, NY where he remained until his death 16 years later in 1999. I called the nursing home and spoke with a staff member who remembered him. "He was a pleasant fellow who lived a sedentary life. He was a wordsmith, very good at crossword puzzles and spelling. In fact, he was the nursing home spelling bee champ." I asked, "Why was he there? Was there something wrong with him? Dementia? Wheelchair bound?" She said, "No. Not at all. He had no apparent health problems. He seemed happy here, having his meals prepared and a place to live." Robert A. White died penniless. Upon his death he had only his final Social Security check of $1000, which was taken by the county administrator and, as with all his monthly social security benefits throughout his years in Elmsford, applied to his nursing home expenses. Since the nursing home cost was $4000 a month, the balance of $3000 was paid by Westchester County. Something seemed unjust about this equation. Mom struggled for nine years during the 1950's to eke out a meager existence with four children on welfare, surviving on less than $2000 a year, all of which was paid back after she died. Yet the federal, state and county government paid more than half a million dollars to have the Elmsford nursing home minister to and wait on Robert A. White for the final 16 years of his life.

Former Army Sergeant Robert A. White was eligible to be buried in a national cemetery. Since there is none in Westchester, the county attorney decided to have him buried in the Long Island National Cemetery in Calverton, New York. The county provided a small wake for Robert A. White at a funeral home in Westchester. Then they transported his remains to Calverton where he was laid to rest among the many thousands of veterans interred there. On a cold, blustery day in the year 2000, I drove to Exit 68 on the Long Island Expressway, found Calverton and visited his grave. Standing on an open, windswept plain in eastern Long Island, amidst thousands of white grave markers, all neatly lined up horizontally, vertically and diagonally, I felt nothing but sadness and loneliness for Robert A. White, a man who had never set foot in Suffolk County, NY, but was finally laid to rest there, after a funeral attended by no one. "Did that cemetery visit bring about any type of closure for you?" a friend asked. Closure? I considered the fact that Robert A. White didn't live much of a life at all, certainly not one of luxury. His was a tragic, mostly empty life. I answered, "Not really. It's hard to close something that was never really opened in the first place."

I have thought hard about whether I should devote so many pages in this writing to Robert A. White and concluded that these stories of him are proper. He suffered from largely undiagnosed and untreated illnesses that caused him, Mom and all of us a great deal of pain and heartache. His troubles were inextricably bound up with our troubles, and that is an integral part of the overall story.

No Father's Day

On Sunday, June 20, 1965, I was speaking on the phone with a young woman named Sharon, my senior prom date from a few weeks earlier. Our conversation was brief as Sharon ended it abruptly saying, "I have to go now. It's Father's Day. We're busy." That was the first time in my life that the words "Father's Day" ever entered my consciousness. I'd never thought about it before. As I sat with the phone in my hands, I realized that millions of sons and daughters were celebrating their fathers, buying cards and gifts, and taking their fathers out to dinner. At the very least, they were thinking about their fathers. I'd never considered the third Sunday of June to be of any importance at all. It was always just another Sunday. I thought, "Maybe I'll be a father someday and I'll know." Ten years later, June 22,1975, was my first Father's Day with my ten month old daughter, Jennifer. This brand new pleasure was mixed with a brand new pain. I'd been stung, beyond my ability to bear, by the sudden loss of Mom the day before.

THE BEGINNINGS OF COMMUNITY SERVICE

The Landers' Kids

During 1966, my sophomore year at Dayton, I was influenced by many professors, books, and the state of the world at that time. With the civil rights movement in full swing, urban rioting, the student rights movement and the growing war in Vietnam, there were tremendous changes taking place. It was then that I embarked on two things that would become the central part of my life's work: teaching and community service. On campus I'd seen a sign saying, "Attention All Students – The Dakota Street Center Needs Your Help – Volunteer Now!" I asked around and found out that the Dakota Street Center was a community center on the west side of Dayton that focused on helping the young people in the area with homework, recreation and a variety of activities. Called the ghetto back then, West Dayton was on the other side of the Miami River from the university and was largely composed of lower income black families. Students from the university were asked to help out at the center with various programs. Long an advocate of civil rights, I decided to volunteer and help with after-school tutoring. One fall afternoon, I made my way to the center which was located in an old wooden building on Dakota Street, a tired-looking, block. Some of the buildings in the vicinity were run down or crumbling. I entered and met Walter Wahl, the director, and a social worker named Nancy. Both were friendly to me and showed me around. The books and arts and crafts materials they had were out of date, few in number, and well worn. Several of the rooms were dark, with the only light coming in from the windows. There was little in the way of furniture, and the few chairs there were tattered. A short while after I arrived, a nearby school let out and a few kids came in. Nancy introduced me to a ten-year-old boy named Mack Landers. I kidded around with Mack for a few minutes, then asked him if I could help him out in some way. Mack seemed quite bright but was in need of assistance with homework and a few other things. Together we looked over his school notebook, which showed that he did try hard in school but struggled with writing. We quickly made friends and as I was leaving I said, "It was great to meet you Mack. If you'd like, I'll come back and we can work some more." Mack seemed pretty enthused and said with a smile, "Nice to meet you too Pete, Mr. White man." He kidded me that my name was White and that besides Nancy, there were no other white people in his neighborhood. I began visiting the center weekly, meeting up with Mack, and doing homework with him.

Once in a while Mack would ask me to walk him home. That's how I met his brothers Ollie, David, and Terry, his two sisters and his parents. Mr. Landers was a WW II veteran, having served in France in the then-segregated U.S. Army. I didn't know what kind of work Mr. Landers did, but the family seemed quite poor. From time to time I'd drop by and see the children home alone. On one such visit I saw Mack and his brothers standing at the lit gas stove, frying what appeared to be a large white ball in a cast iron pan. I said, "What are you guys trying to do?" Mack answered, "Pete, I'm fixin' us some bread." The boys had mixed some flour and water together into a softball-sized wad of dough and were trying to fry it. I could only foresee a round browned wad of paper mache paste. I didn't think that unsupervised kids should be operating a gas stove by themselves, but I could tell they were quite hungry. I went to a local store, bought a loaf of bread, some eggs and syrup and made them French toast. They gobbled up the entire loaf in minutes. Though I had to fit my time at the center into my work and class schedule, I liked going there to help Mack and the other children. Instead of reading about problems in the paper or seeing them on the television news, I felt like I was participating in some type of direct action by visiting the west side, meeting people and getting involved in a positive way.

After my sophomore year, in the summer of 1967 I moved to Hawaii to attend my brother Robert's wedding and enroll at the University of Hawaii. For the next year, I remained in touch with the Landers children through letters. They were prolific letter writers, and not a week went by that I didn't hear from one of them. A year later, suffering from what some call "rock fever," a sense of isolation that comes from living on a small island, after serving an eight-week Army ROTC summer camp at Ft. Lewis, Washington, I moved back to the mainland and returned to Dayton to complete my B.A. in History. My year in Hawaii, from summer of 1967 to summer of 1968, was a tumultuous one, dubbed "American Revolution II" by pundits. It saw the largest number of U.S. servicemen killed during the Vietnam War, the Tet offensive, the assassinations of Martin Luther King and Senator Robert F. Kennedy, the My Lai Massacre, the violence-filled Democratic National Convention in Chicago, where Mayor Daley ordered police to "shoot to kill any arsonist and maim or cripple looters," and much more. During my senior year at Dayton my involvement with the Dakota Street Center grew. My friend Frank Zeccola and I, interested in increasing the number of student volunteers working at the center, decided to hold a meeting to see of we could expand the program. We hung a few simple signs around the campus encouraging students to attend our meeting. To our surprise, more than 200 students showed up, so many that we were overwhelmed and didn't know how to handle them all. Fortunately, there were a few real organizers in the group and we were able to separate these eager volunteers according to their interests, like art, athletics, tutoring, music, etc. This was beginning of my life-long participation in community service. This meeting resulted in groups going over to Dakota Street most afternoon and nights for homework help, arts and crafts, and music lessons. Some members of the university's freshman basketball team visited once in a while to conduct basketball clinics. A few volunteers were lifeguards and swimming instructors, which was of great help when we got the Dayton YMCA to donate the use of their pool one day a week. We were involved with adult activities as well, facilitating dances and other events. While most of our involvement was educational, some was fun. In the spring of 1969, I saw a poster on campus advertising a Bill Cosby concert. The show was for that night, so with little time to act, I called a friend of mine who was part of student government, the group sponsoring the concert, and asked if I could bring some kids from the center to the show, for free of course. He said, "It's last minute, but I'll try." Shortly after that I got a call from Cosby's manager who said, "Mr. Cosby said, 'Tell him to bring as many kids as he can.'" With only two hours to go before the concert, I could only manage to transport a dozen kids. During the show, Bill Cosby, seeing the UD Fieldhouse packed with mostly white college students, couldn't help but notice the only row of black kids there. He pointed us out to the audience, made a joke or two, then called the youngest child, third grader Terry Landers, on stage and made him part of the act. Terry, a bright boy, the City of Dayton Third Grade Spelling Champ, played along very well in several of Cosby's skits and actually stole part of the show. A photographer was on hand and a close up of Terry and Bill Cosby was the centerfold in the next issue of Jet Magazine. Following the success of the Cosby concert, when I learned the Fifth Dimension was coming for a concert a month later, I had more time to plan things with student government. Like Bill Cosby, these award-winning professionals were an inspiration. When I asked about bringing kids from the center, their manager called and said, "Take all you can. Fill the house," and we did. I recruited everyone I knew with a car to go to Dakota Street that night and pick up kids at the center. A convoy of eighteen cars shuttled back and forth from the West Side and transported more than 200 underprivileged poor children to the show, filling an entire section of the UD Fieldhouse. The Fifth Dimension proved to be a very special group of people. During intermission they asked to have several dozen kids come to their dressing rooms where they greeted them, showed all their costumes, and made them feel very special. After the show, when all the college students had left, the group stayed with all the kids for more than an hour to make sure that every child had a chance to meet each singer individually, sit on a lap, have a chat, and get an autograph. I'd been to many events at the UD Fieldhouse, but that was the first time I ever left in tears.

Mack, Ollie, Terry and David Landers after swim in Pearlman's pool.

The Landers kids were wonderful, fun-loving, bright children. Through our pen pal relationship, I offered to bring them to New York for a week in the late summer of 1968. I had enough money to do this, as my income from Pan American Airways was enough for me to pay my own bills and college costs, and to send Mom $150 a month to help her out. The minimum wage at the time was $1.50 an hour, and I was earning $2.75 plus overtime. Since Hawaii was considered an overseas station, I received additional pay for that, bringing me up to near $4 an hour. So while I was not rich by any means, I'd saved enough to provide the kids with this experience. When my Army summer camp was over in mid-August, I flew from Seattle to Dayton, picked up the kids, and escorted them by plane to New York. They had a glorious week meeting my friends and neighbors, and visiting New York City, Jones Beach and elsewhere. Mom loved having the Landers kids around and when the trip was over she became an avid pen pal with them. They wrote her so frequently she couldn't keep up with the volume of mail.

When I returned to the west side of Dayton a few weeks later, I began to observe things that I didn't like, including some dangerous things. Some adults spent what money they had on alcohol and food for themselves and left their kids alone to fend for themselves. A west Dayton man I knew spent two weeks in the county jail on a minor charge because he couldn't afford $25 bail. While riding in a car with a few adults to bail him out, I noticed a pistol in the glove compartment and grew even more worried for the kids. I felt I should get involved, but didn't know how. I wrote a letter to Mom about my concern for the conditions I'd observed and of my intent to get more directly involved, even considering moving to the west side. In her October 1968 response to me, she wrote back,

Dear Peter,

One of the reasons for my writing is to tell you my thoughts and opinions have changed a bit. It happened when I was preparing for my fourth grade confraternity class lesson. There, staring me in the face, was the title of the new chapter, 'Bear One Another's Burdens,' which I feel that I have always done as far as I am able to. However, as I read on and on I noticed that the words in your letter were the same as the words of the book – 'As sharers in the mission of Christ, we Christians prolong and extend His presence in the world. He acts with us, and through us. We, too, are to be men for others, and with others. In a society which is becoming progressively more mechanical and impersonal, Christians should bring to bear the personal concerns and involvement of Christ. It is one thing to read about the sufferings of the sick, the aged, and the poor, or to watch T.V. programs about racial prejudices. It is something else again to learn of these pains and needs through personal contacts, and to do something to remedy evils by personal involvement. Christians are not to remain isolated or detached. Still less are they to be indifferent to the miseries of their brothers and sisters – not if they are to act as Christ Himself did.'

Well, these words haunted me and I feel perhaps you are right and you are doing a very commendable thing. However, you are my son and I am very concerned about you. It worries me that perhaps you are going a little overboard. I do hope you see and understand my feelings.

We were in a similar setup years ago but never did you go hungry while I ate or drank. You children were my main concern. Sad to say this is not true of all parents. Some parents feel that their children are a burden for them. This I want you to know, these parents are in full charge and responsible for their children. We may not always understand their actions nor should we condone them. We may wonder why they are not concerned if and when their children go hungry. Sometimes you cannot interfere so be careful. It is good of you to be concerned. These boys must love you for it, but you do have a life of your own. I want you to realize you cannot run another's life for them. You really don't know all of these people well enough and I am afraid of what may happen. You are 21 now and free to do as you wish.

Love,
Mom

Of my mention that I might leave my apartment near the university and move to the west side, Mom went further, *"I do hope you stay in your apartment. I don't like to see you take such a step. I don't think that it is necessary. What purpose would it solve? Being a concerned friend is more than enough."* On one hand Mom was congratulating me for my involvement, saying she was proud I was doing "Gods' work." On the other hand, she was urging caution, patience and safety. She was being a wise mom.

My experiences on Dayton's west side during that volatile time led me to discover that there were many problems in the world and some of them were solvable. I believed if I continued to learn more about the world and its problems, participated directly, took action, continued my work at the center, and spoke up in class and elsewhere I'd have at least some impact on local and global matters. During the mid and late 1960's, I went through an important change. From the reading I'd done, my life experiences and my recollections of childhood struggles, I'd learned a great deal. I sought Mom's wisdom for she was a woman who faced greater struggles than I, specifically the death of her mom at age two, and her dad at age four, abandonment by her husband, and the daunting task of raising four children alone on little money. She didn't let me down, urging me to get involved in the lives of others, but in a cautious, proper way. I took her advice to heart, didn't move to the west side, didn't become overly-involved in the personal aspects of every family's struggle, yet continued my work with and for the poor for the rest of my life.

Beyond my work at the Dakota Street Center, my involvement in other issues, including some global ones, grew. In 1968, ABC –TV's Peter Jennings visited Dayton and spoke passionately of the atrocities he saw while on assignment in Nigeria during the Biafran War. In what was mostly a tribal conflict, one that also involved oil, more than two and a half million children younger than the age of five starved to death as the breakaway region known as Biafra was surrounded and completely cut off by government troops, most of whom were from rival tribes. The suffering of the children, who were dying mostly from protein deficiency diseases, was unbearable for me to watch without getting involved in some way. I volunteered to show a short, attention-grabbing film in the lobby of the main building on campus. The film contained graphic footage of the civil war and genocide against children in Biafra. I showed the film over and over again hoping to spark student interest and solicit donations. I found this experience to be difficult because many of the students were apathetic, passing by without even looking. Few stopped to watch the film. Even fewer dropped any coins into the collection jar next to the projector. Some criticized saying, "Why are you showing this?

Peter in Nicaragua with friend Marjorie, 2006

What are you trying to do, ruin our day?" One confronted me angrily saying, "Hey. If I invest money in an oil company that does business in Africa, I really don't care about those people, only that business goes on and I make money." The more aware I became of world problems, the more I began to worry about people, especially suffering children. I was hurt by the indifference I saw in so many college students.

At the same time, I received this encouragement from Mom about continuing my community work, albeit cautiously, I was reading The Autobiography of Malcolm X, which contained a message somewhat parallel to Mom's. Malcolm didn't think sincere whites needed to "prove they are with us" by working in the black community. "Where the really sincere white people have got to do their 'proving' of themselves is in their own communities; American's racism is among their own fellow whites. That's where the sincere whites who really mean to accomplish something have got to work." While Mom was teaching me to cautiously remain involved, Malcolm was suggesting not working in the black community at all, but in the white community. After I finished college, I taught for one year in Ft. Greene, Brooklyn where the vast majority of my students were poor and non-white. For the next 35 years I taught social studies and law in Long Island schools, to classes that were more than 95% white. While there, in keeping with Malcolm's message, I took my suburban white students, thousands of them over the years, on field trips to every part of New York City, including lower Manhattan, Midtown, Central Park, great museums and architectural treasures. I also took them to places most visitors don't go, like Harlem, inner city neighborhoods in Brooklyn, homeless shelters, soup kitchens, city-owned housing projects and high schools that were 100% non-white. While on these trips my students, utilizing mass transit all the way, had encounters with people who were from every walk of life, and from every race, color, creed and nationality. These hands-on, on-site experiences provided my urban studies students with a new and different view, one that typical suburban students rarely get. They also led to my work with students and the poor through the club I formed in 1986 called Students for 60000, named for the 60000 homeless persons then in NYC. The club, 30 years old as of this writing in 2016, is alive and well with more than 300 members each year, and continues to provide substantial aid, care and support for the needy, locally and internationally. In 1990, I began leading mostly suburban students and adults on more than 50 field experiences to the impoverished barrios and campos of northwest Nicaragua. Prior to each trip, students gathered tons of medical, educational and household supplies, and raised up to $50000 for each trip's humanitarian projects. When I retired and left Students for 60000 in 2008, my students had raised more than $1.5 million, which built hundreds of houses, several schools and a life-saving children's nutrition project. These trips spawned other trips as well, to the poorest regions of Africa, to live among and work side by side with the poorest people in the world. My teaching philosophy, inspired by my Mom's words and work, allowed me to motivate my students and provide opportunities for them to have real, important, and meaningful life-changing experiences in parts of the world books or videos alone do not take them, to sweatshops, dirt-floor shacks, tenements, primitive schools, and prisons, locally and throughout the world. While many suburban kids were busy with sports, or just hanging out with friends, many of my students were busy uncovering global problems, discussing and providing solutions, and making life substantially better for the poorest in our hemisphere. And, while doing so, they were became the recipients of valuable, life-changing lessons. These activities were greatly inspired by my Mom, my first and most important teacher, through her encouragement and concern, and by being the proper role model she was. While on my many visits to the poorest regions of Nicaragua I've always wished Mom could have lived long enough to join me, to see where her teaching led.

HAWAII

Robert, College and Hawaii

My brother Robert left Levittown in 1957 to become a ninth grade seminarian. He was always an independent-minded, hard worker, one who sought to make his life, and those of others, better. Mom was extremely proud of him. In fact, Robert's work ethic and academic success was always the standard Mom set for the rest of us. He did well as a schoolboy at St. Ignatius, at the Don Bosco seminary and Chaminade High School. Then in 1961, Robert decided to leave Long Island and make his own way in life as an 18-year-old young man. He applied to and was accepted at Chaminade College of Honolulu, some 5600 miles west of Levittown, the middle of the Pacific. Dennis, Jeanne and I were basically still kids and were saddened to learn he was going to live so far away. He'd been at the seminary for three years and was finally home for a year, something we all liked very much. It was like a man had returned to the house. Now he was going away again. This was at a time when Hawaii had just been admitted as our 50th state. Mom had finished two years of college back in the 1930's, and she was extremely proud that her oldest son was about to go further than she toward higher education. Except for Joan and John Larkin, our second cousins, he'd be only the third college graduate in the family, and the first in our immediate family. Mom very much wanted him to succeed, and was quite emphatic about how serious he should take his college studies. In the summer of 1961, just before Robert began packing his bag for the big move to Hawaii, his good friend Bud came over for dinner. Bud had gone to St. Ignatius with Robert, then on to Hicksville High School, from which he dropped out at age 16. He joined the Coast Guard reserves and by age 18 was out of the service and had begun working. Bud, the oldest of eight children, was not the serious student Robert was, but one who mainly sought to have a good time. A few weeks before Robert's departure, Bud joined us for dinner and we chatted about Robert's big move. Always a jokester, Bud said, "Hey, I got an idea. I'll move out to Hawaii too. We'll get a place together and have a blast." Mom didn't know whether he was serious, or whether he was joking. To make herself crystal clear, and without mincing words, she said, *"Robert is going to Hawaii for college, not to have a blast."* Bud, who didn't seem to appreciate Mom's words, smirked and gave her a look. Mom looked directly at Bud and added, *"You're not going to Hawaii."* Not one to hold back, Bud replied, "I'll go where I want." Frosted, Mom stated emphatically. *"You're right. You can go wherever you want. But if you go to Hawaii,…"* She then paused, turned and looked directly at Robert, and finished saying, *"…you're not."* That was a very tense moment, one followed by an awkward silence. It clearly showed that Mom was head of the family and where she stood on serious issues such as the future of her children. Robert didn't counter or argue. He'd worked hard as a student, knew what was expected of him, and understood what was at stake. Mom put Robert and all of us on a pretty straight path throughout childhood and Robert was the first to take such a major step toward adulthood. There was no way Mom could let someone like Bud, who never did move to Hawaii, interfere with that.

Robert and Pit

While I was only four years old when Robert A. White left, Dennis two and Jeanne only an infant, Robert was eight. He'd undoubtedly seen more as a boy than the rest of us had, and this made him appear older to us than he was. It was like he was the adult child in the family and we were the kids. More deliberative, pensive, and mature, Robert was our role model for manhood, since there was none other. When he was a young teenager, Robert did things that seemed like faraway dreams for me, things like going away to Boy Scout Camp in distant eastern Suffolk County, sleeping overnight in a tent with his friend Chuckie in "the weeds" across the street, or going with other teenagers to rock and roll shows in the city. He could also handle himself too. During one visit to Washington Heights to see Aunt Katherine and Aunt Nellie, Dennis and I witnessed Robert standing up to some tough guys in a way we greatly admired. It was like a scene from "West Side Story" or "Rebel Without a Cause." In the mid-1950's, many city teenagers had a tough look. We called them hoods. Boys combed their hair with the classic D.A. look in the back, and shoved a pack of Lucky Strike cigarettes in their rolled up tee shirt sleeves. They cursed and spit and ranked each other out. One such city tough guy was named Pit. We never knew his last name, or even his real first name for that matter. He was just called Pit, the leader of a bunch of teenagers who hung out at William Gordon Bennett Park on Ft. Washington Avenue and 183rd Street. A popular game at the time, played with a knife, was called "territory." Another popular knife game was called "stretch." Lots of teenagers carried knives in those days. One afternoon, Robert was in the park with his two city pals, Eric Mendelson and Donny Shea, both clean-cut, nice guys, not hoods. They watched as Pit, Terry, a goofy guy who followed Pit everywhere, and a dozen or so other teenagers played territory. A rectangular box about five feet by ten feet was drawn in the dirt with a knife. Then a player would throw the knife into the ground trying to make it stick in. If it did, he got to draw a line in the dirt in the same direction as the blade, cutting out for himself a piece of "territory." Then the next player would go. Who ever ended up with the most territory at the end of the game was the winner, ready to accept a challenge from someone waiting to play next. After a game, Pit said, "Who's next?" Robert said, "I am." Pit walked up to Robert, stood nose-to-nose with him and said, "Who are you? We don't know you. You're not next." Robert had only Eric Mendelson and Donny Shea with him. Pit had at least half a dozen in his crowd. Robert didn't back down. Continuing to face Pit he said, "I've been waiting. I'm next." Pit didn't know what to do. Goofy Terry egged him on saying, "C'mon Pit. Don't let him play. He's not from here." Pit looked first at Terry and his other pals, then back at Robert, paused, then handed Robert the knife and, in his tough manner, said, "OK. It's your turn." We never saw Robert fight, but just standing his ground against a tough city guy and winning his turn at territory was enough for Dennis and me, young boys in search of some manhood.

Aloha Robert

With Mom unable to provide any financial help for college and no scholarship, Robert worked the summer of 1961 at a construction job in New York City. Mom's cousin, Bernard McCoy, was a wirelather, a construction worker who installed long pieces of steel into concrete to strengthen it. Moving heavy steel rods all day, then bending down to tie them together was backbreaking work. Robert got a few months' work with Bernard on a project in the city, enough for him to have sufficient funds to begin college. In the late summer of 1961, Robert took off on his long journey to Hawaii from La Guardia Airport. We didn't know it at the time, but it was to be a life-long journey. Still a car-less family in 1961, I don't know how we got to the airport, but somehow we all got to see Robert off. This was an unusual goodbye. Robert was going to the middle of the Pacific Ocean and we knew there wasn't much chance we'd be seeing him again, at least not soon. Even though commercial jets were commonplace by then and a flight to California could take as little as five hours, the cost of a jet flight was greater than that of traditional propeller planes. So Robert boarded a medium-sized propeller plane that had four loud engines on it. As he boarded, we stood on the rooftop deck of La Guardia and waved goodbye. Robert waved back, then disappeared into the plane and was gone. Traveling first to Chicago, then on to St. Louis, then Los Angeles, he arrived in Honolulu nearly 30 hours after his departure from La Guardia. Since a call from a telephone booth cost a lot back then, the best form of communication was through regular mail. We waited more than a week to learn how he made out on his journey. Robert knew no one in Hawaii. Other than someone from Chaminade Collage greeting him at the airport, he was completely on his own. Jeanne was misty seeing Robert leave, "Robert was nice to me when I was a child, and I always felt close to him. So when he was gone I missed him greatly. It was hard for me to adjust to the change of his being so far away."

Robert began classes at Chaminade College in Honolulu, majoring in liberal arts and business. He had enough money saved from his 1961 summer wire lather job to fly to Hawaii, finish his first few months of school and pay rent on a small apartment. To support himself and continue paying for his education, he began a job at a downtown Honolulu bar called Two Jacks Pub, in the Hotel Street district, a part of Honolulu known for its late nights and less-than-fancy bars. As with all of us, Robert could expect little financial help from Mom for college. Paying for higher education was something each of us would have to accomplish on our own. Though she couldn't afford to pay for school, Mom strongly encouraged us and amazingly we acquired a wide range of education. Our ancestors were Irish immigrant bricklayers and plasterers, people without any formal education. So Robert's completion of a bachelor's degree in business, then an MBA from the University of Hawaii was a huge jumping off point in our family history. He paved the way, and the rest of us followed. I received my B.A. in History from the University of Dayton, then two master's degrees and a law degree, passing the bar exams in New York and Massachusetts on the first try. After serving two years in the Marines and excelling at their radio school in San Diego, Dennis studied for two years at Nassau Community College earning an Associates Degree. After completing high school in 1969, Jeanne received training to become a practical nurse. In the mid-1970s' she moved with her daughter, Michelle, to Albany where, over the next few decades, she persevered and finally received her bachelor's, and ultimately a masters degree in Social Work. Jeanne did this the old fashioned way, one course at a time, paid for, as with all of us, entirely by herself.

Robert was more than a continent away and we missed him greatly, especially during those early years. He was our older brother, someone we looked up to, the man of the house. After he left, the man of the house torch was suddenly passed to me at age 13 and I can't say I was prepared for that role. Even though he was such a great distance, Mom couldn't have been prouder of her oldest son. He was a man, living on his own, doing adult things, making decisions, and solving problems by himself, going to college, getting a job, while we stayed home and remained children…for a little while longer. We heard from Robert by phone only infrequently during those early years. A phone call from Hawaii to New York was very expensive. Mostly he and Mom exchanged newsy letters. Whenever the phone would ring and it was Robert on the line calling from Hawaii, Mom would get very excited. House noises, like a radio or television or even a conversation, had to cease immediately. Mom did not want to miss a word of Robert's long distance call, something she considered a real treat. She'd place her finger over her mouth and say, *"Shhh. Quiet. It's Robert, … from Hawaii,"* as if we didn't know. We had to stop whatever we were doing, and hush. Calls were brief, and after Mom spent a few minutes with him, she'd give us all a moment to say hello. We all remember how, after living several years in Hawaii, his accent began to change. With each call he sounded less and less like a New Yorker, and more and more like a kama'aina, a mainlander on his way to becoming a permanent Hawaiian. We joked, calling his accent the "aloha-mali-cali-wali" talk, our version of some of the Hawaiian expressions Robert used. He worked long hours at the Two Jacks Bar, doing most every job there. He would open and close the place, tend bar, clean up, do the bookkeeping, everything involved in operating a small business. After one year of working full time and going to school full time, he came home during the summer of 1962 and was able to resume the wirelather job he had the year before. This involved commuting to the city everyday on the Long Island Rail Road, working with steel rods all day in the heat, and returning home exhausted. So even though it was great that he came home that first summer, we didn't see too much of him. He earned enough money to return to Hawaii and begin his second year of college. The next time any of us would see Robert would be four years later, when Mom made her first visit to Hawaii to attend his graduation in 1966, and to meet his fiancée, Charlotte Gomes and her parents, Ida and Tony.

The Home Front

With Robert gone, all wasn't always easy or quiet on the home front. Dennis, Jeanne and I could see how much Mom missed Robert. We did too. Though we tried to do our best, we were pretty much still kids and things weren't always trouble-free, especially for Mom. But over time we fit into our roles and became the young adults of the house, doing the things Mom needed done. With no man around the house and our older brother gone, at times we may have shown a trace of resentment, like when things had to be done around the house and we were the only ones there to do them. There were also times when Mom would have health or emotional problems and the only ones around to witness them or deal with them and we were three kids with no idea what to do. Mom began to experience bouts of loneliness, sadness, depression, and even some version of PTSD at her plight in life. At times we'd see tears. Those tears and sad feelings abated when Mom's 70 year old adopted mother, Aunt Katherine McCoy, moved in with us. Aunt Katherine was a retired chief operator from the New York Telephone Company and lived alone after the death of her sister, Nellie, and brother, Connie. Mom and Aunt Katherine decided it would be best for all of us if she came to live with us. She gave up her large, well-located, inexpensive apartment in a fashionable part of Washington Heights and made the move to Levittown in the spring of 1960. The next five years were great for all of us, mostly because Mom finally had another adult she could confide in, consult with, or simply talk to, someone other than a child or a teenager. With Aunt Katherine home and Mom less lonely, the three of us felt much more breathing room. A great weight had been made lighter.

We loved having Aunt Katherine stay with us. She was elderly, with silver colored hair. We used to kid her and say her hair looked like George Washington's. While Mom rarely drank, Aunt Katherine had an occasional "highball." We didn't really know what a highball was, but whenever she had one she'd relax and tell stories that made us laugh. It was like having a real grandma, which made us feel good. At last there was some additional laughter in the house. While Mom wouldn't tolerate any profanity from us, at all, Aunt Katherine would slip once in a while, mostly with simple words like hell or damn. We said, "Aunt Katherine, be careful. Mom doesn't allow anyone to curse." In her Irish-Washington Heights manner of speaking, she'd say, "Those words aren't so bad. That's not really 'coising.'" We knew that, to an Irish woman from upper Manhattan, "coise" meant curse, same as "choich" meant church, "poil" meant pearl, "erl" meant oil, and "terlit" meant toilet. Mom made half the upstairs into a bedroom for Aunt Katherine, and even had a toilet and sink added to an upstairs closet, so she'd have some additional privacy. Dennis and I still slept in the adjacent bedroom, formerly known as the "coldroom." We enjoyed being so close to Aunt Katherine. It was like having an adult buddy next door. As Aunt Katherine got older, into her mid 70's, it became increasingly more difficult for her to climb the stairs. But she did, and her door was always open for us. When Mom was too busy to talk with us, overwhelmed with her new job as a teacher, paying bills, or just with the busyness of her day, Aunt Katherine always took the time to speak with us. She'd listen to our problems, tell us stories of what we called "the olden days," give us advice, and even tell us who won the Yankee game that day while we were at school. "Mantle struck out, Maris and Blanchard homered, and Ford got the win!"

Mom's First Trip to Hawaii

By 1966, five years after Robert moved to Hawaii and Aunt Katherine to our house, Mom wanted to visit Hawaii to see Robert, meet Charlotte and the Gomes Family, attend Robert's college graduation, and of course to see the beauty of Hawaii, our 50th state, the Aloha State. I was a freshman at the University of Dayton during 1965-66 and worked three part time jobs, getting enough hours each week to keep up with expenses. While other college kids were having their fun, I was delivering auto parts on Saturdays, waiting tables at the Sheraton Hotel, and running the desk at a less than one-star hotel on weekend nights. I lived frugally, didn't drink or go out much at all, and saved up as much money as I could. By Easter 1966, I'd saved enough to send Mom a rather substantial gift, $500, so she could make her first trip to Hawaii. Mom was very happy with this gift, and also very excited at the possibility of going. In a letter to me, dated April 23, 1966, she said:

Dear Peter,

Your gift gave me a wonderful feeling – it was not the amount that you sent me that made me feel like a queen but the thought of your sacrificing and saving for my pleasure that made me feel your love and devotion to me. You know I never look for gifts and your traditional box of candy always made me happy because knowing you had no money it was the thought that counted. So when you got a job, on your own, and unknown to anyone saved up this large sum, how my heart puffed with pride. You and your brother, who is 23 years old today, have the wonderful virtue of character which cannot be bought for any price. It makes me happy to be your mother…. You and Robert are men now, away from home. I hope you really know what this means to me. I never get gushy but I can say you gave me the surprise of my life. Especially when I had just been discussing wanting you to use your earnings on a car of your own.

Instead you used this money for me. Thank you a million. God will bless you for all your devotion.

Love and prayers,

Mom

Overjoyed as she was about a trip to Hawaii, Mom was faced with a serious conflict. While Hawaii beckoned, Aunt Katherine's health was sinking and Mom felt duty-bound to remain home with her. Dennis, Jeanne and I really wanted to see Mom go to Hawaii, so we promised we'd do our best as teens to care for Aunt Katherine, to make her meals, wait on her, and to make sure she was safe and well. We were no longer kids, but young men and women who knew the responsibility involved, and wanted to assume it. Even though we gave her these assurances, Mom was reluctant to leave Aunt Katherine's side. Then in May 1966 Aunt Katherine's health sank even lower and she had to be placed in Syosset Hospital, about six miles from the house. I had just gotten a summer job as a swimming pool repairman, and Dennis and Jeanne were students in Clarke High School. Mom dropped all thoughts of going to Hawaii, because, as was her style and strong belief, she placed Aunt Katherine's needs ahead of her own. It was Aunt Katherine, sick as she was with a very painful blood disease, who insisted that Mom go to Hawaii. From her hospital bed with Mom and us by her side, Aunt Katherine was adamant, "Catherine, you've taken care of me all along. Now it's your turn. Go to Hawaii. You deserve to see Robert graduate, and he deserves to have you there. The kids will take good care of me. If you stay home because of me, I'll worry the whole time." Mom followed this strong and good advice from her wonderful Aunt Katherine, who had cared for her and so many others throughout her life. Dennis, Jeanne and I felt great that Mom trusted us enough to handle the job of seeing Aunt Katherine through this critical time. Knowing how important attending Robert's graduation was to Mom, her boss, Msgr. Martin O'Dea, allowed her some time off in May. She accepted this kindness, bought a ticket to Hawaii and began packing. While she used my gift to purchase her ticket, Dennis and Jeanne gave her what they could for spending money, and Robert, Charlotte and her parents, Tony and Ida Gomes contributed substantially while she was in Hawaii, with dinners, shopping and gifts. So her trip was a group effort, made possible by Msgr. O'Dea, Aunt Katherine, and all of us.

Unlike Robert's 30-hour propeller plane experience five years earlier, Mom was booked on a TWA jet from New York's JFK Airport to Los Angeles, then on to Hawaii via United Airlines. Maybe it was the flight itself, Mom's first airplane experience, or the excitement of it all, but she was able to fly away in a big jet and leave her concerns aside for several weeks. In the 45-page journal she kept from this first Hawaii visit, Mom described her long flight in heavenly terms:

> *The takeoff was thrilling. We soared up and up where the land below looked like a child's train layout of a village dotted with miniature houses, roads and cars below. Higher and higher we soared until the land looked like a giant map below us. Then on into and above the clouds where you thought you could reach out and touch the cotton-like clouds below. Prisms of beautiful colors were visible from the rays of the sun. This was so beautiful that I felt very close to heaven and was literally out of this world for a few hours. I felt the beauty of God's creation, like an astronaut on a trip around the world. I then plugged in my earphones and had my choice of seven channels of beautiful music to select from. Peace was all around me and I thanked God for being a very lucky person to be able to have made such a trip. I also thank those who made this trip possible.*

Her journal goes on to point out how even the smallest things made her happy, things like being served a nice meal by a friendly flight attendant, having a cocktail on the flight, and seeing an in-flight movie *"in color."* While many grumble when they board crowded planes, especially when they must sit for hours on a middle seat, Mom saw things differently. Of her jam-packed flight from Los Angeles to Honolulu she said,

> *This plane, Flight #198 to Hawaii, was very crowded but the people were lovely. I was seated between a nice young girl and a man, an engineer who was bound for Japan on business. We chatted for the 5 and a half hours and they were very interesting company. We settled back and relaxed as we soared high up to 35,000 feet above the earth and once again I was 'up in the clouds.'*

While in Hawaii, Mom was treated royally by Robert, Charlotte and her parents, Tony and Ida Gomes. They hosted parties, danced the hula, took Mom to dinner at Koko's on Kapiolani Boulevard and other eateries, and brought her to all the points of interest that tourists wait a lifetime to see. In her letters from Hawaii, Mom spoke of the beauty of the ultra-blue Pacific Ocean, and the relaxation she got visiting Waikiki, Waimanalo and other beaches. She was touched by her visit to "Punchbowl," the National Cemetery of the Pacific, and came to tears while standing over the U.S.S. Arizona at Pearl Harbor, recalling the events of December 7, 1941. Mom even went in a glider plane and saw much of Oahu's mountain and ocean beauty silently from the air. Robert, Charlotte and the Gomes' took her to singer Don Ho's nightclub at the International Market Place in Waikiki, and shopping at the huge, new Ala Moana Center, all activities that were basically unavailable to her at home, with her regular work schedule, parenting and household tasks. Photos of this first visit to Hawaii show her wearing a muumuu, a colorful, flowing Hawaiian women's dress, a glowing tan, and the broadest smile any of us ever saw on her face. Her journal and letters to Dennis, Jeanne and me described in detail every joyous aspect of her trip, from Hawaii's natural beauty, Robert's graduation, and meeting Charlotte, who a year later would become her first daughter-in-law. The trip was just what Mom needed, and made all the work and worry that went into getting her there 100% worthwhile. In a letter dated early June 1966, Mom shared her feelings about her first visit to Hawaii and the new people she'd met.

A week and a half has gone by and we are crowding everything in – doing something each day and evening. It has been marvelous! This trip was something I never thought possible and it still seems like a dream to me.... I'll bring home to all of you this beautiful island in pictures and a complete day by day description of all I've seen and done. This would never be possible without Robert, Charlotte and her parents who have planned a wonderful schedule of every place on the island for me to see. I had no idea it was as large and interesting as it is. If I were a tourist coming alone, it would cost a small fortune to see all that I have.... Last night we were invited to Charlotte and Robert's friend's house – Gail Weber. Her father is a retired naval officer. They have eight children and a large and beautiful home. We had a wonderful evening. A neighbor of the Gomes' gave me a white orchid corsage (three orchids!) to wear to the dinner. What generous people.... I'm very glad that I was able to see Robert and know what a fine man he turned out to be. Everyone speaks highly of him, including his teachers.... Jackie Kennedy is arriving here on June fourth and will be staying at the hotel where Mr. Gomes works. Also Joe DiMaggio is here now too.... Tomorrow Mr. Gomes is cooking some Hawaiian dish for me. He is really very nice. We all get along just fine. It is very easy being with them.... Tell Sugar I miss her and won't leave her for such a long time again. Aloha and love to all.

Mom

AUNT KATHERINE

Syosset Hospital

Back home, we had less to smile about. Dennis, Jeanne and I led busy, complicated but meaningful lives during that time. While they went to school each morning, I went to my swimming pool cleaning job, which usually took me until nightfall each evening. When I'd get back to the house, I'd pick up Dennis and get to Syosset Hospital as quickly as I could. Aunt Katherine had bought Mom her first car, the 1960 Ford Fairlane, less than a year before, and this was the first time I was allowed to use it on a regular basis. I remember returning from college for Thanksgiving and Christmas in 1965, thinking I could use the car while I was home. But Mom was emphatic, "I waited all my life for a car, and I'm not turning the keys over to a teenager." With Aunt Katherine in the hospital, family necessity changed that. Mom allowed me to use the car to get to my job and to visit Aunt Katherine, something we did every evening while Mom was gone. Sometimes, when my job kept me until after dark, we'd arrive at the hospital after visiting hours were over and were greeted by a rather unfriendly and strict security guard whom Dennis and I nicknamed "Dick Tracy." "You're too late. No more visiting tonight." Dennis and I became quite skilled in devising ways to either talk our way past him, or somehow maneuver our way to Aunt Katherine's room. Dennis would keep Dick Tracy busy while I'd slip by, or vice versa. Overcoming this challenge was important for Aunt Katherine and us. She was alone all day suffering from a serious illness, so there was no question in our minds that we had to see her, by whatever means necessary. The nurses never had a problem on those nights when we came by late. They knew the value of our visits and how they lifted Aunt Katherine's spirits. And she was always glad to see us. So was her hospital roommate, Mrs. Beach. I don't know what she was hospitalized for, but the more we visited and got to know her, Mrs. Beach grew fond of us and was quite moved to see teenagers showing up every night, no matter the hour, to see their elderly great-aunt. Aunt Katherine and Mrs. Beach developed a special friendship, the kind that is borne out of common struggle, one that continued after their hospitalizations. In fact, after she was released from the hospital, Mrs. Beach wrote a long and beautiful letter to Aunt Katherine in which she described in detail her feelings about her and of our dedication, care and concern. After Mrs. Beach left the hospital, Aunt Katherine grew increasingly more lonely and uncomfortable. I spoke with her doctor who said she had a blood disease that was quite painful for her and for which there was no cure. Due to her age and condition, he advised against any heroic treatments or approaches. Aunt Katherine was born in New York City in 1890 and was just about to turn 76. Frustrated with hospital life and all that ailed her, she cried at times and we felt helpless. What became crystal clear as the days went by was that she wanted to go home, no matter what anyone said. No more hospital. When her itching and other symptoms were at their worst, she'd press the button for a nurse's assistance, and sometimes no one would come. She'd had enough. Inwardly, I believed that Aunt Katherine saw the end of her life coming and she wanted to spend it at home, in familiar surroundings, with her little pet dog, Sugar, whom she loved dearly, and us. One night Aunt Katherine looked directly at me, held my hand and said, "I want to go home." I was never faced with this type of decision before, but I couldn't leave her there against her will. Quite certain of what Mom would do under these circumstances, I assured Aunt Katherine that she'd be home the next day. I didn't bother calling Mom in Hawaii, worrying her, interrupting her time there. She wasn't present to see Aunt Katherine's condition, or her need to be home. The next morning I went into her closet at home, picked out a nice dress and a few other things, put them in a bag and brought them to the hospital. When Aunt Katherine saw what I'd brought, she lit up. Finally, her long days and nights of being hospitalized would be over. I helped her change from her hospital clothes into her dress, grabbed a wheelchair from the hallway, and pushed her straight out of that hospital. On our way out, a nurse asked what we were doing. Aunt Katherine said, "I'm going home." This is what she wanted, and it proved to be the best thing. As soon as we arrived home, almost miraculously, Aunt Katherine was up and around, laughing, talking, eating, enjoying Sugar's company, and even doing dishes. The agonizing itch abated, as did so many of the aches and pains she suffered during her three-week stay in the hospital. To our surprise, she was even able to climb the stairs to her own bedroom. For this brief period, all seemed well. Considering all she'd been through, things couldn't have been better. When Mom returned from Hawaii happy and tan, she was astonished to see Aunt Katherine home, looking as well as she had in years. As good as Aunt Katherine and Mom felt, we felt good too as our multi-pronged mission was accomplished: Mom had her trip to Hawaii, Robert a graduation visit from Mom, Aunt Katherine the care she needed, and we three children of Kay White the chance, once again, to be trusted with important matters.

Mom, nearing age 50, had the trip of a lifetime, her first such vacation since her honeymoon 25 years before. She returned filled with stories of her amazing experiences and the wonderful people she'd met. For a number of reasons, Mom smiled a lot more after her trip to paradise. She'd seen Robert's life and surroundings, been present for his graduation, and was proud that he was on his way toward a career. She'd also met Dave Hamilton, Burt, and several of Robert's other friends, Charlotte and the Gomes family, spent several relaxing, blissful weeks enjoying Hawaii and returned to find out that her three youngest children were capable of making mature decisions under adverse conditions. Most of all, she came home to witness the tremendous improvement in Aunt Katherine's health. For months after her trip, Mom spoke constantly of the Aloha Spirit, about how Hawaii had a laid-back lifestyle, one where there was "no pilikea," no trouble with little things. She enjoyed that people could wear flowered shirts to work sometimes instead of shirt and tie. She played her favorite Don Ho songs over and over, "Tiny Bubbles," "One Paddle, Two Paddle," and loved the one called "Ain't No Big Thing." Hawaii relaxed her, which was good for us to see. She saw how the Aloha Spirit also signified how people in Hawaii get along quite well in their racially mixed environment. For a number of reasons, Hawaii is made up of a blend of many nationalities, ethnicities and cultures. It is not uncommon for an African-American, or someone of Japanese or Philippine ancestry to be married to one another or to a Caucasian. She explained that the largest group is known as the "local" people, or persons of racially mixed ancestry. To her there seemed to be less prejudice in Hawaii than on the mainland, where most schools, neighborhoods and housing patterns continued to be segregated. Although the Civil Rights Act of 1965, which made it violation of federal law to discriminate against a person in a public place for reasons of race, religion or national origin, was only a year old, Mom didn't need a new law or a trip to Hawaii to know that. She had no tolerance whatsoever for bigotry or prejudice, and none was ever tolerated in our house. Mom toted back several physical reminders of her trip and cherished them all. She loved her carved wooden Hawaiian flowers, a gift from Robert and Charlotte, and the framed Japanese prints given to her by Tony and Ida Gomes. These Hawaiian treasures were placed throughout the house as constant reminders of this trip of a lifetime. She had lots of photos too, including her dancing with hula girls at the Kodak Hula Show at Waikiki. This was no problem for Mom, who'd been a dancer and actress in college in the mid-1930's. Her favorite place on Oahu was the view of Honolulu, Diamond Head and the Pacific Ocean from the top of Tantalus Mountain. Robert and Charlotte took her all the way up long, winding Roundtop Drive and showed her all the sights, including the Gomes' house on Bingham Street below. All such trips come to an end, but happily for Mom, she returned to the great news that a happier, healthier Aunt Katherine was home from the hospital and flourishing.

The Loss of Aunt Katherine

In late August 1966, as Mom was about to begin her seventh year of teaching and I was about to leave for my second year of college, things with Aunt Katherine changed drastically. The intolerable itching from her blood disease returned and she grew weak and unable to stand the pain and discomfort. Her health began to decline with each day so we moved her to the small bedroom downstairs so we could keep a constant eye on her. Several times we didn't think she'd last through the night. We even called Father Donovan from Holy Family Church to administer the Last Rites. Mom decided it was best to have her hospitalized again, so she was taken to Long Island Jewish Hospital in New Hyde Park. Doctors said her blood disease, called macroglobulin anemia, was very severe and that only a complete blood transfusion could change things. There was great risk with that however, due to her age and condition. I didn't know what to do about school. Should I skip a semester of college in case I was needed at home? Should I go back to school in faraway Dayton, Ohio, with all this on my mind and in my heart? A boyhood friend of mine from Twig Lane died accidentally in 1958, and an eighth grade classmate died of leukemia in 1961. Death terrified me and the thought of losing Aunt Katherine, whom I loved very much, was a lot for me to bear. I had never lost anyone that close, and her death seemed imminent. Mom had many experiences with death, having lost both her parents as a child and seen the passing of all ten of her aunts and uncles. She was strong and said, *"Peter, go to Dayton and get to work. I'll let you know if you should come back."* With that I packed my bag and left.

Though she had looked forward to and greatly needed her teaching job, Mom had no thoughts of leaving Aunt Katherine alone. She wanted Dennis, Jeanne and me back in school, and she would handle things with Aunt Katherine at home the best she could by herself. Aunt Katherine had been there for so many others, and Mom felt an absolute duty to care for her the best she could. A few days before school was to open, she went to the principal and the pastor, Msgr. O'Dea, and let them know of her problem, and her decision. She couldn't be responsible for the education of 50 children and at the same time care for Aunt Katherine. Faced with this dilemma, there was only one path for her:

to leave her teaching job to care for her loving aunt. Sadly, Msgr. O'Dea accepted her resignation and wished her the best. After six wonderful years as a first grade teacher at Holy Family School, though she earned only a modest salary of a few thousand dollars a year, she was now unemployed and had the task of caring for her seriously ill Aunt Katherine.

Robert, who was in the Hawaii National Guard, had just finished a training assignment at Ft. Ord, California and had a two week leave. Immediately after camp ended, he got a standby ticket to New York and joined Mom at Aunt Katherine's side. As Robert's leave expired and my classes in Dayton were about to begin, Aunt Katherine's condition deteriorated. Mom called me in Ohio and said, *"Come home."* I don't recall how I got to New York, but within a day or two I made it to Long Island Jewish Hospital to be with Aunt Katherine before it was too late. Knowing how special and generous she was to Mom and all of us and to so many others throughout her life, I held her hand and said, "Aunt Katherine, whatever I do in this life, I'm going to do for you." That pledge turned out to be my final goodbye. Our beloved Aunt Katherine passed away that afternoon, September 12, 1966. I have been mindful of the vow I made to her, throughout my life. It has remained a constant guide for me ever since.

We had a wake for Aunt Katherine at Quinn's Funeral home on Hempstead Turnpike in Levittown. Since she had survived all in her generation, it was a small funeral. Mom, Dennis, Jeanne and I, as well as Mom's cousin Francis McCoy, whom we called "Frank the Cop," and cousin Florence Larkin and her children, made up the bulk of those paying their respects to this grand lady. Dennis and I were not used to funerals and didn't like seeing people chitchat with their backs to Aunt Katherine's casket. At one point, Dennis got up and announced his desire that everyone turn their chairs around to face Aunt Katherine. They did so immediately. I was glad that he took command. While others may have experienced death before, this was a tough situation for us, our first loss of a loved one so close. Throughout the

Aunt Katherine's new stone, located directly across from large McCoy family grave, Calvary Cemetery, Queens,

two-day wake, there weren't too many visitors to the funeral home, but there was one unforgettable surprise. During the afternoon of the second day, the mostly empty room in which Aunt Katherine lay filled up with a large group of young men. Dozens of Dennis' teammates from the Clarke football team had entered to pay their respects. Few of them knew Aunt Katherine personally, but all knew of Dennis' love and devotion to her, and so they joined him at her side. Mom had Aunt Katherine buried in Calvary Cemetery, Queens, in an empty grave purchased decades before by her sister, Aunt Nellie. This plot is in the same row as the large McCoy grave, purchased in 1899 by Aunt Katherine's father, Cornelius McCoy, that contains nearly a dozen family members. With no room left in the large family grave, Aunt Katherine was buried alone. At the time Mom didn't have enough money for a tombstone and so Aunt Katherine was laid to rest in an unmarked grave. Regrettably, years passed before Robert, Dennis, Jeanne and I became mindful that Aunt Katherine had no stone. Upon learning she was buried alone and without a stone, in 2008 we purchased one and had it placed on her grave. Our Aunt Katherine McCoy, who took care of so many others during her life, including Mom when she was orphaned, and us when we were fatherless, the generous, unselfish lady who saw all her brothers and sisters through their final years, finally got a stone from us, her grand nephews and niece.

Mom's Aunt Katherine McCoy was a great woman, respected by all who knew her. She was tough when she had to be, and as gentle as possible whenever she could be. She enjoyed a good laugh and was the most generous, patient, caring person I ever knew. She was the first person that I ever truly loved and lost. Her death was very difficult for me.

MOM'S VALUES

Loyalty and Perseverance - The Uniform Store

With Aunt Katherine gone, Robert in Hawaii, and me back in Dayton, Mom was jobless and alone with Dennis and Jeanne who were both in high school. Having resigned from her teaching job at Holy Family School only weeks before, Msgr. O'Dea had already found a replacement. So in mid-September 1966, with little time to recover from the loss of Aunt Katherine, Mom, a single parent of two minor children and unemployed, did the only thing she could. She took the first job she could find, at a store in Carle Place that sold nurses and other types of worker uniforms. The store, which continues to operate today, had a huge sign on the front that said "UNIFORMS" in big red letters. Mom accepted the minimum wage of $1.50 an hour. This was about half the $3.00 an hour her modest paycheck would have been from Holy Family. She willingly went to work for this pay cut, with no benefits, because she had to and because she believed that it was the right thing to do. At the uniform store, she unpacked, stocked and folded uniforms, swept floors, and did whatever else was needed. She did these menial tasks without any grumbling or whining, well aware that she was doing what she always taught us to do, her best. Whether she knew it or not, she was living the true meaning of Gandhi's words, that "all work is honorable." In her letters to me, she never complained at all about this humdrum job or the substantial reduction in income she suffered. She accepted life's ups and downs with grace and strength, content with the knowledge that she was doing what she had to do as a parent. Dennis and Jeanne pitched in more around the house, and we all contributed money when we could. She was accustomed to the task of belt-tightening and understood that she'd simply have to get by with less, something she'd learned as a young woman during the Great Depression, and as a welfare mom throughout the 1950's. Luckily for Mom and all of us, within a few months of this drastic, downward change in circumstances, Msgr. O'Dea called her with some good news: a teacher suddenly resigned for personal reasons and there was a job opening. The principal did a little shuffling around of teachers' schedules and Mom was brought back at Holy Family School as teacher of the same first grade class she would have had had she not resigned.

From Mom's many hardships connected with Aunt Katherine's illness, giving up her job, losing her adopted mother, and working for minimum wage, we saw firsthand the meaning of perseverance, loyalty, bravery, patience and character from our ultimate teacher. By this time we were no longer children, but young men and women old enough to see the reality of our family's plight. From then on, we would find it difficult to complain about not getting enough when we witnessed Mom making her way with so little, and always for our benefit. What many might have viewed as a form of degradation, an educated, professional, head-of-household working for minimum wage, was something Mom did silently, patiently, and with great dignity. She accepted this job change without complaint because she knew it was the right step, the only step available at the time, toward making her life better. Today I see many who run into tough times, whether they be the poor who become frustrated and give up, working folks who get laid off in these days of economic downturn, upper income people who lose their waterfront homes to natural disasters, or wealthy Wall Street bankers whose companies fail, always expecting government or someone else to come along and provide for them, to bail them out, to make them whole. Mom expected no bailouts or handouts. She saw things differently, believing that her life would only get better if she made it better.

Courage and Strength

Raising four children alone is a difficult job. It requires attention to many details, especially the necessary tasks of providing food, clothing and shelter, and directing the health, safety, and educational and moral growth of children. Parents know that there are times when consulting with one another is the best course, when two heads are better than one. As a single parent, Mom didn't have that opportunity. When important decisions had to be made, there was often no one else for her to consult with. On occasion, situations arose that made it necessary for her to confront people or institutions. Not to confront such people or institutions, in her mind, would have been to allow major wrongs to go unchecked. To halt those injustices, Mom had to gather the facts and assess the matter at hand, organize her thoughts, decide on a course of action, and then confidently, courageously and boldly, face things directly. Three such situations come to mind where I watched Mom stand up to others without fear because she believed it to be necessary and right to do so.

Mrs. A.

As kids, we lived in a hand-me-down household, with not much in the way of new toys, bikes or other things. When my sister Jeanne was four years old she received a new doll, something very special to her. She played with it constantly. For some unexplainable reason the six-year-old son of one of our neighbors, Mrs. A, tore the doll to pieces, ripping off both legs and both arms. Jeanne cried. Mom was furious when she saw that the doll had been destroyed. Without hesitation, she steamed out of the house heading straight for Mrs. A's house, mutilated doll in hand. She didn't go out the front door to the sidewalk, but took the quicker path, out the back door, across the next-door neighbor's back yard, directly to the side of Mrs. A's yard. I could foresee what was about to happen. As she marched across the lawns, I followed begging, "Mom, Stop. Please." I didn't like confrontations and was afraid, partly for her, and partly for me. Mom, straight faced and paying no attention to my pleas, continued on. In addition to the six-year-old doll vandal, the A's had a nine-year-old son, a bully whom neighborhood kids feared. I thought if Mom took on Mrs. A over the doll, she'd get shouted down, maybe even hurt, and I'd become the older boy's next victim. Mrs. A could be loud and confrontational, and no stranger to profanity. Few would mess with her. Mom never uttered a curse word. It would be an unfair fight. Mrs. A would easily out-scream and overpower Mom, and when it was over, I'd pay the price. A giant hedge surrounded the A's house, at least four feet wide and four feet tall. Mom stood on one side of the hedge, and called loudly for Mrs. A to come out. Moments later, she appeared. Mom held the doll straight out across the wide hedge toward Mrs. A and, without mincing words, demanded, *"Your son did this. I want to know what you're going to do about it!"* As was foreseeable, Mrs. A did not like being confronted or shown this evidence, undisputed as it was. She shouted back at Mom, loudly, offensively, and with the predicted foul language. Refusing to back down, Mom stood her ground and continued to make her point in plain, non-profane language. At times she raised her voice, but only so as not to be out-yelled. Hearing the fracas, neighbors came out and tried to calm the two women down. After a few verbal volleys, Mom reached across the hedge, placed the doll in Mrs. A's hands, demanded that she make things right, then turned around and walked quietly back home. I followed, shaking…partly for Mom, and partly for me. I'd never seen anyone take on Mrs. A before. Few had the courage. Few were brave enough to feel the sting of her lash. In the end, the doll was replaced and I never did get beat up.

Kay White had faced Mrs. A and won. If she had money, Mom easily could have replaced the doll and spared herself and the neighbors the noise and tumult. But that was not the case. There was more at stake. There would be no new doll unless someone stood up. Only in part this was about replacing Jeanne's doll. It was also about doing the right thing when confronted with a problem, about standing up and being counted, about calling "a popgun a popgun," and letting the chips fall where they may. I discovered that day that there are times in life when one must speak his mind, even when it is difficult to do so, even when unearned suffering may result.

"Good Friday"

During his years at St. Ignatius Loyola School, my older brother Robert was a successful student, a fine scholar who took pride in his work. His attitude toward his studies pleased Mom greatly. In 1957, during the spring of eighth grade, he entered a school-sponsored poetry contest. The subject matter of students' submissions was to be an Easter theme. Robert took the contest very seriously and began writing a poem he called "Good Friday," about the days leading up to the crucifixion of Jesus, the holiest and saddest day of the Catholic calendar year. After his initial draft, he began the process of going back, over and over, constantly refining his work. Night after night for weeks, we three kids and Mom could hear Robert from behind the closed door to his bedroom, reading his poem aloud, stopping only to make subtle changes here and there, crafting each word so that it meant precisely what he wanted it to mean, and getting it all to rhyme perfectly. He worked hard every day on "Good Friday" until the deadline came.

Proud of his work, he read his final version to Mom and us before submitting it. We were all very proud of his accomplishment. The first place prize was $10 and a religious statue. Far more than the $10 and the statue, first place would be an honor. Days before the Easter vacation, the eighth grade nuns, led by the intimidating, four-foot, 11-inch Sister Rose Dominic, nicknamed "Rosie" by her students, posted the winning submissions for all to see. "Good Friday" wasn't among them.

The winning poems weren't very good. Most lacked polish and apparently were written hastily by kids who couldn't have put in a fraction of the time Robert had. One of the posted poems joked, "And sisters and priests eat bread made of yeast," an inartistic line, perhaps written by someone who was clowning around. Robert's poem was about a serious topic, the crucifixion of Jesus. In contrast, one of his lines stated, "For three sorrowful hours, from twelve until three, He hung on the cross for our eternity…" a much better expression. Any neutral person could see that the winners' poems were poor compared with Robert's excellent work. So why was he not recognized? Why hadn't the nuns acknowledged his fine poem, or at the very least spoken with him about it? Robert was not a complainer or a whiner and simply accepted the fact that his poem didn't win. Though he was disappointed, he'd been taught at home that in life you don't always win. Sometimes people work harder or have more talent. But that wasn't the case here. The other students couldn't have worked any harder than Robert, and their work showed very little talent. He was expected to do his best, and he had. He was a levelheaded, determined boy who served his family, church and community well as son, altar boy, paperboy and Scout. Any success or accomplishments he achieved in life came not from luck or politics, but the old fashioned way, from the sweat of his brow.

Disheartened, Robert shared the unhappy news with Mom, "I didn't win. They picked other kids." Mom, who was well aware of the time and effort Robert put into "Good Friday," and the quality of his work, asked, *"Those other poems must have been very good if yours wasn't chosen."* Robert explained, "I didn't think they were very good." Upon hearing this, Mom grew skeptical and decided to contact the school. She was rarely intimidated, not the least but faint of heart, and though Robert hadn't asked her to intervene, would have no problem speaking with the authoritative Sister Rose Dominic. None of us asked for Mom to get involved whenever an injustice came our way. We were taught to fight our own battles, or to accept life's disappointments when they came along, then offer such suffering up to God. But Mom was a justice-seeker and so she decided to go and see for herself, to get the facts. She wouldn't be going there to complain or demand that her son win. If the winning poems were better, and if the judging was fair and impartial, then Mom would be the first to say that Robert shouldn't win. But if not, then perhaps there'd be some justice to meat out. Sensitive to her son's feelings and the possibility that an injustice may have taken place, a few days later off to St. Ignatius she went.

St. Ignatius Loyola School is an old 1880's structure. To enter, one walks up several rows of brick steps through the main doorway into the dark, aging lobby. Once inside Mom noticed the collection of winning poems hanging for all to see. For a few minutes she stood alone and quietly waded through the mostly mediocre verse, stanza by stanza, and noticed something disturbing. None of the poems approached the quality of Robert's fine work. She immediately went to the office and asked the school secretary, Mrs. Shiffmacher, if she could speak with Sister Rose Dominic. Mrs. Shiffmacher obliged and Sister arrived moments later. The two chatted cordially at first. *"Good afternoon, Sister."* "Good afternoon, Mrs. White. What brings you here?" *"Sister, I came to read the winning Easter contest poems, which I've done. Quite frankly, I'm not impressed."* Sister responded, "We weren't either, but we were limited. We thought we'd get much finer submissions than we did." Mom replied, *"Not to grumble, but I watched my son work for weeks on his poem. I heard his final draft. The ones you've selected don't compare. I don't understand why his work wasn't included."* The veteran nun responded, "Oh, that. We didn't include your son's poem in the contest. When we read it, it looked too good to have been written by a child. We agreed that it must have been plagiarized, so we kept it out." This infuriated Mom because she knew the truth about Robert's work, something the eighth grade nuns hadn't even bothered to seek. With all deference she countered, *"Sister, you are mistaken, and by your mistake you've hurt a child. I stood outside my son's door for weeks, monitoring his work, listening to him hone his words night after night until he was satisfied that he'd done his very best. Anyone can see that Robert's poem, written entirely by him, with not one plagiarized word, is far better than what you've posted here. I can't believe that at the very least you didn't speak with him about this before discarding his work."* Then Mom left. She'd had her say. She demanded neither a review of the contest, nor that Robert be awarded a prize. She'd come for the truth and to point out what any reasonable, fair-minded observer should have seen, that Robert's work was far superior, and that if they believed it was copied, they as educators had a duty to address that with him. Moreover, she'd come to stand up for her son against bureaucratic injustice, and she'd done just that.

Abraham Lincoln won the election of 1860 with the slogan, "Right makes might." Mom always fought for what was right, and to me, that made her one the mightiest women I knew.

Retarded?

The third story that demonstrates courage and strength involves something my ninth grade math teacher wrote in a note to Mom and how she responded. Prior to attending Clarke High School, I went to St. Ignatius, where math instruction was rote and the teaching methods involved memorization and mostly low levels of learning. Perhaps this was because there were 88 children in each classroom and the teachers had to make sure we all kept quiet and did our work. Imagine if 88 kids were allowed to talk, or walk around the room? Consequently, there was little time for our teachers to get to know us well, or to try and provide us with any individualized instruction. School was often an exercise in drudgery and fear. Everything seemed to be centered around work, work, work, as in, "Peter is slow in finishing his work, or "Peter daydreams. He doesn't seem to be concentrating on his work." During my eight years at St. Ignatius I was always afraid of school. Terrified to ask questions to make sure I understood things fully, I just did what I had to in order to get by. Constantly made to do thousands of little arithmetic examples involving simple skills like addition, subtraction, multiplication and division, usually timed by the nun's watch, there was little opportunity to become challenged or reach higher levels of learning like understanding and analysis. When I began ninth grade at Clarke High School, my Elementary Algebra class had 30 students in it, far smaller than at St. Ignatius. Beginning with the first day of school, my math teacher, Miss B, used words I'd never heard before, a completely new vocabulary. I was clueless when she spoke of binomials, trinomials, axioms, algebraic functions, the quadratic equation and the "y intercept." It was as if I spoke English and she spoke Swahili. Not wanting to sound like the dumb new kid, I never asked questions in class, nor did I seek extra help. Instead, I tried to do what so many adolescents do when they are frightened: master the skill of hiding so as not to get called on. I learned how to fake it, …for a while. The day before Thanksgiving vacation 1961 was a day that would radically change my life. That was the day my teacher discovered that I had absolutely no idea what was going on in her class. With about five minutes remaining in the period, Miss B peered at the clock, then the class, looking for someone who hadn't been up to the board in a while. "Peter White. Go up to the blackboard and take us through problem 11 on page 45." I shook as I turned to page 45 and noticed that problem 11 was complex. Finally caught by Miss B, I sank in my seat for a second, trying to stall. "Come on. Come on. Time is running out. Let's go Mr. White." I dragged myself to the board knowing that within the next five minutes, my teacher, my whole class and, in my mind, possibly the whole school would know that I didn't know a thing about algebra. I stood alone in front of the class, put the problem on the blackboard, got part of the way through it, then, when I could go no further, I stopped. Miss B grilled me about the next step to take as my classmates stared with big smiles on their faces. She screeched, "Use the addition axiom." I didn't know what she was talking about. More Swahili. I stood speechless before my smirking classmates until I was finally told to sit down. Numb with humiliation and embarrassment, I trudged to my seat and slumped down in my desk. Moments later the bell rang and all the kids headed joyously toward their school buses for the four-day vacation. It had rung too late for me. As the others flew out the door, I was the last to leave. This was a good thing because none of the others were around to witness what happened next. As I neared the door, Miss B stopped me. "Come back here. You don't really know what's going on in here, do you?" I said, "No, I don't understand a lot of this." Then she said something devastating, something I never thought I'd hear. "When we get back from this vacation, I'm going to give you a test. If you don't pass, I'm going to ship you back on the boat to Basic Math." Then, looking directly at me, she said, "Do you understand me?" As she spoke, she pointed down the hallway toward the junior high wing of the building, where the 7th and 8th grade had their classes. I said, "Yes, I understand." She then took out a slip of paper, wrote a short note and placed in an envelope addressed "Mr. and Mrs. White." "Here. Give this note to your parents." I didn't bother letting her know that there was no Mr. White. That really didn't matter at the time. Nervous, empty, and shaking, I took the note and left the room. I knew Miss B meant that if I didn't pass whatever test she would prepare, I would be removed from her ninth grade Algebra class and placed in an eighth grade general math class, that I was essentially going to be "left back" in math. When I got on the jam-packed bus, all the kids were happy to be heading home for the school break. I was in another world. Dazed, I looked out the bus window, feeling nothing. I wished I were in Siberia. At home Mom greeted me, *"Peter, it must feel so good to finally have a few days off. Why don't you go on out and see what your friends are doing?"* I answered, "Mom, I don't feel good. I'm going upstairs." She must have thought I was sick. In a way I was. Dennis and I slept upstairs in "the cold room," a half-finished, unheated attic space. The cold room was our escape, our privacy, a place we liked being. There was a small desk up there, with a little lamp that hung over it. With no particular plan in mind and clueless as to what to do about my dilemma, I sat down, took out my algebra book, and began doing something I hadn't done much of during my first three months at Clarke High School…read. I started on page one. It didn't seem too difficult; in fact it was pretty straightforward, almost easy. I quickly learned that algebra, something that looked so complicated, actually was not. I also discovered something else for the first time, that there were sample questions at the bottom of each page, and the answers were provided in the back of the book. After I read the first page, I answered the questions, then checked my answers with the ones in the back. I got them all correct. "Now that wasn't too hard," I said to myself," and I went on to page two, then three, and so forth. I didn't know it at the time but by working my way through those first few pages, I was building a foundation of important concepts. One was the addition axiom, the one Miss B stumped me on when I was in front of the class – "If equals are added to equals, the results are equal." I thought about this for a second then said to myself, "This is really not too hard to understand. In fact, it's pretty logical." Too bad I didn't know this the earlier, when all eyes were upon me. With this new foundation, the ensuing pages got easier. Crucial concepts seemed to build upon one another and I continued getting all the answers right. Truthfully, I grew excited with each new page, reading the rules of algebra and getting the answers to the sample questions right. I remained in the cold room for most of that four-day vacation, reading page after page, solving problem after problem, completely on my own, coming out only rarely, like for Thanksgiving dinner. The rest of the class was up to about page 50 or so in the textbook. That's what we said back then, "What chapter are you 'up to' in social studies?" "Oh, we're 'up to' the Civil War.' What is your class 'up to'?" With my four day, self-taught, cold room clinic, I didn't just catch 'up to' the rest of the class. I went well beyond it, all the way "up to" page 80. The further I went, the easier the algebra got. As those four days and nights went by I continued to get all the practice answers correct. My confidence grew. Toward the end of the holiday weekend, a new feeling came over me, one of relaxation, knowing that I no longer had anything to fear from Miss B or my classmates. I breathed easier, knowing that I wouldn't be shipped on that boat back to basic math. What would Mom have thought if I'd been moved down to eighth grade? Thanks to my private, homespun effort, I didn't have to face that question for I'd read and understood the work, and moved well beyond the rest of the class.

Busy for most of the holiday weekend with my simple but effective, self-taught math clinic, I'd forgotten to give Mom Miss B's note. On Sunday, four days later, I finally gave it to her. As she read the note, her mood changed. It said, "Dear Mr. and Mrs.

White, Your son is struggling in my math class and needs to do quite a bit to catch up. This may be impossible. If he cannot do so, we may have to change his schedule and place him in an 8th grade math class. He may be retarded." The note also mentioned that she'd be sending a similar note to the assistant principal and my guidance counselor. Mom was stunned. At first I didn't know whether she was upset with me for not giving her the note sooner, or because I'd fallen behind in math class. I told her that for the first few months of school I was bashful and afraid to ask questions in class in front of so many kids I didn't know. I also told her that I'd just spent the past four days catching up and was now confident in my newfound understanding of elementary algebra. Mom was not pleased with me for falling behind and for not sharing the note sooner, but she was far more upset with Miss B for her choice of words. She couldn't understand why or how a teacher would use the word "retarded" in such a manner, in writing, and forward it to other school officials, when I wasn't retarded, just behind in math. Not wanting the teacher's word to end up in any permanent file of mine, the Monday after the vacation, after work, she made her way to Clarke High School and had her say. *"I'm a teacher too, and I know there's a great difference between a retarded child and one who simply falls behind in his work. I don't understand why you've clearly misused a very serious word when it comes to a child's development.. You shouldn't throw words like that around, in writing, so easily and unnecessarily, especially when you're wrong."* Miss B tried to explain that she was using the word in a benign way. "The word retarded, according to the dictionary, means 'to impede, to delay, to detain.'" She went on to say that because I was behind in algebra, I might be retarded, in other words held back from moving on with my class. Mom answered, *"Then you should have used words like delay or detain, not retarded."* Mom reminded Miss B that, in most people's minds, the word retarded refers to someone with less than normal intellectual competence, one who is extremely slow intellectually and emotionally. *"Mental retardation is something doctors and experts diagnose, not math teachers based on a few classroom quizzes. I'd like you to apologize and get that note back from the assistant principal immediately."* Miss B did.

Although this entire experience was one I wished never happened, it brought with it an important silver lining. After Monday's class, before Mom spoke with Miss B, I took her much-feared, personalized algebra test. I'm quite sure she expected me to fail so she could eliminate me, the apparent struggling student, from her class. Doing so would make her life easier, and cave mine in. But after my self-taught, cold room clinic, I solved all the problems she gave me within minutes and, as I'd done with all the practice questions, I got every one correct. Puzzled she asked, "How could you get all these right so quickly today, and last week you didn't have the slightest idea of how to even begin?" I explained, "Easy. I did something I should have done a long time ago. I finally read the book." From that day on I became a successful math student, finishing algebra then going on to easily pass in geometry, intermediate algebra, trigonometry, advanced algebra and calculus in high school and college. My S.A.T. scores on math approached 700. While Miss B used fear as a motivator, a disfavored approach, one I never used during my 36-year teaching career, it worked in my case so many years ago. My success on that quiz left me with a great feeling, that I could succeed if I could just focus my time and energy correctly. This was a basic value Mom taught, but as a shy 9th grader, I'd forgotten. Something else arose from this situation, an awareness that I had a strong adult by my side, one willing to stand by me when an injustice occurred.

Religion

Mom was from a religious family. Orphaned before the age of five, she was raised by her Aunt Nellie and Aunt Katherine, two strong, generous, hardworking women. Nellie and Katherine were devoted Catholics and regular churchgoers, and Mom became one too. She went to the Incarnation School in Manhattan and graduated on

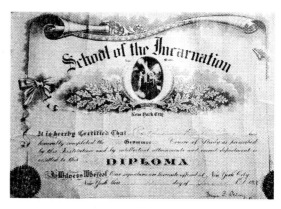
Mom's elementary school diploma, 1931.

Mom's graduation from College of St. Vincent, 1937.

June 21, 1931. From there she went to All Saints Academy in Riverdale, Bronx, where she did well academically, starred in the school's senior play "Racine's Esther," and graduated on June 21, 1935. While most women didn't go to college in those Great Depression days, Aunt Nellie and Aunt Katherine gave her as much educational opportunity as they could. After high school she attended the College of St. Vincent and received an associate's degree on June 21, 1937. It is a sad coincidence that she graduated from all three schools on the 21st of June, and decades later died on June 21, 1975.

The Catholic school background and religious upbringing she received from her adoptive parents remained with her throughout life. Under the direction of Father Edward Kellenberg, she became a volunteer confraternity teacher in Harlem for several years. She was well known in her parish, St. Elizabeth's Church in Washington Heights, for going door-to-door through the Depression era, collecting for Catholic Charities. During high school and college summers, she served as a counselor at church-run Camp Sunset in New Paltz, New York. In January 1942 she was married at St. Elizabeth's Church. She raised her four children Catholic as well, managing to send them all to Catholic schools, despite struggling with the most modest of tuition payments. Her friends were mostly religious people, including Father Edward Kellenberg and his brother, Father Walter P. Kellenberg, who went on to become the first bishop of the Rockville Centre Diocese.

Mom was not a religious fanatic; however she took her Catholic faith very seriously. So as children ours was a very religious household. Most of the kids in our neighborhood practiced some kind of religion, but their parents didn't seem to require the same level of participation and devotion as Mom. Levittown was composed mostly of Catholic and Protestant families. A few were Jewish. The Hoffmans, the Schwartzs, the Bergers, and the Polanskys sent their kids to Hebrew school and had them make their bar and bat mitzvahs. I attended a few at the temple on Carman Avenue in Westbury. While I didn't understand exactly what those ceremonies were all about, nor did I understand the Hebrew songs that were being sung, Mom taught me to respect all religions and that I should go and bring a gift. I recall walking to Bobby Hoffman's bar mitzvah at Temple Emanu-el in Westbury and handing him a card with a $5 bill inside. It was my own money, and it was all I had to my name at the time. Mom encouraged such acts of giving. Some of the Protestant families sent their kids to Sunday school or church. We were a Catholic family, and the rather inflexible rules of our religion directed many aspects of daily life. We all went to Catholic elementary school, and Robert to a seminary for three years and then Catholic Chaminade High School. When Dennis, Jeanne and I went on to public high school, we attended religious instructions, also known as confraternity, through the 12th grade. Robert and I both graduated from Catholic colleges. As kids, Robert and I were altar boys, serving Sunday and weekday masses for years. Mom took great pride in seeing us on the altar, wearing our cassocks, and assisting the priest at crowded Sunday mass. While we had to pay close attention to the Latin words from the priest so we could follow with the correct Latin responses, ring the bells at the right time, and move the priest's large missal from one side of the altar to the other, Mom enjoyed when we turned around from the altar, spotted her and brandished a momentary smile. She'd whisper to her friends at mass, *"That's my son up there. The altar boy."* Robert served the mass when I made my First Communion at St. Ignatius in 1955, and assisted the bishop when I made my Confirmation there in 1959. One neighborhood altar boy I remember was Joseph Madden. Joey, who was two years older than I, taught me the altar boy "actions" and the Latin phrases and prayers said at mass so that I could pass the rigid altar boy test. For several weeks preceding the test I'd walk down to Joey's house each day and practice my actions and Latin with him. We'd use his bed as our practice altar, and his large geography book as our missal. Joey was a fun lover, a smiling, carefree young man who liked to have a good time. At the young age of 13 Joey Madden was struck by a car while crossing the Wantagh Parkway and killed. His death jolted us all. He was the first of several in our neighborhood to die young.

There was little opportunity for us to forget the strict Catholic teachings Mom provided for us. As a constant reminder of those teachings and Christ's suffering, she placed a crucifix over each of our beds and a few holy statues in various parts of the house. After Palm Sunday mass, we'd receive a piece of palm. Mom showed us how to place it behind our crucifixes to commemorate Jesus' triumphant entry into Jerusalem. We said morning and nighttime prayers, including Grace before meals, went to mass every Sunday and on holy days of obligation, regularly prayed the Rosary as a family for world peace, went to confession at least monthly, whether we needed to go or not, delivered the Catholic newspaper, The Tablet, every Saturday to dozens of customers, sold the Tablet after masses yelling "TAB-LET, TAB-LET," and closely followed all church rules, like abstaining from meat on Fridays, giving up things for Lent, and putting Christ before

Santa Claus at Christmastime. We made all our sacraments and took them seriously, never used profanity, and ended our day with Mon's words, *"Say your prayers and go to bed!"*

Mom tried to protect us from what she believed were bad influences. Sometimes we felt too protected. When it came to the rapid changes that were taking place in American culture, like movies, music and dress, Mom was very traditional, and quite strict. She had a very clear list of do's and don'ts for us, mostly don'ts. In the 1930's, when Mom was a young woman, the Catholic Church established the Legion of Decency in order to combat immoral movies. Each year on December 8, the Feast of the Immaculate Conception, Catholics took the Legion's pledge not to go to objectionable movies and avoid theaters that showed them. The Legion, which had a huge influence on the movie industry, rated movies according to their decency. It had a very strict interpretation of what was objectionable and what was not, and Mom was raised to follow that interpretation. In 1947, the Christmas film "Miracle on 34th Street," starring Maureen O'Hara and Natalie Wood, won four Academy Awards. It received a "B" rating by the Legion, meaning morally objectionable in parts. We weren't supposed to see it. To do so would have been a venial sin. The movie, still popular today, seven decades later, was a cute Christmas story about the Macy's department store Santa, Kris Kringle, asserting that he was the real Santa. The Legion objected to the portrayal of the mother, played by Maureen O'Hara, as being divorced. Making light of or excusing divorce was a major taboo back then. Even Mom thought that rating was silly and we were allowed to watch "Miracle" whenever it came on TV. Several Elvis Presley movies were given B ratings as well. Elvis was a huge star by the mid-1950's and we really wanted to see some of his movies, but couldn't. Movies that received a rating of "C" were condemned, meaning no Catholic could see them. We were taught to believe that to do so would have been a mortal sin, that we'd be damned to hell for all eternity if we ever saw a movie condemned by the Legion of Decency. So as to remain free from mortal and even venial sin, any time any of us wanted to go to the movies, we had to check the Tablet first, then with Mom, the ultimate arbiter.

Though fundamental Catholic teachings had a serious presence in our house, we weren't really made to eat, breathe and sleep religion. Religion was a guide, a blueprint, something that grounded us and provided a foundation upon which to base the way we conducted our lives. Notions of doing the right thing, caring for others, and living an honest, decent life grew from this foundation. While Mom provided us with this religious base, she never pontificated or pushed religion on others. Faith was a private matter, something we practiced as individuals and as a family. Mom was never very concerned with what "other people" were doing or thinking, but with what we were doing and thinking. When troubled, she'd turn to God for help. She took her devotion to God seriously, and she required that we did as well. In 1952, when we were small children and Mom was left with the task of raising us alone, she brought us to church and had us dedicated to the Blessed Virgin Mary. With little else to hope for, Mom trusted that Mary, the Mother of God, would see us through.

During the 1950's and 1960's, before the age of détente, perestroika and the breakup of the Soviet Union, Cold War headlines were in the news daily. We knew that an "iron curtain" had descended upon Europe, that the proliferation of nuclear weapons could end the world, and that Hungary's Cardinal Jozsef Mindszenty was imprisoned for opposing communism. We watched "Honest Joe McCarthy" on the television news tell us that our own government was filled with communists. Many Americans, including two right in our neighborhood, built expensive fallout shelters in their backyards so they'd have a place to flee in case of a Russian nuclear attack. Mom couldn't let those fears get in the way of her job as parent. She laughed at the idea of a fallout shelter and had us say the Rosary instead. As a family we'd pray, bead after bead, decade after decade, on our knees, for world peace. The Rosary was a very serious family activity. There was no snickering, laughing or interruptions allowed when the family Rosary was being said. We'd take turns saying the first part of each Hail Mary, then the whole family would respond with the second part. During one such family Rosary session, someone knocked at the door. It was Robert's friend, Bernard Nygren. Mom paused from the Rosary briefly, and allowed him in…not to excuse Robert to go out with him, but to have Bernie join us. He came in, knelt down in the living room with the five us, and together we finished the Sorrowful Mysteries. We took Lent seriously, including following the stringent rules about no meat, no snacks, "giving up" certain things, and doing good works. We said "Grace" before meals, as a family, and could expect a stern look from Mom if we were to take a bite of our food before the mealtime prayer was said. Our bedtime prayers were not necessarily about something "for" us, but an opportunity for us to close our day with a prayer. We were taught to pray for others, for the sick, the suffering and the dying. We actually knew our prayers too. The every day prayers like the Our Father, the Hail Mary, and the Glory Be were easy. We also had to know the longer, more difficult ones too like the Act of Contrition and the Apostle's Creed. Frankly, though we learned the words to these prayers, we didn't always understand their meaning. Depending on which teacher we had, this misunderstanding about the meaning of prayers continued through the years. In fourth grade, I had a nun who must have suffered from some serious sexual hang-ups because she couldn't say the word womb. Every day she'd lead the class in saying a decade of the Rosary. We'd all take out our rosary beads and sister would say the first part, then the 88-member class would respond saying the second part, essentially asking for Mary to intercede on our behalf, to "pray for us sinners, now, and at the hour of our death. Amen." I always thought I was a little young to be contemplating my own death at that young age, but several times a day I was made to do so. Sister added to our general confusion over the meaning of this simple prayer by intentionally mispronouncing a very important word in the prayer. Instead of saying, "blessed is the fruit of thy womb, Jesus," she'd say, "blessed is the fruit of thy "coomb", Jesus." We all knew the word contained in the Hail Mary was womb, so why was sister changing it to something else that wasn't even a word? She was a very strict, autocratic nun, so none would question her about her word change. Though we were only nine-year-olds who knew little of wombs, we knew nothing about "coombs." By the end of the year, half of our very confused the class was saying womb and the other half "coomb".

More important than the memorization of basic prayers, however incorrectly the words were pronounced, we were made aware of the important messages contained in Jesus'

Sermon on the Mount, the Eight Beatitudes. "Blessed are the peacemakers,… Blessed are the meek, … Blessed are the poor in spirit,…." We also knew the importance of the corporal works of mercy, "to feed the hungry, give drink to the thirsty, clothe the naked, visit the sick, harbor the harborless…," and so forth. In our Catholic schools we memorized the traditional English and Latin church songs like "O Salutaris," "Immaculate Mary Our Hearts Are On Fire," and "Holy God We Praise Thy Name," which we sang aloud on First Friday mass, after which we could buy not only white milk but chocolate milk as well, and a crumb bun for a dime, … if we had one. A few times each year Mom sent us by bike to Holy Family Church to watch films like "The Robe," "The Ten Commandments," and other movies with religious themes. We respected our church leaders very much, always praying for the pope, our cardinal and bishop. In October 1958, Pope Pius XII passed away. Mom cried when she learned the news, and so did we. I was 11 years old and wept as if a member of our own family had passed away, perhaps because Mom did. We watched newsreels of the pope's funeral on TV, not live and in color as families can today. The miracle of videotape wasn't invented until 1961. After the funeral, we watched the nightly news and waited anxiously, day after day, until we finally saw white smoke puffing from the chimney above the Sistine Chapel. Mom rejoiced at the news that, John XXIII, who would go on to revolutionize so many of the church's practices, had been elected Pope by the College of Cardinals.

It was important to Mom that we followed Catholic rules and traditions. Mostly they were rooted in the Golden Rule, "Do unto others as you would have them do unto you." Based on the Ten Commandments, they provided us with a path for knowing what was right and what was wrong. In a way, Mom didn't really have to make too many rules; God had already done that. Our Baltimore Catechism taught us that God was a Supreme Being who made all things, that He made us, was everywhere and was always watching. We believed this to be true, so there was really very little opportunity for us to be involved in bad acts because … either Mom or God was always watching. However beneficial this religious upbringing was for us, we sometimes thought that Mom's strict interpretation of Church doctrines placed too many rules on us, and often wished we could do some of the things that other neighborhood kids were able to do. But we didn't really fight her over it, probably because deep down we respected her for her values and her religious devotion, and probably because we knew that to fight her would be a losing cause. When we wanted to play organized baseball, she made us join the CYO Baseball League (Catholic Youth Organization) instead of the municipal Little League like the other neighborhood kids. Her reason was something we disagreed with, but had to follow. *"Kids in Little League curse,"* she said. *"You can play CYO if you want to play ball."* Though we tried to tell her, "Mom, Catholic kids curse too," and disliked the fact that the nearest CYO program was held at the distant Hicksville Junior High School, several miles from our house by bike, CYO it was.

Dutch Lane and Ivory Soap

Any use of profane language was clearly an unpardonable error in our house. Mom didn't curse, nor would she allow us to, nor did she want us hanging out with kids who did, or visiting the households of kids whose parents did. If any of us accidentally hit our finger with a hammer, we couldn't let off steam with a few choice curse words. Restraint under those circumstances was considered a virtue. It wasn't that hard to follow this rule because television shows back then were far cleaner than cable and network shows are now, and we weren't bombarded with the language young people face today in songs, movies, and social media. There were no exceptions to the no cursing rule that I can recall. There was simply no cursing, period. But for one time, I followed this rule right up until my college and Army days, when I went to great lengths to make up for my clean-spoken childhood and teen years. As an 11-year-old sixth grader, I biked with a few friends and Dennis to Dutch Lane School in Hicksville. While we were all playing on the monkey bars, I slipped, in more ways than one. From the top rung of the monkey bars, I lost my grip and plunged several feet to the ground. During my decent, meaning to say "shoot," I mistakenly blurted out something for the very first time in my life, the "s" word. The other kids were shocked because they'd never heard such a word come from my mouth. For the rest of the afternoon they poked fun, not letting me forget, annoyingly singing, "Ah ha, Peter White cursed." I was traumatized and in great fear of what might happen if Mom found out. Was God really watching? Was I a sinner? How many years would I have to suffer in purgatory for that unintentional, spontaneous utterance? In one quick, blundering moment I'd managed to offend both God and Mom. Dennis continued to play, but was silent. I knew he heard my slip, but what would he do about it? Would he keep it a secret? Would he tell Mom? I didn't know. I didn't want to compound my sin by asking him to lie. That would be another sin. So though my insides were all churned up, I continued to play. I didn't have to wait too long for the answer to my questions. Mom was a very tolerant person, but not when it came to us falling short of her behavioral expectations. As we walked in the door, Dennis, in a singsong manner, said, "Ma-a, Peter said 'sh-it.'" He told on me. I expected he would because to cover up such a transgression might have been a sin for him too. Mom's eyes widened. There were no questions, no hearing, no opportunity for me to explain the accidental nature of my error. Mom gestured toward the bathroom and said, *"Get in there."* Like Ralphie from "The Christmas Story," I knew what was coming next. Mom unwrapped a brand new bar of Ivory soap and said, *"Open up,"* then shoved that medium sized white cake into my dirty mouth, pushing it back and forth, in and out, to clean it good. I gagged a bit, cried, but took this punishment as an expected consequence of my conduct. Even though unintentionally, I'd sinned, and this was the price I had to pay. I tasted those soapy bubbles for days and they served as a reminder to be more careful and in control of myself in the future. While this cleansing was happening, I thought, "Why was my use of the "s" word, a mere slip of the tongue, so wrong, when Dennis could stand in the kitchen and intentionally say the same word without getting into at least some trouble?" The answer to this question came quickly. Not tolerating his use of the word either, regardless of the context, Dennis was next. *"Open up."*

First Penance

As a young boy, some of the religious rules I learned at St. Ignatius and at home bewildered me. I wasn't always comfortable speaking with Mom about certain topics, like those commandments that made it a sin to covet they neighbor's goods or his wife. I was seven years old and didn't even know what the word covet meant. And what were the goods the commandment was referring to? And weren't my second grade friends and I many years away from having wives? I also didn't know what the word adultery meant, but was expected to follow rules forbidding it. In the spring of 1955 I was the recipient of some very strict training from the nuns in the months leading up to my first confession. Some of the things the nuns taught back then seemed to be pretty irrelevant, like how my hands had to be folded with my right thumb crossed over my left throughout my confession. What if I placed my left thumb over my right instead? Would that have been a sin? My folded hands were to be pointed upright, toward God, and kept under the little shelf in the confessional box, not above the shelf. I was taught that this was so my hands didn't get in the way of my words, so the priest could hear my sins clearly. Though it was dark in the confessional and the nuns couldn't see me, I lived in great fear of what might happen if I got caught with my hands folded incorrectly or located above the shelf. We were drilled in what to say to the priest when we first entered the confessional: "Bless me father, for I have sinned. This is my first confession and these are my sins." A simple line, but at such a nerve-wracking time, a seven-year-old might easily stumble and forget a line like that. After that opening sentence we were supposed to recite all the sins we'd committed, like "I argued with my brother," or "I disobeyed my mother." This was actually difficult for me because there wasn't much room for sinning in Kay White's house. Cursing was prohibited, and none of us dared to steal or inflict harm on others. And there certainly was no coveting of anything or anyone. Consequently I felt I had to stretch things a bit for the priest. In addition to some squabbling with my siblings, I made up a few small sins just to have something to say. Then, at the end of my confession, I was required to confess to my biggest sin, the sin I was most sorry for. In other words, I had to save my worst sin for last. I really didn't have any big sins so I decided to come with one anyway. I took a good look at the Ten Commandments from my <u>Baltimore Catechism</u> and searched for one to use as my big sin.. I picked the easiest and shortest one, the sixth commandment, "Thou shalt not commit adultery." Without the slightest idea of what the word adultery meant, I ended my first confession saying, "Father, I am extremely sorry for these and all my sins, especially my most serious sin." The priest said, "What sin is that, son?" I said, "Adultery, Father." I figured this had to be a common big sin because it was one of the Ten Commandments and the word "adult" was in the word adultery. Maybe it had to do with bratty kids who were trying to act like adults. The priest chuckled behind the confessional screen, then asked, "I see. And how many times have you committed adultery, son?" I responded, "Twice Father." "Well then, you say three Our Fathers, three Hail Mary's and three Glory Be's and try not to do it again." I said, "Thank you, Father," and left the confessional to take my place before the altar of God. There I knelt and immediately said my prayers. I promised God that I'd try real hard to be a better boy and that I would never commit adultery again. While I was saying my penance, I noticed my friend, Billy Corrigan, praying next to me. He stayed at the altar rail much longer than I, so I figured he had broken several commandments. With me saying my penance for so long, the nuns probably figured I was a bit more of a sinner than they'd thought. When I got home from making this serious sacrament for the very first time, Mom asked me how it went. I told her everything, focusing on what I thought were the important things, like how I folded my hands and where I placed them. When I got to the part about my two adulteries, Mom howled laughing. Of course, I didn't understand what was so funny until years later. In a conversation about religion many years after, I mentioned the tale of my first confession to a friend who was 20 years older than I. She said that the nuns who taught her during the 1930's in Rochester, NY had her believe that her first confession would leave her soul completely clean and innocent, like that of a brand new baby. Afterwards, she'd be so pure and free from all sin that she'd feel like an angel, able to soar with them. She believed what they said, went home after her first confession, put a ladder to the roof, and jumped off to fly with the angels. Luckily she broke only her arm.

Some of our religious practices left us sad. Every Good Friday, Mom would take us to jam packed Holy Family Church for services that took at least three hours. The church was usually mobbed, so more often than not we'd have to stand that whole time, constantly shifting our weight from the left foot to the right, then back to the left, for hours. If we got there early and got a seat, Mom always required that we give it up so another, usually an elderly person, could sit down. Good Friday was a sad day, the day Jesus died. Several priests would be on the altar together, wearing black vestments, like at the funeral masses we served. The tabernacle, where the blessed hosts were stored and safeguarded, was left open so that all could see. It was empty. No hosts inside. No Body of Christ. Jesus had died. From noon until three p.m., the hours Jesus hung on the cross, we worshipped and, though the entire service was in Latin except for one line in Greek, we were saddened beyond description. Some adults cried during this long, sometimes stiflingly hot service. We did this every year because it was part of our religious training. Leading up to Easter was of course the 40-day period of Lent. We were taught to suffer, and to offer that suffering up to God. The message was, if Jesus could suffer the Crowning of Thorns, the Carrying of the Cross, and the Crucifixion, we could certainly take on some petty discomforts like giving up snacks, or missing a meal, or being nicer to others. This period of minor suffering wasn't really so bad for us because we didn't have a whole lot to give up. We weren't given snack money or allowance, so we couldn't very well give those things up. Lent also meant giving money. Every year the nuns sent each of us home with a small, foldable, cardboard box called a Mite Box. Our job was to fill it with coins and bring it back before the Easter vacation. Some kids, maybe those with generous allowances, brought in Mite Boxes jam-packed with coins. The nuns celebrated those kids as very pleasing to God. That wasn't the case for us. Spare change to stuff into our Mite Boxes was a rarity, but we did our best. Overall, Lent reminded us of the suffering of Christ, something Mom took quite seriously. We really didn't mind the Lenten period because it made the rest of the year seem that much easier.

The Gugliano Letter

Mom wasn't a religious scholar but she knew a great deal about religion, at least in the everyday, practical sense. She didn't major in theology, nor did she read erudite spiritual or philosophical works. But from the religious upbringing Aunt Katherine and Aunt Nellie provided, she developed powerful moral convictions that guided her throughout life. It was those convictions that she transferred to us and to her many pupils at Holy

Family School. A wonderful demonstration of this is contained in a letter written to Sister Eileen McMahon, Principal of Holy Family School by the parent of one of Mom's former students. Dated June 23, 1975, two days after Mom died, it reads:

Dear Sister Eileen,

This letter should have been written years ago. I put off writing it for various reasons, mainly because I felt that my complimentary remarks might be interpreted as flattery to gain favor. I thought I would wait until all of my children were finished with grammar school. But now it is too late! Mrs. White is gone.

When Holy Family School was in the planning stages I prayed that my sons would be accepted for admission. When it opened, that prayer was answered. We were informed that two or maybe three sisters and one lay teacher were to be assigned to each grade. Until that time lay teachers in Catholic schools were rare, and I am ashamed to admit that I was prejudiced. I hoped my son would have a sister teaching him in first grade. My hopes were fulfilled. He was assigned to Sister Martin Joseph's class.

Each noontime I would pick my son up and bring him home for lunch and after I brought him back at one I would stop and make a visit in church. One day while I was kneeling there, Mrs. White came in with her class. She took them around to each Station of the Cross and explained each one to them, bringing out meditations of the Passion of Christ that I had never thought of before and in a way that these young minds could understand. It was so beautiful and so impressive. The experience brought tears to my eyes. I remained in church after she left to ask God to forgive me for thinking the way I did about lay teachers in Catholic schools. When the time came for my next son to go to school, his first grade teacher was Mrs. White and I learned to appreciate her even more. As my children went through Holy Family School I had many, many times good reasons to write and thank sisters and lay teachers for the important dimensions they added to my sons' spiritual and intellectual development. I have always remembered them in my prayers, but I can see now that I should have thanked them personally.

I will always remember Mrs. White because she was en exemplary Catholic and because she helped me become a better Christian. I'm sure everyone who came in contact with her was affected by her goodness and she will continue to influence Holy Family Parish from her honored place in heaven.

Sincerely,

Lillian Gugliano

Only Sister Eileen, who passed away a few years ago, my brothers, sister and I have ever seen this letter before now. It is something we cherish deeply because it explains, in words no one could ever misread or misunderstand, just how truly exceptional and devoted a teacher and a Catholic Mom was.

Catherine White Award and Hall of Fame Honors

In the spring of 2013, 38 years after Mom's sudden, tragic death, Ms. Maryalice Doherty, who succeeded Sister Eileen as principal of Holy Family School, informed me that Mom had been selected for induction into the newly established Holy Family School Hall of Fame. This wonderful, posthumous honor confirmed the words of Lillian Gugliano, written so many years before, that Kay White "continues to influence Holy Family from her honored place in heaven." I attended the Holy Family School Awards Night in 2011 and 2012 to present the Catherine White Award, something we as a family do each year to keep Mom's memory alive. Formerly a $500 award provided by Robert, Dennis, Jeanne & me and given to a needy and deserving student, by 2016, with more family members participating, the award increased to $1,650. I was anxious to attend the 2013 ceremony because, in addition to presenting the award, Mom was being honored with this Hall of Fame induction as well. On, June 10, 2013, I entered the church and the first thing I noticed was that it had been completely renovated. The altar had been turned to face the old auditorium, making it the main part of the church. I sat in the former main chapel, now more like a transept, an arm of this newly renovated church. Alongside me sat my loving partner Kathleen, my daughters Jennifer and Meredith, my son Brian, and my niece Lisa and her daughter Allie. I was proud of Mom and very happy that several

Certificate of Mom's induction into Holy Family School Hall of Fame, awarded June 10, 2013.

Holy Family Church, Hicksville, New York, a mainstay in Mom's life.

family members were on hand as Mom's beloved Holy Family bestowed this wonderful honor upon her. As I waited, nostalgic thoughts and images swirled through my head. I looked at the altar, now turned 90 degrees to the east, toward the Holy Land. It was the same altar where I served mass as a young boy in the 1950's. I stared at the spot that was once occupied by the second pew, the same pew Mom sat in during my wedding in 1971, the pew from which she stood up and headed straight to the altar to give me the sign of peace during the wedding mass. It was also the pew where Dennis, Robert, Jeanne and I sat during Mom's funeral mass. I looked around the chapel for the Stations of the Cross, the original ones which Lillian Gugliano so poignantly wrote about in 1975, but those small, simple, unpainted wooden carved figures that depicted the last days of Jesus had been removed. When the induction ceremony was over, I walked through the auditorium, now the main aisle, or nave, of the church. The Stations weren't there either. I asked the pastor, Rev. Gerard Gentleman, "Father, congratulations on the renovation of the church. May I ask what happened to the Stations of the Cross that lined the old chapel?" Father answered, "Don't worry, Peter. We still have them. They're being cleaned up and will be back soon, good as new." Six months later, I attended Christmas Mass at Holy Family and was happy to see that the very same Stations Mom so eloquently and caringly used to teach those "young minds" about the life of Jesus were placed prominently in the newly renovated church. I gently ran my fingers across one of the stations and said a prayer. Doing that made me feel closer to Mom.

STRUGGLES AND DECISIONS

Health Problems and Recovery

In 1972, Mom began to experience some difficult changes. She became annoyed with little things and was crabby at times. Dennis, Jeanne and I were puzzled. Initially we thought it was something people just go through, a type of mid-life crankiness. She was irritable and cried a lot. She criticized Dennis, Jeanne and me for the slightest of things, even though we did our best to be there for her whenever we could. I was married in early 1971, lived nearby and taught in Holy Family with her. Mom was not only my mother, but also my colleague. It was terrific knowing that her classroom was just below mine and that I could see her every day. Sometimes however, being so close on a daily basis was not so good. When problems arose things could become unpleasant. One cold gray winter morning, the principal, Sister Eileen, came to my door with a grim look on her face. I thought I was in trouble for something. Right in front of my entire class, sister demanded sternly, "Where's your mother?" I was troubled by her question, her tone and at the thought that maybe something might be wrong with Mom. I stepped out into the hall away from my 50 sixth graders and said, "I don't know. I thought she was in her classroom, as she always is." Sister responded, "She didn't call in sick and she's not here. She's a half an hour late." Now I was worried because Mom was rarely late. That morning sleet and ice had covered everyone's car windshields. I scraped the windshields of my wife Jill's car and mine, not thinking to call Mom or go over to her house to see if she needed help. It didn't cross my mind earlier that if I had a problem scraping ice from our cars, Mom must have had the same problem with hers. In her new fragile state, she couldn't handle all that and wound up late for work. As Sister Eileen and I talked, I saw Mom's car pulling up to the side of the building. I asked Eileen to watch my class while I went down to greet Mom. All bundled up and looking awful, she entered the building with a scowl on her face. I could tell she'd been crying. I apologized for not thinking of her and she responded by bursting out, *"I had to scrape the ice by myself. It took half an hour. Then the car wouldn't start. I'm alone. No one cares. Go away.*" She turned from me and slowly walked to her classroom. I felt terrible that I hadn't thought of her, but it was icy cold that morning and I had my own job to get to. Mom's words stung. This is just one example of how her growing health problems were intensifying and taking a toll on her daily life and her ability to get up in the morning and out of the house on time. Dennis had moved to an apartment in Westbury with some friends. Though he kept late night bartender hours, he visited Mom's regularly, kept her company and did whatever jobs he could around the house. Jeanne was married, but lived in distant East Rockaway, visiting when she could. We could tell Mom didn't like being alone and tried to convince her that she'd done a great job as a parent, that she should begin to feel less lonely and more free. "Mom, you worked hard and struggled for so long to raise us. Now we're grown up. You should think of yourself more and us less." Mom liked certain aspects of having an empty house. She'd say, "*I'm OK here by myself. Don't worry about me. I can watch what I want on television, keep whatever hours I want, clean the house when I want to, or not.*" But we knew that wasn't completely true. She was suffering and her problems went beyond empty nest syndrome. When we were about to leave after visiting her, she'd say things like, "*Where are you going? I thought you came over to paint the bathroom ceiling. You didn't finish,*" or sarcastically, "*That's it. Go out and have fun. Leave your mother home alone.*" With our own lives to live and our jobs, we were stumped. Something was wrong and we didn't know what it was or what to do about it. Without consulting Mom, completely on our own, Dennis and I visited her doctor, Juan Wilson, M.D. We explained the symptoms we'd observed and which were growing more intense as the days went by. Dr. Wilson thanked us. "Boys, you did the right thing by coming to me. I haven't seen your mom in a while. I'll call and tell her it's time for a physical and take it from there." Mom followed the doctor's orders and had a comprehensive physical. The preliminary results were inconclusive so Dr. Wilson recommended that she spend a night or two in Meadowbrook Hospital for additional tests. A good patient, Mom complied. From this battery of tests, Dr. Wilson determined that she had hypoglycemia and was experiencing some bouts with depression, hence the crankiness and mood swings. He put her on a strict diet and prescribed several vitamins and hormones. Mom didn't give in to her problems, nor did she fight the doctor's diagnosis. Instead she strictly followed Dr. Wilson's advice, diligently took the vitamins and hormones, and began eating a better diet. Instead of three meals a day, she'd have snacks of apples, nuts and other healthy foods in between meals. Gone were the junk foods. No more cake, ice cream, or other unhealthy treats. During this time, the beginning of her recovery, I'd walk by her classroom and see her teaching her class while eating an apple. The school had a "no snack" rule, but the principal allowed Mom her snacks because they were doctor's orders. Mom would look at me and smile, and I'd smile back, knowing that she was on a better health course than before. As result of Doctor Wilson's intervention and the seriousness with which she took this new health program, Mom quickly began to look younger and feel better. Within months she became more vibrant than we'd ever seen her. A dancer from back in her college days, she began attending weekly dance classes in New Hyde Park. She wanted to re-acquaint herself with the old steps and learn some new ones. Mostly she wanted to change her life a little, to get out and meet new people. The dancing took place on the second floor of a building. On the first floor was a lounge that served drinks. Mom would occasionally stop by and enjoy a few things she hadn't been able to do in decades: socialize, laugh, relax, have a drink. Though she went to these weekly dances alone, she did meet new people. Some were men, and more than a few asked her out on dates. At first she was shy, perhaps afraid. It had been years and she was a middle-aged woman in her 50's who hadn't been on a date in more than 25 years. Not fearful but careful about this new life, she asked Dennis, Jill and me, *"What should I do? I'm so inexperienced with all this."* We said, "Mom, as long as it's safe for you, that some of these guys don't take advantage or hurt you, we think you should give it a try. Why not?" Mom decided to go for it, but cautiously. One of the gentlemen who asked her out was named Jack, a big man with white hair and a big smile who looked like the actor Ernest Borgnine. Jack began asking Mom out on a regular basis, and she continued to say yes. We didn't know much about him, but if Mom was happy, we were too. Finally, after a few months of dating, Jack came to the house and we met. It seemed surreal. After never seeing a man in Mom's life or having one in ours, we found ourselves in the position of having to approve of this man who was so interested in her. We smiled as Jack introduced himself to us as Mom's "boyfriend." In September 1974, Jack accompanied Mom to my first child, Jennifer's, christening. As if he were a member of the family, he sat in the front row of the chapel at Holy Trinity High School as Father Patrick Young baptized one-month-old Jen. Outside the chapel, Mom had a broad smile as she stood with Jack while waving to the camera for home movies. Still married, at least in the eyes of the Church, Mom felt the need to remain guarded and keep her relationships strictly platonic. She continued her dancing, dated occasionally, and appeared to be having more fun than we'd ever seen. We enjoyed the times she spent with her friends from the dance group, seeing her excited when she came home after having met and danced with some very fine gentlemen, and even visiting Gatsby's Pub for a drink, sometimes with Jack, sometimes with other friends. Once she came home later than Dennis and I and we asked, "Where were you last night? You came in pretty late, didn't you?" Mom smiled and answered, *"Never you mind."*

Despite the excitement and joy this new view and restored health provided her, Mom's religious background made it difficult for her to let go of the fact that she was still married. Dennis and I disagreed. "Mom, you've been alone for more than 20 years. You're not really married." We encouraged her to contemplate the annulment process, to give it some time, and if that didn't work, to see lawyer-cousin Vin Nicolosi and file for a civil divorce. Mom said, *"I know you care about me. Thank you. I'll think about it."*

The McCoy's, Dinner with Dennis, and a Name Change

Mom, age 3, with her dad, John McCoy
Rockaway Beach, summer 1920.

Even though my last name was White, I liked Mom's maiden name, McCoy, better. So did Dennis. Though Robert A. White's parents emigrated from Ireland, the name White sounded bland, while the name McCoy revealed our Irish ancestry more clearly. And why the name White anyway? We didn't know Robert A. White, nor did we know his two brothers, his sister, or any of the Whites. On the other hand, we did know several of the older McCoy's growing up. Around St. Patrick's Day every year, Mom did her best to remind us of our proud Irish heritage. She'd make a corned beef and cabbage dinner, put some Irish music on the old Victrola, and make sure we watched Jack McCarthy emceeing the big parade on channel 11. I liked these visible reminders of our roots and deep down wished that we had a more Irish-sounding name. Our great-grandparents, Cornelius and Mary McCoy, were Irish immigrants. They came to the United States in the early 1870's and had 11 children. Cornelius, Mom's grandfather, was listed in the New York City Directory, a document published before there were telephone books, as a plasterer. He lived on W. 57th Street near Tenth Avenue, on the west side of Manhattan, an area known as Hell's Kitchen. He then moved uptown to E. 116th Street in East Harlem, and finally settled in Washington Heights, an area populated my many Irish immigrants after the Independent subway line, the IND A train, extended that far north. This is how our family became established in Washington Heights. The oldest of Cornelius and Mary's children was our grandfather, John McCoy, a bricklayer, who died in 1922. John traveled to find work, including the Panama Canal Zone at the turn of the century. He often brought Mom, then a little girl, along with him as he sought work. John's brother, Peter McCoy, my namesake, also worked as a bricklayer on the canal and died young of an illness related to his work there. Joseph McCoy was an officer at Engine Company 20, Fire Department of New York. Old photos show him with his fellow firefighters in front of the old firehouse which, in those days, used horse-drawn fire engines. Both Peter and Joseph died before 1920. There were also two McCoy sisters who passed away before we were born, Anna McCoy and Mary McCoy Duffy, mother of Mom's cousin Florence. James McCoy, whom I barely remember, died in 1950. We were fortunate to know the remaining five McCoys, all of whom lived until old age. Cornelius McCoy, Uncle Connie to us, was a highway inspector. Bernard McCoy lived in Washington Heights and gave driving lessons when the automobile was first introduced into the American culture. Agnes McCoy Gordon lived with the Larkin's in Flushing until she was 87 years old. Aunt Aggie was born ten years after the end of the Civil War, when Ulysses Grant was president. We only saw her once or twice a year and loved it when she told stories of the olden days, especially the one about being snowbound for five days when she worked at a Manhattan department store during the Blizzard of 1888. Finally, there was Ellen, or Nellie McCoy, and Katherine McCoy, the two aunts who adopted Mom when she was a little girl. Nellie was the homemaker of the family and Katherine was the breadwinner, working for many years as a chief operator at the New York Telephone Company until she retired in her late 60's. So while Mom was orphaned at the age of four, with all these aunts and uncles there was no shortage of adults in her life.

Dennis and I had great hope that Mom would get a church annulment for her own emotional well-being. We wanted her to experience a sense of freedom she'd not had in years. She said, "If I'm granted an annulment, I think I'd like to return to my maiden name, McCoy." We were excited about the possibility of such a change in our family. Only weeks before Mom died, Dennis made a pact with her and wrote the following about that challenging time in Mom's life:

In February 1975 I received a call to hurry over to my friend Bill's house. When I arrived there were police present. Bill was going crazy after learning that his dad had suddenly passed away. The police warned me to stay outside. Bill's mom was there and assured them that it was ok that I try to talk with Bill. I approached Bill in the kitchen and it was obvious that he was having a breakdown. He punched the brick fireplace so hard it caused his hand to bleed and swell. He was in pain in his body and his heart. Bill grabbed me, hugged me, and pointed his finger in my face saying, 'You go home to your mother and tell her how much you love her, right now.' I promised him that I would and made him promise to calm down and get to a hospital to get his bleeding hand stitched.

I went straight to Mom's house. She was watching TV by herself. We weren't the type of family that went around saying 'I love you' very much, however seeing Bill struggle with his father's sudden death served as a real wake up call. I suddenly realized how much Mom meant to me and wondered how I would handle life without her. I took advantage of this moment, held Mom and shared how my friend lost his father and I wanted her to know how much I loved her and how much I appreciated all that she had done for all of us. She understood, and we cried together. We also agreed to spend more time hanging out together.

About a month later, Bill and I took our moms to dinner and a movie. We saw "The Sting" with Robert Redford and Paul Newman, then went back to the Bill's home where his mom played the organ. Mom really enjoyed that evening, and so did I.

A few months later, I took Mom to a fancy dinner. She was beginning to realize that she was a single lady and wanted to enjoy herself more, laugh and feel more like an adult. She began understanding that her job as a parent was mostly done and that she should focus on her future plans. She had gotten a bit healthier in the previous two years, lost some weight and had even begun to date a few gentlemen. She enjoyed some hobbies, like sewing, and made some of her own outfits. She was quite talented. I still have a green tie that she made me for St. Patrick's Day. We went to the John Peel Room at the Island Inn where they had food and live music. Sometimes there were celebrities there, like Johnny Mathis or Perry Como, when they were in town. I remember kidding her about how one of them might come along and sweep her off her feet. We had a few cocktails and Mom was truly at ease and comfortable. It was probably the best conversation I ever had with her. She asked me about dating, and what I thought about certain things. I shared that she had done a marvelous job of raising us and it was time for her to enjoy herself. I honestly think that she felt a new spirit as we danced together and laughed. We then began talking about the church and the strict rules that she had always believed in, and how the church granted annulments to rich and famous people while ordinary people, who were quite deserving, had to wait. Mom said that she would consider applying for an annulment and if approved, revert back to her maiden name - McCoy. When we finished the evening, we made an agreement: if she changed her name, I'd change mine. We clinked glasses, and smiled as though we had just signed an important pact. In a way, we actually did. We felt a great sense of accomplishment.

Mom was never able to change her name, but I was. After Mom died, I became Dennis McCoy. Family members and close friends know why I changed my name. I had no real connection to my father, Robert A. White, but I had a strong connection to my mother. So to me the change made perfect sense. Also, it was the fulfillment of a promise that I made to her. I'm proud of my name and glad I did it. And now, years later, there are new family members with that name: my wife Beth McCoy and children Lisa McCoy,, Katelyn McCoy Peterson, Daniel McCoy and Matthew McCoy.

Annulment Decision

While Mom's strong religious beliefs and practices served as an important guide for her, they sometimes held her, and us, back. In January 1942, a month after the attack on Pearl Harbor, Mom married Robert A. White. They remained together for ten years. For much of that time Robert A. White was not present. Though Mom wanted very much to keep her marriage together, certain unpleasant conditions existed that caused her to insist on a separation. Of this time in her life, Mom said of Robert A. White, *"I can't honestly say that he understood my needs. I was left quite alone and felt rejected. The children and I were without the presence of a father and husband. We were left to do for ourselves. It was a most distressing time for us."* Though Mom believed she gave him many chances to be more of a husband and father, she came to realize that his poor behavior, which mostly involved drinking, staying away from home, and some dangerous conduct, left her and us at risk. When he wouldn't or couldn't change, she felt he could no longer continue to live with us. He'd have to either change or leave. He left. At the time they separated in early 1952, it was difficult to obtain a divorce from the state, and even more difficult to obtain an annulment from the church. Spouses vowed to take one another for better or worse, and both the state and the church interpreted that vow strictly. Despite the separation, as a strict Catholic Mom continued to view herself as married throughout the years that followed. Her religion held that unless she could have her marriage annulled, she was married, alcoholic husband or not, abandoned or not, for better or worse. Throughout our entire childhoods, we witnessed Mom struggle day to day with no husband, no male companionship, no boyfriends, and little social life to speak of. In 1972, wanting only to see her happy after so many years of fear, anxiety and loneliness, Dennis and I urged her to seek an annulment from the church. Reluctant at first, perhaps due to stigmatization, Mom agreed to go forward with the difficult, time-consuming application. She came to believe that Robert A. White, perhaps not meaning to, had misrepresented himself to her from the outset, that he was in fact a very different man than the one he originally portrayed himself to be, and that grounds for annulment existed. In order to be granted one Mom was required to submit a lengthy, cumbersome request to the Rockville Centre Diocese's marriage tribunal, the church committee that made annulment determinations. Part of this complex application required Mom to write a 40 page biographical sketch of Robert A. White and herself, and include a number of authentic letters of support proving the truth of certain facts. Mom worked hard for many months on this task, writing, in her own pen, a straightforward, passionate document that tells the story as only she could. The sketches describe how she did everything possible to make a good life with her husband and children, and how Robert A. White increasingly became a man she didn't know. Mom felt completely justified as she set out on this annulment journey. Though she took the church's maxim "What God has joined together, let no man put asunder," very seriously, there was no other man in the picture. No one was trying to "put asunder" her marriage. In essence, there really was no marriage. Once Mom submitted the biographical sketches and other paperwork to Father Bernard McGrath, head of the diocesan tribunal, he frequently wrote back, always unsatisfied with what she'd submitted, always needing more proof. Mom wearied of Father McGrath's repudiation of her submissions. She faced the difficulty of claiming in the 1970's that things were seriously wrong decades earlier, in the 1940's, and found it difficult to prove things after the passage of 20-30 years. In letter after letter, Father McGrath demanded testimony and corroboration that Mom found difficult and sometimes impossible to produce. Many of the people from whom she requested letters of support lacked sufficient memory of events that occurred three decades earlier, were unreachable, or had passed away. At the time Mom was going through this process, it became common knowledge that certain important people were obtaining annulments, while ordinary Catholics were either rejected or made to wait forever. While Mom toiled on her application and the diocese dragged its feet, a member of the Kennedy family got a rapid annulment. So did former New York City Mayor Robert Wagner. Mom grew frustrated with the process, and began to develop a sour taste toward the church hierarchy. But rather than whine or quit, she persevered and followed through with all that Father McGrath required of her. She wrote letters to relatives, former neighbors, and old friends like the esteemed Henry Viscardi, Jr., founder of Abilities, Inc., a not for profit corporation that trained persons with disabilities and found jobs for them. Henry was an old friend. But he, as with a few others, wrote Mom saying they could be of little help since so many years had gone by, or their recollections had become so vague their testimony would be unreliable. Despite these setbacks, Mom continued her struggle until she found the proof she believed would satisfy the tribunal. Finally, after two years of preparing her statements, seeking letters of support and other proof called for by the tribunal, Mom completed her application the best she could, submitted it to the diocese, and patiently awaited the results. Sadly, no response ever came. Mom died before Father McGrath and the tribunal made a determination.

Final Note on Father McGrath

Father Bernard McGrath, the priest with whom Mom had the most contact during her ordeal with the diocesan tribunal, was an inflexible man. He authored most of the letters saying the materials she provided in her annulment application were insufficient. His letters were never encouraging, always dispiriting and sour sounding. Bizarrely, while her application was pending Fr. McGrath left the tribunal and was appointed pastor of Holy Family Parish, essentially becoming Mom's boss for the last two years of her life. In 1975, after Mom passed away, her attorney, cousin Vincent Nicolosi, asked me to obtain a few of Mom's employment records from Holy Family. For some reason, Father

McGrath seemed reluctant to meet with me. Finally, after making several calls to him, he agreed to meet. Unfortunately, our appointment didn't go very well. When I mentioned who my Mom was and that I was requesting her records, he didn't seem to care that she was a dedicated teacher and a respected, charter member of the Holy Family faculty. He didn't seem to care that we sought only a few documents that were easily retrievable. He simply refused to cooperate and I had no idea why. I said to him, "Our attorney thinks it would be helpful if we could get certain records for his file." Father responded angrily, "No. You can't have them." I pushed, "Why? Mom was a dedicated teacher here. We're not asking for much." With that, McGrath grew livid, "I don't have to, and there's not a judge who will make me." I never figured out why Father was so adamant about refusing my request. Maybe he was just a stubborn man. Maybe he was lazy. Or maybe as a new pastor he just didn't want to get involved in things that occurred before he took the helm. Following this nonsensical and illogical repudiation, I got up to leave. As I did, I looked down at this sad man and said, "My mother was devoted to this church and the children of this school. She deserves better than this. What kind of man are you?"

As a Holy Family School Hall of Fame inductee, Mom's name has been inscribed on a large plaque in the main hallway of the school. Ironically, right across the hall from this handsome plaque is a portrait of her former pastor, the rigid, reluctant repudiator, Father Bernard McGrath.

Mom's Catholic faith, beliefs to which she was extremely loyal, formed a solid foundation upon which she based her life. The church's teachings and traditions were her rock, and served as an important beacon, lighting the way when she had to make certain hard choices. Sometimes however, those teachings and traditions confined her, much like a bonsai tree, harnessing her into 25 years of marriage to no one. As she grew into middle age, she became a more open-minded, flexible thinker, one capable of altering or changing her views as her life went along. I'm certain, had she lived longer, that the recent revelations of pedophile priests and the bishops who protected them would have appalled her, and that she'd be outspoken in support of the victims, the oppressed children. And I believe she'd be extremely proud of the new Pope Francis from Argentina and the many changes he's bringing to the Church. On Palm Sunday 2013, during the first week of his papacy, Pope Francis could easily have been quoting Mom when he said, "Never give way to discouragement; ours is not a joy that comes from having many possessions. Don't let anyone rob you of hope." Mom never let discouragement get the best of her, never focused her life on material things, and always kept hope alive.

FOND MEMORIES

Easter in The Heights

Mom's adopted mother, Aunt Nellie McCoy, Asbury Park, New Jersey.

Throughout the 1950's we spent many Easters visiting Mom's Aunt Katherine and Aunt Nellie at their Washington Heights apartment. With no school the week before Easter, we'd make our customary trek from Levittown to their apartment in Manhattan. Nellie and Katherine lived at 106 Pinehurst Avenue, Apartment C-35, New York 33, New York. That was before five digit zip codes came into use. Today that zip code is 10033. The memories I have from those childhood visits are as clear to me today as if they happened yesterday. I remember the contents of Aunt Nellie's kitchen drawer. In fact, I still have her poultry shears, large scissors that I use to this day. I remember her small "icebox," the appliance that once required a block of ice, delivered by an ice man, before it was converted into a small, gas-powered refrigerator. Nellie and Katherine continued to call it their icebox. We weren't allowed to drink soda at home. Mom said it wasn't good for us, and she couldn't afford it. But when we visited Nellie and Katherine's, the icebox always contained a few six-packs of 12 ounce Pepsis, their treat for us. I remember the wooden secretary desk where their phone was located. Next to the phone were a few green automatic lead pencils. On top of each pencil was a round silver ball that spun. Telephone operators like Aunt Katherine were able to dial numbers more quickly with those round-top pencils. Nellie and Katherine's phone number was Wadsworth 3-8323. Wadsworth Avenue was less than half a mile away and Aunt Katherine was chief operator at the Wadsworth branch of the New York Telephone Company. When she came home from work, she'd talk about the girls, or "goils" in the office, the young operators under her supervision. I remember the wonderful smells that emanated from Aunt Nellie's kitchen back then. Nellie was an excellent cook and, whether it was turkey, roast beef or leg of lamb, she was always roasting something when we visited. I remember the way Nellie set her long dining room table in the wide hallway. It had a fancy lace tablecloth, her best dishes, silverware and glasses, and a large platter upon which she'd place the meat she'd carefully prepared. There always seemed to be more food than we got at home, more than we could even eat. Sitting at Nellie's table, I felt like I was a rich person. I remember the antique looking porcelain bathroom sink and tub, and black and white tiles on the bathroom floor. We'd laugh at their television set with the long rabbit ear contraption they'd rig up for better reception, and were fascinated by all the women's effects they kept on their dresser tops, like powder puff things, broaches, hair pins and an antique music box. That century-old gray music box sits on my dresser to this day and it still plays the same tune I remember so well from childhood. Once in a while I give the frail old crank on the bottom of the box a few turns and provide myself with an authentic, aural reminder of childhood days. Nellie and Katherine were hard-working, generous, non-flamboyant, religious women. Their choice of house decorations included a large living room mirror, some comfortable chairs, a few vases and lamps, and a religious picture and crucifix in each of the three bedrooms. We felt safe there, and very happy to spend time with these two patient, loving women.

Getting to see Nellie and Katherine wasn't easy. After packing our things the day before, our journey began by lugging suitcases and packages up Twig Lane to Newbridge Road where we waited for the bus to the Hicksville Station of the Long Island Rail Road. In the early 1950's the LIRR was still powered by big steam locomotives. It was exciting to see the enormous black engine come clanging into the station, puffing its giant plumes of steam into the air. By the mid-1950's the LIRR replaced its steam locomotives with diesel trains. From Hicksville we'd pass all the stops, Westbury, Carle Place, Mineola, New Hyde Park, then wait to hear the conductor say, "Jamaica next. Change at Jamaica." Then it was on to Midtown Manhattan's Pennsylvania Station, or Penn Station, designed by the famous New York architects McKim, Mead and White in 1909. Modeled after the Second Century Roman Baths of Caracalla, this great old train station had vaulted ceilings that seemed to reach the sky, with light pouring through the giant windows and solid brass stairway railings. Penn Station was and still is the busiest transportation facility in the United States. Sadly, this architectural treasure was torn down in 1963 to make room for the new Penn Station with the ugly Madison Square Garden and the uglier One Penn Plaza office complex built on top. Of the old Penn Station and the new one that replaced it, it's been said, "Through it one entered the city like a god…. One scuttles in now like a rat." When we finally arrived at Penn Station, with its thousands of "Dashing Dans," as commuters were called, we knew we were in the great big city and on our way to a few days of holiday happiness. We'd struggle up the stairs to the main concourse, head west past Nedick's, where Mom sometimes allowed us to get a hot dog and an orange drink that came in a cone-shaped paper cup, to the Eighth Avenue express, the A train, which we took uptown to 181st Street and Ft. Washington Avenue. Each of us was responsible for at least one bag to haul. We loved riding the subway, seeing the names of the stations fly by as our express train roared through all the local stops, up Manhattan's west side, through Harlem, then on to Washington Heights. As stressful as the trip was, hurrying from here to there as young children while dragging heavy bags, we loved it because we couldn't wait to see our two great aunts and the special things they'd have for us when we visited. In addition to the Pepsi-Cola, we awaited the little cakes called marigolds they'd buy from Cushman's Bakery on 181st Street and chocolate lollipops called lollicones from Barricini's Candy Shop, also on 181st Street. Those were special things we didn't get back home but Nellie and Katherine were sure to have. We knew when we'd arrived at the right station when we saw the large "181st Street" signs emblazoned on red ceramic tiles every few feet on the walls. As we stepped off the train we were greeted by the familiar subway station scent and the millions of white tiles that formed the long, rounded tunnel that seemed to go on forever. The 181st Street station on the IND Eighth Avenue line is the deepest in the entire New York City Transit system, nearly 200 feet below the ground. It is so deep that passengers cannot take stairs or escalators up to street level. There are none. Instead they must take a large elevator operated by an elevator man who always had a smile for us. We loved that ride too. Even the elevator had its own, unique, musty, smell. Once we stepped off, our excitement grew. We were now only minutes away from arriving at Nellie and Katherine's. Through the big wooden turnstiles we'd go, then out onto Fort Washington Avenue. Outside the subway station was the familiar newspaper stand and the large, white temple next door. Immediately we'd be smacked by the different smells of the city. Levittown was mostly lawns and trees, and the smell of cut grass dominated the spring air. Uptown Manhattan's smell was mostly a mixture of diesel fumes from the many buses and smoke from the trash burning in the incinerators of the many buildings. For some reason I liked the city smells because they were evidence I was really there, back in a place I was familiar with and loved, "The Heights," as Mom's Aunt Katherine and Aunt Nellie referred to their safe and attractive Irish and Jewish neighborhood. On our way from the subway to their apartment, we'd cut through Bennett Park, a historic Revolutionary War site that was an important outpost for General George Washington as he was leaving New York in 1776 to escape the British. In addition to its historic importance, Bennett Park holds another distinction: it is the highest natural point in Manhattan. Located on the Pinehurst Avenue side of the small park, inserted into the Manhattan schist, the bedrock foundation of New York City, is a plaque that states:

**THE HIGHEST
NATURAL POINT
ON MANHATTAN
265.05 FEET
ABOVE SEA LEVEL**

Mom always let us stop for a second so we could climb up the large rock with the bronze plaque. We'd be excited knowing that at that very moment we were standing taller than anyone else in the city.

I loved the history and beauty of the Heights. Bennett Park was our stepping-stone to their apartment. It was named for the famous 19th Century newspaper publisher, William Gordon Bennett, whose mansion stood where the beautiful Hudson View Gardens apartments were built in the 1920's, between Pinehurst Avenue and Cabrini Blvd. from 183rd to 185th Streets. Bennett and his competitors wrote over-sensationalized stories at the turn of the Twentieth Century that caused critics to coin the phrase "yellow journalism." After cutting through the park, our next anticipated sight was "the alley," a narrow space between Nellie and Katherine's building and the ivy covered stone cluster of buildings of Hudson View Gardens. We'd peek down the alley between the buildings to see if Nellie and Katherine were leaning out and waving from their bedroom and kitchen windows to greet us. Somehow, a half century before the invention of cell phones, they always seemed to know exactly when to be at those windows, because every time we visited, they were there with giant smiles and arms waving from three stories up to greet us. We couldn't wait to see these two bighearted women, women who, besides Mom, had the most to do with caring for us and keeping us safe when we were young. We had no key to get into the building, so we'd tick the button next to the name on the directory that said, "McCoy C-35," then wait a few seconds until we heard a loud buzzing noise coming from the door and we were able to push the door open. The lobby had little sunlight, only that which peered through the stained glass windows. Set in a medieval motif, the dimly lit entranceway had large, ornate chairs that we thought kings must have used as their thrones in the olden days. The lighting fixtures and other décor gave the formal room the look of a medieval court. The lobby was the crossroads of three wings, A, B, and C. We turned right, then left toward C-wing, then pushed the elevator button and waited for it to come. When the red light came on and the metal bars automatically opened, we'd enter. There were no elevators in Levittown so cramming into this small car with our luggage and packages was exciting. One of us would push the button numbered "3" and within seconds we were at Nellie and Katherine's door. The third floor hallway was actually a gloomy-looking, poorly lit space with black and white floor tiles and dark brown stucco walls. The smells of cooking coming through the doors from the six apartments on the third floor of C-wing permeated the air. Right next to their door was the incinerator hatch, which led to the chute where Nellie and Katherine and the other five tenants on their floor deposited their garbage. One of us would ring the bell and after a few seconds, perhaps to extend our anticipation or just to check and make sure it was in fact Mom and we kids at the door, the little peephole would open and an eyeball would appear. Then the door would fling open and both of these grand ladies would greet us with big hugs and smiles. Entering that apartment, being welcomed by those two special women, was one of my best feelings as a child. Nellie was Mom's adopted mother and the homemaker, so Mom called Nellie "Mother." Since Aunt Katherine worked nights a and slept days, we had to keep quiet much of the time. But Easter was special and Aunt Katherine didn't mind that we banged away on her piano, watched TV, and stayed up a little later than we did at home. The night before Easter Mom, Nellie and Katherine would have us put some carrots and a lump of sugar on the windowsill for the Easter Bunny. While I no longer believed in the Easter Bunny, I was always puzzled by the fact that the carrots and sugar were gone by the next morning. We'd wake up on Easter morning and see the jam-packed baskets Mom, Nellie and Katherine had prepared for us. But before we were allowed to invade them, church, or "choich" as Nellie and Katherine would say, came first. We'd dress up in our best clothes, which we carted from Levittown, and walk, as a group, to either St. Elizabeth's Church on Wadsworth Avenue and 187th Street, or to Mother Cabrini Chapel on Fort Washington Avenue and 190th Street, which was closer. We liked going to mass at Mother Cabrini Chapel inside Cabrini High School because the remains of the first saint to be canonized from the United States, Mother Frances X. Cabrini, the Patron Saint of Immigrants, are located in a glass case under the altar for all to see. The sight of Mother Cabrini's remains, preserved in an airtight vacuum, always intrigued us. Once mass was over, everyone was overjoyed that the pain of Good Friday had ended, the Lord had risen and we could now head back to our aunts' for the holiday.

The steps leading from 181st Street to upper Pinehurst Avenue. Aunt Katherine's building 106 Pinehurst Avenue, is second building on left, top of steps

Easter always meant a big meal, and Aunt Nellie was the chief cook. And of course…there was the candy. Nellie and Katherine were very generous toward us at the holidays. They didn't purchase cheap candy from a local supermarket or discount shop. Instead they shopped for our jellybeans, chocolate covered eggs and other treats at swanky candy stores like Loft's and Barricini's. A foil wrapped chocolate bunny and lots of smaller candies were hidden in the grasses of the colorful baskets. There were some other special things about our visit that we loved.

We thought Aunt Katherine was a millionaire because whenever we visited she gave each of us a dollar bill. This was a rare treat for us because we didn't receive any allowance at home. Many of our Levittown friends received 25 cents or even 50 cents a week. So this single dollar made us feel rich. And since Aunt Katherine said we could spend it on anything we wanted, for one brief moment we felt empowered. We had control of our own money. In the 1950's, a dollar went a long way. Candy bars and cokes were five cents, and a comic book was ten cents. Those were the pre-crack, pre-Columbine, pre-9/11 days, when parents trusted their kids to leave the apartment, cross busy streets by themselves, and make their way to the local stores unsupervised. When we visited Nellie and Katherine, we'd be allowed to walk down the street to "The Steps," as we referred to the three flights of granite stairs that led from upper Pinehurst Avenue to 181st Street below, then continue east for several blocks, past the little "rock garden church," the RKO Coliseum movie theater with its palatial lobby, maybe half a mile or so to Woolworth's 5 & 10. There we would spend five cents of our dollar on a serving of frozen vanilla custard with a big spoonful of chocolate syrup on it. Sometimes we'd have two and come back with our stomachs too full to eat Aunt Nellie's big supper. We called it supper back then, not dinner. The trip to Woolworth's, which involved crossing Broadway, a major

Grand children Brendan, Merry, Brian and Jen on the steps 1986

thoroughfare was more than a trip to a different neighborhood, it was like taking a trip to a different country. Broadway was, and still is, a dividing line separating a few groups. West of Broadway, almost everyone back then was of Jewish or Irish ancestry. Aunt Katherine's neighbor, Mrs. Katz, was an Eastern European immigrant who had fled from war, pogroms and other holocaust-related catastrophes. She and so many others in the Heights spoke with thick Yiddish accents. Others, with names like Duffy and Shea, had Irish brogues. They were either Irish immigrants, or first generation Irish-Americans.

Many, like all in the McCoy family, moved uptown from Hell's Kitchen on Manhattan's west side when the Eighth Avenue subway was completed in the 1930's. For these urban pioneers, moving to Washington Heights was like going to the country. They were still in Manhattan, linked to the center of the city by express subway, but miles away from the hustle and bustle of Midtown. East of Broadway, Washington Heights was like a northern extension of East Harlem, where there was an influx of newly arriving immigrants from Puerto Rico and the Dominican Republic. Along 181st Street east of Broadway, most everyone spoke Spanish. As Levittowners, we never heard Spanish spoken at all. We laugh to this day at the time, while walking on busy 181st Street after leaving Woolworth's with our stomachs full of vanilla ice cream, six-year-old Jeanne loudly called out to Dennis and me, "Mullagijiba." I stopped and looked at her and said, "What?" Surrounded by Spanish speakers, Jeanne again called out, "Mullagijiba. That's my Spanish." Jeanne had made up her own version of the Spanish words she was hearing from passersby along the busy street. Dennis and I whisked her away quickly.

In addition to providing all they could for Mom when she was young and parentless, and helping her provide for us when Mom was struggling alone, Nellie and Katherine cared for their own father and all their brothers and sisters when they grew old and needed help. When we were kids, their brother Cornelius McCoy lived with them. Uncle Connie, as we called him, was in his late 70's but looked older and couldn't walk. He stayed in his room all day, which he kept dark with the shades pulled all the way down. Occasionally I'd peek in and all I'd see was the glow of his cigar, and the thick layers of cigar smoke permeating the room. He'd say, "Come in here sonny." I'm not sure whether or not he knew my name, but I'd spend time with him, listening to live radio shows like "Flash Gordon," "Amos and Andy" and the "Green Hornet" on his big brown radio. Uncle Connie allowed me to go through his drawers and snoop around. This was the first time I ever got to see the kind of things men keep for themselves, like razor blades, shaving equipment, colognes, a wallet and other men's things. His wallet was stuffed with small bills and an official-looking gold badge. He'd say, "Give me that wallet, sonny. That's my pension in there." I didn't know what a pension was, but Connie was a retired city highway inspector who carried a badge. Sometimes he'd give us a dollar too. Uncle Connie was considered quite a character during his inspector days. He had a reddish facial complexion and white curly hair. In his three-piece suit with a cigar stuck in his mouth, and an entourage of other inspectors surrounding him, he gave the appearance of being quite important, like a big-time city political figure. He'd go wherever he wanted, including Yankee Stadium during the World Series, which he jokingly called the "World Serious," have one of his men flip his badge and say, "Make way for the commissioner. Make way for the commissioner," as they'd enter and seat themselves. Troubled by severe arthritis, which he called "Arthur-itis," Uncle Connie would say, "I got wires in my legs, sonny." Unable to walk anymore, he'd sometimes fall in his room trying to get to the bathroom and neither Aunt Katherine nor Aunt Nellie could pick him up. They'd have to call the police for assistance. Finally, in the late 1950's, unable to care for him, Aunt Katherine had her brother Connie placed in the Bronx V.A. hospital where he lived the last few years of his life. He passed away in April 1960 from severe burns inflicted when an orderly accidentally dropped a lit match into his pajama cuff after lighting his cigar.

I felt a wonderful sense of independence whenever I visited Nellie and Katherine's. It was also good to see Mom relax more than she was able to at home with so many burdens upon her. She loved spending time with her aunts and being able to put her troubles aside for a few days. While the adults relaxed, we kids usually occupied ourselves quite well in Aunt Katherine's bedroom. There were no toys to play with, but we improvised quite well with whatever we found. Aunt Katherine kept a folding bed that we used when we visited. During the day, the bed would be folded up and shoved out of the way. It had wheels and one of us would ride on top while the others pushed it all around the wooden floors of Aunt Katherine's room. That folding bed became the car we didn't have, our garbage truck, fire truck and anything else we wanted it to be. We joke to this day about how we'd "drive" the folding bed up to our imaginary gas station and put our imaginary gas in, then take off again for a different part of the room.

Nellie and Katherine's apartment had three bedrooms and a long wide hallway in which we played hide and seek and other games. It also had ten windows from which we could see vast uptown stretches. Since Pinehurst Avenue is geographically higher than all the other streets in Manhattan, we looked down on the rooftops of adjacent buildings, saw hundreds of pigeons roosting on the brick ledges of Hudson View Gardens, and watched passersby from a distance. It was very majestic. With the magnificent Tudor-style buildings of Hudson View Gardens next door, we felt like we were in Europe, or what we thought Europe would look like. From those windows we also had spectacular views of the Hudson River, the George Washington Bridge, and the tall, sheer cliffs of the New Jersey Palisades across the river. Just north of the Jersey side of the bridge, jutting out into the Hudson, we noticed a peninsula that we thought was a dude ranch because we could see trees and a log cabin. When I was 12 and Dennis ten, Mom let us walk across the George Washington Bridge to investigate this "dude ranch" that we wondered about for so many years. Mom knew that the bridge has a pedestrian walkway with a steel railing, so there was no real danger of us falling. We were happy to be given her trust. First we walked south on Pinehurst Avenue to 178th Street, then out onto the bridge's pedestrian path. As we made our way from the Heights, out over the Hudson, we were amazed at how high up were actually were, 212 feet above river level. A sign told us that when it was completed in 1931, the George Washington Bridge was the longest suspension bridge in the world, nearly a mile from tower to tower, and its exposed steel towers rose a dizzying 60 stories high. It was windy out there but we didn't think about that. We concentrated instead on the magnificent views from so high up. They were worth it. First we looked back to where we'd just come from, at the red brick cluster of buildings known as Castle Village, behind them at the ivy-covered Tudor buildings that make up Hudson View Gardens, then at the gray brick 106 Pinehurst Avenue, our city home. We looked up the Hudson to Fort Tryon Park and the castle-like tower of the Cloisters, the medieval branch of the Metropolitan Museum of Art, piercing through the treetops. North of Fort Tryon was 200 acre Inwood Park, the only virgin woodlands still in existence in Manhattan, untouched by four centuries of development. Farther up river, almost out of sight, a little portion of the Tappan Zee Bridge, which connects Westchester with Rockland County, was visible. We looked south, toward Midtown and lower Manhattan, at the splendid skyline. When we reached the mid-point of the bridge, we stopped at the sign that says New Jersey to the left and New York to the right and smiled as we took turns straddling the line that separates the words, knowing that we were standing in two states at the same time. And then there was the bridge itself. French architect Le Corbusier said of it, "It is the most beautiful bridge in the world. Made of cables and steel beams, it gleams in the sky like a reversed arch. It is blessed." When we got to the Jersey side of the bridge, we hiked about a quarter mile north, along the rim of the steep Palisades where we found a sign leading to a path toward a long stone and wooden staircase. Hundreds of steps later we arrived at the bottom, river level, and there it was, our "dude ranch." In fact, it wasn't a dude ranch at all, but a few barren acres of land with an empty brown house in the middle. Dennis and I were the only two people there. There were no swings, no playground, nothing but that closed-up brown house and some open space. There was something there for us though, breathtaking vistas of the river, the Manhattan skyline and the George Washington Bridge. I learned later that our "dude ranch" was really named Ross Dock, a peninsula built on sunken barges and other landfill from when the area was a stone quarry. In the 1930's it had been a summer camp for New York City families. Today it is called Ross Dock Picnic Area, a much nicer park maintained by the New Jersey Park Department. Though our journey didn't turn out to be what we'd expected or wanted it to be, at long last we knew what we were looking at from our window at 106 Pinehurst. Now we had the daunting task of climbing back up the hundreds of steps to the top of the Palisades, then back out on to the bridge and our long walk home. As we made our way back to Nellie and Katherine's, we noticed the little red lighthouse adjacent to the bridge on the New York side. It's only 20 feet tall, but from where we stood, 212 feet above the river, it looked like a toy. The sight of it called to mind the influential children's storybook Mom sometimes read to us called The Little Red Lighthouse and the Great Gray Bridge. It was written in 1942 by Hildegarde Swift to call attention to the fact that the U.S. Coast Guard was not only extinguishing the Jeffrey's Hook Light, as it was officially known, but also taking the tiny lighthouse down completely. The soaring towers of the bridge, 604 feet tall, had made the little red lighthouse obsolete. However, neighborhood people, especially children, were familiar with it, loved it, and didn't want it removed. Swift's book, which gave a human personality to the lighthouse and the towering "great gray bridge," caused such a public outcry, the Coast Guard kept it lit until 1948 and never demolished it. Now an official landmark, The Little Red Lighthouse still stands, and is a part of Fort Washington Park. It sits proudly on a rock mass at the edge of the Hudson River beneath the Manhattan tower of the famous bridge.

Before we exited the bridge and walked up the steep incline of 181st to Pinehurst Avenue, we took one look back at the Jersey side of the bridge. There, just south of the Jersey tower, we saw the roller coaster, the Wild Mouse, and other rides at the world famous Palisades Amusement Park. Whenever we visited our aunts during spring or summer, Mom usually took us to Palisades by bus, which cost ten cents. When Robert was old enough, he took us. Once in a while we walked across the bridge to get there, not just to save the dime, but for the adventure. Admission to Palisades Park was free then. We only had to pay for the rides we went on. Some were only a dime. Thank God for Aunt Katherine's dollar bill. Rides and ice cream cones were cheap too, maybe a dime, so we could do a lot with the little money we had. Palisades had a swimming pool, with a waterfall at one end that caused small waves to lick the shore at the other end, onto an artificial sand beach. We were impressed knowing that it was "the world's largest outdoor salt water swimming pool." That pool is where city teenagers, who'd been encouraged to "Come on over" by the Palisades Park jingle, laid down their towels, worked on their tans and listened to the newest rock and roll songs on their transistor radios. Everyone in the New York area was familiar with the Palisades Park jingle, which played constantly on TV and radio ads,

> Palisades has the rides, Palisades has the fun, Come on over;
> Shows and dancing are free, so's the parking so cheap, Come on over;
> Palisades from coast to coast, where a dime buys the most,
> Palisades Amusement Park, swings all day and after dark.

One of those rock and roll songs, written in 1962 by Chuck Berris of "Gong Show" fame, was actually named "Palisades Park," and sung by Freddy "Boom Boom" Cannon. The hit song, which reached #3 on the Billboard charts, boosted the park's attendance. It also included genuine amusement park sound effects like screams heard from the roller coaster, and spoke excitedly of the "swinging place called Palisades Park," the place "where the girls are," the place where you could "dance around to a rocking band." The bands he was referring to were the hundreds of rock and roll

Pinehurst Avenue and 181ˢᵗ Street, an important family center for us.

bands that Palisades brought in for their regular teen shows emceed by New York's "Cousin" Bruce Morrow. The 40-acre Palisades Park, one of the most visited amusement parks in the country, closed in 1971 to make way for a few dozen high-rise residential buildings. Whenever I head west across the George Washington Bridge these days, I look left and see, not the place where we were so happy as kids, but rows of giant condos.

Palisades wasn't always a joyous place for all. Before we began visiting in the 1950's, Palisades had a Jim Crow history. The "World's Largest Outdoor Salt Water Pool," was racially segregated. Whites were sold tickets while blacks were refused admission. This lasted until 1950 when, after a decade of protests by C.O.R.E. and other groups, the park's owners finally changed the rules.

We weren't really upset that our "dude ranch" turned out to be an empty space. We'd had our adventure. We'd filled ourselves with the sights of the Heights and the Hudson from the Palisades and the bridge. Mostly, our adventure allowed us to feel free, and that freedom came from Mom trusting us to go on that journey and others like it. Whenever we visited Nellie and Katherine's, we were free to go Bennett Park where we played and met a few new "city" friends, or hike up to Fort Tryon Park to see the Cloisters, which we thought was an actual castle left over from medieval times. We were free to spend a quarter of our dollar at the extravagant RKO Coliseum movie theater, with its opulent chandeliers, drapes and fountains, dripping with excess. It was there, in that air-conditioned palace on 181st Street and Broadway, where Mom first met Robert A. White during the 1930's when he worked there as an usher, that we saw the lengthy film "Twenty Thousand Leagues Under the Sea" twice in one day. We were free to go to the old-fashioned bowling alley above Lynn's Department Store on Broadway, where they still used pin boys to reset the pins after each frame. We were trusted to do the shopping for Nellie and Katherine at the butcher's, Cushman's Bakery and Tony the Greengrocers, or to Hye's Candy Store to buy whatever we wanted for ourselves with what remained from Aunt Katherine's dollar. Whenever we visited the Heights, we had fewer rules imposed on us than at home. We were free.

During Easter week, Mom would sometimes take us by bus or subway to places like the Indian Museum on 155th Street and Broadway, Grant's Tomb at 122nd Street and Riverside Drive, or to Central Park. During Christmas visits, we'd skate at the park's Wollman Rink, sometimes at night and enjoy the skyscrapers all brightly lit up and snowflakes coming down. Once in a while, undoubtedly with a gift from Aunt Katherine, she'd take us to the circus or the ice capades at the old Madison Square Garden on 50th Street and Eighth Avenue. Knowing I liked cowboy things as a boy, Mom gave me the surprise of my life one year, tickets to the rodeo at "The Garden." At that great old venue I got to see my favorite TV hero Roy Rogers, the "King of the Cowboys." With the spotlight on him, Roy, wearing his trademark cowboy hat, fringed shirt and red bandana, galloped into the darkened arena on his golden palomino Trigger. I was thrilled. Then his wife and co-star, Dale Evans, rode out on her horse, Buttermilk, to join him as they trotted around, smiled and waved to the thousands of young fans in attendance, singing their theme song, "Happy Trails To You." Following Roy and Dale came their lightning-fast "wonder dog," Bullet, and Roy's comical sidekick, Patrick Aloysious Brady, driving his jeep Nellybelle. We watched bronco and bull riding, calf roping and steer wrestling for hours, just like kids out West got to see, as thousands of city kids twirled their little red souvenir flashlights in the darkened Garden.

Aunt Katherine and Nellie's third floor apartment overlooking the Hudson River.

Our visits to the Heights were the best times of our childhoods for, as with 55 Twig Lane, there we were happy. Mom, Aunt Katherine and Aunt Nellie did everything they possibly could to brighten our holidays. It is with enormous thanks, the utmost respect and a few joyous tears that I remember the great lengths those wonderful women went through to make those days special for us.

Washington Heights Postscript – A Brick from 106 Pinehurst

I go back in Washington Heights on occasion. It's still a very nice neighborhood. Though some of the buildings are nearly a century old, many actually look better than they did when I was a boy in the 1950's. Hudson View Gardens, Bennett Park and "The Steps" that lead from lower Pinehurst Avenue to upper Pinehurst Avenue remain unchanged. Some places, like Fort Tryon Park and the Cloisters, look better than they ever did. In May 2005, one month before my retirement from teaching, I led more than 100 students on my final field trip to New York City. After organizing more than 1000 trips during my 36-year career, this was my last. The students had been assigned certain special tasks that they were to do in lower Manhattan in groups, without me. This allowed me a couple of hours to spend with Sean, a special education student who required one-on-one supervision. He chose to stick with his teacher aide, Pat, and me. Sean loved lighthouses and wanted very much for me to take him to see the Little Red Lighthouse. I jumped at the chance to please Sean and have a few hours to visit that old, familiar area once again. We took the A train, an express, and within minutes arrived at 181st Street station, then made our way west on foot toward the Hudson. The walk from "The Heights" to the river below involves a steep descent of more than 250 feet. No problem going down. Sean effervesced as we got closer and closer to the little, red historic landmark that sits beside "The Great Gray Bridge." After climbing on the rocks that surround the lighthouse and taking a few peeks inside the small round windows, Sean who had a brief attention span said, "That's it. I'm done." With that, we began the long ascent back up to 181st Street. On the way I mentioned that I used to live nearby, that my first boyhood home was only a short walk from the subway station. Sean thought this was "cool" and asked if I'd show him my old building. "Please, Mr. White. Please?" "Of course," I said. Actually, I was glad he asked me. I'd take any opportunity I could to see the old place one more time. After trekking up from the river to street level for about 20 minutes, then scaling the three flights of steps to upper Pinehurst Avenue, Sean, Pat and I arrived at the building I lived in as a child, the building where I was so happy to visit Aunt Katherine and Aunt Nellie so many times, my first home, 106 Pinehurst. While I was explaining a few things about the neighborhood and what it was like to live there 60 years ago, like seeing the junk man who parked his horse-drawn wagon at the end of cobble- stone Pinehurst Avenue, yelling "Junk for sale," I noticed a large dumpster in front of the building. It was full of chunks of cement, wood and other debris from construction work being done at 106. It dawned on me that there might be some good stuff inside, so I decided to do a quick dumpster dive. Sean, growing impatient didn't know what I was doing and kept saying, "OK. Let's go Mr. White. Time to go." I said, "One more minute, Sean. I want to check this out." I hoisted myself up the side of the large steel container and saw mostly scraps of wood, garbage, and…some large, gray bricks. "Hey," I thought. "These bricks are original pieces of 106 Pinehurst Avenue. Some could be from my very apartment." I grabbed one, rescuing it from oblivion. Pat asked, "What are you doing? It's just a brick." Sean repeated, "C'mon Mr. White. We got a train to catch. C'mon. Time to go." I explained that I really wanted to take this discarded brick, garbage to most but a treasure to me, home. Pat understood and just happened to have a shopping bag with her. This brick, part of the original 1920's construction, was made of cement not clay and was much larger and heavier than a standard brick. Sean, Pat and I took turns hauling the bag and its precious contents to the subway, then Penn Station, then all the way to Northport. When I got home, I wore a broad smile. I'd become the proud owner of an actual piece of 106 Pinehurst Avenue. I decided to place my prize in an easy-to-observe spot in the garden, right behind the house next to another city treasure of mine, a discarded, hexagon-shaped slate from Brooklyn's Prospect Park. I dug a spot in the garden for the new brick, making it part of my growing collection of mostly stones and other permanent reminders of the many places I've visited and cherished throughout my life. Since 2005, I've lived at 16 Stony Hollow Road, Centerport, NY in a house situated on nearly two acres of land. I've worked hard over the past decade to clear away many of the thickets, vines and creepers that had invaded the yard, and planted gardens to my liking. Throughout these gardens, I've placed dozens of stones and other esteemed and venerated objects from places I've lived or visited. They serve as a constant reminder of where I've come from, where I've been and what's important. In my outdoor stone museum, one stone is from Mom's grave. Another is from the grave of her dad, my grandfather John McCoy. There are stones and other meaningful items from all around the world, places like Bash Bish Falls, and my friend Gary's place at Garnet Lake in upstate New York. There are twigs and other objects from nearby places like Bethpage State Park and far-away places like the shores of Oahu and Maui, and the green fields of Ireland. Leaves from the grave of my first friend, Les Joy, who lies buried in Punchbowl National Cemetery in Honolulu, have been mingled with leaves in my very own gardens. No matter where I go in my own yard, I take comfort in knowing that I am surrounded by these physical reminders of what's important from my past. One stone, slightly larger than my fist, is dark gray, speckled with spots of lighter gray and white. It is from Nuevo Amanecer, Nicaragua (New Dawn), a community of 68 very poor families, about 350 people, in northwestern Nicaragua, just north of the volcano Telica. I brought that special stone here in 2003 after my student group purchased 55 acres of land and provided the money for and helped build 68 houses, a school, a community center and a water system for the poorest people in our hemisphere. Each day when I walk outside, get in my car and set out to go wherever it is I'm going, I glance down at that speckled rock and am reminded of the great struggle of the poor and of what's important in life. Of all these physical reminders of the past, the rock from Nuevo Amanecer and the brick from 106 Pinehurst Avenue are my two favorites.

Christmas

Mom always did a good job trying to mix the religious aspects of holidays with fun. Christmas was first and foremost Jesus' birthday. A nativity scene always had a prominent place in the house. It went up during Advent, before the Christmas tree or the outdoor lights. Attending mass always came before any gifts could be opened. Santa came, but Jesus came first. Whether or not we got what we wanted didn't really matter that much to us, we were just glad to have Christmas. I don't know how Mom was able to buy a Christmas tree each year, or to put gifts under it, but she did. She'd let us decorate it, first by stringing the colored lights throughout the tree, then hanging the many ornaments she'd gathered over the years. I can still hear her voice directing me, *"Peter, don't put all the lights on the end of the branches. Try to put some of them farther in."*

She knew what she was doing because our tree was quite beautiful every year. I'm certain that by being thrifty and saving a few cents here and there, and with some help from her cousin Florence Larkin and Aunt Katherine, Mom was able to do some shopping for us. She also got a little holiday help from Holy Family Church. By typing letters for the priests on her old Royal portable typewriter, selling raffles tickets for the church every month, and doing whatever she could to be of help, Mom was well known as a parish helper. When holiday times came around, Father Fagan or another priest would stop by and drop off some things, some new, some used, which we were not supposed to look at. Mom always found a way to make sure that Santa came, and to make things nice for us.

Mom emphasized that Christmas is more about giving than receiving. Though as kids we had little to give, we always tried to come up with something for Mom, whether it was a home-made gift, or doing some type of extra work around the house. Whenever we had any money at all, like the change left over from the dollar Aunt Katherine would give us, we'd go to Mister B's 5 & 10 store next to our Grand Union supermarket. Two elderly folks, Mr. B and his wife, Mrs. B, ran the store. We'd have ten or fifteen cents in our pockets and enter like we were big shoppers, walking up and down every aisle, looking over all of the merchandise to see what we could afford, something we could wrap up and have Mom open on Christmas morning. Often, guided by Mrs. B herself, we'd pick out some useless, junky looking plate or ashtray, even though Mom didn't smoke, bring it home, hide it for days, then give it to her on Christmas morning with broad smiles on our faces. She'd open it and sometimes cry. We weren't sure whether she was shedding tears of joy, or whether she was really upset that we'd be foolish enough to spend the little money we had on something so useless.

Halloween

We loved Halloween. In those early Levittown days there were hundreds of kids in every neighborhood, all out in costume, all together, all smiling, all collecting as much candy as they could. It was a joyous day. Of course, Halloween was the day before All Saints Day, a Catholic holy day of obligation. As Catholic school kids we always had November 1st off from school. Halloween was sometimes a theatrical experience for us. Our costumes were homespun, and Mom took great care in making them. She'd find material, old clothing and even rags, anything lying around, and create very colorful, accurate costumes. I remember wearing Robert A. White's old army hat and being a soldier one year, and a hobo the next, complete with a scuffed up dirty face applied by Mom from a burnt piece of cork. I can still remember the smell of the burning cork. Dennis was Superman, with a big 'S' on his chest and a flowing cape one year, and a pirate, with bandana, mustache and eye patch the next. We'd knock on door after door, proudly show off our costumes and gladly accept the candy, apples and even loose change that came as we trick or treated. It was a safe, fun holiday, and though we couldn't afford store-bought costumes, Mom took the time and had the patience to make it great for us. As we got older, we were allowed to stay out later, and even leave our neighborhood to trick or treat blocks away. We'd be out pretty late for us, since we normally had to be home from play when the streetlights went on. When I was 12 years old, almost too old for the costume and candy scene, I was very interested in gathering a record amount of candy. I went with friends who were more interested in smashing pumpkins than collecting candy. I could have none of that. Under no circumstances could I smash the pumpkin of a neighbor or stranger, get caught, and be brought home by a neighbor or cop to face Mom. No way. So when my friends approached a house with a pumpkin out front they'd say, "C'mon. What's the matter White? Are you afraid? Chicken?" I'd just answer, "No. Sorry. I can't." Not only was I taught that such destruction was wrong, I believed I could never, ever be caught doing such a thing. Not with Mom at the helm. So I went about trick or treating, and they went about smashing pumpkins. One year, a kid from Branch Lane smashed our pumpkin, one we'd carved as a family and placed out front with a candle in it. When I came home from trick or treating and saw how upset Mom was, I walked around the block to his house and saw his mother sitting on the lawn with a pumpkin on her lap, waiting to give candy to the kids as they passed by. I told her how upset my Mom was that her son smashed our pumpkin. Before I was able to ask her what she was going to do about it, she placed her pumpkin into my hands and said, "I'm sorry my son did that. Take ours, please."

Saturday August 31, 1957

For a kid, achieving the age of ten has its rewards. For one thing, at ten you're out of the single digits and well aware your teen years are right around the corner. At ten you can have a paper route and be trusted with lawn mowing and other jobs. And greatest of all in our neighborhood, at ten a Levittown kid can get into the municipal pool without an adult accompanying him, a huge sign of growing up. On Saturday August 31, 1957, while visiting Aunt Katherine and Aunt Nellie in the city with Mom, Dennis and Jeanne, I turned ten. We were to spend the night, then on Sunday go to see Robert up at his seminary in Haverstraw, NY. It would be our first visit to see him and we were all excited to be going "upstate," even though Haverstraw was just 20 miles from upper Manhattan by bus. But Saturday was my day. I'd just finished fourth grade and would be starting fifth grade a few days later. Since my birthday is so late in the summer, my gifts usually were back-to-school things – a new schoolbag, new white shirt for St. Ignatius, maybe some school supplies. To my surprise, on Saturday morning Mom asked, *"Peter, It's your birthday. How do you want to spend it?"* With no time to prepare for what sounded like the beginning of a special day, the first thought that popped into my head was how much my Twig Lane friends, Bobby and Freddy Hoffman, liked going to Coney Island. They went there every summer and came back with tales of the famous Parachute Jump, the Cyclone, Steeplechase Park and lunch at the original Nathan's, where the hot dog was actually invented half a century earlier. It didn't take me long to ask, "Can we go to Coney Island?" Mom looked at Aunt Katherine, who gave an affirmative nod then said, *"Sure!"* Aunt Nellie decided to stay back with Dennis and Jeanne. I bubbled with excitement. I was going to see with my own eyes the most famous amusement area in the country, go on rides, get a glimpse of the ocean, and be treated special, all day. This would be a lot better than getting a schoolbag or new white shirt. A short while later Mom, Aunt Katherine and I found ourselves speeding downtown on the A train, through

Manhattan, under the East River and into Brooklyn, changing somewhere for the D train to the Coney Island-Stillwell Avenue station. I'd never been to Brooklyn before. I'd heard a lot about it from Drew Keenan, Les Joy and a few other former Brooklynites but this was my first time to that famous place. The ride from Washington Heights, at the very top of Manhattan, to Coney Island, at the very bottom of Brooklyn, is long, very long, and we seemed to be on the subway forever. But, when we finally arrived and the doors to the elevated train opened, in swept a wonderful smell that was new for me, a mixture of salt water air, French fries, cotton candy and dozens of other fast food aromas. It was an intoxicating smell. Millions had gone to Coney Island each year for decades. I was now finally one of them. We walked the boardwalk and looked west, down its two and a half-mile span, and there it was, just as I imagined it to be. Coney Island. People of all races and ethnicities sped by, bobbing and weaving their way along the crowded boardwalk, stopping at different sideshows and games of chance, and lining up for rides and food. I couldn't wait to get started. "Where should we go first?" Mom answered, *"It's your day Peter. We're following you."* We were near Steeplechase Park so that was my first stop. Aunt Katherine gave me $1 and I bought the ticket I'd need to enter. It was about six inches round and had ten punch holes on it. There were dozens of rides inside this old building and each time I went on one an attendant punched one of the holes out. Inside the building I went on nine rides, including a magic carpet ride and a spinning barrel where kids tumbled all over one another. I saved my last punch for the Steeplechase, the fast moving, wooden, mechanical horses that followed a race course around the entire building. After getting strapped in tight by an attendant, a loud bell rang and we were off. I held onto my horse's reins for dear life as we went at breakneck speed, round and round each bend. I never experienced anything more exhilarating in my entire life. Bobby and Freddy weren't kidding when they said how fast these steeplechase horses really go. Aunt Katherine and Mom sat on the boardwalk while I played, alone but completely happy. After Steeplechase, we headed west to the Cyclone, world's fastest and steepest roller coaster. I barely made the height requirement and was a little frightened by the sign that said, "HOLD ON TO ALL HATS, KEYS AND WIGS," and another that warned riders to stay seated and keep hands and arms in, especially during the famous 60-degree drop. Another life thrill I never expected to have. Next was the Wonder Wheel, the largest Ferris wheel I'd ever seen, at least 15 stories high. Mom joined me on that ride. After that, we walked a block over to Surf and Stillwell Avenues and the original Nathan's for hot dogs and a Coke. I could tell that Aunt Katherine and Mom were hot and getting tired of traipsing and waiting, so I asked for just one more ride, Brooklyn's Eiffel Tower, the Parachute Jump. Mom said, *"OK. It's your birthday."* The 250-foot tower is visible from all over Coney Island, and much of Brooklyn. As we got closer and closer, the gigantic red icon seemed to grow larger and larger. I thought I was brave enough for this, but when I finally stood next to it and looked up, I got scared. I think Mom and Aunt Katherine were too. We watched for a while as the twelve parachutes, each with their two daredevil passengers strapped into their little canvas seats, continued to float down, one after the other. I saw the steel wire that guided each one down, but the only thing that slowed its descent was the open parachute itself. What if mine didn't open? I could see the shock absorbers that cushioned each rider's landing, but there was 250 feet of nothing but space between the top and those shock absorbers below. What if mine didn't work? I didn't want to punk out, but my ten-year-old better judgment told me not to go. Fortunately for me, and I think Mom and Aunt Katherine too, I didn't have to face the choice of whether to go or not. As I passed by the height requirement sign an attendant stopped me and, in his thick Brooklyn accent, said, "Hey sonny. Hold it right there. You're not tall enough. Come back next year sonny." Relieved, we headed to the subway and the long ride back to Washington Heights. I'd had the greatest day in my young life. While it was important for me to finally do what Bobby and Freddy and others in my neighborhood had done, and while it was fun to finally experience the sights and sounds and smells of Coney Island, and thrilling to go on the world famous rides, this was a great day for a more important reason. I got to spend an entire day with the two most important people in my life at that time, two loving women who, by their kindness and patience, placed my wants and needs ahead of their own. Better than any store-bought birthday present, they gave me their time and their love.

My Best Night as a Kid

On Halloween night 1958, I stayed out quite late trick or treating. Thinking that I'd be scolded or punished for overdoing it, the exact opposite happened. As I entered the house all was quiet. The only light I saw was from the glow of a single candle on the kitchen table. As Mom entered I thought I was in trouble. Then, in the candlelight, I noticed that the table was set with some Halloween decorations and a beautiful homemade cake. Instead of a reprimand, Mom looked at me, smiled and said, *"Welcome home, I'm glad you're safe. You must be tired, relax."* She went upstairs and got Dennis and Jeanne, who were in bed already, and we all had a piece of cake. I wasn't in trouble after all. Mom was happy to see me. That moment, Halloween night 58 years ago was very special for me. In addition to the usual fun associated with Halloween, like costumes and candy, and staying out a bit later, that particular Halloween, with Mom taking the time to really care about me, created a feeling of happiness inside that's hard to describe. That moment, Halloween night so long ago is one I'll always cherish; it stands out as one of the most memorable of my entire childhood. For that one moment, I was at peace. All seemed right in my world. And it wasn't because Mom baked me a cake and put a Halloween candle on it; it was because she cared.

Chinese Food and the World Series

My friends' families had cars, occasionally went out to dinner, and took trips to places like Jones Beach, the Catskills, Maine and even cross-country. Except for our visits by train to New York City to see Aunt Nellie and Aunt Katherine, we did not go to very many places, nor did we ever go out to dinner. Two stories point out the affect this had. On a Friday afternoon in the summer of 1957, I was playing in the back yard of friend, Robert. His house was on Branch Lane, almost directly behind ours. Suddenly, Robert heard the slam of a car door coming from the front driveway and said, "You have to go home now. My dad's home." I said, "Why? What's wrong?" He replied, "It's Friday. Every Friday my dad brings home Chinese food and we love it. Our whole family sits down together and has a big Chinese meal. I gotta go now." Robert ran around to the front of the house to greet his dad, who had a big smile on his face as he held up the brown bag full of Chinese food. They both seemed so excited as they entered the house together. I stood alone for a few seconds, wondering what Chinese food tasted like. Then I squeezed through the fence that separated Robert's yard from the Polansky's, hurdled the Pearlman's fence, and arrived back at my house, where soon I would be enjoying our usual Friday night fare, tuna fish sandwiches. I wondered what it would be like to have a dad bring restaurant food home for the family. As I sat at our table with Dennis, Jeanne and Mom, I enjoyed my Friday night tuna fish sandwich. It was a speedy, inexpensive meal that involved very little clean up, and it got us back out playing again pretty quickly. I knew there was no way I could ever have what Robert had, but I did have a Mom who did her best to make our Friday night meals special. Actually, I liked tuna fish sandwiches just fine back then. In fact, I still do. They're a great reminder of those simple Friday nights from long ago.

The second story involves the historic 1955 World Series, when the Brooklyn Dodgers beat the New York Yankees in seven games for their first World Series championship in franchise history. Almost everyone in our Levittown neighborhood came from New York City, which back then had three major league teams. Those of us who hailed from Manhattan or the Bronx were generally Yankee or Giant fans. All the Brooklyn kids were Dodger fans. The rivalries sometimes caused arguments among us, which team was best, whether the American League was tougher than the National League, who was the best center fielder, Mantle, Snider or Mays, and on and on. On a beautiful October morning in 1955, I was an eight-year-old boy standing at the corner of Twig and Bud, waiting for my school bus when a two-toned black and white Ford sped down the block. It was the Joy's car. As it passed by, a boy's head popped out the window. It was my friend, Les Joy. As they sped down Twig, Les called out, "We're going to the Dodger game!" I fixed my eyes on Mr. Joy's new car until it faded down the block then turned onto Newbridge Road. A familiar feeling came over me as I watched it disappear. I wondered what it would be like to go to a Dodger game, especially the World Series. I also wondered what it would be like if we had a family car, especially a new one like the Joy's got every few years. And I wondered what it would be like to have a father. Les had all three of those things at the same time.

Thoughts of that incident came back to me once in a while through childhood. They used to make me feel that I was somehow deprived. But as my life went on and I gained valuable experiences with people all over the world, I came to realize that I wasn't really deprived. I may not have had a World Series experience, or come from a family who got a new car every few years. But I had something that new cars and ball games could never replace.

CHURCH AND COMMUNITY

Generosity and Community Service

Despite her financial struggle, Mom was a very generous community servant, regularly giving of herself to others. For a number of years as a New York City teenager and college woman, she volunteered to teach religion under the direction of Father Edward Kellenburg. She was very active in her parish, St. Elizabeth's Church in Washington Heights, tutoring children in Harlem, collecting door-to-door for Catholic Charities for several weeks each year, and serving as a camp counselor at Camp Sunset in New Paltz, New York. As young children we'd sit next to her during Sunday mass. When collection time came and the ushers would pass the basket down each row, Mom would open her purse and search through the little money she had, trying to figure out what she could afford to contribute. Regardless of how broke she may have been, she strongly believed in supporting her church and giving all she possibly could. She'd give us a few coins to put in the basket too, so we could learn from the experience of giving. Whenever someone came to the door collecting for one charity or another, after asking a few questions about the charity, Mom would always give something. When she learned that poor children in Ft. Greene, Brooklyn had to spend their summers in sweltering tenements, she volunteered to have some come to Levittown to spend a few weeks with us, go to the Levittown pool, and enjoy backyard barbeques and safe play. It was quite inspirational to see a poor woman, who had to rely on welfare for ten years of her life, host poor children, despite not having enough herself. Levittown began in the 1940's as an all-white community, so we saw few black people growing up. Mom broke new ground by hosting black girls from Ft. Greene, Brooklyn during those summers. I doubt any of our neighbors disapproved of Mom inviting the girls to stay with us, but if they had, it wouldn't have fazed her in the least. Never one to back down, Mom would have halted any such critic in his tracks. I never, ever heard Mom say anything unfavorable about a person's race, religion or ethnicity, and she wouldn't tolerate any such disparagement from us or others either. When we were quite young, an elderly black man knocked on our door. He was canvassing the neighborhood, passing out religious pamphlets. When Dennis opened the door and the well-dressed man appeared, he exclaimed, "Mom, there's a colored man here." Mom was embarrassed. She was from the city, where encounters with people of different races, religions and nationalities were common. We were among the shortchanged children from all-white segregated suburbia, where the "N" word was sometimes hurled around. The expression "colored" was a common reference we heard frequently from other kids, their parents, the media, and even from some of Mom's older aunts and uncles. We didn't know any black people personally. The only knowledge we had of them was from others, or from movies and television shows like "Amos and Andy," which portrayed blacks as lazy and conniving. Mom was humiliated and apologized to the very kind man, who looked at us with a smile as he handed her one of his pamphlets, then left. I'm not sure whether or not she took Dennis into the bathroom for some Ivory soap treatment, but she may have. Either way, the message was clear, *"Never say such a thing again."*

Courtesy

Mom was a courteous, kind and proper woman. She knew when to dress fancy and when to wear her casuals, when to smile big and laugh hysterically, and when to be subdued and guarded. So many aspects of her life demonstrated the kind of appropriate and decorous woman she was. At her funeral, a friend of Mom's took my arm and said, "Your Mom was a proper woman, the epitome of polish and respect." I believe all who knew her would agree. It was very important for Mom to teach us those values. We were raised to be courteous, not just when we had to be, like when company came, but all the time, even when people weren't looking. During the years I was away at college, Dennis was a high school boy. He recalled how with every winter snow, Mom would have him go across the street and shovel Mrs. Ahearn's driveway. Mrs. Ahearn's husband had been sick for years, and then passed away, leaving Mrs. Ahearn alone. Mom reminded Dennis not to accept any money. *"Just do it as a favor,"* she'd say. Without argument or complaint, Dennis did so every time it snowed. After a few snowfalls, he needed no reminders. When it snowed, he'd grab the shovel, head across the street, and make the snow fly. By doing so, he learned how placing the needs of others ahead of his own was not only good neighborliness; it was the essence of the lessons he'd been taught at school and church and from Mom. Dennis, who's never forgotten the times he helped Mrs. Ahearn, said, "Shoveling her driveway for free made me feel far better than shoveling the other driveways for which I got paid."

The lessons Mom taught about courtesy extended beyond snow shoveling. Whenever we rode on a subway in the city or a crowded Long Island Rail Road train, Mom would have us get up and offer our seat to an elderly person, a woman, especially a pregnant woman, or anyone standing who looked like they needed a seat more than we. We didn't mind. In fact, we liked seeing the smile that would come across the face of the newly seated person, and we liked being thanked. We also liked the reaction of the other passengers as they witnessed Mom training her children properly. As with the snow shoveling, after a few such trips, we didn't have to be reminded by Mom to be courteous toward elderly or needy passengers. We'd get up automatically, as we were expected to do. Once my attempt to give my seat to an elderly woman backfired. Noticing the standing woman, I stood up as usual, turned to get her attention, and said, "Excuse me, Ma'am. Would you like to sit down?" She looked at me oddly and answered, "Where? What seat?" That's when I saw that a selfish commuter had jumped into the seat I'd left empty, stealing it before the elderly woman even noticed it. I said to him, "Excuse me mister. I got up to give my seat to this woman." He didn't even look up. His rudeness and indifference bothered me, and it infuriated Mom who said, *"I can't believe you'd do such a think to this boy and this woman. What kind of man are you?"* With that, the man got up and the woman took the seat.

When Jeanne was a seven-year-old second grader at Bowling Green School, one of her close friends was a Chinese girl named Koon Fong Mae. Koon was a very nice girl, extremely polite, and the shiest, quietest little girl I ever met. She was a neighborhood girl, but didn't live in a house like most Levittowners. Instead, she and her family inhabited a room behind their laundry business at our local shopping center less than half a mile away. Koon would sometimes visit with Jeanne after school to play and do homework together. In winter, when it would get dark as early as 4:30 p.m., Mom wouldn't allow Koon to go home unescorted. She'd call, *"Peter, Dennis, one of you. Time to walk Koon home."* Sometimes in winter, when a deep freeze would follow a wet snow, the top of the snow would turn to ice, strong enough to hold up our weight. As I'd walk and slide along on the ice-covered snow I'd hear the sound of Koon's little footsteps, crunch, crunch, crunching one after the other. I'd try talking with her, but would get little response. Maybe a yes or a no to something I asked about, but not much more. Once I got her back to her family's store, I'd walk back home, alone in the cold and dark, but with the feeling of being supremely happy at having helped bashful, humble Koon. Inspired by Mom's sense of kindness and courtesy, and knowing that we were helping people like Koon, Mrs. Ahearn, or even total strangers on the train, we were able to experience the good feeling that a simple act of kindness can bring about. By the end of his first year at school, strongly influenced by his very dedicated teachers, the great educator Booker T. Washington said, "At school I got my first taste of what it meant to live a life of unselfishness, my first knowledge of the fact that the happiest individuals are those who do the most to make others useful and happy." Though I don't think Mom ever read Up From Slavery, she knew that fact quite well, well enough to teach and require it from all of us.

Sometimes the lessons taught by Mom left me a little confused. For example, as with all kids, we were taught not to take food or candy from strangers. Whenever we visited Aunt Katherine and Aunt Nellie in the city, we'd take the subway up to Washington Heights. The A was an express train, meaning that it didn't make every stop, it only stopped at the big stops like 42nd Street and 59th Street/Columbus Circle. Then it would fly at a high rate of speed all the way to 125th Street and St. Nicholas Avenue in Harlem, some 71 blocks, or 3.5 miles, in a matter of seconds. From 125th Street it would then make stops at 145th and 168th Streets. Most of the passengers getting off or on the train at those stops were black, often leaving us the only white people on the train. It was good to be exposed to the people of Harlem because such an experience was non-existent in the suburbs. On one uptown subway trip, I sat next to a middle-aged black woman who smiled nicely at me. As the train rumbled along, she opened her pocketbook and took out a package of Chicklets, then placed a piece in her mouth. In doing so, she made eye contact with me, reached back into her bag, took out another Chicklet, then extended her hand and offered it to me. I looked at her smiling face and accepted the small, square treat. I'm sure this woman had nothing but the kindest intentions as she did this, but I was confused. Not knowing immediately what to do, I held onto it for a few seconds, then looked at Mom, who was smiling. But I still didn't know what to do. On one hand, I was taught to be courteous and kind to others, especially to those who were kind to me, and to never hurt people's feelings. On the other hand, I was taught not to take candy from strangers. With little time to think, and being only a five year old, my choices were limited. I didn't want to break the cardinal rule of eating something that came from a total stranger on a New York City subway. In this brief moment of childhood panic, I handled the situation poorly. Wham! I threw the Chicklet onto the subway floor. The woman's smiling face turned to one of disappointment. Mom's happy look turned to one of shock and embarrassment. She apologized to the woman, then swiftly and publicly admonished me. "How could you do that? How could you be rude to this nice lady?" Why I did what I did I'll never know, especially when there were other choices available to me. I could have simply handed the Chicklet to Mom. Or I could have put it into my pocket. Instead, in one split second of uncertainty and thoughtlessness, I hurt the feelings of a perfectly nice woman, and disappointed and embarrassed Mom. I never meant to hurt anyone, but I had. I learned an important lesson that afternoon on the A train, more than 60 years ago, one that has stayed with me ever since. I learned to think things through more before acting. To this day, whenever I think of that kind lady, I become saddened by my act of childhood thoughtlessness. What must that kind lady have thought of me? What must she have thought of little white boys from the suburbs, or how they were raised? I've long wished that I could find that generous Harlem lady and apologize.

Booster Club Captain

With four small children, Mom somehow managed to serve her community in many ways. When we were cub scouts, she served as den mother, hosting a dozen active kids every week for meetings. When St. Ignatius School needed volunteer parents for playground duty or to serve as a substitute teacher, Mom stood ready. Without a car, she'd walk to Newbridge Road and take the bus to Hicksville, at her own expense, to work all day for free. She did that on and off for years whenever the principal asked. There was a *quid pro quo* of sorts. The principal, Mother Adelaide, accepted whatever sum Mom could afford each month instead of the regular tuition. A Catholic school education was not part of the welfare budget. While teaching first grade at Holy Family for 15 years, she volunteered to stay after school one, sometimes two days every week to teach confraternity classes to public school children. Holy Family, as with most churches, was always in need of funds. The parish had a monthly Booster Club, basically a raffle which cost $1 a ticket. There were several dozen Booster Club captains, each responsible for selling 50 raffle tickets a month. Mom was a proud and successful Booster Club captain. She dutifully walked the streets of our neighborhood selling all her tickets. There were a number of $50 winners each month, and the grand prize was $500. The captain who sold the winning ticket received a 10% prize. One time one of her boosters, a neighbor about ten houses away, won the top prize in the monthly drawing. When Mom found out that one of her boosters won and that she would be receiving a $50 bonus, she cried with happiness. She had the honor of walking the enormous sum of $500 up Twig Lane to the winning family, and the joy of receiving $50 herself as the seller of the winning ticket. To Mom, on her bare-bones welfare budget, that $50 was found money, manna from heaven, money that came to her with no strings attached, no forms to fill out, nothing to pay back. It was as if she won the grand prize herself.

Working with Special Education Students

In addition to her involvement with her church, Mom gave to the community in some very private and uncommon ways. In the early 1960's, I came home from school one day and saw that Mom wasn't there. She left a note saying she was down the block at the house of one of her first grade students. This was fifteen years before the term "special education" came

Mom with her class on a visit to Mexican Fiesta Day 1972.

152

into the lexicon. Children who were ADHD, slow readers, or who had any type of handicapping conditions or disabilities, no matter how slight or how severe, struggled, and their teachers had to work much harder to reach them. Those were the days when 50 children in a first grade class was not uncommon, making teaching special needs youngsters that much more difficult. Mom had a little girl in her class who tried very hard but who had difficulty keeping up with the class. I needed to ask Mom something, so I walked down to the girl's house and knocked on the door. The child's mother answered and brought me into the living room where I saw Mom and the little girl sitting at a table full of workbooks, pencils and papers. Mom was tutoring the young girl, trying to keep her up with the rest of the class. Later she explained, *"That child works so hard and struggles so much. My heart goes out to her. It seems no matter how hard she tries, the concepts just don't come to her. She needs extra help, so I offered to do what I could."* The school didn't require that Mom give this extra help, and neither the school nor the parents were able to pay her anything. Today, such one-on-one tutors charge $75 - $100 an hour. Mom did it for free, week after week, because the child needed help and Mom was a professional and a committed community servant.

Mom sought ways to improve her knowledge and skills by taking additional courses, some of which she paid to take, and none of which enhanced her skimpy salary. She was especially moved by the plight of children with special needs. In a letter dated February 26, 1969, Mom said to me,

> *I'm rushing off to an in-service course at the Burns Ave. School, Hicksville. It's called 'The Problem Child.' Much of the course is about perception, trying to define it. It is good for me as I am in with public school teachers and feel at home. The course also is an aid in understanding and helping slow developing children. More should be done for them.*

Mom with her first graders, December 1967.

Six years before the term "special education" was first spoken, before Congress passed Public Law 94-142 requiring that all children had to be educated in "the least restrictive environment," Mom was aware of such children and took steps on her own to be better prepared to provide for them. She was the first special education teacher I ever knew, years before Congress made it a national requirement.

The Veteran's Hospital

Mom's community service didn't always involve education or church work. In July 1968, when I was away at an eight week U.S. Army ROTC summer camp at Ft. Lewis, WA, Mom wrote to tell me that she decided to become a volunteer at the Veteran's Hospital in Northport, NY. Northport was approximately 20 miles northeast of Levittown, and she had never been there before. She became aware of the need for volunteers to work with elderly veterans, some of whom had psychiatric problems. In letter dated July 29, 1968 she wrote,

> *Dear Peter,*
>
> *Right now Sugar (her pet dog) and I are sitting out in the back yard under a tree and enjoying our leisure. I intend to relax all I can and still get the work done before school starts, but on Wednesday I volunteered to go to Northport Veterans Hospital and do what I can. I saw an article in the L.I. Catholic newspaper asking for volunteers. Everyone discouraged me but since I had already made plans to meet the director I went anyway. I got lost and took two hours to find the place but the drive was beautiful. The director said he could use me. I went again on Friday and stayed about two hours playing checkers with a patient named Charlie. We played three games when he had to go and take his shower. I went out on the porch and visited with the other old men – age 70 to 80. Most of the older ones are W.W. I veterans. This is a mental part of the hospital. I was a bit frightened but it wasn't so bad so I am going every Wednesday, which is visiting day, and try to let them see a new face. I asked Dennis to come along as they have a large pool table and they need people to play with them. Pool, cards, or any such game. Maybe you could go too when you get back. When I was on the porch I looked out. It didn't look very beautiful. The men don't look their age because of the wonderful care they are getting. I keep thinking of Aunt Nellie when I see these men.*
> *Love,*
>
>
> *Mom*

Mom was very familiar with the suffering people with mental illness must endure. Ten years earlier, in the late 1950's, her adopted mother, Aunt Nellie, had to be confined to a state mental facility in Rockland County. Aunt Nellie developed a severe form of cognitive impairment. Mom was horrified at the way Aunt Nellie had to spend her last years, however neither she nor Aunt Katherine could keep her at home safely.

While Mom gave freely of her time and talent, I found her act of volunteerism at the V.A. Hospital particularly interesting. She was not driven by politics. She wasn't providing service at a government-run Veterans Hospital for elderly W.W. I vets because she was "for" or "against" a particular position, but rather because these elderly, sick men were in need of company and, as she said, seeing "a new face." In reading her 1968 letter, I found it a pleasant coincidence that she had made her way to Northport of all places. Little did she or I know then that six years later, I'd become a teacher at Northport High School for the next 32 years, only minutes from the sprawling Veterans Hospital that she had such trouble finding, and that I'd work with the veterans myself for years as a lifeguard and volunteer. Moreover, her letter calls attention to another important part of Mom's character. Despite being discouraged by friends and others, long before GPS and google maps were invented, Mom willingly traveled alone to a town she'd never been to, with no training in caring for psychiatric, geriatric patients, and served as a volunteer, because, as with everything else she did in life, it was the right thing to do. She embraced what others were afraid to even consider.

Politics

Mom held certain beliefs dear. In addition to the Ten Commandments and basic Christian tenets, she believed in American principles like justice, fairness, the rule of law, and the freedoms found in the Bill of Rights. But she was not a political zealot. She voted regularly, but her vote was private. She never pontificated or tried to sell others on her viewpoints. Mindful of the plight of others, wherever they were located, Mom embraced those from other countries and cultures. Whenever we visited Washington Heights, she took us to the chapel and shrine of Mother Cabrini, the patron saint of immigrants, located on 190th Street and Fort Washington Avenue. Mother Cabrini was a late Nineteenth Century Italian immigrant who became a U.S. citizen and devoted her life to serving others, mostly poor immigrants. Mom was greatly inspired by Mother Cabrini, the first American canonized saint. She also loved the Maryknoll Fathers and Sisters, who had missions all over the world, and supported them and similar organizations whenever she could. She loved it when missionary priests came to Holy Family to tell of their work with the worldwide poor.

Mom was born in 1917, three years before the 19th Amendment to the Constitution of the United States established the right to vote for women, and 50 years before the ratification of the 25th Amendment which extended the right to vote to citizens 18 years of age or older. She cast her first vote at the age of 21 in 1938, during the second term of President Franklin D. Roosevelt, right in the middle of the Great Depression. As with an overwhelming majority in the nation, she favored Roosevelt's New Deal and the many programs he established to bring relief to millions of suffering Americans. However, like many Americans, as Roosevelt ran for unprecedented third and fourth terms in office, she began to think less of him and believed two terms were enough. Evidently the American people, the Congress and three fourths of the state legislatures agreed because the Constitution was amended in 1951 for the 22nd time stating: "No person shall be elected to the office of the President more than twice…." Upon Roosevelt's death in April 1945, early in his fourth term, Vice President Harry S Truman succeeded him. Mom believed Truman was brave, bold and bright, however she didn't like his style. She thought he had a bratty, sometimes vulgar demeanor. She believed those who serve at the highest level should meet the highest standard, and as successful as Truman was as president, she favored a more courteous and likeable leader. In 1952 she, like millions of Americans in the post-war period, liked Ike, General Dwight D. Eisenhower. Ike won two terms, serving throughout most of the 1950's. When I was a boy, television was brand new. I remember how Mom, Aunt Katherine and Aunt Nellie howled when former president Truman's daughter Margaret played piano and sang on television programs like Ed Sullivan's "Toast of the Town." They'd laugh and Aunt Katherine would say, "Who said she could sing?" In 1960, after Mom had more or less shifted from being a Roosevelt Democrat to an Eisenhower Republican, Massachusetts Senator John F. Kennedy, a Catholic, ran against Vice President Richard Nixon. Mom, a political moderate in most respects, didn't vote on religious or strict party lines, but for the candidate she thought would be best for the job. That year Mom voted for the more experienced Nixon and not the Catholic newcomer, John F. Kennedy. I was in the eighth grade at St. Ignatius at the time and our class held a mock election. As with the nation, our class was split 50% for JFK and 50% for Richard Nixon. Not too politically aware myself, and knowing Mom favored President Eisenhower, I lined up with the Nixon- Lodge ticket. When JFK-LBJ surprisingly won by the slightest of margins, I was upset. Mom quickly admonished me, *"Peter, President Kennedy is our leader now. You may have wanted the others to win, but our job is to get behind the new president. He'll need all the help he can get."* I sensed that she wasn't really abandoning her candidate as much as she was being open-minded, a good citizen first and a member of a political party second.

The Issues

Mom's views on the issues facing society were mostly traditional, yet she was capable of adapting with the times. She took a liberal view and stood for fundamental fairness when it came to issues of civil rights and racial relations. The sight of little black children in Little Rock, Arkansas having to be walked to school by federal troops, innocent people in Alabama being beaten, hosed down the street and attacked by police dogs for demonstrating or marching to integrate restaurants, theaters and even libraries appalled her. The sight of segregationist governors in Mississippi, Alabama, Arkansas and other states blocking the doorway to colleges so black students couldn't enter, disgusted her. She considered those governors to be awful role models. Mom rarely followed the crowd and was not terribly concerned with what her neighbors or others thought, or how they'd view her if she disagreed with them. She listened to the facts and made the most well-reasoned decisions she could on matters that concerned her and society. In 1973, the Supreme Court of the United States, in the landmark case of Roe v. Wade, made first and some second trimester abortions legal. Most Long Island Catholics were anti-abortion. Mom was too. However, she didn't join the church-sponsored anti-abortion groups on their protest trips to Washington D.C. or place "Abortion is Murder" bumper stickers on her car. She was aware that there were individual and privacy issues surrounding a woman's right to choose and that there was often more than one solution to a problem. She studied contemporary issues quite carefully, often reading about the questions facing society and listening to informational and thought-provoking TV shows like David Susskind and Edward R. Murrow. She and I didn't always agree, but we frequently discussed the issues of the day. From our chats, I could tell that she tried hard to balance her own knowledge and feelings with the church's positions on controversial matters to come out with a view that she could accept. Aware that not all things are black and white, she often sought middle ground and allowed for compromise. She based several major decisions in her life, not solely on church leaders telling her how to think, but on her own personal knowledge and judgment. Her views on controversial issues were hers, arrived at independently, and not the views imposed on her by others. When she disagreed with me, which she frequently did, she always spoke her mind and was sure to back her position with a well-reasoned knowledge of the facts. Mom was neither an advocate of the Vietnam War, nor an opponent. She trusted and supported our leaders, not unquestioningly or blindly, but enough to believe that at the very least they were trying to act in the nation's and world's best interest. Gay rights was not the major issue then that it has become today, yet she did treat all people, regardless of their color, creed, nationality and sexual orientation, respectfully and as equals. If she were alive today, she might have family members or close friends who are gay and lesbian. I believe her relationship with them would be based on her personal knowledge of them and their character, not on what others said or expected. In other words, Mom was open-minded enough to think for herself. We never heard her speak badly about anyone based on race, religion or national origin and she wouldn't accept anything but fairness and acceptance from us. Aunt Katherine, who was born in 1890 of Irish immigrant parents, was more or less "old school" when it came to certain issues. On a few occasions she used the word "colored" to describe black people, a taboo in our house. When Aunt Katherine moved in with us in the spring of 1961, Mom immediately brought such talk to a standstill the first time she used the word colored saying, *"We don't talk like that in this house."* I'm confident that Mom, whose own mother didn't live long enough to enjoy the right to vote because of her gender, who believed in standing up for the underdog in society, who despised seeing people denied a cup of coffee at a coffee counter because of the color of their skin, would be pleased with the progress we've made as a nation in many areas of social justice.

The Flag

Holidays were more than just days off from school for us. Whether it was Abraham Lincoln's or George Washington's Birthday, Memorial Day, or Veteran's Day, Mom made sure we understood why we were off from school. On those holidays, first thing in the morning Mom would get out our aging, faded 48-star U.S. flag and lead us in a respectful, family flag-raising ceremony. This ritual began by one of us, usually Robert, erecting our tall wooden flagpole into the cement-anchored pipe Mom had dug into the middle of the front lawn. This may sound easy, but most often we'd have to find the pipe in the lawn first. Grass would grow over it so the first few minutes were always spent on hands and knees, poking fingers into the lawn to locate the pipe. Once one of us found the elusive narrow tube, Robert would thrust the pole in and foul-smelling brown water would shoot out, the accumulation of weeks of stagnant rainwater. With the flagpole in and the water out, Robert would then unfurl the flag in the dignified manner he'd learned in Boy Scouts, fasten it to the ropes that swung from the pole, then slowly hoist it upward. As he did this, we, including Mom, would stand at attention with our hand placed over our heart. When the flag reached the top, Dennis and I, wearing our Cub

Scout uniforms, would snap a salute. While this flag-raising ceremony was fun, Mom required it to be formal and solemn. No giggling or talking was allowed. Old-fashioned, maybe even corny to some onlookers, this ceremony was Mom's way of teaching us to respect not only the flag and our country's values, but also the person or event we were celebrating.

Moon Landing

On July 16, 1969, astronaut Neil Armstrong Jr. and his crew took off for the moon. A mission like that sounds routine, almost commonplace now, nearly five decades later, but back then, it was a monumental event. Only 12 years earlier, in 1957, commercial jets first flew passengers across the country in five hours, and the Soviet Union launched the first unmanned satellite, Sputnik into orbit. The very thought of a human walking on the moon was beyond belief. With all the media hype, Mom and I were excited to know we'd not only be seeing this historic event, we'd be seeing it in color. Prior to 1969, we didn't have a color TV, only the little 12-inch black and white Admiral TV that came with the house in 1950. But by the night of the moon landing we had a color TV. Just before he joined the Marines in January 1969, Dennis rented one because he wanted to watch a lot of shows and movies before he went away. Mom kept this rental for the next few months, even though it was expensive. On the night of July 20, 1969, with Dennis away at U.S. Marine radio school in California, Mom and I sat in the back left room of our Levitt house, which Dennis had converted into a den just a few months before, riveted to the TV. As the spacecraft descended to the moon's surface and touched down, we clapped at Armstrong's words, "The Eagle has landed." Moments later, as he exited the capsule and took that historic first step saying, "One small step for man, one giant leap for mankind," tears welled up in Mom's eyes. Along with the rest of the world, she was watching history being made once again and she knew it. Something else struck Mom and me as we watched in disbelief. She said it reminded her of the day 42 years earlier when Charles A. Lindbergh made his solo flight across the Atlantic Ocean in his small single-engine plane, "The Spirit of St Louis." Mom attended the city's 1927 ticker tape parade as Lindbergh rode up the "canyon of heroes." There was something else that struck us. There were so many changes taking place in technology at the time that it was hard to keep up with them. So many things awed us then, and this moon landing was the pinnacle of them all. It was new for us to be watching color TV, together, in our own home. Live and in color, we watched a humble man from Wapakoneta, Ohio land space equipment developed by Grumman Corporation, in Bethpage, NY, right next to Levittown, safely on the moon and, for the first time in human history, walk on its surface. We listened to the astronauts' words as they spoke to a worldwide audience, picked up moon rocks, hit a golf ball with a six iron, and planted the American flag. And while all this was happening live and in color, in the upper right hand corner of this color TV screen we saw President Richard Nixon speaking from the White House with Neil Armstrong as he walked about the moon. That three-way communication from the White House to the moon to our den, seemed so impossible to believe, and yet it happened right before our eyes, and it captivated Mom and made her happy and proud.

MILITARY SERVICE

The Military

Robert, Dennis and I all came of age during the 1960's, as the Vietnam War was escalating. All three of us served in the military. Robert was first. After graduating from college in 1966, he joined the Hawaii National Guard, did his basic training at Fort Ord in the Monterey Bay area of California, and the required six months active duty in Hawaii. After he got married in July 1967, as result of the U.S. escalation in Vietnam, the Hawaii National Guard was called into active duty. So even though Robert had fulfilled his military obligation, it began anew with this added two-year Army hitch. Because he could type and had a college degree in business, he was made a company clerk and served at Schofield Barracks, in the middle of the island of Oahu. During this assignment he was promoted several times and became Sergeant Robert J. White. Half the Hawaii guardsmen were sent to Vietnam. Fortunately for Robert, Mom and all of us, he was part of the half that remained at Schofield.

I was second to serve. While I was at the University of Dayton, I was required to take the Reserve Officer Training Program, otherwise known as ROTC. Every physically able male had to take this training at all land grant colleges, meaning colleges like the University of Dayton that received land from the federal government. The first two years were called the basic course, and all but those with physical disabilities were made to participate. The final two years, called the advanced course, were voluntary. I chose to enter the advanced course because there was a stipend of $80 a month, and every dollar counted. I also figured I would probably wind up in the service anyway, so why not learn some leadership skills along the way and serve as an officer. By the late 1960's I found myself increasingly opposed to the U.S. involvement in Vietnam and yet I was contractually bound to fulfill my military obligation. I received my commission as a second lieutenant in April 1970 and was assigned to the infantry branch. In spring of 1971, I was ordered to the U.S. Army Infantry School at Ft. Benning, GA for four months of BOIC, the basic officer infantry course. Upon my graduation from the Infantry School, as a brand new second lieutenant I was told I had a 90% chance of being an infantry platoon leader in Vietnam, commanding 40 men. This was difficult news for me because I was 23 years old, married, had finished college, read a great deal, and worked for two years including one as a teacher in inner-city Brooklyn. Philosophically I was conflicted about the mission of the infantry: to close with and capture or destroy the enemy. By that time in my life, I believed that there were other solutions to the problems of human existence besides war, in particular the Vietnam War. In the late spring of 1971 I drove from New York to Ft. Benning, reported to the Infantry School and was assigned to something called The Student Brigade, or TSB. My entire battalion was composed of young lieutenants and captains, some of whom had served several years in Vietnam as helicopter and fixed wing pilots. They attended the infantry school to prevent being released from the Army. With the war beginning to wind down and the new policy of Vietnamization, whereby the war was increasingly being fought by South Vietnamese soldiers and less by American soldiers, the Army needed fewer pilots. These men needed to qualify in another branch in order to stay in. The Army was their livelihood, their job.

This new policy of Vietnamization didn't work favorably for them, but it did for me. With the Army needing fewer young officers, upon completing the BOIC program, I was offered a choice: serve six months active duty with an overall reserve commitment of eight years, or serve two years active duty, undoubtedly go to Vietnam, then have an overall reserve obligation of six years. I chose the six-month active duty option, then spent the next eight years as a teacher serving part-time in the Army reserves, attending some training weekends and a few two-week summer stints at Camp Drum in Watertown, NY. When I graduated from the Infantry School in the late summer of 1971, I flew Mom down to Ft. Benning, GA to be on hand. She was very proud of me, even though I hadn't done much soldiering except for going to school and serving a few months as the assistant executive officer of a training company. In 1978 my honorable discharge listed me as Captain Peter C. White. This seemed bizarre to me because when I was on active duty I was a second lieutenant, not a captain. I was promoted to that rank on paper. By the time I began active duty in 1971, the Pentagon Papers had been published, the world had learned of the My Lai massacre, and more than 70% of the U.S. population was opposed to the war. Dissent had become consent. Peace talks between the U.S. and North Vietnam were underway in Paris and it was just a matter of time before the U.S. would be getting out of Vietnam.

Dennis was last to serve, in a way. I say "in a way" because while I was in the Army reserves before Dennis joined the Marines, he began active duty before I did. It was just the way things worked out with college and the needs of the military. In January 1969, when I was a senior in college, I received a letter from Mom with the usual hometown and family news. I also noticed a second letter in the envelope. It was from Dennis. At the end of her letter Mom said, *"That's it from me. Dennis has a lot to tell you, Love Mom."* In his letter Dennis went on to say,

Pete,

Well I finally completed high school and have also made some important decisions. The most important decision was that of my military obligation. I told you I went to see the Army recruiter. Well I did and he gave be a big line of bull about Army OCS (Officers Candidates School). So, what I did was to do what I feel is the right thing. I enlisted in the United States Marine Corps for two years. I guess you could say, "I'm doing my own thing." I sincerely felt I made the right decision. So do me the favor of not condemning me but rather respect me for doing what I think is right. I will be leaving in the middle of March.
I hope that everything is ok with you and no one is protesting your protests (joke). I hope the Dakota Street Center is doing well. It should be with my brother as coordinator. Say hello to all the kids, black and white. P.S. I will see you before I leave.

In Friendship,

Dennis

Dennis' mention of no one "protesting my protests" refers to the fact that by 1968, I had become increasingly opposed to the Vietnam War, including participation in a peace vigil on the campus of the University of Hawaii.

Dennis joined the Marines because he felt it was a good place for him to begin his adult life. He also felt it would make Mom proud of him. He had no plans of going from high school right into college as Robert and I had done, so this was his way of showing Mom he was serving his country and entering adulthood. She saw it differently. She was aware that the two previous years, 1967-1968, were the busiest and bloodiest of our involvement in Vietnam, and that the war dragged on and on, never seeming to have an end in sight. She was certain he'd be sent to Vietnam. So while Mom was very proud of Dennis for many reasons, she became extremely worried.

Once Dennis finished the last of his high school requirements, he went into the USMC, as had several neighborhood and school friends. Our Twig Land pal Les Joy served in the Marines for four years, including a one-year tour in the most busy and deadly combat zones in Vietnam during 1967 and 1968, Con Thien and Khe Sahn. Dennis' high school friend Al Anderson served two tours in Vietnam. Dennis became part of a growing fraternity of young men from the area who were doing what they believed their country was asking of them. He played football and lacrosse at Clarke High School, so he felt he was in good enough physical shape to fulfill the requirements of boot camp at Parris Island, SC. When he arrived there, bulked up from high school football and weighing 200 pounds, he learned that the Marines had different plans for him. He was given a very rigorous training schedule and placed on a strict diet of healthy food and no snacks. He said the training staff referred to it as a "fat body diet." When he finished boot camp in the summer of 1969, Dennis was a trim, muscular 180 pounds and had made a number of good friends, some of whom he corresponds with to this day. The training was difficult, and the spring and early summer months at Parris Island were unpleasantly hot, muggy and buggy. Dennis was not a complainer, but, like Mom, he believed in standing up for himself and others when and if necessary. Basic training can be a form of harassment at times, testing soldiers to see how they'll behave when things get tough, or circumstances don't go their way. Once a member of the training cadre ordered Dennis to assist in a certain task, which he did. By doing so, he arrived a few seconds late for a formation called by his drill instructor. The DI singled him out to his platoon as a late marine, "part of the 10% that's going to get you killed in Vietnam." Dennis, a hard working trainee, was embarrassed at being singled out, and upset at the characterization that he could be responsible for harm to others because of his lateness, when in fact he was ordered to help with another task. Marines are taught not to talk back, however they are also taught to be honest. Dennis spoke out to his DI and platoon members, "Permission to speak?" The DI allowed him to, and he said, "The private wasn't late on his own, sir. The private was ordered to help another marine." The DI was impressed with Dennis' willingness to stand up for himself and to be truthful, and allowed him back into the formation with no punishment or further embarrassment.

I wrote Dennis a few times during boot camp and suggested that he work hard in order to create options for himself. He followed this advice and did quite well at Parris Island and on various placement tests. As result, he qualified for U.S.M.C. radio school in San Diego, CA, where he excelled in a program that lasted several months. Shortly thereafter, he was ordered to Vietnam. Through the miracle of videotape, Mom had seen her fill of death and injury on the nightly news. Dennis spent most of his one-year tour, between late 1969 and late 1970, in Da Nang, a large US base. From there, his unit would go out by helicopter several times a week, be dropped off at various landing zones, conduct their operations, then return to Da Nang by helicopter. In the spring of 1970, these operations, which sometimes lasted only a day or two and other times 30 days or more, took him into Laos and the Queson Mountains of Cambodia. Of the one week he served at a location called Hill 165 Dennis said, "Even though it was only one week, I really didn't like it there. Lots of shells went off. It was a pretty dangerous place." When time permitted, he sometimes visited orphanages, playing with the children and giving them snacks. He often brought other marines along with him on these visits. Most marines carried 40 pounds of equipment with them. With his normal pack and heavy radio gear, Dennis carried 77 pounds. He did whatever his superiors required of him, including volunteering for various patrols, even though that was not his primary specialty. During this period, I had finished college and moved back home. While Vietnam was a dangerous, hot, far-away place for Dennis to be, it was not easy to live with Mom during that time. Every night we'd watch the news together. When vivid images of an ambulance or stretcher appeared on the news, Mom would leap from her seat, run to the TV screen, point and say, *"That's him. Doesn't that look like him? Oh my God! What if that's him?"* I'd try to calm her down and reduce her worry, reminding her that if anything happened to Dennis she'd be notified officially. "Mom, those newsreels could be weeks old. They could be from areas hundreds of miles away from where Dennis is. Stop worrying." But she worried every minute, and grew more and more puzzled by the increasingly unpopular war. She spoke with several mothers in the neighborhood whose sons also served. One, Jimmy, was a year older than Dennis, and was drafted into the U.S. Army. He had a nervous condition that caused his hands to shake. When he couldn't hold a rifle steady enough in basic training to pass the marksmanship requirements, the Army gave him sedatives to calm him down, making sure he passed. His mom thought her son would be in danger if he were sent to Vietnam and given a combat infantry assignment. She became an outspoken critic of the war. Jimmy went anyway. Several months later, after having been hit by shrapnel in the ear and shot through the hand, Jimmy was sent home.

Not all of Dennis' service involved combat communications. In April 1970, while serving in Di La Pass, a little humor found its way into things. While on patrol, he and his fellow marines had rocks thrown at them by small ape-like animals they dubbed "rock apes." I wrote him, "What do you do when they throw rocks at you?" Dennis answered, "We pick up the rocks and throw them back." Sounds funny, a rock fight between U.S. Marines and a bunch of monkeys, but Mom didn't think so. She became especially upset when an a senior officer asked Dennis to build a box-like trap to catch one of the apes. She had read how some American casualties resulted from soldiers sometimes doing unnecessary things. The last thing she wanted was to see Dennis injured doing something he didn't have to do.

Even though Neil Armstrong, Jr. had walked on the moon in July 1969, the technology for soldiers trying to speak with family members back home was quite primitive. Letter writing was the chief form of communication. Today soldiers in Iraq and Afghanistan can email, text and even Skype with family members back home. Nothing like that existed for those serving overseas back then. In order to hear Dennis' voice and have direct communication, Mom purchased two little tape recorders and sent one to Dennis. Every few weeks, Mom, Jeanne and I would gather to say something to Dennis on tape, then mail it to him half way around the world. Dennis could listen to our taped messages, then record his voice onto the tape and mail it back to us in Levittown. These were inexpensive, low quality devices that didn't always work. But when they did, Mom was ecstatic. Hearing Dennis' voice, which sometimes showed his sense of humor, was very uplifting for her and helped make his year overseas go by far more quickly. When he made a joke on one of his messages, we knew it was the same old Dennis and that he was ok. Mom's tapes were not impromptu or ad-libbed. She carefully prepared each one, writing out her messages, reading them aloud for practice, then speaking her words very deliberately into the recorder, slowly, enunciating every syllable. *"Hel...lo Den-nis, ... This...is...Mom."* Jeanne and I couldn't help but laugh. Mom would hush us up and go on. Having an unbroken communication with Dennis was serious and important business to her.

When he was nearing completion of his ninth month in Vietnam, Dennis was happy to learn that he might be sent home three months early. Sadly he missed the cut-off by a few days so he had to serve the whole 12 months as ordered. On the other hand, he was told that since he'd be completing his full tour, he'd be released from active duty upon his return to San Diego. This meant he'd be discharged from the Marines six months early. Mom found little comfort in that. She wanted him home and safe. Dennis finished his full tour and when he arrived back in San Diego, he was disappointed to learn of another surprise from the Marines: the early discharge he was promised was reversed. He'd get a few weeks leave, then report to Camp Lejeune in Jacksonville, NC for six more months. This was upsetting to him and all of us, especially since the six months was really unnecessary. He was trained, he served, and he was finished his tour. Instead of being released early as promised, he was ordered to participate in "project transition," a Marine Corps program designed to help returning veterans with training to prepare them for civilian life. Dennis was a mover and shaker who had his own transition plans, and he saw the additional six months at Camp Lejeune as a waste of time. But he was a good marine and reported to Camp Lejeune as ordered. Upon his arrival he was confronted with yet another complication: the Marines determined that while he was overseas he was overpaid and as result they'd be withholding a substantial part of his pay. This didn't provide him with sufficient income to pay for the off-post trailer he rented, so he got an after-hours job at a local bar called the Dixieland Club in downtown Jacksonville, NC. By day, he installed moldings around doors and did other jobs as part of project transition. By night, as with Robert at the Two Jacks Bar in Honolulu eight years earlier, he learned the bar business. Eventually this nighttime job contained a silver lining and became his real project transition. Upon his final discharge he began working as a bartender and waiter at a tavern in Westbury NY called Gatsby's Pub. Within a few years Dennis became manager, and ultimately the owner of Gatsby's.

Today Dennis considers himself a proud veteran and looks back on his service as an important and worthwhile part of his youth. However, when he was winding up his two years of active duty, he didn't see things exactly that way. At Camp Lejeune, he resented the attitude of some brand new but higher-ranking marines ordering him around. He resented the Marines' bungling of his pay. And he saw the requirement that he participate in project transition as bothersome and unproductive. While in San Diego, he got a small tattoo on his forearm that read "U.S.M.C." When he got out of the service, he had it removed the old fashioned way, by having his forearm painfully scraped until all the ink was gone. Most importantly to Mom and all of us, Dennis came home safe, uninjured and free to go about living his life. That made Mom happiest of all.

Robert served in the military the longest, two and a half years, mostly at Fort Ord, CA and Schofield Barracks, HI. I served the shortest, only six months at Ft. Lewis, WA and Ft. Benning, GA. Dennis served for two years and was the only one deployed to a combat zone. The 1960's were very trying times for us. But for Mom, with all three of her sons serving throughout much of that decade, they were the most trying times all.

"A Sister Prays"

As a teacher from 1960 – 1975, Mom's career spanned the entirety of the Vietnam War. While she was patriotic and supported our troops and our country's leaders, regardless of political party, she was concerned about the potential of someday seeing her six-year-old first graders serving on a battlefield. In a small metal box, where Mom kept some of her most personal things, I found a poem written in the early 1940's by an anonymous Catholic nun and printed in a New York City newspaper during WW II. Perhaps as a teacher of young children, and because she could relate so directly to the words written on this yellowed paper, Mom preserved this poem over the many years. Entitled "A Sister Prays," it reads:

> I taught him Lord, in the parish school, something of You and the Golden Rule;
> It's not long since that my work was done – Yet now he is dead ere his youth is run.
>
> It seems dear Lord, so pitifully weak, this teaching a boy how to write, how to speak,
> And things he needs for a life full of years – today he is dead and there's room for tears.
> I tried to help in building his mind, in making him gentle, loving, and kind,
> Yet giving him strength which he lacked before – but they shot him down in a game called war.
>
> I doubt if he thought of the recess yard, as he lay with his face in the enemy sod,
> Or our Christmas party, our Halloween mirth, as his young blood crimsoned the earth.

For the papers an item, for his mother a star,
And little much else with the way things are –
Yet there must be more that a teacher can do
For a bright-eyed lad whom she taught of You,

These others, dear Lord – young, hopeful and shy –
I must teach these, too, how to live, how to die.

Give me, then, grace and strength for my part,
As I teach them of You – and the love in Your Heart.

THE WELFARE YEARS

Welfare

Welfare. The very word ought to conjure up a positive feeling, since it comes from the word "well." Welfare means prosperity, happiness and success. The Preamble to the Constitution of the United States, the "supreme Law of the Land," states as one of the six reasons for our nation even existing, "to promote the general welfare." Yet today, perhaps because welfare often refers to government aid in the form of money or

Dennis, 2, Jeanne, 2 months, Robert, 8, Peter, 4,
Christmas 1951.

necessities for poor people, the word conjures up a negative feeling to many. Sometimes welfare recipients are referred to as "cheats," or are not welcomed into many neighborhoods. Not long ago a neighbor of mine, upset that a nearby house was about to be rented to a family on public assistance, said to me, "If we let one in, the whole pack's coming." Fortunately for our family, in 1952 when Mom was without any resources at all, we lived in New York, an enlightened state when it comes to providing for the needy. During the New Deal of the 1930's, the federal government, along with many state and local governments, enacted laws requiring that needy people have at least some means by which to live. In New York, the Department of Social Services (DSS), or more commonly, welfare, administers those means. It is designed for people who fall between the cracks, people who may have exhausted all other remedies, people without sufficient family support systems, people who are mentally ill, or parents caring for young dependent children, or disabled, or otherwise unemployable persons. The majority of the recipients of welfare are parents, mostly women, and their dependent children. In January 1952, Mom was such a person, a single parent completely willing to work, but who could not because there were four young children in her care, ages two months to eight years. Although her husband Robert A. White was ordered to pay $35 a week as child support, none came, so Mom was without any source of income.

Though Mom tried to get Robert A. White to pay child support, he repeatedly failed to appear for Nassau County Family Court appointments. A Family Court judge advised her to apply to the DSS for some relief. With no other option available to her, she did so, reluctantly and only out of absolute necessity. Only 14 years earlier, prior to the existence of the DSS, there would have been no governmental opportunities for assistance. But in 1938, the New York legislature re-wrote the state constitution to include Article XVII, which states, "The aid, care and support of the needy are public concerns and shall be provided by the State...." This was basically a New Deal-minded inclusion into our state's highest law, and it was designed to make sure New York residents, especially those out of work or in situations like Mom's, didn't die in the streets. Some countries have death carts that patrol their streets each morning to pick up the dead. Fortunately New York adopted a more modern, enlightened approach that provided at least some means to avoid such disaster. Article XVII is one of the reasons we have a number of social welfare programs in New York, including Aid to Families with Dependent Children, which we received, food stamps, which we didn't receive because they didn't exist until 1964, and other government help for shelter and food. When Article XVII was being debated in the New York legislature in 1938, its sponsor stated,

Here are words which set forth a definite policy of government, a concrete social obligation which no court may ever misread. By this section the committee hopes to achieve two purposes: First: to remove from the area of constitutional doubt the responsibility of the State to those who must look to society for the bare necessities of life; and secondly, to set down explicitly in our basic law a much needed definition of the relationship of the people to their government.

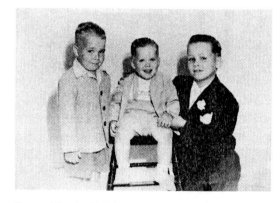

Peter and Dennis with Robert on his First Communion, May 1951.

If we were all 14 years older, prior to the existence of DSS, Mom, a very private person, would have been at the mercy of church groups or other philanthropies, in other words, the proverbial poorhouse. Instead, she was able to feed us and keep the roof of 55 Twig Lane over our heads by applying for and accepting AFDC – Aid to Families with Dependent Children.

No Profiting

This welfare assistance was important but not quite a grant. Mom purchased 55 Twig

Lane with Robert A. White in September 1950 for the sum of $8000. They made a minimal down payment and financed the rest through the Bowery Savings Bank. After one and a half years, when Mom made her application for assistance from DSS, there was very little equity in the house, only a few hundred dollars. Nevertheless, since Mom's name was on the deed, DSS placed a lien on the property and she had to turn the deed over to the county. That was a condition that all owners of real property, no matter how much or how little they owned, had to accept in order to receive DSS assistance. In effect, Mom would be receiving a loan, not a grant or a gift, and she could never sell the house without the DSS being paid back in full from the proceeds of the sale for any and all aid she'd receive throughout the period she accepted benefits. So while the common thinking may be that welfare is a gift, something government freely hands out to people, that is not the case for anyone whose name is on the title to real property, or who owns, or may potentially own anything of value. The rationale for this is logical. Welfare is supposed to be for emergencies and was designed to be temporary in nature. People are not supposed to profit from it by using public money to pay off a mortgage. Mom received payments of about $150 a month during the beginning years in the early 1950's, and between $180- $200 toward the late 1950's. Of that meager sum, she'd have to spend $90 a month, or about half of her check to pay the mortgage. On a 30-year mortgage, each month she was on welfare, she'd essentially be buying 1/360th of her house, using government money to do so. This was not allowed, hence the lien on the property.

A Visit to DSS

In 1971, after ten years of teaching and being off welfare, making mortgage payments by herself from her own salary, Mom became concerned that Robert A. White's name remained on the deed to the house. She thought this was unfair since he made none of the mortgage payments and failed to make any child support payments over the years. She grew troubled thinking that, in the event something happened to her, he could take the house. I made an appointment for Mom and me to meet with a lawyer from the Nassau County Attorney's office to see what he could do about Robert A. White's name still being on the deed. The county attorney was very knowledgeable and polite, and tried to be helpful. We explained Mom's plight, that she'd lived in the house for 20 years and that although welfare benefits paid the mortgage for nine of those years, she paid for the last 11 years herself from her wages. Robert A. White had made no payments, yet his name was still on the deed. We also explained how, over the course of those nine years she received only $19000 in benefits and half of that sum, about $9500, went toward paying the mortgage. The other half went toward food, clothing, heating oil, doctors and other necessities. We emphasized that there were never any extravagances, no car, no vacations, no restaurants, only the basics. We questioned why, if only half the modest welfare payments went to the mortgage, and the rest for necessities, she had to pay back the entire sum in order to satisfy the lien and get her deed back. Why couldn't she just pay back that portion which went toward the mortgage? The county attorney understood that only a portion of Mom's welfare benefit went toward the mortgage, but said his hands were tied. He explained that if it were not for the government's assistance, our family wouldn't have been able to stay in the house at all, that the house was worth

$8000 in 1952 and by 1970 it was worth more than $20000, and that a recipient couldn't realize a profit resulting from accepting government benefits. He also explained that the county had no means available to find Robert A. White or to require him to take his name off the deed. That would have to be done privately, by us. So we left the attorney's office with an explanation, but no solutions. The county still had a lien on 55 Twig Lane, and Robert A. White's name remained on the deed... for a while longer.

No Sale

Mom knew that she was lucky to have a nice, safe house to live in and raise her four children. But she also knew that, unless something changed for her financially, she could never sell it. The sale of 55 Twig Lane would have been foolish and imprudent and cause her to lose any equity she had in it, so she felt more or less chained to the house. If she sold the house for the market price just before her death, she would have gotten about $22000. By law DSS would have taken between $18000 and $19000 of that, leaving her with very little. So long as she stayed in the house, she had a place to live, but not the equity that other homeowners built up after years of making their mortgage payments. Mom was 57 years old at the time of her death, and, while she was still a vital woman and successful teacher at that time, she did have concern for her future and took steps to secure it. She had no retirement accounts, no 401k plan, no pension to rely on or savings to fall back on. All she had was a little equity in the house, maybe $2000 - $3000 after DSS recaptured it's money, and some shares of AT&T stock that Aunt Katherine had left her. She also had some debt. In 1974, shortly before her death, Mom looked forward and took a big risk. She borrowed a substantial amount of money to have the upstairs of 55 Twig Lane dormered and made into a small apartment. She did this to produce some rental income and give her a modicum of financial security. In the months before her death, she rented the upstairs to a very nice couple for $200 a month, the going-rate back then. This sum was nice for her to receive while she still worked at Holy Family School, however she was well aware that this $200 rental income would not take the place of her salary when she could no longer work. She thought about her old age and recognized that her options were limited. She had no idea in the early 1970's that only a few years later the Long Island housing market would experience significant inflation. Within a year of her death, the price of a typical Levitt house soared from $20000 to $50000, then a year later to $80000, and a few short years later well into the six figure range, topping out in the early 2000's at $350000-$400000. Had she reached old age, she'd easily have been able to sell, settle with DSS, and have ample resources left for her retirement needs. She also could have relied on us, Robert, Dennis, Jeanne and me, for help. But in the early 1970's such considerations were years away. She knew she would have to stay at 55 Twig, with the county-imposed lien hanging over it, because it would be far too costly for her to sell. Ultimately, Mom stayed at 55 Twig Lane for two reasons. She had made it into a lovely home for herself and she was happy there. She also stayed because she had to.

Sheetrock and Steak from the Blender

While this economic uncertainty and welfare obligation was nerve wracking for Mom, sometimes a bit of humor crept its way into the picture. In 1973, when she decided to convert the second floor into a rentable apartment space, Dennis and I wanted to help. We were not trained professionals, but we wanted to save her some money. "Mom, we'll help in any way we can. Why not let us at least do the sheetrock and spackling?" This was right after Dennis had gained some construction experience, having helped cousin Bill Fowkes build his new house in Port Jefferson. I had some, not much, experience with spackling. Mom said yes, so we went ahead with our best effort at sheet rocking and spackling. After several days of work, due to the many angles and corners in the newly dormered space, Mom, Dennis and I realized that our best effort weren't good enough. With our primitive tools and lack of experience, we were leaving too many spaces and the job didn't look neat. Mom grew less and less pleased with our work. She understood that the working conditions weren't the best. During summertime, it was hot, humid and very uncomfortable in our former "cold-room." Also, Dennis could hardly breathe or speak. He had his mouth completely wired shut as result of a broken jaw he suffered in a softball game. About half way through the job, Mom made a change and decided to have the rest of the work finished by professionals. This would mean adding to the cost of the renovation. We were disappointed that we weren't more successful, but also relieved knowing that at least Mom would have the job done better and more quickly. Days later, two professional sheetrock men came in at a cost of $80 a day. I watched them work, like magicians, as they fixed up our gaps, straightened out our crooked places, and finished sheet rocking the entire upstairs in one day. They came back the next day and applied two neat coats of spackle, giving the place a real professional look. Mom smiled and was very happy with the outcome. She thanked us for our good faith try by barbequing a nice steak, forgetting that Dennis' mouth was wired up and that he was on a completely liquid diet. The smell of the steak on the grill was too much for Dennis, who really wanted some. So Mom improvised. She cut up a few small pieces of the juicy steak, placed them into the blender, and liquefied them. The sight of Dennis trying to no avail to drink steak from a blender is one I'll never forget. It didn't work, and only made him more frustrated. But it showed how we did what we could to try to help Mom, and how she'd do whatever she could to please us. Today, when I face a decision that scares or worries me, I think of how fearless Mom was, borrowing money to invest in her future, adding a dormer to her house despite the presence of a large lien, and allowing two untrained sons to tackle a big sheetrock job. Then, inspired by Mom's strength and confidence, I go forward with much more certainty.

Robert A. White and the Deed

In 1972, still concerned about the issue of there being two names on the deed, Mom contacted her cousin's son-in-law, Vincent F. Nicolosi, Esq. Vinnie, as we called him, was married to Florence Larkin's daughter Lois and was a prominent Queens attorney. In the late 1960's, Vin served as a Queens County Assistant District Attorney in the homicide bureau. We'd see him regularly on the television news commenting about major cases. His most successful prosecution was that of Alice Crimmins, a Kew Gardens woman who was convicted of killing her two children. Vinnie not only knew many people, he also knew how to get things done and was a very big help to Mom whenever a legal question loomed. Mom asked Vinnie for help and he zoomed into action. Within days, he did something neither she nor I could do – he located Robert A. White in New Rochelle, and spoke with him about the wisdom of taking his name off the deed to 55 Twig Lane. Robert A. White was resistant at first and not pleased being pressured by a lawyer. Vinnie explained to him that there would be a legal action commenced against him for his failure to pay any child support for so many years and that arrears plus interest over several decades would be an astronomical sum. With that, Robert A. White cooperated and signed what was necessary to have his name removed. Vinnie accomplished in days what Mom had worried about for years. He was a godsend to her, and, though she didn't live to know it, he continued to be of help in the months and years after her death, settling her affairs with DSS and sale of the house, and handling a claim with the insurance company of the driver of the car in which she was killed on June 21, 1975. I'm sure Mom would love knowing that, right up to his death in 2014, Vinnie and his daughter, Maura, who became his partner in the Nicolosi law firm, continued to be of great help to her family, the children and grandchildren of Kay White.

Marigolds

Mid July 1956 was like most other summer times on Long Island, hazy, hot and humid. I was outside playing "catch a fly you're up" with a few of my buddies. Mom was gardening. She didn't ask for my help, so I was free to keep playing. When she needed or wanted my help with jobs around the house, I usually knew. She wasn't one to beg or plead. She'd ask once. If I didn't come quickly enough, with a good deal of certainty in her voice she'd say, *"Peter, I mean now!"* We all knew that now meant now. Other times she'd give a look that needed little explanation, one that said, *"Can't you see I need help with this?"* This day Mom neither asked for help nor did she give a look. She was happy planting marigolds out front, and I was happy playing with my fifteen-cent, high bounce rubber ball, which we called a "Spaldeen," against the side of our carport. Our house still had the original 1950 Levitt carport, a plain, roofed structure that hung over an open space next to the house. A few families still had carports in 1956, but by then most had converted them into enclosed garages. For us it didn't matter whether we had a carport or a garage because we didn't have a car, just the empty carport with the original blue slates William Levitt provided to cover the dirt floor. As my friends and I played, Mom smiled and hummed as she planted her yellow and orange marigolds. She liked tending to the garden and worked hard to make our house and yard look as nice as the others on the block. Marigolds are inexpensive compared to other flowers. They are also hardy flowers, resilient and strong. Once the flower of a marigold died, Mom knew she could save the dried-out black and white seeds in an envelope to make more plants the next year. As she planted and I played, a car slowed down in front of our house, then came to a stop. I looked up for it was rare that anyone visited us by car. From down on her hands and knees, Mom turned around and looked too. A well-dressed young woman got out of the car and, standing erect like a soldier, scanned her eyes left, then right, as if she were inspecting our house and yard. Without smiling or waving or even looking our way, this woman marched briskly toward our front door. Mom got up, dusted off her grassy knees, made her way toward the door and greeted the woman with a smile. On her way inside, Mom gestured my way, letting me know to stay outside and leave her alone with this straight-faced visitor. So I did. It was my turn to be up anyway. About 20 minutes later, the woman left in much the same manner in which she came, all business. Inside I found Mom crying. "What's the matter, Mom? Who was that woman? Why are you crying?" She collected herself and stoicly said, *"Never mind. It's nothing. You can go back out and play."* I did as I was told, but I was confused. This was not the first time someone I didn't know came to our door and I had to remain outside. There were other times. Once in a while a man would come, but mostly women. They always came in cars and they always carried a briefcase. This incident passed, but the memory of the woman who made Mom cry stayed with me. A few years later I became curious about a few things. Other families in the neighborhood had dads with jobs. Mom didn't have a job, so how did we live? I questioned Mom about a few of these things, and about those visitors. "Who are the people with the briefcases who come over here?" She said, *"They're social workers from Nassau County. They come by every month to check on us."* Still not understanding why total strangers would come to check on us and not the other families in the neighborhood, I continued, "Mom. Do you remember the time a woman came here and you cried?" *"Yes. That woman wasn't very nice to me and I got upset."* The more I questioned Mom the more mixed up I became. Finally she said, *"Peter, I don't want to confuse you, so I might as well tell you what some of this is about."* For the first time in my life I began to understand how we actually went about living as a family. Mom explained things that had always puzzled me, how with four kids and no money we had to rely on the county for help. She didn't make this sound bad at all. *"Don't worry. Our situation is only temporary. We'll be fine someday."* Growing up we knew that there were times when we had to tighten our belts, that we sometimes ate simple foods like spaghetti with a small can of Hunt's tomato sauce poured over the top, or eggs and a piece of toast for dinner. We knew that our school lunches were plain, like peanut butter and jelly, or just jelly if that was all there was, but we really didn't know why things were the way they were. Mom went on to explain what happened the day the county lady made her cry. *"You know I do my best to shop well and never waste money, and when I send you or the others to the grocery store, I ask that you do the same. Usually at the end of a month there's no money left, but once in a while, if I shop well, there's a dollar or two left over, which I save."* I began to feel frightened listening to Mom explain all this to me, mostly for Mom, but she must have felt that such a talk was necessary and that I was old enough to hear it. *"Once in a while, very rarely, when there are a few dollars left over, I buy something small to help make our house look nice, like the neighbors' houses. That month I was able to buy a few marigolds, the cheapest, brightest flowers I could buy, and I was happy to be planting them. When that county woman came to visit, she saw how nice our house looked with the lawn mowed and the marigolds in the front garden. Instead of saying something pleasant, she said to me, 'Mrs. White, if you have enough money left over to buy flowers, it's obvious that we're overpaying you.' This woman didn't ask about how I scrimped and saved just to have $2 left over at the end of a month. She didn't compliment me on how we kept our house or how well you children were doing. She didn't try to get us any more help. Instead, she cut us down because of a few* *flowers."* So there it was. Someone Mom didn't know punished her for simply trying to make the house look nice. Mom's words made me feel badly for her and angry with the cruel county woman, a woman Mom didn't know and might never see again, a woman who could control Mom's life without even bothering to find out the whole story. Mom was a powerful woman, but she could do little about such things and had to go on for almost ten years like that on welfare, living cautiously and vigilantly, so no one else would come along and make things worse.

Payback

As far as closing the books on the years Mom reluctantly but necessarily accepted government benefits, it is important to emphasize that every cent Mom received from welfare was paid back, in full. After she died in 1975, Dennis lived in her house for about a year. For several months, Jeanne and her infant daughter, Michelle, lived there too. Soon after, Jeanne moved upstate New York, to the Albany area, where she continues to reside to this day. Dennis bought the house from the estate of Catherine White and lived there for a couple of years before selling himself and buying a condo in Plainview. When the estate sold the house to Dennis, the first order of business at the closing was to satisfy the lien imposed by Nassau County. There could no transfer of title from the estate to Dennis without first paying back the county, in full. The bill was $18500. A quick review of the math shows that the five of us lived on that $18500 for the entire nine year period from 1952-1960, about $2050 a year, or $170 a month! Impossible as that may sound, Mom was able to make the mortgage payment of $90 a month, and pay all the other bills, like food, clothing, heating oil, doctors, and medicine with the remaining $80. Those are the facts and they explain why there was no such thing as us receiving an allowance, or going on a family vacation, or making unnecessary phone calls, or having a family car. We lived on the edge, and we made it. We were poor, but as kids we really didn't know it. We played with other kids, rode bikes, swam in the Levittown pools, went to school, and did most of the things the other kids did. We just did it with a lot less. Growing up we didn't have many worries; Mom did that for us.

Tonsils and Braces

In reviewing the statement the DSS provided at the house closing, I noticed that the sum due to the county of $18500 included not only the monthly payments Mom received for rent and food over the nine-year period, but also a few larger, special items, like my having my tonsils removed at Meadowbrook Hospital in 1957. Welfare paid for the tonsillectomy and got reimbursed 18 years later from the sale of Mom's house. I also noticed an entry for the braces Dennis wore on his teeth for a few years as a kid. Welfare paid that expense too, and got reimbursed years later, in full. Happily, I noticed that during the late 1950's, there was a reduction of about $2000. I asked about this and the attorney representing the county at the closing explained that DSS tried to locate Robert A. White from time to time over the years and was usually unsuccessful. One time they were successful and found that he had a few thousand dollars in the bank, which they took and applied toward the overall welfare debt.

Welfare Myths and Realities

When government first conceived of a welfare system in the 1930's, it was intended to be a temporary program, something to hold individuals and families over until better times came along. In my experience as an attorney and as an advocate for the poor, I've found that most welfare recipients, due to circumstances beyond their control, are truly needy. Their situations, like Mom's, call for them to seek government assistance. Millions of Americans are now part of our country's 5% who are unemployed. They are eager to work but have gotten laid off or are disabled or, like Mom, are single parents with young children. They need help. Others, a minority in my view, abuse the system. Some work off-the-books jobs for cash, show no income, and are able to apply for and receive some level of benefits. They have become skilled in gaming the large, bureaucratic system. There are many myths about welfare too, like what the critics refer to as the "Welfare Cadillac," as if everyone who receives welfare is a lying cheat who uses food money to buy extravagant items. Something talked about a lot these days is corporate welfare. In this era of bailouts and economic stimulus, a great deal of government money, perhaps more than is provided to the poor, goes to large banks and corporations to make sure they don't fail. Mom neither lied nor did she game the system. She wasn't in line for a handout, or a bailout of any kind. She was one of the "truly needy," as President Reagan described the actual poor, and rightly deserved the temporary help she got. We, Robert, Dennis, Jeanne and I, were the lucky ones, first hand observers to and participants in the struggle she faced trying to successfully make it from one day to the next. We watched, often without knowing the whole truth, as she stood strong, refusing to become consumed by the circumstances she faced. We knew we were a little different from the other families in our neighborhood. We knew about living without certain things that were common for other families. But such things were out of reach for us. Because Mom shielded us so well, we didn't suffer. She made us feel ok, so we believed we were ok, and that made us ok.

The Merry Mailman

August 31, 1953 was my sixth birthday. Birthdays were never big extravaganzas for us, but we always got something and Mom tried real hard to make them fun, by either having Aunt Katherine and Aunt Nellie come out from the city, having some neighborhood kids over for a kiddie party, baking a cake, or doing something to make sure we had a special day. Since my birthday was usually a day or two before school would start, I knew what to expect as a birthday present, a new schoolbag or something related to the start of school a few days later. I'll never forget the smell of those new schoolbags. If my schoolbag was still in good shape from the previous school year, I'd get a new white shirt or blue pants to go with my St. Ignatius school uniform. On the morning of August 31, 1953, surprisingly, nothing happened. No one said happy birthday, there were no presents, not even a new white shirt or schoolbag. There was no cake baking in the oven either. I was disappointed. It was a sunny day and my friend Leslie called for me. I wanted to go out and play with him but Mom said no. I didn't understand. "Mom, I want to go out and play." *"No,"* she said. *"Stay inside and watch the Merry Mailman."* The

Merry Mailman was a show that began a few years earlier in 1949 and starred Ray Heatherton as the Merry Mailman. It was actually a quality children's program with games, songs, stories, puppet skits, magic tricks, and of course cartoons, like the standard Terrytoons and the new Crusader Rabbit cartoon. Television was fairly new in 1953, a culture-changing technological advancement. Levittown kids watched a lot of it because each Levitt house came with a 12-inch Admiral TV embedded in the living room wall. I wanted to go out and didn't understand why Mom was making me stay in just to watch the Merry Mailman, something I could do any day. And it was my birthday. I begged and whined for her to change her mind and let me play outside, but she was adamant. For reasons she did not share, she confined me and insisted that the only thing I could do was watch The Merry Mailman. In my six-year-old mind, I was having the worst birthday possible, punished rather than celebrated, for no apparent reason. Each time I stepped away from the television or got distracted, Mom insisted that I pay attention to Ray Heatherton, The Merry Mailman, who spoke directly to his young listeners in much the same way Fred Rogers did decades later on "Mr. Roger's Neighborhood." Not understanding any of this, I reluctantly did as I was told. Near tears, I stared at the TV and watched the mailman host his cartoon show until it was nearly over. Then, seconds before it was about to end, to my sudden and joyous surprise, something unforgettable happened, something I'll remember always. I looked at the TV set and the Merry Mailman looked directly back at me. Then he said the most beautiful words a six year old could ever hear. With thousands, maybe millions of kids watching he said, "Oh, one more thing boys and girls, I want to wish Peter White a very happy birthday. Peter, I'm sure you're watching, so go to your room right now and look under your bed. You'll find a big birthday present, just for you. Happy Birthday Peter!" Following the Mailman's instructions, I dashed to my room, got on my hands and knees, looked under the bed and found a huge box decorated with bright wrapping paper. Ecstatic, I tore the paper off the huge box and there it was, a toy gas station set complete with little cars and trucks, signs, and garage doors that opened and closed. Mom came into the room and hugged me. That was a special moment, just the two of us, hugging in the unlit bedroom beside this big, brand new toy. My sadness had turned to bliss as my worst birthday turned into my best. Creatively and thoughtfully, Mom changed something normal into something unique and unforgettable. Neighborhood kids may have gotten more gifts than I on their birthdays, but none could say that they got theirs on live TV, straight from the Merry Mailman himself. I was too young at the time to make all the connections that brought about that happy moment, like Mom having to think about me and my birthday weeks before, calling the Merry Mailman show and making arrangements for the announcement, shopping without a car for my big toy, wrapping and hiding it, and then making sure I was present, in front of the TV at that precise moment to get my surprise. As time went by, I came to realize how loving Mom was, always placing our needs ahead of her own. Though we were on welfare and the budget didn't call for new toys, Mom, who mastered the art of providing for us while shielding us at the same time, figured out a way. Once again, she made me feel ok, so I believed I was ok, and that made me ok. Considering the circumstances our family faced, we lived remarkably normal lives, mostly because the hard stuff was left to Mom.

Living on $1 a Day

"I bet you I could live on $1 a day," said my 11-year-old friend Robert Taormina. "No way," I said. "It must cost at least twice that." We were young boys from the neighborhood who had no idea of economic reality. Robert had no knowledge of what his father, a tool and die maker, earned, and I had no knowledge of what my Mom lived on. Robert's "$1 a day" theory rested on him being extremely thrifty, following strict rules that included buying only basic, filling foods like bread, fruit, milk and cereal. He believed if he ate only those basic, cheap foods, and slept out in the tent we owned together, he could survive on $1 a day. I went home I told Mom of our theories and said we'd like to test them out, to see which one of us was right, Robert's $1 a day plan, or my $2 one. Mom said, *"Peter, try if you like, but I can tell you it takes a whole lot more than $1 or even $2 a day to live."* Knowing she didn't work outside the house, I asked, "Then, how do we live?" That day she began sharing more bits and pieces of the reality we faced, of our existence on welfare. That day I began to learn more about real life.

Final Thoughts on Welfare

Mom was a reluctant welfare recipient. She only sought the aid of the county because she had to; necessity required it. Life on welfare wasn't easy. There was a lot she had to give up to make sure our needs were met, and she did so willingly and lovingly. Just visiting DSS in Mineola or being visited by DSS workers was stressful. Anyone who has ever visited a busy welfare office knows it can be an unfriendly, uncomfortable, businesslike environment. It's often a stark, bleak place, crowded and noisy, with long lines of downtrodden-looking people waiting to be seen by busy, often frustrated welfare workers. DSS staff members don't always refer to prospective recipients in hospitable terms, but sometimes impersonally bark orders like, "Come on people, move down. Next! Is there a next?" So for Mom, a polished, educated, willing-to-work woman, visiting the DSS office in Mineola was a taxing experience, especially when she had to take any of us with her, which sometimes was the case. Just entering the Nassau County DSS building is degrading. Architecturally speaking, it is drab and plain looking, situated below ground level nearby several large and powerful looking courthouses. The courthouses sit up, higher-than-ground level, like Greek or Roman temples. To enter those halls of power, one ascends a stairway, giving the visitor the feeling that what goes on in there is important. The DSS building sits in a hole. To enter, one descends a flight of stairs to the main doors below, giving the welfare recipient visitor the feeling that what goes on in there is unimportant, something to be hidden. I don't believe this is an accident. Throughout history, there are many examples of society hiding its poor. Mom wanted to get off welfare as soon as she could, but it took nine long years, until Jeanne was a third grader and she was comfortable leaving us alone for periods of time, for her to begin her career as a Catholic school teacher.

Mom was private about the economic aspects of her life. She kept the welfare experience away from others, and from us for as long as she could, believing that if we knew and understood the situation earlier, we'd be troubled by it, feel sorry for her or ourselves, or blab our family business to others. Of this trying time in her life, Mom said,

> *I never did tell my children of the great difficulties we were facing, as they were*
> *too young. I felt I should try and keep this discouraging news to myself as long as*
> *possible. I wanted to rise up above all of these problems and make a peaceful life*
> *for us and hoped I had the stamina to withstand all these tribulations. I also*
> *wanted to keep this in our own family and did not feel the neighbors had to know*
> *of our misfortune.*

While the overall struggle with the DSS was unpleasant, uncertain and often degrading, it did help Mom maintain a household, keep us alive and allow us to move forward. In other words, welfare saved us. I've often thought what would have become of us if it weren't for welfare. If there were no such program, we might have been homeless, or raised in a slum, or if we were lucky, perhaps a housing project. We would have gone to different schools than St. Ignatius, Holy Family, Chaminade and Clarke High School. We would have had a different peer group and may not have turned out the way we did, each becoming law-abiding, college-bound, educated men and women. If it weren't for welfare we wouldn't have had the safety and security we had at 55 Twig Lane, with its well-kept yard, its 12-inch Admiral TV set, its beloved cold room, and enough space for the five of us to live safely as a family. If it weren't for welfare we wouldn't have had the basics – like food, clothing, shelter, heat, and health care. If it weren't for welfare we wouldn't have played on safe streets, taken bike hikes, or gotten to know the hundreds of friends with whom we played hide-and-go-seek, ringalevio, and stickball, or explored our enchanting weeds – the wooded nature sanctuary in our neighborhood. If it weren't for welfare, we wouldn't have been able to live the healthy life we did, with clean water and basic safety. So while it is true that DSS got every cent back that it provided Mom, that the welfare existence was often quite a degrading experience, that welfare workers made Mom nervous, uncomfortable, and even cry, it is also true that welfare saved our lives.

Of this nine-year period, something stands out clearly to me. As a child I never really felt inferior to anyone or deprived of basic safety and security. Thanks to Mom's wisdom, attention to details, tenacity and forbearance, and notwithstanding the welfare system's many flaws, we were able to participate in the overall Levittown experience like thousands of other kids. Mom's struggle, worry and tears gave us that safety and security. I've always looked back at those times, when things were really quite uncertain, as the happiest and most secure time in my life.

Facing Things Alone

Mom faced many struggles throughout her life, from losing her own mom at the age of two in 1919 and her dad two years later, to putting up with the mistreatment and inconsistent behavior of her troubled husband. She frequently faced the uncertainty caused by economic struggle and the monumental task of raising four young children. While she was able to confide in her loving, adopted mother, Aunt Nellie, her helpful and generous Aunt Katherine, and her reliable cousin, Florence Larkin, she saw them only infrequently. The day-to-day struggles of raising four children, keeping house, paying bills, shopping, preparing meals, getting all of us up and out to school each morning, and to bed each night, she met alone. There were no nights off for Kay White. She had to handle all of life's experiences, its many boredoms and despairs and its infrequent joys, alone. Neighbors sometimes helped her out in a pinch, like Kitchie Schley, who had some Red Cross experience and seemed to know about nursing when one of us got sick. Other neighbors pitched in too, like when Mom needed to borrow something or make a minor repair. But for the most part, she was alone. With no spouse, brother, sister or parent, there were few shoulders upon which she could lean when difficulties arose. As we grew older, we tried to fill that void, but we were far from experts at fixing things, and we could do little to give her the kind of emotional relief that real adult companionship could provide.

Mom liked to laugh and have a good time. Once in a while, usually around the holidays, she'd be invited to one of the neighbor's houses for a party where she'd have a drink and some laughs. There was never alcohol in our house, so there was never any drinking at home. When a neighbor did have a party and Mom was included, there was sometimes a down side. The Kaisers had a holiday party one year, and Mom was pleased to be invited. She got dressed up, put on a smile, and walked across the street to the Kaiser's house at 56 Twig Lane. In part to see her having a good time, I made up a reason to knock on the Kaiser's door and ask Mom something. From the Kaiser's vestibule I could see Mom sitting in the living room with a "highball" and some snacks on a little table in front of her. She was smiling away and laughing out loud. Satisfied that she was ok, I waved to her and told her I'd see her later at home. "Have a good time, Mom." Later on she came home and we were anxious to see her glow. We thought a few cups of cheer, some laughs, and some adult conversation would cause her to come home with a smile. Instead Mom entered the kitchen and burst into tears. Puzzled, we asked, "Mom, you just went to a party. We saw you having a good time. Why are you crying?" She said she had a good time and enjoyed herself very much. But when she came home, she was sad. Yes, she'd relaxed and had some laughs. But when the party was over, all the other neighbors went home as couples, the Schleys, the Chiffers, the Flynn's. Mom left unaccompanied and went back to facing life alone. In the 1950's, Levittown was full of young families raising children. We were the odd family with only one adult. Sometimes, no matter how good things might have appeared, the bright light of joy would quickly dim.

Aside from attending occasional parties by herself, Mom did most things alone. Without the benefit of advice or corroboration from a spouse or significant other, Mom made most decisions single-handedly. While we saw her as a strong, capable and determined woman, at times she saw herself as fragile and frustrated by her situation. Of her mostly solitary existence during this time she said:

> *Handling it is difficult, especially for me with no one to rely on or ask for direction. Sometimes I'm not able to do my household duties. I become depressed when I think about my problems. Then, in a day or two this feeling leaves me and I have renewed strength to resume my chores and a sense of relief that my frustrations are over. It takes a lot to make me angry. I am normally quite*

peaceful but when too many obstacles present themselves I feel anger. After this gets out of my system I am calm and realize the foolishness of it all.

GOOD TIMES

The Larkins

Despite years of struggle scraping by on welfare, there were good times. Mom took great delight in keeping up the best she could with her small family. She traveled several times a year to Manhattan to see Aunt Katherine and Aunt Nellie and once or twice a year to Flushing, Queens to see her cousin Florence Larkin and her children. These Queens experiences involved a degree of struggle with transportation and cost, but Mom handled it. We loved visiting the Larkin's in Flushing. They lived on 169th Street near Francis Lewis Boulevard. Across the street was a vacant lot where we sometimes played. By the mid-1950's, Holy Cross High School was built on that lot. Of our visits to the Larkin's, Jeanne remembered,

Mom, age 3, with cousin Florence Duffy (Larkin), 1920.

We had so much fun with our cousins Kathy and Bob. We played hide and go seek in their attic, and did talent shows where Dennis, imitating Ed Sullivan, would be the host. Mom, Florence and the other adults really enjoyed watching us do this. Most importantly, Mom had good times there.

The most difficult place for us to visit was Rockaway Beach. Quite far from Levittown, a trip to Rockaway involved taking the bus to Hicksville, the LIRR to Jamaica, then several buses to meet the Larkins at the beach. After going on a few rides at Rockaway Playland and a snack, we'd have to sit on the hot sand and not be allowed in the water until hours later. Mom took the "no swimming after eating" rule very seriously. A graceful swimmer, Mom sometimes went into the water while we sat on the burning hot sand. We'd watch her swim out into the ocean, by herself, well beyond where the waves were breaking. She did the backstroke and other strokes quiet gracefully, reminiscent of Esther Williams from the aqua shows. I worried that she was out too far, that something could happen to her. But I'm sure she was only trying to create a little private time for herself, relaxing in the water and getting a rare break from the tensions of her daily life. With sunburned and tired children in tow Mom dreaded the gruesome, multi-bus and train trip back to Levittown. Uncle Joe, as we called Florence's generous and thoughtful husband Joe Larkin, sometimes handed Mom a ten-dollar bill, no small sum back then, enabling us to go straight from the Larkin's or Rockaway all the way to Jamaica by cab. Struggles aside, those rare family outings were good times for us and important to Mom. She did all she could to make sure that we had some relationship with Florence and Joe Larkin and their children, Joan, John, Lois, Kathy and Bob, our second cousins and the only relatives we knew.

One summer Dennis made a sleepover visit to the Larkin's. Florence was a very proper woman. Her vocabulary was superior to most, and her tone the most elegant. As he was ascending the stairs on his way to bed, Florence wanted to know if he was ready for a good night's sleep. She said, "Goodnight Dennis. Oh, by the way, did you have a bowel movement?" Dennis said, "A what?" She said, "A movement. A bowel movement." Dennis had absolutely no idea what Florence was talking about. In our house, we didn't use such formal expressions for our bodily and bathroom functions. Florence repeated herself, "Maybe you should try to have a bowel movement." Now knowing what a bowel movement was, Dennis thought Florence was saying the word "bow," that maybe Florence wanted him to take a bow before bed. So, standing at the top of her stairs, he placed his right hand behind his back, his left hand in front of his waist, then bent all the way forward, giving Florence his most elegant and unforgettable "bow movement."

The Fowkes Family

Mom was very happy that Bill and Joan Fowkes decided to move into a house right down the block from us. Joan was the oldest daughter of Mom's cousin Florence Larkin. In 1959, Joan married Bill Fowkes, a teacher at Chaminade High School in Mineola. By 1960 Joan was pregnant and she and Bill began house hunting on Long Island. Mom knew of a well-kept Levitt house on our block that was being sold by an elderly immigrant couple we all called Pop and Penny. Bill and Joan bought Pop and Penny's house at 18 Twig Lane and became more than neighbors for Mom, they became Mom's good friends. After being surrounded by children and teenagers for so many years, Mom finally had some adult relatives close by, additional shoulders upon which she could lean. Though 20 years younger than Mom, Bill and Joan were more like peers. They often dropped by to chat with her, relax, talk about adult things, and just make company. This provided Mom with an important sense of security, just knowing that a close, caring couple was right around the corner. Joan and Bill became active members of Holy Family Church and Bill eventually became a member of the Holy Family School Board, a newly formed organization. Prior to its formation, the pastor called all the shots. Now parishioners had a say. Mom was still car-less at the time and Bill and Joan helped her with errands, took her on outings, and helped her with things she'd never been able to do before. Bill also embraced Dennis in a special way, including taking him along on their family's summer-long cross-country trip in 1964. Dennis had just graduated from St. Ignatius School and, with some money he'd saved from folding newspapers at the local luncheonette, was happy to go. Since that trip he's traveled to and lived in many places throughout his life, but to this day he says that was the nicest trip he was ever on. He was inspired by the Black Hills of South Dakota, and "awestruck" at the breathtaking beauty of the lakes in Custer State Park. Bill, an important male influence for Dennis, helped him in several ways, including letting him and cousin Bob Larkin, Joan's youngest brother, hike by themselves down to the bottom of the Grand Canyon and back up again, a 20-mile excursion – wearing the new cowboy boots they'd bought. When Bill, an English and driver education teacher, became fatigued from the heat and boredom of driving hours through the Mojave Desert, he gave Dennis a few driving lessons and handed him the wheel. Dennis, not yet 16 drove the final two hours through the desert. While walking along Sunset Strip in Los Angeles, Denis ran into Yankee Hall of Famer Yogi Berra, with whom he had a pleasant chat. In addition to the experiencing the beauty and sheer size of the United States, Dennis also learned some things he couldn't have on Long Island. After taking the northern route going west, Bill drove a southern route back to New York. Though the Civil Rights Act of 1964 was enacted in January, throughout many places in the south Dennis saw signs saying "white" and "colored," the final vestiges of many decades of Jim Crow laws in the U.S. This Fowkes Family cross trip was the journey of a lifetime for Dennis, something special that Mom could never have provided him.

Once in a while Mom would be invited to a gathering at the Fowkes' house, or offered some type of much-needed assistance. In 1961, Dennis and I talked about becoming high school athletes, and to get fit, we wanted a set of barbells for Christmas. Mom said, "We'll see." Somehow, undoubtedly with Aunt Katherine's help, she made it happen. Of course, she faced a major problem. Without a car, carrying such a heavy gift, a few hundred pounds of iron, was an impossibility. Bill and Mom didn't know that on a snowy evening a few days before Christmas, Dennis and I watched from our cold room window as Bill lugged several very heavy boxes into the house, then helped Mom hide them until Christmas Day. Though we knew this gift was coming, we acted extremely excited on Christmas morning to have gotten something so big that we wanted so much. In 1971, after living on Twig Lane for ten years, Bill and Joan bought a wooded acre of land in Pt. Jefferson and began building a new home there. Dennis, who remained close with Bill throughout high school and his time in the Marines, helped Bill with the construction. For several months, Dennis traveled to Pt. Jefferson where he worked side by side with his cousin Bill, hanging sheetrock and installing floors, windows and doors. With the experience he gained from building his own rather large house, Bill eventually became a successful contractor, building many houses on Long Island's east end. Even though the Fowkes' family left Levittown, they didn't forget Mom. From time to time they invited her out to Pt. Jefferson to have dinner at the clubhouse, which was part of their Belle Terre community. Bill and Joan respected Mom a great deal. In an e-mail to Dennis, written in April 2010, a year before he passed away from a sudden illness, Bill said,

> After our many travels, we finally arrived back on Long Island to the house that you helped me build. I often think how your life might have been different if you joined me in the building business when you left the USMC…. I also want to thank you for giving me a copy of Catherine's letter to the Diocesan Tribunal. I had all I could do to keep my eyes dry. I can tell you now that I was there. I was a player in the saga of Kay White. I was only 22 years old and didn't know how I could help but whenever she called I came over to listen and give her whatever support I could give. To this day I feel that I was a good friend and confidant to your mother. I spent many visits laughing, smoking my cigar and having a drink with Catherine. These are cherished moments that I will not forget. The one thing

that bothers me to this day is, as attentive as I was to your mother, I did nothing for her kids. I feel that I could have been there for movies, ball games, school things….or just been there. For this oversight I ask your forgiveness.

Bill Fowkes

Dennis answered Bill with a similar heartfelt expression. Greatly respecting their father-son relationship, he replied:

Dear Bill,

Your note touched me more than words can say…. There is nothing to be sorry about; you were very good to my Mom and for this I will always be grateful. What you don't realize is how important it was for me to spend time with you and how you influenced me during my early teenage years. I genuinely love you and your family. I have shared with many others, including Mom, that when I was growing up, you were like a father to me. I thank you for all you did.

Family forever,

Dennis

Since the early 1960's, and continuing to this day, I've loved the game of golf. Bill Fowkes, an avid and fine golfer, introduced me to the game. The first round I ever played was in 1961 at Eisenhower Park, then called Salisbury Park with Bill, Joan and, believe it or not, Mom. While I would have to admit it wasn't quite championship golf that was played that day, it was fun and that first round has become a very special memory. I did pretty well with the pointers Bill gave me, and seeing my enthusiasm for the game, a week later he took me to Bethpage State Park where we played the Green Course. The greens fees were only $1.50 back then. After we finished walking the full 18 holes, Bill encouraged me with a rare male pat on the back saying, "You've got a lot of good golf in you, Peter. Stick with it" After we finished the 18th hole, Bill noticed that there was no one teeing off the first hole, so he asked the starter if we could go out and play a few extra holes. The starter nodded yes and we played until dark. Bill Fowkes did more for me that day than Robert A. White did in a lifetime.

Holy Family School

A very happy part of Mom's life was her teaching career. She made friends easily and found much joy in her involvement with church and school activities. Despite the workload and the many children assigned to her, usually at least 50 kids a year, she

Mom on Holy Family stage with first graders performing "Charlie Brown" skit.

enjoyed the classroom experience very much, especially seeing her first graders go from babies to becoming eager, young learners. She also enjoyed the many relationships she had with her adult colleagues at Holy Family School. Several were serious intellectuals who were well read on the issues of the day. Mom liked taking part in the faculty room skirmishes with them, discussing everything from politics and current events to their students' progress. Many of her colleagues were fun to be with, party people who made her laugh. She took great pleasure in working side by side with these women, and a few men, and also sharing some outside school activities with them, like the trips she took with Mrs. Alice Reilly and her family. Third grade teacher, Lucy Deegan, was from Ireland, home of Mom's ancestors. Mom liked Lucy a lot, and smiled each time she heard her authentic and colorful brogue. Lucy brought a new, liberal perspective to many controversial matters, and Mom, a conservative thinker on certain issues, accepted many of them, showing she was flexible and capable to altering her views. About half of Holy Family's faculty was made up of nuns whom Mom loved very much. Together the nuns and lay teachers formed a good, solid staff. All worked for less than half the salary of their public school counterparts, and all were greatly devoted to their students and their vocation. Holy Family School, only a mile from 55 Twig Lane, was a wonderful place for Mom, a place made all the more special for us now that she's been permanently enshrined in the Holy Family School Hall of Fame.

Kids' Activities

Mom holding granddaughter, Michelle in August, 1974. Mom made the christening dress, which has been worn by several grandchildren afterwards.

Mom encouraged all of us to become involved in a number of activities outside of school. Robert, Dennis and I had paper routes, and played CYO baseball. We were all either members of Boy Scouts, Cub Scouts or Girl Scouts. Dennis and I played high school football, and Jeanne played bagpipes in an Irish marching band. Throughout our lives, Mom shared in our involvement. She attended scout meetings and ball games whenever she could when we were young, even with the limitation of having no car. Somehow, some way, she made it to most of our activities. She took great pride in the fact that we were serving mass on the altar, giving things our best out on the baseball or football field, marching in a parade, or participating in some sort of activity with other boys and girls. Encouraging us to participate was her way of making sure we were involved in, and learning from the normal activities of young people. So much of her life and ours dealt with struggle that whenever some type of normalcy came along, she embraced it, cherished it and it brought a smile to her face.

Mom also made sure that each of our birthdays was special. I vividly remember my fifth birthday. Mom had all the neighborhood kids over for cake, ice cream and something we never had unless it was a special occasion, Coca-Cola. More than a dozen kids from age three to age eight were there, crammed into our kitchen, wearing party hats, eating ice cream, cake and drinking from their own bottle of Coke. Toward the end of the party, probably through the kindness of Aunt Katherine or Mom's cousin, Florence, something special happened. Mom hired a small fire engine to come by and give each child a ride around the block. It wasn't a real fire engine, but a pickup truck painted bright red with a ladder hung along the side to make it look like a fire truck. The "fireman" who drove the truck gave each child a bright red felt fire hat and drove around and around Twig and Branch Lanes until every child had gotten a ride and had a chance to pull the switch to sound the siren. It was a very hot day, and all the parents laughed when they saw the bright red color of their kids' heads when the ride was over. The dye from felt hats mixed with our beads of sweat and streamed down our faces and necks, painting us all red. Another unforgettable birthday was in 1959, my 12th. All the neighborhood kids were there, but this time they brought their Hula Hoops, the craze at the time. Mom organized contests for everyone, including the traditional Pin the Tail on the Donkey, not only blindfolded, but while twirling a Hula Hoop at the same time. Of Mom's efforts to make birthdays special, Jeanne remembered,

> Mom would always make us a birthday cake and let us have friends over. We would each receive cards and presents, and a special card from Aunt Katherine who would put money inside, sometimes as much as $20, which was a lot of money back then. Singing Happy Birthday, making a wish, and blowing out the candles was so exciting too. I remember as my brothers got older and moved away to college or the Army, Mom would call them up and we would sing Happy Birthday to them over the phone. Believe it or not, my brothers and I still do this on each other's birthdays. This memory from Mom continues in our lives.

Mom was resourceful and knew how to accomplish a lot with a little, especially when it came to making holidays exciting. When we were too young to stay up until midnight on New Year's Eve, she found a way for us to celebrate that didn't involve confetti, noisemakers or fireworks. We'd go to bed at our regular times, but around 11:45 p.m. she'd wake us up, hand each of us a pot or pan and spoon, and take us go out on the front lawn at the stroke of midnight to bang away, ringing in the New Year the best way she could. Life was simple then. We wanted for very little.

Bagpipes and Irish Feis ('fesh')

When Robert and I were working and going to school in Hawaii and Ohio, and Dennis was involved with his high school friends and sports, Jeanne was a young teenager and often the only one home with Mom. At Mom's encouragement, she took up the bagpipes and became a member of an Irish marching band. Jeanne's memories of this time in her life show Mom's dedication to our activities:

> During my time at Holy Family there was an opportunity for me to take Irish step dancing after school. The group was called the Barrett Pipers and Dancers and was from Baldwin, NY. The group consisted of adults, teenagers and children as young as ten. I joined and learned how to do the Irish jig and other dances. I enjoyed myself very much and met new friends. After some time I was invited to learn to play the bagpipes and began weekly lessons. Eventually I became a member of the Barrett Pipe and Drum Band, traveling quite a bit with the band to competitions and much larger Gaelic arts and cultural festivals called Irish feis's, sometimes out of state. We won several gold medals and marched in parades, especially around St. Patrick's Day. This was a very exciting time in my life and Mom was so proud of me and happy to be involved herself. She would attend most of the feis's and parades with me and became friends with many of the band members' parents. Whenever company would visit, Mom would have me play the bagpipes for them…. The years that I was involved in the band were wonderful and I am so happy that Mom was able to be a part of it.

Jeanne often practiced the bagpipes in our backyard without fear, hesitation or embarrassment. The pipes were loud and when she practiced, we'd smile and wonder what the neighbors thought, even those several blocks away. We liked hearing Jeanne play because she was very serious about it, showed great improvement as she went along, and was doing something that Robert, Dennis or I had not done. She was the only one in the family who learned to play a musical instrument. Mom loved Jeanne's involvement with the band. Extremely proud of her Irish heritage, she saw Jeanne's participation as a great way for both of them to connect with it. The only member of the family that didn't appreciate the pipes was Mom's beloved dog, Sugar, who howled and shook with the shrill sound. Sugar was a sweet dog, but she didn't understand what was going on in her backyard during practice time. Mom, whose favorite song was "Danny Boy," loved the sound of the pipes, the Irish step dancing, the parades, especially the St. Patrick's Day Parade, and most of all, the fact that Jeanne succeeded in accomplishing something extraordinary that connected to our family's cultural background.

No matter whether it was sports, scouts, altar boys, Irish dancing or any other activity, and no matter which one of us was involved, Mom was our biggest fan.

A Big Regret

There was one time when Mom tried very hard to make me feel good and to feel good about me, and I took that moment's happiness from her. In the fall of 1961, I was sometimes an unthinking, immature, 14-year-old boy. New to Clarke High School, I made the freshman football team. Our first game was at home after school one September day, and Mom, who was in her first year as a teacher at Holy Family School, walked the two miles from work to the game. Inexperienced and new to the football program, I sat on the sidelines for most of the game, frustrated. I was very disappointed at not being given much playing time because I worked hard, didn't dog the drills, never missed a practice, and tried my best. The coach, Mr. Jack McDonald, played the boys whom he knew had prior football experience from 7th and 8th grade football. I wasn't one of "Jack's pets," as some of Jack's favored veteran boys were called, but an unknown, unproven new kid. I was embarrassed in front of my new peers, some of whom had even missed a few practices, yet got more playing time. I'd long known that life wasn't always fair, but I was upset and humiliated at the situation. I had worked and worried for weeks about the big first game, only to end up sitting on the bench until the final quarter, when the outcome had already been determined. As I sat with a few other "benchwarmer" teammates, Mom approached me with a big smile. I tried to hide. Bad enough as it was to be a second string player, the last thing I wanted at that time was to be seen as a mama's boy in front of my teammates. Mom had no way of knowing how I felt at that moment. She was happy to see me in my team uniform and proud that I was the first in the family to play a high school sport. I turned my head away, and through the facemask of my large, leather helmet, I noticed Mom stepping closer. She walked right up behind the bench and tapped me on my shoulder pad. Out of sheer embarrassment and frustration, I said something that came out nastier than it was meant. "Not now, Mom. Go away." With those five little words, I changed Mom's proud, bright smile into a look of dejection and heartbreak. I didn't mean to hurt her, but only to end my brief moment of adolescent grief. At that young age, I didn't think about how piercing my words might be, especially to one who loved and cared so much, one who was proud of me no matter how many minutes I played, who went to such a great effort to be my only fan. Wounded and teary eyed, Mom did an about face and began the long trek back home. As bad as I felt about not playing much, I was now doubly pained, ashamed of myself for the way I treated my mother. I don't remember how I worked it out with her later that night, but I do know that it was very difficult to take back that kind of hurt. That incident occurred in 1961, yet I remember it like it was yesterday. I've never forgiven myself for taking that moment of happiness away from her.

Household Laughter

On his 1950's TV show "Candid Camera," host Allen Funt used to try to catch unsuspecting people in "the act of being themselves." Occasionally, we would catch Mom being herself and it was quite humorous. Thinking she was alone in the house, Mom would sometimes sing along with songs on the radio. If she didn't know the words, she'd make up her own. In 1969, singer Mark Lindsay had a top ten hit called "Arizona."

Mom liked it. It was the number one song for many months. When it came on the radio Mom would turn up the volume as she vacuumed or did other work around the house, and sing along, loudly. As Lindsay belted out the word, "ARI-ZONA," Mom would loudly sing, *"Here Comes Mona,"* or *"Bill and Joan-a"* instead. I'd laugh and tell her she got the words wrong. She'd laugh too and say, *"I can sing any words I want. Besides, I like my words better."* Then we'd laugh together. Aunt Katherine had a good sense of humor too; one Mom didn't always appreciate, especially if we, "the kid's," were around. At the dinner table one evening, Dennis mentioned that a family down the block decided to shorten their name from Lipshitz to Lipp. Our neighbor Freddy Lipshitz was soon going to be just plain Freddy Lipp. When she heard this, Aunt Katherine smiled and said something we'd never be allowed to say, "If his Lipshitz, what does his ass do?" Mom gave Aunt Katherine a stern look, but she followed up with another joke instead saying, "What's the matter, did somebody knock the 'shitz' out of him?" Mom never allowed any foul language from us, but we howled at Aunt Katherine's jokes. Mom knew Aunt Katherine's spontaneous jokes weren't meant to be harmful, but funny. And I deep down, I'm sure even Mom enjoyed a laugh of her own once in a while whenever Aunt Katherine felt her oats.

Tissues in the Parking Lot

The funniest moment I remember with Mom took place in the late 1960's on a hot summer Sunday afternoon in the parking lot of Holy Family Church. Mom and I attended a late mass, and by the time we got back to her car, we were both perspiring greatly. Her little Ford Fairlane didn't have air conditioning, so to dry the moisture from her face she began dabbing the beads of sweat with some tissues. While she was busy dabbing away, she spotted Frank Saracino walking toward his car. Frank was a social studies teacher at Clarke High School and a good friend. Mom knew him through Holy Family, where he was the president of the newly formed school board. It was unbearably hot and I wanted to get going, so I waved to Frank and started the car. Mom said, *"Wait a minute Peter. I want to say hi to Frank."* It was very important for Mom to give a big greeting to the president of the board. Mom began calling, *"Frank, Frank, yoo hoo!"* What she didn't know was that, from her attempt to dry the perspiration from her face, hundreds of little tiny pieces of tissue paper clung to her wet face causing her to look like a ghost. Trying to spare her some embarrassment, I said, "Mom, Mom, wait a minute. I have to tell you something." Mom would not be interrupted and kept saying, *"Shhh. That's Frank. I have to say hello."* She waved me off and continued calling out the window, *"Frank! Oh Frank!"* Again I interrupted, and again she shh'ed me. Frank heard Mom calling and walked with his wife Joan toward our car. I made one last attempt to get Mom's attention, but she waved me off for the final time, got out of the car, greeted Frank with a big smile, then chatted with him and Joan for a few minutes. I watched helplessly, knowing that I tried my best. Frank and Joan had the broadest smiles on their faces during this chat, and so did I. When Mom got back in the car, she said, *"Aren't they the nicest people? Did you see the way Frank and Joan just smiled and smiled?"* I said, "Of course they smiled. Take a look in the mirror." She looked at herself in the car mirror and let out a loud shriek. Her entire face was covered with hundreds of tiny white tissue flakes. I couldn't contain my laughter, and she scolded me for not telling her. "I tried, Mom. I tried," I said as I kept laughing. On the way home, Mom laughed too. She had the ability to appreciate those times when the joke was on her.

Clem and Maude

In 1962, Mom was blessed to have a wonderful elderly couple move next door, Clem and Maude Randbeck. Clem, an immigrant carpenter from Denmark, spoke English with a very strong Danish accent. His wife Maude was a smiling, happy woman who provided first Aunt Katherine, then later Mom, with precious and important friendship and companionship. Clem and Maude were extremely giving people. In addition to being available for Mom and Aunt Katherine, they took great care of Maude's sister, Irene, a retired legal secretary who was nearly blind. So with three older folks close by, Aunt Katherine and Mom found very wonderful and caring friends right next door. They all seemed to need and rely on one another. We were happy too, because with Mom working, Aunt Katherine could walk over to the Randbeck's house and pay a visit, have a nice chat, and depending on the time of day, maybe even a cocktail. Maude was a corpulent woman who had difficulty walking, so Clem did the most of the household chores and all the yard work. He also prepared the snacks and meals, and when he made Manhattans, he often included Aunt Katherine and Mom for a libation. This was something we'd never seen before, Aunt Katherine and Mom looking forward to something, laughing, having fun…and it was all right next door. After Aunt Katherine passed away in September 1966, Mom's friendship with the Randbecks became closer and stronger. She viewed them as much more than neighbors, but as an older brother and sister. Dennis, Jeanne and I enjoyed the Randbecks too, and could always count on them when we needed help with almost anything. Clem was a magician when it came to tools, woodworking and mechanics. When he was in his early 80's, he installed an in-the-wall air conditioner for Mom. Thinking that he was too old to do it alone, I offered assistance. Clem said, "That's ok, Peter. I'll do this." I insisted, so Clem allowed me to help. The unit was going into a hole that Clem made in the living room wall that opened to the carport. I was worried that such an elderly man was cutting a hole in Mom's house. "Clem, are you sure you have the measurements right? Can we double check?" Clem seemed bothered by my questions and doubt. Then I tried holding up the machine from my side so Clem's burden would be less. Again he got annoyed. "Peter, let go. I'll put it in." While I struggled to hoist the machine into place, Clem effortlessly picked it up and inserted it by himself. It fit like a glove into the space he'd cut, so tightly no daylight could be seen and no caulking was necessary. Clem wasn't just a carpenter. He was a master craftsman. The Randbecks were very fond of Jeanne, Dennis and me. We frequently dropped by to chat, borrow something, to be of help if they needed us, or just to see if they wanted some company. I loved going upstairs with Clem to the workshop he had in his unfinished Levitt attic. As a very skilled carpenter, he would make gifts out of the most ordinary of materials, like scrap pieces of paneling or molding. From scraps like these Clem made a beautiful household plant holder for me. I still use it and cherish it to this day. I was in awe at how he could take a section of a tree branch that fell during a storm, cut it to size, dry it out for months, then put in on his lathe and make the most beautiful furniture pieces and works of art from what others would burn in the fireplace or put into the garbage. Dennis' best memory of Clem and Maude was from the night he returned home from Vietnam.

> When I got home, I had a great time. Mom sewed a huge sign saying 'Welcome Home Dennis,' and hung it from the roof for all to see. All the flags were up in the neighborhood, and I remember kissing the green, green grass of home. That night I had a terrible ear infection and hadn't slept in a number of days. I was really tired, but I remembered that Clem had made me promise to come over for a special drink when I returned. So Mom, Peter, Jeanne and I went over to the Randbeck's to say hello and have our long awaited toast. Word got around that I was back because over the next few hours, this little old couple ended up hosting an open house party for nearly a hundred young people who came to welcome me home. The Randbecks were fine with hosting their first open house, knowing that I was home safe with friends and family.

Mostly we enjoyed the Randbecks because they provided Mom an important shoulder to lean on, an adult sanctuary, a place for Mom to go for a nice time, advice, or just to feel secure and happy.

One, Two, Three Laugh

Whenever any of us would fight or argue, Mom would promptly chastise us and say, *"Stop it! You're just like the fighting Whites."* Apparently, Robert A. White and his family members argued a lot. Mom enjoyed a good laugh and wished there were more of them. On our way home from visiting Aunt Katherine in Long Island Jewish Hospital during September 1966, Mom, Dennis, Jeanne and I stopped at a restaurant for lunch. Saddened by Aunt Katherine's condition, we weren't saying much to one another or having a very good time. After ordering, we sat quietly and waited for our food to come. All the other people in the restaurant were talking with one another, smiling, and having a nice time. We were sullen, unable to appreciate or savor the moment. Dennis broke the ice saying, "Look at all those other people having a good time. We should too. On the count of three, everyone laugh." He counted, "One, two, three," and we all began to laugh. What began as a brief bit of contrived chuckling continued, becoming real, uncontrollable laughter and it was contagious. People from other tables looked over, perhaps wishing they were having as good a time as we, and began laughing too. Soon most of the people in the restaurant were laughing. No joke or funny story was told. We just laughed at the count of three for no other reason than Dennis said to. And it worked. That was one of our funniest times with Mom.

Hawaii Visits

Mom dining with Robert, Charlotte and "Granny" Ida Gomes, Honolulu, 1966.

Many of Mom's best times took place 5600 miles from Levittown, in Hawaii, a place she visited several times beginning when she was nearly 50 years old. She loved her first visit there, to attend Robert's college graduation in 1966 and meet his new fiancée, Charlotte Gomes. Mom immediately liked Charlotte, then a student at Chaminade College, Charlotte's parents, Tony and Ida Gomes, and their large family of cousins, aunts and uncles. She also loved the beauty and enchantment of the Aloha State. When she came back from her first trip, and for months afterwards, she talked nonstop about the beauty of Hawaii, the sweetness and tolerance of the people, the relaxed environment of the "Aloha Spirit," and of the hospitality shown to her by Robert, Charlotte, Tony and Ida. As nice as her neighbors in Levittown and work mates at Holy Family were, nothing compared with how she felt when visiting her soon-to-be-family members in Hawaii, the Gomes'. They prepared special meals, sang and danced, told stories, laughed, enjoyed "a cold drink," as Granny Ida used to say, ate out at Koko's and other Honolulu restaurants, and even went to Duke's, the nightclub owned by Duke Kahanamoku, to hear the popular Hawaiian singer Don Ho and his Swinging Alii's perform "Tiny Bubbles" and "Pearly Shells." As much as the Gomes' were great to Mom, she brought smiles to everyone when she visited Hawaii. Charlotte said, "Everybody loved her." Charlotte was also very impressed with Mom's green thumb. Mom, who loved flowers a great deal and had more than average success with her Levittown gardens back home, was awed by the elegance, beauty and colors of Hawaiian flowers. When Mom returned from her first trip, she glowed. She wore the muumuus that Robert, Charlotte and the Gomes' purchased for her whenever she could, even to work. Her bird of paradise plant, photo albums and other reminders of that wonderful first trip to "paradise," were on constant display at 55 Twig. Dennis, Jeanne and I couldn't completely relate to what she must have been feeling. But we were happy to see her smile.

Peter, Jeanne, Robert, Mom, and Dennis toast at Robert and Charlotte's wedding, Hawaii, July 1967.

189

Best man Peter toasting Robert and Charlotte in
Waikiki, July, 1967

A year later, in July 1967, Robert and Charlotte got married, and we all found a way to get to Hawaii for the wedding. I was proud to be Robert's best man, and, once I made the decision to go to the wedding, I transferred from the University of Dayton to the University of Hawaii, thinking I might stay there as Robert had. Dennis and Jeanne saved up what they could to pay for their airfare. Mom was happiest of all because she was going to her son's wedding where all of us would be in attendance, and… she was going back to her beloved Hawaii. It was Mom's second trip, and our first. The wedding took place in Honolulu, at

Sacred Heart Church, and the reception in a room with a beautiful view of Waikiki Beach. Mom smiled broadly as she posed for pictures with all of us together, and sang "When Irish Eyes Are Smiling." The wedding photo with all five of us in it, taken at Robert's wedding in 1967, is the last photo of the five of ever taken. Mom, Dennis and Jeanne stayed on in Honolulu for a month in a small apartment nearby Chaminade College. Dennis got a

Dennis escorting Mom at Robert & Charlotte's wedding
Sacred Heart Church Honolulu, Hawaii July 1967

Mom dancing with the Groom, Robert July 1967

summer job in the Dole Pineapple cannery in downtown Honolulu, an experience few Long Islanders ever had. I got a job at Pan Am Airways at Honolulu International Airport, working mostly midnight to eight a.m. This schedule made it tough for me to join all the family activities, but I tried. At first I was a porter in the flight kitchen, then as a port steward working in the galleys and cabins of the big planes. At the same time I maintained a full time schedule at the University of Hawaii. After living and working for a year in Hawaii, I returned to the mainland in June 1968, attended a six week ROTC training camp at Fort Lewis, WA, then went back to finish college in Dayton.

Though Mom had fewer good times than most, she created her own bliss wherever and whenever she could. All the photos we have of Mom as an adult show her wearing a broad smile.

Mom on Florida honeymoon, January 1942.

Beauty

As the covers of this book shows, Mom was a very beautiful woman. One look makes this clear. Childhood photos of her show a cute young girl, but often without a smile. She was an only child with no siblings, saddened and confused at the loss of both parents before the age of five. By high school and college age, photos reveal a great smile and a glamorous look. During the years we knew her as our Mom, despite not having a large wardrobe, she always dressed and carried herself with elegance and dignity. She'd do her hair nicely, usually by herself as she couldn't afford a beauty parlor, and wear appropriate earrings and jewelry so she would look good and fit in wherever she went. In addition to her own beauty, she also liked beautiful things, liked the beauty of nature. Colorful flowers, neat gardens, graceful cloud formations and the stars of the night sky exhilarated her. She was elated at her first airplane ride, and commented in her diary at length about the beauty she saw while soaring high above the clouds, as if she were in heaven. Her elegance wasn't limited to her physical appearance, smile, dress or appreciation of nature. She was a graceful dancer and swimmer. Active on stage as a young woman, Mom starred in high school and college plays, especially where dancing was part of the show. She mastered the popular dance steps of her youth, like the Charleston and the Lindy, and was no stranger to the dance floor whenever the opportunity presented itself at a wedding or party. In her 50's, with the job of raising young children done and all of her children having left the nest, she grew depressed. Dennis and I encouraged her to get out more, meet people, and start doing things she liked. We told her she'd done a terrific job as a parent, and that she deserved to devote some time to

Mom (r) starring in All Saints Academy high school play, May 1935.

herself. She took our advice and began doing something she liked so much as a young woman, dance. She began attending a dance group in New Hyde Park to re-learn the old steps with which she was once so familiar, to learn new ones, and to make new friends. Once a week she'd drive to New Hyde Park in her little Ford Fairlane to meet new people, including some men, and dance with them. She'd always come home with a smile. Of the friends she made there, most were women, but some men began calling her at home, which was a completely new experience for Mom. We were very happy to see her excited about dancing and meeting new people, and finally doing something pleasant, something other than housework and teaching.

Mom was not a vain woman, nor was she a show off or one to steal the show. While she liked to have a good time, she was a decorous, appropriate woman of good taste, one who always said and did the right thing at the right time. The way Mom looked and expressed herself was, in my view, the epitome of refinement, elegance and distinction.

The years have taken their toll on many of my memories of her in a physical sense. I have to think hard sometimes to remember the sound of her voice and laugh. For a few reasons, I remember her legs. Because she never had a car until she was nearly 50 years old, Mom did a lot of walking throughout her life, which undoubtedly produced strong legs. As a small child I marveled at how she would sit in a living room chair with us on her lap, extend her legs together, downward to the floor, and let us slide down. We'd do it over and over again, laughing. Alone as she was with small children, she found ways to create fun for us, and all it took was a strong, willing pair of legs. They were the graceful legs of an athlete, a gardener and a dancer. They were the strong legs of a woman who, out of necessity, walked most everywhere she had to go as a New York City schoolgirl, suburban homemaker, community servant, parent and teacher. And they were the legs that I last saw at the Nassau County Medical Examiner's Office on the late afternoon of June 21, 1975, the legs that eliminated any doubt that it was she who was the victim of the accident that took her life that day.

VALUES

Strength, Patience and Acceptance

Mom had to deal with many hardships when we were small children, almost always alone. It would have been completely understandable if she complained a lot. However, we rarely heard a grumble or murmur from her. She was a tough, focused woman, never one to whine. Sometimes, not frequently, she'd go into her room, close the door and cry. It was her way of letting off steam from time to time. She always had to scrimp and save, to borrow from Peter to pay Paul, but she always found a way through, quietly. She never displaced blame, as so many do, by saying that her problems were the fault of others. She accepted things as they were, and dealt with them honestly, the best way she could. When there was not enough money, she tightened things up and made do. I'm sure there were many times when she'd have preferred to have a steak, but we'd have eggs and toast for dinner instead, or one of our favorites: spaghetti with a can of Hunt's tomato sauce on top, and maybe some scrambled eggs on the side. Mom was the master of making the food dollar stretch quite far. And when we did have steak, it was usually the $.29 a pound chuck steak, rather than the $.89 a pound sirloin. Cold cuts from a deli were never the school lunch fare. We ate the standard peanut butter or cream cheese and jelly sandwich. There were no complaints though, something we learned from her. We got to like plain food better than fancy food. Our favorite night was Friday night. As a Catholic family, we respected the meatless Friday rule in those days. While some may have gorged themselves on lobster, or a nice piece of swordfish or salmon, we preferred our tuna on white, primarily because we knew what to expect, and also because it was a quick meal, almost no cleanup, and we could be back out playing all the more quickly once we finished eating. Tuna Fish Fridays were the best.

Mom understood that life was often unfair, that some had more than others, and some had less, that some had an easy life, while others suffered greatly. She wasn't one to become consumed by her problems. Instead, they toughened her. She faced and overcame obstacles and disappointments with a deep faith that her situation would get better someday. She exuded great hope and confidence, no matter how dark the hour. When we brought our petty complaints to her, she'd listen, try to console us, but then, with a smile, say something like, *"Well I guess that's that,"* and we'd know it was time to move on. She accepted hardships patiently and with hope that the future would be brighter. What she couldn't provide, she'd do without, or try to find help from Father Fagan at Holy Family, or Aunt Katherine, or someone somewhere. Most of all, she clung tenaciously to the belief that no matter what she had to endure, God would see her through. When I wrote her about something that troubled me during college, she responded by telling me that everything would work out, that God would provide the answers. She understood the concept of trial and error quite well too. When Nassau County officials were of no help in getting Robert A. White's name off the deed to 55 Twig Lane, she didn't fall apart. She simply steered another course and found an alternate way to accomplish her goal. She mastered the ability to adapt to almost any situation, and we learned a great deal by watching her do that. Problems were seen as opportunities, not insurmountable obstacles. Upon reflection, I think Mom's situation was as dire as anyone who had been abandoned by his or her spouse and left with no resources whatsoever. Yet, by the dignified, steady, solid, unwavering way she lived her life, she persevered, always turning lemons into lemonade, always finding a different, better, straighter, honest path to accomplish whatever needed to be accomplished. And she did this without feeling sorry for herself or displacing blame. She never said a negative word about Robert A. White or how his conduct cost her and all of us so much. She never sobbed to neighbors or relatives about her plight. In fact, she never told neighbors anything about her situation. She was our tower of strength, our Iron Lady, years before Margaret Thatcher was dubbed with the title.

Nightmares

As strong and experienced as Mom was, the tension that weighed upon her sometimes produced nightmares. They didn't happen on a regular basis, but when they did they were loud and sometimes woke us up. As kids we were afraid, not for ourselves, but for how upset she must have been during some still and quiet nights. We'd be roused by shrieks of *"Chinamen! Chinamen!"* or other alarming shouts, and hurry to her room in the dark to see what was happening. She'd hug us, and let us know that there was nothing wrong, only that she was only having a bad dream, then send us back to our beds. One summer, when Dennis was in high school and I was home from college, Dennis was sound asleep in the room next to Mom's when one of her nightmares occurred. Alarmed by the screaming, Dennis flew from his bed and ran in the dark toward Mom's door, which was closed. He banged his head full force and collapsed to the ground. By the time I came downstairs and Mom woke up to see what the loud bang was, Dennis had come to. We were all glad to see each other and that everything was ok. Another of Mom's nightmares occurred while I was away at college. In her sleep, Mom got up, left her room, closed the door, and then began shouting. Dennis awoke and tried to comfort her. She dreamt that there was a man in her room, and that she was afraid to go back in. Dennis said, "Mom, this is only a dream. There's no one there. But if it makes you feel better, I'll go in first and check." Just to make sure, he went to the kitchen, grabbed his lacrosse stick, and bravely entered the room. After inspecting the empty room with stick in hand, both he and Mom enjoyed a good laugh together.

Jeanne, now a social worker, believes Mom's occasional nightmares involved some sort of PTSD. No matter how strong Mom appeared to us, she often felt alone and some underlying, suppressed fears may have been coming out at night in her dreams. As for the reoccurrence of "Chinamen" in her dreams, that was always confusing because Mom was not the least bit prejudiced or fearful of any nationality or ethnicity. She loved all cultures and had several small Asian statues in the house, as well as a number of Japanese prints hanging on the walls, and her bright red living room drapes were covered in Asian scenes. She also loved the Japanese, Korean and South Pacific people of Hawaii, whom she described as "lovely."

Mostly Fearless

Outwardly Mom seemed fearless, but every once in a while a little fright crept its way into her life. The main thing that caused this apprehension was the thought that some injury or harm might come to one of us. She was the protector and our safety came first. Coping with the task of raising four small children by herself often made it difficult to accomplish even the simplest of tasks without assuming some calculated risks. An example of Mom having to take a risk that other parents might not have had to take occurred in the early winter of 1953 when I was a five year old. Mom walked Jeanne, 1, Dennis, 3 and me to the Sunrise Supermarket, which was part of the West Village Green, to do some shopping. The Green was on the east side of Newbridge Road across from Levittown Parkway and was composed of three buildings, each with a few stores. There was a small swing park behind the stores. For trivia buffs, singer/songwriter Billy Joel grew up two blocks from the West Village Green, a place he mentioned it in one of his songs. It's where we shopped before they built the Grand Union supermarket on the west side of Newbridge. Probably for reasons of facility while shopping, Mom brought me to a small playground behind the Sunrise Supermarket and gave me very specific instructions. *"Peter, I'm going into the store with the kids. You play here for a while and when I'm done, I'll come out and get you."* This was one of the first times I was ever trusted to be alone, and I'm sure this made me feel excited. It was like Mom was telling me I was a big boy. As she spoke, my attention drifted to the swings and slide, so I really wasn't listening to what she said. She left with Dennis and Jeanne, and I began to play. Unmindful of Mom's instructions, that she'd be right back, after about 15 minutes I looked around, didn't see her and thought, "Hey. She must have gone home without me." I didn't cry. I just figured she forgot and that I'd better get going home. I knew the way, and began the three quarter-mile trek, including crossing busy Newbridge Road alone for the first time. I made my way to Twig Lane and walked as far as my friend Leslie's house at 65 Twig where I saw him and some other kids, and began playing with them. After about half an hour, a blue and orange Nassau County police car pulled up in front of Leslie's. The officer rolled down his window, looked carefully at all of us, then got out. He was looking for a five-year-old blonde boy wearing a green winter coat and brown leather hat with earmuffs. I fit the description. "Is your name Peter," he said. I didn't know if I was in trouble or not because I'd never been asked anything by a policeman before. I said, "Yes it is." Most of my young friends were speechless. Not Leslie. He taunted me a bit as the officer told me to get into the police car with him. He drove me back to the playground where Mom was crying hysterically. Until she laid eyes on me, she'd been thinking outrageous thoughts, that I'd run away, or been kidnapped. She hugged me and was very happy to know I was ok, then she scolded me for not paying attention and leaving the park. I could see the fear in her face and I'll never forget her words as she hugged me, *"How could you do this? How could you do this?"* I'm sure if she had to do that moment over again she'd have done it differently, but those were the innocent 1950's and parents then sometimes had to do things that parents might never consider doing today.

I can only think of one other time when I saw Mom afraid. As a single parent, the thought of losing a child or having one of us injured was her greatest fear. Little else seemed to frighten her. She faced all obstacles in her way with strength, determination and an uncommon bravery. In the mid 1950's the Mid-Island Shopping Center, now called the Broadway Mall, was built about a mile north of downtown Hicksville. The mall contained a giant department store named Gertz, and many other shops like Newberry's, National Shirt Shop and Flagg Brothers shoe store. The bus from Newbridge Road and Levittown Parkway took us there for fifteen cents. One day, while we were quietly window-shopping at one of the stores, Mom suddenly grabbed each of us and swept us away to another part of the mall, then on to the next bus back home to Levittown. We were young and puzzled. I later learned what caused the sudden panic. As we gazed in the large store window, Mom saw what appeared to be the reflection of Robert A. White behind her. Intrepid Mom, fearful of little, lived in apprehension of such a possible encounter with her former husband because, as she told me when I was older, such sightings happened a few times and she didn't want him coming back to upset the peace of our house. While most Long Islanders lived a life of safety, free from fear, Mom had to live on constant tiptoe stance, never quite knowing when she might not be able to make it financially, when one of us would have a problem we or she couldn't handle, or when the unstable, unpredictable Robert A. White might re-enter the picture. Somehow she was able to conquer or circumvent her fears when she had to. One thing is certain; she never gave in or succumbed to them.

Privacy, Humility and Gratefulness

Mom was a very private, modest person. Few knew of her plight. While she did have a few confidants, like her Aunt Katherine and cousin Florence Larkin, her teacher friend Mildred Sannosian, and the priests from Holy Family Church, she kept her problems to herself and trusted in her own ability to overcome them. As a devoted Catholic, she believed that God and Mary, the Mother of God, would guide her and help her find her way. As a young boy and later a teenager, I was puzzled by Mom's need for such silence. It must have been evident to all that we were a family with no dad, no car and little else. Neighbors had to be aware of the hardships and pressures we faced. I thought that if some people knew more of the story, they might be willing and able to be of help. However, Mom was a proud woman, in the good, proper and dignified sense, not the least bit haughty. She was an educated woman with two years of college, something few if any other women in the neighborhood had. She knew she eventually would be able to make a contribution to society and earn her own living once we were old enough, and therefore she didn't want to become the recipient of charity or to become reliant on others. Mom was not ashamed of her situation, but she kept her problems to herself for her own reasons, which we respected, but didn't always understand. In 1952, after Robert A. White left and failed to provide or was unable to provide the $35 a week child support he was ordered to pay, Mom described her need for privacy in these words:

> *I was advised by the judge in Family Court to apply to the Department of Social Services, something which was necessary for me to do. I had to go about so much all alone and was frightened and unsure of our future. I had to hand over the deed to my house and my life insurance policies to the county. This was a most upsetting time for me. I never did tell my children of the great difficulties we were facing as they were too young. I felt I should try and keep this discouraging news to myself as long as possible. I wanted to rise up above all these problems and make a peaceful life for us and hoped I had the stamina to withstand all these tribulations. I also wanted to keep this in our own family and did not feel our neighbors had to know of our misfortune.... I am quiet and would rather let others do the talking. I lead a very personal life, not divulging too much of my life to others. I also don't inquire into the personal lives of others as I believe privacy is most important to everyone.*

So the question "Why was Mom so private about things back then?" was answered by Mom herself. It was to protect us. She thought we kids would be dealing with enough with no dad and little family income. Almost all the other kids in the neighborhood had dads. I can only think of one who grew up without one: Joy Gillen of nearby Branch Lane. Many of the dads in the neighborhood did more than go to work and bring home a paycheck. They put in long hours commuting to the city and came home late. But when they did come home most would be up to their ears taking care of their kids, their houses and their yards. They'd wash the family car, fix things that broke at their homemade garage work benches, help bathe kids, assist with homework and the other jobs of parenting, coach Little League, serve the community as volunteer firefighters and ushers at church, run errands, bring home take-out food from the local pizza place or Chinese restaurant, take the family to Yankee, Giant or Dodger games, or Jones Beach or to far away vacations spots like the Pearlman's had in Ellenville, NY, plant flowers in spring, trim hedges in summer, rake leaves in fall, shovel snow in winter, help kids go from training wheels to two wheelers, and light the barbeque for family cookouts. Mostly they taught their kids that they had a dad, one who would be there to listen to their joys when they succeeded, or their problems when they were hurting. Mom knew we would be missing much of what other kids had. She believed that was pain enough and there was no need to provide young children with all the reasons. So while in one way we grew up a little emptier than our peers, in another way we were protected by a woman stronger than most. She bore many burdens alone, so we'd have fewer to carry. Despite her willingness to spare us, it was sometimes complicated for us. When kids would ask me, "Where's your father?" I'd answer, "I don't have one." They'd say, "You have to have a father. Everyone has a father." I'd say, "Well, I don't." We were who we were. Mom's requirement for privacy arose from her desire for us to be free to live normal lives, go to school, have friends and be healthy and safe. She faced life's troubles and fears herself, with great humility, leaving us out of it the best she could.

Mom accomplished a great deal during her lifetime. She was an excellent parent, hard-working housekeeper, devoted member of her church, faithful friend, dedicated, award-winning teacher, and dutiful community servant. When I compared her with other women I knew or observed, which weren't too many, none seemed to come close. It was not because the other women weren't good. They did many of the same things Mom did, but were able to do them without the fear and struggle that seemed to accompany every aspect of Mom's life. They had husbands, incomes, cars, insurance, refrigerators, even freezers full of food, savings accounts, visited beauty parlors, went dress shopping and never had to worry about where the next meal was coming from. Mom had it different, and we knew it. Everything she and we did involved some type of struggle. Whenever we had to go somewhere that was any distance away, it was always an ordeal that had to be planned days, even weeks in advance. Nothing was easy. No matter what the issue, it always seemed like a disproportionate amount of life's injustices were heaped upon her. When I first began teaching at Northport High School in 1974, my salary was $11,800. There were teachers, many of them women whose salaries served as second incomes in their families, who earned more than $20000. Mom was teaching for 15 years and her salary at Holy Family was less than $6000 a year, about a third of what my colleagues in public school earned. I thought it was terribly unfair, that Mom was being cheated. She didn't really see things that way though. She was happy in her house, even if welfare did possess the deed, happy with her family, and happy teaching in a wonderful school, even if the pay was low. She wasn't looking over her shoulder to see how others were doing, but was more than thankful to God and her community for what she did have. I saw Mom's many successes as a parent, teacher and community servant as heroic, partly because I knew what she had to overcome to accomplish them. She didn't see herself as a hero, but rather as an ordinary woman who was handed a different kind of life, one that called for more patience and tenacity than others. She went about her life with a genuine sense of humility, doing the best she could with the circumstances she was handed. Rather than be resentful for what she didn't have, she cherished her life and was extremely grateful for what she did have: four healthy, decent kids, a house to live in, a job, and a good community. Critical as her situation often was, it never led her to feel jealous of anyone else, or less than anyone else, or ashamed, or afraid to show her face, or hang her head. Rather, she cherished her life, accepted what was, and worked hard to better things for herself and others.

Duty, Virtue and Life's Goal

During the 1920's and 1930's, Mom was raised well by Aunt Nellie and Aunt Katherine. Of her upbringing, she wrote,

> *Orphaned in 1922, my two wonderful aunts took on the task of caring for, educating and loving me as their own child. During my youth, I remember having lots of playmates and school chums and being a happy and well-adjusted child. My school life was a pleasant experience. My marks were always good and I worked hard at my studies through college. Then I began dating and planned to marry. As I was a happy child, I do not remember being fearful in my childhood or in later life or else I could never carry out the tremendous task of raising my four children alone. I had a wonderful religious background and placed my hope and trust in God's Providence to see me through life.... My life goal was to be a good Christian and have a large family and teach them to love and serve God in their own way. Not having brothers or sisters, I had hoped when I did find the right man I would never let a child be alone in the world. Even though I was happy, I thought a brother or sister to share my thoughts and experiences with would add to my happiness.*

(Note: Mom had a number of half-brothers, including some from her mother's first marriage who were born in the late 19th Century, who died many years before she was born. She knew little of these distant half-siblings.)

Mom describes what was a good and innocent childhood, an ethical one in which proper morals and cardinal virtues were important. She showed the utmost respect for her adopted parents Aunt Nellie and Aunt Katherine, and frequently spoke of how well they raised her. Undoubtedly, Mom's right-thinking, dutiful, virtuous behavior came from the lessons provided her by these two special women, to whom she gave great credit. These important values, which stemmed from her upbringing and religion, guided all aspects of her life, and she made sure they spilled over to us. She followed a strict moral code, one she expected of us as well. Mom often had to be a strict, no-nonsense parent who set bedtimes, curfews, and other rules, and established definite consequences if we violated them. When Dennis and I shared the cold room together, we sometimes would continue talking after Mom thought we should be asleep. She'd come to the banister in the living room, tap it a few times with the round wooden paddle from a paddle ball game, and state firmly, *"I'm coming up."* Her words and the crisp tap of the paddle were enough to quiet us down and get us to sleep pretty quickly. Mom was a pretty good delegator. She handed out everyday chores like washing and drying dishes, grocery shopping, taking out the garbage, mowing the lawn, shoveling snow, normal things that most suburban kids did. But, as mentioned previously, she gave us monumental jobs too, like painting the house, paneling a room, making repairs, or assuming other adult responsibilities while still quite young and inexperienced. Though we were still kids, we enjoyed this adult empowerment and the trust she often placed in us. Following the strict moral code Mom established was ingrained in us and became a major part of our personalities. Essentially, we had to behave well because Mom expected us to, and so we did. Looking back, Mom's approach, while strict to us then, provided us with a clear view of right and wrong, something from which we benefited greatly throughout our lives.

Religious and Racial Justice

Similar to her zero tolerance policy for the use of foul language, Mom showed absolutely no leniency for the use of racial epithets or ethnic or religious slurs. No "N" words could be hurled around, no Italian, Polish or other ethnic jokes told, and no anti-Semitic remarks made. As a result, if a kid in the neighborhood told an off-color or racial joke, probably one he learned from his parents, we'd feel uncomfortable. During lunch hour at St. Ignatius one day, a classmate of mine named Paul told an anti-Semitic joke. A few kids chuckled, most did not. I was a nine year old in the fourth grade and didn't understand Paul's joke, which contained the "k-word." When I got home I told Mom about it. As she listened, her expression turned grim and her response was firm, *"You're never to repeat that, do you hear me? And you are never to play with Paul again."* Even when a punch line was funny, we were taught that it was wrong to make fun of or laugh at the expense of others. Though our neighborhood was mostly made up of Christian families, there were a few Jewish families, the Hoffman's, the Pearlman's, the Schwartz's, the Berger's and the Polanski's and we played with all the kids in those families. Everyone did. Some friction was inevitable because of the segregated pattern that came with our new, historic suburb. William Levitt, the developer of Levittown, himself Jewish, believed Christians wouldn't move into largely Jewish neighborhoods, so he sold mostly to white non-Jews. Black families were excluded at first by restrictive covenants in the original Levittown deeds, and later, after court action, by plain old racial discrimination. Once the covenants were found to be unlawful and courts said black families couldn't be excluded, white communities stayed white as realtors steered black families away to New Cassel, Hempstead, Roosevelt and other towns. Most early Levittown kids, toddlers fresh from the city, didn't have much contact with people who were different from them. So it was understandable that some prejudice might enter the minds of kids in our new, suburban community. From time to time, guys told "wop" or other ethnic jokes, mostly for the cheap laugh and usually at the expense of an Italian kid. It wasn't until I was in college that I learned that the term "wop" referred to a potential Ellis Island immigrant who was without papers (W.O.P.) and likely to be deported. Mom, who taught us to be tolerant and accepting of others, disallowed the telling of such jokes.

We'd cringe when someone would shout "dumb Jew" when a Jewish kid struck out in a stickball game. Mom served as neighborhood referee once in a while, like when she observed Jewish Freddy Hoffman sitting on top of Catholic Richard Urban, pounding away at him with both fists. When she ran out to stop the beating, Freddy looked up and said, "He called me a mockie." Mom said, *"Oh, that's terrible, Richard. But Freddy, stop beating him up. That isn't right either."* Given the behavioral standard Mom set, we considered such remarks cruel and intolerable. Consequently, whenever the older kids bullied the younger, weaker ones, which they often did, we'd find ourselves sticking up for the underdog. Sometimes a few others stood by me when I'd challenge a bully, which was usually enough to call his bluff, and the bully would let up. Sometimes not. But such was life for Levittown kids who grew up with different parents and different value systems. I learned from Mom that it was right to intervene. In fact, after doing so a few times, I discovered it wasn't that hard to do. Neighborhood kids regarded me as a "goody, goody kid", "Mister Justice," but that didn't really bother me. I was glad I had the values Mom taught and didn't suffer from the bystander mentality.

The New Section

Slight tensions grew in our neighborhood with the coming of the "new section," a more upscale residential subdivision built adjacent to our more modest, less expensive neighborhood. Our Levitt houses were built in 1950; this new, more expensive, split-level cluster of several hundred brick homes was built in 1954, so it quickly became known as "the new section," a name that has stuck until this day. The new section was built on the 28-acre farm formerly owned by the DeMonaco family. We loved the farm and were sorry to see it sold. Prior to the coming of the new section, we could look across the street from our kitchen window at the farm, with its endless rows of beets, cabbage and other vegetables and see all the way to the large smokestack atop Meadowbrook Hospital on Hempstead Turnpike. As kids, we loved playing in DeMonaco's fields, being given tractor rides by farmers' Dominic and Freddy, seeing the crops grow, running under the huge sprinklers, and having dirt bomb fights with clusters of soil left by the plows. Our fun ended when the DeMonaco's sold the large parcel of land to a developer who constructed Westbrook Park, the official name of the new section. New houses in Westbrook Park cost $16000 each, compared to the $8000 cost of a Levitt house. During the many months of construction, before the new families moved in, we took advantage of the situation, playing every game possible inside the freshly poured cement foundations and on top of the piles of scrap lumber, and making friends with some of the workmen. Older kids hustled tips by bringing them soda and water. We used the leftover scraps of wood and the thousands of nails we found all over the ground to make our pushmobiles and other projects. But by 1955, when all the houses were completed, things changed. With the arrival of families with slightly more money, an economic war of sorts began. Many Levitt house kids began to resent the new section kids and the rivalry was on. The people that moved in came with higher salaries, fancier cars, better bicycles, and even one and two-car garages built right into their houses. And unlike our neighborhood, most were Jewish.

While the biggest division between the kids from our neighborhood and the kids from the new section was in my view economic, the separation took on another shape. A group of homeowners from the new section lobbied the Town of Hempstead to have their section named Westbrook Park and be given it its own zip code, rather than be associated and on par with us Levittowners. They even erected a sign on Newbridge Road saying "Welcome to Westbrook Park." Though we laughed at their sign and push for their own zip code, we were no longer welcome on land that had served as our playground for years. We'd come home from school and see new section kids playing on the ball field that we built in "the weeds", the name we called the vacant lot between De Monaco's farm and the Wantagh State Parkway. New section kids didn't show the place the reverence we did, calling the weeds the Pinecone Forest instead. A self-imposed segregation grew; kids from the new section didn't play in our neighborhood, and we didn't play in theirs. New section parents didn't want their kids catching the school bus in our neighborhood and successfully had the bus stop moved to their neighborhood. There were only three ways into and out of the new section, and one was to cut through the center of our neighborhood. All year long, dozens of us would be out on Twig and Branch Lanes every day playing stickball, two hand touch, tag, ringalevio and other games. New section drivers would whiz right through our games, honking their horns to move us out of their way. Some reacted by yelling at the drivers, throwing their baseball gloves at the speeding cars, or taking their sweet time to move out of their way. And while people from our neighborhood rarely ventured across the divide into the new section, some Westbrook Park people even walked their dogs on our streets and failed to clean up. They may have had more money and bigger houses, and their fathers may have had better jobs, but we never saw ourselves as any less. Seeing new section kids as rivals and their more upscale development as an encroachment into our way of life, some kids, and even some adults, dubbed the new section the "Jew Section," "Little Israel," and other slurs. Mom would not tolerate us using such phrases. We were all seen as God's children, and that was that. Actually, as the years went by many of us got to know new section kids like Peggy O'Neill and Linda Cirillo quite well. In fact, they have become life-long friends. I delivered the paper to some new section families and they were quite generous. One Twig Lane girl, Lisa, married a new section boy and they continue to live in the old neighborhood to this day.

Upon reflection, I believe we were well-behaved, basically good kids who followed Mom's rules, partly because they were right and proper guidelines by which to abide, and partly because we, the children of Kay White had to. Despite normal peer pressure to sometimes do things that were wrong, with all the responsibilities and duties heaped upon Mom, we had little choice but to do that which was right. Not to do so would only cause her and us embarrassment and add to her problems. We willingly complied with Mom's rules, not solely out of fear of punishment, even though she sometimes did use punishment to correct behaviors and to serve as a deterrent, but because she taught us about responsibility and duty, and she expected us to carry out her lessons. It rarely, if ever, entered my mind to cross Mom, to try to get away with things behind her back. As Mom stated in her own words above, her religious background was a major part of her existence, and her trust on God provided the path that would see her through life. She made sure this path was abundantly made clear to us, *to know and serve God in our own way."* In looking back at how she lived her life, and at our adult lives, with our many involvements in education, community service and poverty work, it's plain to see that dutiful, virtuous, accountable Kay White carried out her life goal quite well.

A RALLY AND AN APOLOGY

Background

Like a lot of American high school students in the spring of 1965, my senior year, I considered myself to be a patriotic young man. I was taught to love my country and believe that its values, like "truth, justice and the American way," were right. When it came to fighting just wars like WW II, our fathers, members of America's "Greatest Generation," stopped the Nazis and Imperial Japan. What could not be right about policies such as that? But twenty years later, our involvement in Vietnam presented a different state of affairs, with issues that were less clear-cut. By the mid-1960's the escalation of war in that tiny country began to highly polarize our citizenry. In high school, I'm embarrassed to say, I knew too little of world events and yet I ignorantly formed political opinions based on emotion and not on fact. I hadn't read very much history by then, and admit to being persuaded by a handful of friends and a cousin to adopt some rather weak and poorly thought-out viewpoints. I wasn't very open-minded and believed "America right or wrong" was a valid maxim, mostly because I hadn't given much serious thought to the times when America wasn't right. In late 1964, the U.S. was just beginning to escalate the war in Vietnam, a place few in my social studies class ever heard much of or could even find on a map. In 1963, during John F. Kennedy's last year in office, the United States had approximately 16,000 advisors there, and few combat troops. Four years later, under President Lyndon Johnson, we would have more than half a million combat troops in Vietnam, under the pretext that they were necessary to protect our advisors. In 1965 I found myself, a 17-year-old, self-appointed know-it-all, defending U.S. Southeast Asia policy, even though I really knew very little about it. In my heart I thought I was being patriotic, trying to support our troops, trying to do what was right. Instead I was really exposing myself as a close-minded, exuberant inexperienced young man. Perhaps I'd seen too many movies, where the good guys were easily distinguishable from the bad guys, and the U.S. was always the good guy. I believed if there was a choice between saying "my country, right or wrong," it was far more patriotic to just say it was right, rather than delve further. In 1964 the Gulf of Tonkin Resolution, which allowed the president to send combat troops to Vietnam, sailed through the U.S. Senate by a vote of 98-2, giving President Johnson the power to add a much larger, more conventional military force. Following the Resolution, Johnson and a few Pentagon advisors began a tremendous military buildup that would ultimately cost hundreds of thousands of Vietnamese and American lives. At that time the vast majority of the people in the U.S. believed what our government was telling them was true. They hadn't yet learned that the Gulf of Tonkin Resolution, which would be repealed in 1971, was based, at least in part, on exaggeration and falsehood. They hadn't yet learned of events that would cause a majority of Americans to oppose the war, events like the My Lai massacre in 1968, where U.S. Army soldiers killed hundreds of men, women, children and babies in cold blood. They hadn't yet been made aware of the Pentagon Papers until 1971, when the New York Times and 17 other newspapers published a collection of leaked documents that revealed the U.S. had knowledge that the war could not be won and that "demonstrated that the Johnson Administration had systematically lied, not only to the public but also to Congress," in order to escalate the war. A so-called war "hawk" in 1965, I became a rather active "dove," by 1967. By then I'd read more and been influenced by college professors and a different peer group. But in 1965, shortly after the Gulf of Tonkin Resolution set the big U.S. buildup in motion, I blindly followed the then popular line of thinking.

The Rally

One evening in early 1965, seven of my classmates decided to attend a Vietnam War event at nearby Hofstra University in Hempstead, NY. Knowing most of these guys to be war hawks, not doves, when it came to the Vietnam War, I asked why they were going. The owner of one of the two cars going, a guy known for expressing himself loudly and often crudely, said, "I'm not going to support the anti-war crowd. I'm going to sound off, to be heard." I wasn't a troublemaker, but I did believe that America was a land where all points of view should be tolerated, including mine, and even theirs, so I went with them. I thought we were going to be part of a give and take, that there would be some people who were against the war, some people who were for it, and some who were neutral. So I got in one of the cars and we headed to Hofstra. I didn't know what to expect. I'd never been to a rally of any kind before. When we arrived, we noticed that the event was taking place in the Hofstra Playhouse, a rather large theater. The eight of us entered and sat toward the back. The theater was packed, mostly with well-dressed, professional-looking, middle-aged folks, not many college or high school students. Several of the guys I was with wore their high school jackets, an easy giveaway as to who we were and where we were from. There were several speakers including a very passionate Vietnamese Buddhist monk who was on an anti-war hunger strike, and U.S. senators Wayne Morse (D-OR) and Ernest Greuning (D-AK), the only two members of the U.S. Senate to vote against the Gulf of Tonkin Resolution a few months earlier. I quickly learned that this was strictly an anti-war event; there was no give and take. All the rhetoric came from the stage to the audience, and audience members clapped as each anti-war statement was made. We seemed to be the only ones with differing views and a few of my friends began yelling things out. When the Buddhist monk was introduced, the most boorish guy in our group rudely shouted, "Throw him a lamb chop!" Audience members shushed him. He smiled, apparently happy with himself for getting their goat. His outbursts continued as the senators spoke. Finally, ushers came to our row and directed all of us out of the auditorium. From their comments to the ushers, I realized some of the guys I was with weren't interested in listening to the speakers at all, but only in disrupting things. Angry at being kicked out, they waited in the parking lot until the crowd broke so they could continue yelling. I was uncomfortable with this, thinking things might get even more out of hand. Not long after we were given the boot, the crowd began to exit the theater. As rally-goers left the parking lot, our group followed their cars, honking horns and yelling things out the window. One guy shouted, "Go home commie." I was offended by what they were doing and thought, "This is not what I came for." But I was in it with these guys. I had put myself in the car with them, and I didn't know how to get out. At one point, a short distance from the Hofstra campus, we pulled up alongside a car that was stopped at a light. Someone in the front seat rolled down the window and shouted, "Jew bastards!" Those two words rang out like a clap of thunder. Shocked and embarrassed, I shrank down in my seat, wishing with all my might that I was not in the car with those guys, that I'd not gone to Hofstra with them. I had no idea that one of my classmates was going to blurt out such an awful thing, but it was too late. The remark was made, loudly and clearly. One guy in the car laughed, others were in disbelief. I'd never heard anyone say anything so cruel and offensive. To make things worse, if that were possible, I knew the victims of this brutal remark. It was the Davis Family, Jewish neighbors of mine. They lived seven houses down from me on Twig Lane. The Davis' were a wonderful family. The father, Sy Davis, was the brother of Mrs. Edith Pearlman, my friendly next door neighbor who had helped my Mom out so many times. Sy's wife, a lovely woman, was in the car too. In the back seat was their 11th grade daughter, Susie, a very nice kid who rode the school bus with us. I found myself trapped in a car with a bully who'd hurled this horrible, vicious comment, and I was unable to get out. I tried saying something, but it was not enough. "Cut it out, you guys." "Leave them alone." My words were too little, too late, and went nowhere. The damage was done. I had been in the wrong place at the wrong time with the wrong people, and innocent people were hurt. I never felt lower in my entire life then at that moment.

The Apology

When I got home I said nothing about any of this to Mom, partly because I didn't need to. I knew exactly what she'd say. *"Peter, if you did something wrong, you better do what you have to and make it right."* I went to bed but had a hard time sleeping that night. I was upset about a whole lot of things, like how a so-called friend could be so mean, how I, even though passively and unknowingly at the outset, could have been involved by being in the car with them, and how awful I felt for the Davis Family. I spent the next morning down in the dumps, ashamed of myself, an emotional basket case. Instead of explaining the whole episode to Mom, telling her what happened, what I was thinking, how I felt, and seeking her counsel, I took an important step by myself. I knew the lessons she'd always taught about how others should be treated. I knew how she had little tolerance for bullies, bigots and ignoramuses. I knew that in our household, there were certain unpardonable errors, and harming people like the Davis family, especially with a religious slur, was such an error. Confident and armed with that knowledge, entirely on my own but with Mom's values as my guide, I made an important decision. I walked out the door and proceeded down Twig Lane, past the seven houses that separated our house from the Davis', until I reached their driveway. Without hesitation, taking no time to rehearse, I knocked on the door. I had to act quickly because I couldn't let this matter remain without immediately trying to right the wrong that had been done. A few seconds later the door opened and Sy Davis stood in his kitchen looking directly at me. He didn't greet me. He didn't smile. He said nothing, perhaps wondering what I, of all people, was doing at his doorway. As Sy stood quietly with his arms folded, I trembled. The conversation would have to begin with me. It was an icy situation, a 17-year-old boy with the need to explain something important, standing face to face with a fit-looking, muscular, experienced, educated, middle-aged man whose family had been harmed. I'd heard that Sy Davis was a weight lifter. His chest and shoulders showed it. I didn't think about that, only how to begin talking. After a few seconds of silence, I finally said, "I was at Hofstra last night, in a car with a few kids from the high school." Sy said, "I know. I was there with my family. We saw you." There was another brief pause. Then I looked into his face and, with my voice quivering a bit, said, "Mr. Davis, I'm terribly sorry. I was raised better than this." I didn't make excuses, didn't blame the others or try to exculpate myself. I was there, and that was that. Whether actively or passively, I was involved. I didn't tell Sy that I tried to shut some of those guys up, or how I wished I could have been a million miles away from Hofstra that night. I just said I was sorry. The goal of my visit to the Davis household was not to take the blame off my shoulders, but to tell the truth and to utter some words that might possibly make Sy and his family feel better. After my acknowledgment and apology, there was another pause. I didn't know what was going to happen next. Sy could have said, "Get out," or yelled at me. He did neither. Instead he looked right at me, smiled and spoke a few reassuring words. I don't remember them exactly, but he seemed moved that a teenage boy would come alone, stand face to face with him in his own kitchen, and admit what happened. Sy shook my hand and put his other hand on my shoulder, then said, "Thanks for stopping by, Peter. My family and I appreciate it." I left the Davis' house that day feeling a whole lot better than I did on the way there. I walked the seven houses up Twig Lane, toward home knowing that, despite what happened the night before, I tried to right a wrong, to be honest, to do the grown-up thing. I tried to do what my Mom, Kay White, would have done if she faced that circumstance. In retrospect, Mom never would have faced such a circumstance because she never would have gotten into a car with such a guy, and if somehow she did, she'd have yelled a lot louder than I did to get out.

I've often reflected on that night from a half century ago. I've thought about what transpired from the time I decided to go to Hofstra with guys I considered friends to the time I left Sy Davis' kitchen, and how much can happen and how much can be learned in such a short period of time. I've thought about how much I'd have hurt Mom and my aging and sick Aunt Katherine if they found out I was involved in such a thing. I've thought about how easily bullies can hurt people with their words. I've thought about the fact that, even though I didn't do the bullying, I didn't do enough to stop it. I've thought about the kindness and forgiving nature of Sy Davis, and the powerful lesson he taught me with a simple smile, a few words and a handshake. Mostly I've thought about Mom, and how she worked her whole life to establish a good name for herself and our family, and how I came close to tarnishing it with one bad decision, one brief moment of thoughtlessness and fear. One thing that needs no thought is this: I am so happy that I had a Mom who taught the values she did, the values that guided me that day down Twig Lane to Sy Davis' kitchen. That day I became a much more mature young man, more responsible for myself and my actions, more accepting of whom I was, and far less concerned with what others thought of me.

A FEW FLAWS

Mom, who nobly persevered through economic and personal struggle to survive and succeed as a parent, teacher and community servant, was not perfect. Even the most courageous hero has her flaws. While Mom stands out in my mind as a pillar of family and community, her blemishes may lie not in anything she did wrong, but in what she omitted to tell us, what she didn't prepare us for.

Facts of Life

The task of raising four children alone was vexing for Mom. When problems with various aspects of our lives arose, she had no other adult to consult with or seek guidance from. Robert, Dennis, Jeanne and I were entering our teen years by the late 1950's and early 1960's. This presented another problem for Mom: how to present the lessons kids need to become normal, fully functioning adults. Since so many of the lessons we learned were centered around religious and moral themes, dealing with topics such as the birds and bees, dating, and adult issues may have been more difficult for her and were mostly avoided. Without a husband, Mom may have been nervous about how to approach three boys and a young daughter about such topics. So, they were never really addressed. We were on our own to learn what we needed to learn, whenever and however necessary. As for learning the so-called facts of life, of course I had a natural curiosity about such things, but never felt comfortable asking Mom any specifics. We just didn't discuss personal topics like that in our household. Mom may have felt that, when the right time came, we'd be ready to learn those things and the proper conversations would take place. In 1957, I was a forth grader with absolutely no clue about anything remotely connected to human reproduction. Some of the kids in the neighborhood knew some things, but not the whole story. One neighborhood friend, fourth grader Robert Taormina, said his mother explained something to him about a man having a seed, and that seed going into a woman somehow, and a baby growing inside. That was all he knew. That's all his mother told him. We were puzzled. Neither of us could figure out exactly how that seed transfer worked. We guessed that this seed grew on some part of a man, maybe the size of a sunflower seed, and the woman would take it like a pill and, like plants in the garden, next thing you know, a baby would begin growing inside. After discussing the obvious harm that could come to the baby when the mother digested food, we rejected this theory. How could mother and baby share that small space and there be no harm? But at that time in our lives, we were satisfied with knowing just that much, and resumed the things that were more important to us, like playing stickball and hide and go seek and sleeping out in the tent we bought together with money we'd saved. A year later, while walking down the hall in St. Ignatius with a few classmates, fellow sixth grader, Paul Flynn, explained much more of the birds and the bees story, the whole story, and I remember being pretty shocked, especially with the rough, graphic way Paul explained it. After these revelations from Paul, I did not go home and double check with Mom about what I'd learned. Like I said, some things just were not discussed.

Social Awkwardness

Learning these things in such an informal, coarse manner from other kids wasn't really that helpful in educating me about grown up matters. Instead it left me feeling that all the other kids knew things that I did not, and that I was therefore less mature and behind in some way. We were not provided the same experiences as other kids in the neighborhood. As children, we never saw our Mom go out with another man. We never saw a man, period. There were no men's things in our house, no men's deodorant, no men's underwear in the laundry, no men's shaving equipment. No smell of a man. We never saw adults acting like a couple. There was no male-female holding of hands, kissing or hugging. No man and woman sleeping in the same bed, or even bedroom, and no terms of endearment like "honey" or "dear." No signs of affection as in other households, like anniversaries and Valentine's Day. No flowers or gifts to put a smile on the other spouse's face. Socially speaking, we went blindfolded into our teen and adult years, at least compared with how other kids were entering them. As an eighth grade boy, my close friends were Bob, Drew, and Gary. Gary lived on Branch Lane and we frequently hung out at his house. As we sat watching TV in Gary's living room one day, something awkward occurred. The bathroom in a basic Levitt house is just across the hall from the living room, and adjacent to the kitchen. Gary's dad, Elio, a psychologist whom all the kids in the neighborhood loved because he was so supportive and active with us, was taking a bath. Since everything is so small and close by in Levitt houses, we could hear him humming in the tub as he splashed around. When he finished he called out to his wife, "Dammit, I forgot to bring a towel. Jeannette, can you get me one?" I looked up, surprised to hear Elio shout out a profanity. We didn't do that in our house. There was no cursing at all. Gary's mom, Jeannette, quickly said, "Yes dear." I looked up again. I didn't live in a family where there were two spouses, with one calling the other "dear." Jeannette got a towel, opened the bathroom door, entered and handed it to Elio, who had just bathed, and was obviously naked. My eyes nearly popped out of my head. "Did you see that?" Gary said, "See what?" I said, "Your mother. She just went into the bathroom!" Gary said, "So." I said, "Your father is in there." Gary said, "White, they're married." The three boys laughed at me for my naiveté. I was embarrassed. But I was learning, slowly, about my ignorance.

When my own four children were growing up, I was reminded of how awkward it was for me to uncover these pre-teen and adolescent secrets, and discussed things with Jill, my wife and mother of my four children, Jennifer, Brian, Meredith and Brendan. When we thought the time was right to begin discussing such topics, the kids were quick to point out that we needn't bother. "Dad, you don't have to go into all that stuff. We've seen the famous 'fifth grade film' in health class. We know all we need to know." Whew.

The Elevator

On one of our many trips to New York City to visit Aunt Nellie and Aunt Katherine, something frightening happened, something I was unprepared for and ill-equipped to handle. After dinner one summer night, Aunt Katherine realized that there was no ice cream in her icebox. That's what they called their small, gas operated, 1920's refrigerator, the icebox. She asked me to go to the local store and buy some vanilla, chocolate and strawberry ice cream. I was ten years old and always eager to accept such jobs when asked. I took the elevator from their third floor apartment, C-35, to the main lobby, a dark place with stained glass windows and a very formal looking medieval décor, a place we thought kings and queens dwelt in "the olden days." After exiting the building and walking a block to the very southern end of Pinehurst Avenue, I arrived at the spot we called "the steps," a three flight, white granite staircase that descended from Pinehurst Avenue to 181st Street below, the neighborhood's main commercial artery. The steps gave this area of Washington Heights a look similar to the many hilly streets of San Francisco. Less than a block east from the steps was a small luncheonette named Hye's, run by an elderly Eastern European man of the same name. He had a strong accent, one I could hardly understand. There were few supermarkets back then, only small individual shops like the butcher, Tony the greengrocer, Cushman's Bakery, and so forth. As I entered Hye's, I noticed a man, maybe in his 40's or 50's, about to enter at the same time. I'd never seen him before and he looked a little scruffy, but I did what I'd been trained to do, I held the door open for him and he entered the store along with me. Hye's had the usual soda counter with the round, stainless steel seats that twirled, shelves of candy bars, racks of magazines, and a small frozen food section that had ice cream. I selected the three small containers, one chocolate, one vanilla and one strawberry, paid Hye for them and headed toward the door. As I was about to leave, I noticed that the man I held the door for was just standing there. He wasn't shopping for anything, speaking with Hye, or doing anything. He was just standing there. As I left, this man left with me and, trained to be polite, I again held the door for him. I thought this was a little odd, but I wasn't alarmed. Maybe it was just a coincidence. It was nighttime, and I walked alone with my package along 181st Street back toward the steps. The man walked in the same direction as I, but stayed about ten yards behind me. We were the only two on the dark street. The dubiousness of this scene began to cause me to think something wasn't right. "Maybe when I turn up the steps, this guy will go straight," I thought. I turned and went up the steps, and the man did too. Now I really wanted to get back to Aunt Katherine's and to be rid of this strange character. I began walking more quickly and hoped he'd either enter the building before 106 Pinehurst Avenue, or continue on past 106. I turned into our building and the man did too. What should I do? I'm a kid and he's a grown man. Questions popped into my mind. Should I be honest and say to this man, "Hey, are you following me?" Should I show fear and shout? What if he's a nice man and I shout for no reason at all? Confused and worried I decided to continue home go. What other choice did I have? In the foyer to the building, there was a set of intercom buttons, one for each apartment. The stranger stood by as I scanned the list of names and apartment numbers, pressed C-35, went to the door and waited to be buzzed in by Mom or Aunt Katherine. When the buzzer ticked away loudly, I pushed the door open and entered, and the man followed through with me into the dimly lit lobby. My worry now turned to fear. I didn't know what was going to happen next. Of all the buildings in Washington Heights, how could this man from Hye's just happen to still be with me, right in Aunt Katherine's lobby? I kept hoping that maybe all this was a coincidence, that he was a friendly neighbor, who possibly forgot his key. But since he was with me ever since the candy store, common sense told me this wasn't right. My heart began racing as I went to C-wing, carrying my precious package. I didn't make eye contact with the man, hoping he would go to A or B wing, but he did not. He came right to C-wing with me. Neither of us spoke as I stood at the elevator door and pressed the button. Moments later the elevator came and I felt a little relief knowing that in a matter of seconds I'd be at the third floor, safely back at Aunt Katherine's. Outwardly I showed no fear, but inside, I was afraid of what might happen during those seconds. As a ten year old, coming from a family that didn't talk openly about certain unmentionable or taboo topics, I knew nothing about perverted behavior and had no training at all about how to react when faced with a sex offender, pedophile or other dangerous character. The elevator had a large heavy door that I opened after the metal iron gate opened automatically. I entered the elevator, and the man followed me in. Now it was just the two of us. No one else was present. I pressed the button for the third floor, and, praying that this was all a coincidence, hoped he would press a button for a different floor. He did not. As the iron gate closed and we were locked in, this sinister-looking man cornered me in the tiny elevator by spreading his arms and legs widely and placing his hands on the walls with me in between. Completely confined by this man I was locked in with no means of escape. As this white, old-looking, unshaven man looked down on me, I cowered below. He pressed his body against me and I could smell the odor of stale booze coming from his breath. He immediately placed a few of his fingers in between my legs and began to touch my genital area. I did not know what he was doing, or why, but I knew this behavior had to be wrong. "What is happening? Why would some want to touch me there?" Finally, the man uttered the only words I heard him speak, "Doesn't this feel good sonny?" I said, "No it doesn't. Leave me alone, mister." He continued touching me and I could feel his fingers against my skin. I remembered that there was a small hole in my pants just below the bottom of the zipper. The man found it and inserted a couple of his fingers through the hole. That's when I yelled, "Cut it out, mister. Cut it out. I have a hole in my pants there!" Then, luckily for me, even though only a young boy of ten, I was able to push him away just as the elevator reached the third floor and the iron gates began to open. Maybe he was drunk, or maybe I'd shoved him off balance, but he didn't grab me and I was able to exit the elevator and knock on Aunt Katherine's door. The man stayed in the elevator and then disappeared. I went into the apartment with the ice cream and said nothing. I must have looked a bit shaken and unnerved because Mom questioned me immediately. *"What's going on? Is something the matter?"* Since I wasn't hurt and just thought I'd met a bad man who behaved oddly, I kept quiet, handed Aunt Katherine the ice cream, made my way to her couch in the living room, grabbed a comic book and began reading it. I wasn't bleeding or injured and really didn't know what to think or even how to explain the episode that just took place. Mom was more perceptive, repeating, this time more emphatically, *"What's the matter, Peter? Did something happen?"* I looked up and couldn't lie. I said, "Yes." She said, *"What?"* I told her that there was a man in the elevator. Frightened, Mom loudly demanded, *"Did he touch you?"* I said, "Yes." *"Where?"* I rolled up my comic book and pointed to my genital area. She screamed. Now I really didn't know what to think. Was I in trouble? What did I do wrong? I just sat there. Mom called the police, then went out with a broom in her hand to see if the man was anywhere to be found. He was long gone. The police came to Aunt Katherine's apartment and asked me some questions, which I was embarrassed to answer in front of Mom. Again I was from a family that didn't talk about sex, body parts, or other adult topics. They were the quiet topics that we'd learn about later rather than sooner in our lives. Given all the excitement with the police coming, I don't remember eating any ice cream that night, but I do remember being left with a lot of questions and a newfound fear of strangers. I decided that I would no longer isolate myself or make myself vulnerable, that I would be more aware of my surroundings and keep my eyes open for things and people that looked suspicious, and that no one would get behind me. I learned these important lessons the hard way. Following that incident, I made changes in my life. In a classroom, I'd always situate myself so no one was behind me. The same is true for restaurants, subway stations, everywhere. No one gets behind me if I can help it.

After the passage of some time I came to realize that what took place in that elevator wasn't my fault but the behavior of a troubled, drunken man. I was just a boy on an errand who encountered a bad man who scared me. And though I wasn't hurt physically, there was a scar. I thought of what might have happened if the man were bigger or stronger, or if I wasn't able to push him off me. What might have happened if Aunt Katherine lived in a high-rise building and the elevator ride was longer? What might have happened if he blocked me from getting out the door, or took me to another floor, or the roof? While I came away from this uninjured in the physical sense, there was a different kind if injury, a psychic impairment, one that has lasted a lifetime. Back on Long Island a few days later, I told my friends on Twig Lane of my elevator adventure, and they weren't kind. While sitting with a group of neighborhood kids, my friend Les said, "Ah ha, White got queered in an elevator." The kids laughed. I did not.

Dating

Learning about the birds and the bees, couples coupling, and the danger pedophiles could inflict was a difficult and awkward process. Dating was also difficult and awkward because it involved actually putting oneself on the line, taking a personal risk. Robert had both boy and girl friends in eighth grade at St. Ignatius, and even had a few girls from Hicksville come all the way to Levittown to visit once in a while. In 1956 and 1957, when some of these girl and boy friends came over, I was just a fourth grader. Dennis was in second grade, and Jeanne in kindergarten. Robert's eighth grade friends weren't doing much more than hanging around, riding bikes, and listening to the latest rock and roll songs like "All Shook Up," "Wake Up Little Susie," and "Be-Bop-A-Lula." But to me, it looked like dating, since there were teenage girls involved. They laughed a lot and even had nicknames for one another, like Sugarino, Tiny Terror and Pigeon Man. Seeing Robert in mixed company was my first view of any type of male-female coupling. Mom even allowed him to go to rock and roll shows in the city where he and his friends were part of thousands of young males and females enjoying the new music of a new age. Those teenage observations ended abruptly for me when Robert entered a prep-seminary in the summer of 1957. The Don Bosco Juniorate was all male and didn't include rock and roll shows or girls named Tiny Terror.

By the time I reached eighth grade in St. Ignatius, 1960-1961, I liked girls and wished I had the knowledge and experience some of the other boys had. But with no role model to follow, and my big brother gone to a seminary for three years, driven by ignorance and the fear of rejection, I really didn't try getting too close to girls. I was good friends with many of my female classmates, but when it came to intimacy or closeness with them, I was mostly an observer. When we had our eighth grade trip to Rye Beach Playland, I envied the cool boys who seemed more sophisticated and mature, guys unafraid to ask a girl to go on the rides or hold hands. There were other impediments in the way of my social advancement. One was geographic. Most of my classmates at St. Ignatius lived in Hicksville, near one another, and were part of the CYO athletic programs there. They had a much easier time being with one another. If there were parties, they'd know about them and go. I lived in distant Levittown, too far away to walk or bike at night. So, with such little knowledge and experience, and no role model, I was more comfortable staying in my own neighborhood, playing sports, riding bikes and hanging out with my friends. Dating would have to wait.

When I entered Clarke High School, I was in a totally different world than that from which I'd come. Class sizes were smaller; only 30-35 students in a class, not 50-90 as in St. Ignatius, and all but gym classes were co-ed. Though there was a dress code that required boys to wear shoes, slacks, and shirts with buttons and collars, and for girls, skirts, blouses and shoes, there were no official school uniforms. Sneakers were for gym class only. These were the days before the courts ruled that dress was part of free speech and kids could express themselves with long hair, tee shirts, sneakers, and shorts. In the early 1960's, many of the girls dressed well and looked older to me, like women. For a fraidy-cat boy like I, such girls were unknowable and untouchable.

I lived nearly two miles from school so when social things were happening, once again it was difficult for me to be part of them. By senior year, when a few friends got their driver's licenses, they could borrow their parent's car to get around, but that was never an option for me. I walked or biked everywhere I had to go, all the way through high school. Sometimes I resented seeing my peers drive by as I walked, but for the most part I believed there was something admirable and self-reliant about being a young man who could get where he had to on his own, without the help from mommy and daddy that so many others seemed to have. Even though I had a driver's license, I didn't have any real opportunity to drive until I bought my first car for $90, a well-used 1951 Dodge Meadowbrook, when I was a sophomore in college. Nicknamed by my friends at the University of Dayton "The Purple Tank," my '51 Dodge had something called fluid drive. There was a clutch, but I only had to depress it when changing from reverse to either forward, or low, which was also called "hill, mud and snow".

Though fear and lack of transportation were two reasons dating was made more difficult, there was another: money, or rather the lack of it. One needed a few dollars at the very least for whatever costs were involved in dating, like admission to a school dance, or a movie, or a burger or ice cream at Jahn's Ice Cream Parlor on Hempstead Turnpike. With no experience, no role model, no car, and no money, I found myself better off hanging out with my guy and girlfriends in group settings. I was happy just being part of the crowd, involved in skating at the Roosevelt Field ice rink with no one in particular, but part of a big, co-ed group of 20 or so friends. Such group activities provided safety in numbers, and there was little risk of failure or rejection.

Things changed during the fall of my senior year and I was a starter on the school football team. While walking down the hall one morning, completely by surprise, one of the most popular, beautiful girls in our school, Christina, the captain of the cheerleading squad, approached me and said, "Hi Pete. Would you like to go to the dance with me Saturday night?" I stood there stunned and didn't know what to say. I'd heard that Christina's parents were professional dancers in New York City and my first thought was, "This could be way out of my league." Nevertheless, the words, "Sure, terrific, yes, thank you" leaped from of my mouth, and I was now the proud possessor of an official date. As a dating neophyte I walked away from this brief encounter with Christina thinking, "Great. I have a date with the most gorgeous, popular girl in school. Now all I have to do is figure out how to make it happen." I'd have to find at least some money, a scarcity for me. I'd have to pick her up somehow, but was without a car. And of course, I'd have to figure out how to dance. None of these tasks would be easy. Fortunately, a friend named Jeff was going to the dance with his girlfriend and he agreed to give me a ride. I was actually quite happy to have been asked by Christina, and, despite the obstacles I needed to overcome, I began to look forward to the big night. Jeff and his girlfriend picked me up, then drove me to Christina's. I knocked on the door and Christina opened it and smiled at me as she came out. "So far so good," I thought. I didn't really know what I was doing out on the gymnasium dance floor, but I watched all the other kids and faked it pretty well. For the most part, I survived the dance but afterwards I got very nervous about how to handle things. I'm not sure if we stopped anywhere after the dance. If we did, I don't remember it. The reason my memory fails me on that point is because I was terrified by a couple of things. If we went to a diner or ice cream place after the dance, I'd have to talk with her. Though she was very nice and very pretty, a genuine member of Clarke royalty, I didn't really know Christina very well, nor her likes and dislikes. What would I say? I knew I couldn't be silent, but dreaded the possibility of bungling a conversation or putting my foot in my mouth. There was another thing I feared, something I'd seen many times in movies: the doorway scene. I was completely unskilled and had absolutely no idea of what to say and what to do when the evening was done and I'd find myself standing with Christina at her doorstep. I remember walking her to the door but I don't recall whether or not anything was said or done at that moment, whether we embraced or shook hands or even looked at one another. I do remember that the manner in which I left that very nice young lady at her front door was quick and probably clumsy and embarrassing. When I got back to the car, the others were laughing. I'll leave it at that.

The whole thought of bringing a girl home seemed too complicated and nerve wracking for me, and something better off postponed until a different time in my life. So even though I did socialize and have friends who were girls, as a teenager I never had a girlfriend. Instead, I went about my life having fun with the rest of my non-dating friends, playing ball, taking bike hikes, working, and mostly avoiding things like dating, that made me feel awkward and nervous. Perhaps Mom was wrong not to have spoken with us about the topics of growing up, the birds and the bees, pedophiles, dating and so forth. But she was alone and had to handle everything by herself. Maybe she was just too busy and didn't know how to present these topics, so she just postponed discussion of them.

MARY

Mom was very devoted to the Blessed Virgin Mary, the mother of Jesus. Mary meant very much to her and was a major influence on her life.

Earlier, I quoted a letter from Mom to me in the fall of 1965, when I was a brand new freshman at the University of Dayton. Thinking I was unhappy or homesick, she wanted me to know that, no matter how difficult the situation, I should never despair, always exude confidence, and have great hope. Mom's words bear repeating:

> *When I was first left with four young children to rear my first act was to bring them to church and all of you were dedicated to Mary. This was a solemn ceremony performed by the priest. I thought she could help me and I don't think she has failed me.*

I don't know exactly why Mom chose Mary for this dedication, nor do I know anything about that ceremony. I was only a four-year-old boy at the time. It's likely that the four of us sat quietly in church while a priest said prayers, blessed Mom and us, and gave Mom the utmost confidence that she was not alone in this task. Perhaps Mom felt that since Mary was chosen to be the mother of Jesus, she was the best person to provide her the guidance she'd need for the serious job that lie ahead. Mary raised her son Jesus in a simple manner, as the son of a carpenter, and suffered a great deal herself, especially seeing her own son die on the cross. Mom also may have chosen Mary because many Catholics believe in her capacity to intercede on behalf of those who pray to her. So our connection to Mary goes back to the very beginning of our family, and it didn't end there.

Mom's family members, the McCoy's of Washington Heights, also were influenced by and devoted to Mary. More than a century ago, Mom's grandfather, Cornelius McCoy, purchased a double plot in Calvary Cemetery, Queens, NY when his wife, Mary, Mom's grandmother, died in 1899. Though the grave spans two plots and contains the remains of nearly a dozen members of the McCoy Family, there are no names etched on the wide gray stone. Instead there are only four words inscribed:

McCoy
One Hail Mary

Mom explained that her grandfather wanted all who visited the grave to remember his wife Mary and say that prayer.

Mom's connection to Mary spanned the Cold War days of the 1950's, when she led us in praying the Rosary to Mary for world peace. The family rosary beads were kept in

Mom's white plastic statue of Mary that had a blue screw-type bottom. There are other connections to Mary in our lives. When Robert left the prep-seminary in West Haverstraw in 1960, he came back home to Levittown and attended Chaminade High School in Mineola for his senior year. Chaminade was a Catholic school run by the Marianist fathers and brothers. It was named for Father William Joseph Chaminade, who founded the Marianist order, also known as the Society of Mary. After high school, Robert attended Chaminade College of Honolulu, where he met his future wife, Charlotte. The Society of Mary runs Chaminade and other colleges throughout the country, and has missions worldwide. I graduated from the University of Dayton, where I minored in Theology and Philosophy. Dayton is also run by The Society of Mary.

Mom loved the Maryknoll Fathers and Sisters, brave priests and nuns who do important missionary work throughout the world, mostly in the poorest regions imaginable, and who are dedicated to the Blessed Mother. Whenever a Maryknoll missionary came to Holy Family or a neighboring church to speak, Mom was sure to attend. She was inspired by their hard work and dedication. Mother Mary Joseph Rogers founded the Maryknoll Sisters in the 1920's. When Mother Mary selected the land for her new order in Ossining, NY, the local bishop saw the site and said to her, "This is Mary's knoll." The order has been known as Maryknoll ever since. Maryknoll's director of communications told me that "Mary figures prominently in all our activities." Interestingly, when I first traveled with my mentor, Dick Streb, to rural, impoverished Nicaragua to begin my decades of humanitarian and educational work there, I was introduced to two great women, Maryknoll Sisters Joan Uhlen and Elizabeth Salmon. Joan and Liz served as an important liaison and helped me with the many groups I brought to Central America from1990 until I retired in 2008. Recently Joan and Liz returned to their Mother House in Ossining for health reasons. Since I lost Mom when I was young and never had any aunts or uncles, Joan and Liz have become the very important "aunts" I never had. I relied greatly on the wisdom and knowledge of these great Sisters of Mary during my 50 trips to Nicaragua with more than 1500 students from Northport High School. Sister Joan, who spent more than 40 years in Nicaragua, lived in Hawaii for many years beforehand and was principal of St. Ann's School in Kailua. St. Ann was the mother of the Blessed Virgin Mary and the grandmother of Jesus. Before arriving in Nicaragua, Sister Liz lived in Hawaii for many years too, serving as a music teacher at the Maryknoll School in Honolulu. One day, while walking on a hot, dusty camino in the campos of Nicaragua, Sister Liz told me a very interesting "small world" story. She had taught my niece and nephew, Ann Marie and Robbie, while she was a teacher at the Maryknoll School. She also said that that she knew my brother Robert and his wife Charlotte quite well. I thought, "How wonderfully interesting it is that I'm in the hottest, dustiest, poorest place in our hemisphere, 2100 miles from New York and 5000 miles from Honolulu, and I'm learning about my own family members from a woman I've just met." Liz raved about what good students Ann and Robbie were. Their mom, Charlotte, also attended the Maryknoll School in the 1950's. The Maryknoll Sisters, these wonderful daughters of Mary, have been a tremendous influence on me and many other members of the Kay White Family.

Another link to Mary is probably more of a coincidence than an actual connection, but worth sharing. I swim several days each week at the Suffolk County Community College pool in Brentwood, NY. During the winter of 2012, when leaving the pool one afternoon, I noticed what appeared to be a chunk of cement sticking out from a bunch of tall weeds and debris that surrounded a lamppost in the college parking lot. Curious, I spread the weeds away and discovered that the very old, worn, cracked piece of cement was actually a discarded two-foot tall statue of Mary. It looked to be a very old, worn-down version of the kind of statue that is sold by nurseries to people who want to display a religious object on their front lawn. It was so worn down that there was no face left on it. As I stood in the college parking lot, I thought of Mom dedicating us to Mary as little children, and of the other connections to her and decided that driving away and leaving this statue amidst the weeds and litter wouldn't be right. I carefully placed the crumbling statue in my trunk and took it home. About 150' behind my house, high up on a hill in a patch of ivy, I propped up this statue of Mary with a few large rocks and faced it toward my house. This statue has remained in this quiet, secluded spot ever since, and unless I pointed it out, no one else would know it's there. Mary looks down on my house, in a way I believe Mom would favor, and I can observe her from almost anywhere in the house or yard. Whenever I have the need to be alone with my thoughts, or require a reflective or prayerful moment, I have this sanctuary, this outdoor "Mary knoll" to bring me peace.

Mary was a constant, unwavering force in Mom's life and it gives me great happiness knowing that these connections to her exist. In a metal box containing some of Mom's most cherished, personal things, I came across this poem:

Image of Blessed Virgin Mary, Holy Family Life magazine

"Mary"

When you follow her, you will not go astray;

When you pray to her, you will not despair;

When you think of her, you will not err;

When she holds you up, you will not fail;

When she protects you, you will not fear; When she leads you, you will not be fatigued;

When she favors you, you will arrive safely; She keeps her Son from striking us;

She keeps the devil from hurting us; She keeps our virtues from escaping us;

She keeps our merits from being destroyed; She keeps our graces from being lost

St. Bernard….

Mom, as a single parent of four, may have had concerns about such things as despair or failure. St. Bernard's words about Mary undoubtedly gave her the strength she needed to continue and succeed.

Compassion for Others

Worrying about her day to day struggles, her lesson plans and report cards, and raising the four of us, Mom sometimes appeared to be all business. When I think back to my boyhood, the image that comes to mind is of her sitting at the kitchen table with papers spread out all over, wearing her reading glasses, working. She was forever balancing her checkbook, paying bills, writing letters, or doing schoolwork. That was the business side of her. There was also the passionate side. Her passion was never the mushy or fake kind, but the sincere, meaningful kind. This level of care and concern was usually shown when things went awry for someone else or their family. She was always willing to help, even if she didn't have much in the way of resources or the means to do so. She cared deeply about the suffering of others, locally and worldwide. While she could do little about the problems of the world, she could, and did, care and pray for those persecuted and oppressed. She often did this whenever the TV news or papers covered tumultuous events going on in the world. Even though her family was small and her resources were few, she cared very much for her aunts, cousins, and other family members. On August 9, 1958, the phone rang. It was one of Florence Larkin's daughters. Florence was Mom's first cousin. Her husband was Joe Larkin, a wonderful man whom we called Uncle Joe. Even though Florence and Joe, a corporate lawyer who traveled around the country much of the time, had five children of their own to raise, they were very big helpers to Mom, especially in the 1950's when she had few places to turn for help. Within seconds of answering the phone, Mom let out the loudest shriek I'd ever heard from her. Moments later, she hung up the phone, then burst into tears and cried uncontrollably for most of the day. I was ten years old, Dennis eight and Jeanne six. We didn't know what was happening, or what to do, so we went into her bedroom, hugged her and began crying too. We didn't know why we were crying; we just knew that if something made Mom that upset, it had to be very bad. It was. Mom had just learned that Joe Larkin had died, suddenly, accidentally, in his own home. Without preparation or warning, she had just lost one of her family's most decent, caring members, and her impassioned response to this shocking news was something we'd never seen in her before.

Usher Jim Schmidt escorting Mom at Peter's wedding, February 14, 1971

Mom reacted in much the same way in June 1973 when she received a call that my good friend, Jim Schmidt, had been murdered in Chicago. Jim and I met at the University of Dayton. In 1967, I decided to transfer to the University of Hawaii and Jim joined me. We lived together for half a year in Hawaii, then Jim went back to Chicago and we remained close friends, writing to one another in the ensuing years. Jim was an usher at my wedding in February 1971, and Mom grew very fond of him. She asked him if he would walk her down the aisle at my wedding. Two years later, Jim told me he'd gotten engaged and asked if I could come to Chicago to be in his wedding party. I was honored. Jim, whom friends called "Schmitty" was a wonderful man, a great friend, and a brilliant scholar. In June 1973, he and his fiancée, Dorothy, were traveling on Chicago's I-57 on route home from a family event. Noticing what he thought was a stranded motorist, Schmitty, as was his style, pulled over to offer help. In fact, it was not a stranded motorist, but a member of a murderous gang posing as one. The couple was made to lie face down on the side of the road, relieved of their valuables, forced to have one last kiss, then shot through the back with shotguns. Mom loved Jim, and viewed him as family. She cried uncontrollably at first, then found the strength to comfort me. The man who killed Jim, who became known as the I-57 killer, was apprehended, convicted, and sentenced to the longest prison term in Illinois history.

Mom's demonstrations of compassion weren't limited to the loss of loved ones. She cared very much about everyone, and tried to be of some help to all whenever she could. She cared very much about the poor, bringing inner city children from Brooklyn to stay for weeks at a time during several summers, even though she didn't have the money to treat them to very much. She saw the plight of others, and always responded the best way she knew how. It was very natural and normal for her to give all she had, from the heart, since she had little in the way of material things to give.

In the spring of 1968, Mom's cousin Florence passed away at Columbia Presbyterian Hospital in upper Manhattan. Though she was a fairly new driver, Mom made her way to the city as frequently as possible so she could be by her cousin's side during her final weeks. Florence's son Bob was just 16 years old at the time and recalled the following:

> My mom was unresponsive during her final days in the hospital. We all took turns sitting by her side, waiting for the inevitable. When cousin Catherine visited, I was very impressed. She'd sit on my mom's bed, hold her hand, and speak to her, even though she wasn't awake to hear anything. I said, 'Cousin Catherine, she can't hear you.' Catherine responded, 'Of course she can, Bob. Come and sit with me. Take your mom's hand and talk to her. I'm sure she'll hear you.' I did as she suggested and am forever grateful that Catherine helped me at that difficult time.

Mom's much-loved pet, Sugar.

As kids, with the exception of a few parakeets, we never had a pet. Mom couldn't allow it. With four children to raise alone, she was unable to add any more expense or worry to her already stressful life. That changed in the summer of 1963, when a neighbor's dog had puppies. Jeanne came home with one of them and begged Mom to allow her to keep the little white mixed-breed dog. Aunt Katherine lived with us at the time, and Mom was about to begin her third year as a first grade teacher. Perhaps she thought a cute little pet would be good company for Aunt Katherine since she spent many hours alone in the house, or perhaps she just felt sorry for the pup and didn't want to see her go to the wrong home. Mom approved and we had Sugar. For the first three years, Sugar became Aunt Katherine's pet. She was a wonderful companion for her while we were at school all day, following her all around the house as she did her chores. Aunt Katherine loved Sugar and had dozens of her own homespun names for her, including Sugar-Pie, and other sweet sounding nicknames. We loved seeing Aunt Katherine happy and excited to be with Sugar, and vice versa. That little doggie was better than any medicine the doctor could have ordered. The two were inseparable until Aunt Katherine passed away in 1966. Mom then assumed the role of being Sugar's keeper and the same, close relationship developed between the two of them. As we grew up and began our adult lives outside the house, there was always Sugar, so excited to greet Mom when she came home and content to be with her at all times. In the late 1960's, Mom wanted a wooden fence built around the entire back yard so Sugar could get proper exercise and experience the freedom dogs require. I worked weeks on building a picket fence, making each picket myself with only a few old hand tools. As Mom requested, I primed and painted this sturdy, redwood fence white, and Sugar had her yard. Mom's joy with Sugar ended in 1974 when she developed a few lumps and the veterinarian's news was bleak. Years later, in the metal box filled with her personal things, I found a handwritten note from Mom that said:

"Sugar passed away March 22, 1974 at age 11, my dearest pet and constant companion. No words could express how I loved her. I will miss her always"

Mom was a sensitive and passionate woman.

DECLINE AND RESUGERENCE

During the early 1970's, Dennis was just out of the Marines and had begun working in the bar business, a job that caused him to keep late hours. As a young man, he was also in need his own space, so he got an apartment with a few of his friends, moving first to Amityville, then to Westbury. I married Jill Papa in February 1971 and had an apartment in nearby Westbury. Jeanne married Ernie Champagne in the summer of 1971 and lived in an apartment in East Rockaway. Robert lived in Hawaii. So with all of us out of the house, Mom now lived by herself and increasingly began to feel more and more lonely. We made it a point to visit her as often as we could, and we'd sometimes find her cranky and crying, often for light or trivial reasons. We felt like we were on a tightrope, unable to tip one way or the other. On one hand, we couldn't avoid or completely put aside our new marriages and new jobs, and on the other, we couldn't stand by watching Mom, who had given so much to us, suffer. Her emotions changed frequently. One day she'd be fine, smiling, seemingly together and feeling good, and the next day she'd be stressed out, cross, and unsteady.

Juan Wilson, M.D.

Dennis, Jeanne and I began seeing Mom's fragile behavior as a sign of weakening health, so we sought the opinion of Dr. Juan Wilson, a very bright and gentle man. He had a wonderful manner with patients, young and old, and something that benefited Mom and us over the years, a social conscience. Since Mom had so little money, he oftentimes accepted less than his normal fee, and sometimes no fee at all. He even made house calls when necessary. We explained Mom's behavior to Dr. Wilson, and how we felt guilty about her having to live alone. He reassured us saying, "She's a survivor. She's been through a lot and isn't the type that will let something like this get her down. I'm sure she'll be able to move forward." We felt so much better knowing that a professional with a good heart was going to take charge, and that things could only get better for Mom. Within days, Dr. Wilson called and Mom agreed to a complete physical exam. He determined that Mom was suffering from hypoglycemia and some level of depression, and immediately put her on a very strict diet that included lots of fruits and other healthy things. He also prescribed certain vitamins and hormones. Mom took Dr. Wilson's advice seriously, and strictly followed her new diet. Within weeks, almost miraculously, things changed. She became a new woman, smiling more, less tired, and shedding fewer tears. She looked better, actually glowing at times. She lost weight and did her hair differently. Her face and smile appeared more youthful and natural. We thought Dr. Wilson was a magician. His diagnosis and suggested remedies worked. Mom's life was transformed greatly, and so was ours.

Sewing

Mom enjoyed sewing. When we were kids, we'd see her sewing once in a while, mostly out of necessity, stitching holes in our pants, or darning our socks to save money. But as part of the new life she'd discovered after Dr. Wilson's diagnosis and treatment, she began sewing for herself. She found it fun to be inventive and express herself through following traditional patterns, and creating some of her own original designs. Sewing became her newfound hobby and an important outlet. First she started with simple projects, then moved on to more complex patterns, eventually making much of her own clothing. In part, she did this to save money by not having to buy new outfits. But mostly she sewed because she liked to. She was proud of the clothing she made for herself and others, and liked the praise she'd receive from colleagues at work, friends and us when she made something really nice and showed it off. The more things she made, the better she got at her new craft. She'd go to shops and find patterns, cut them out, and have blueprint papers strewn all over the kitchen table, always measuring and cutting away. Daily, she'd sit at the new Sears sewing machine she bought for herself, a fine machine encased in a wooden table, and finish off her many blouses, skirts and other articles. Shortly before her death, she was working on a bright green tie for Dennis to wear on St. Patrick's Day. She never got to complete it. To this day, Dennis wears his unfinished green tie on St. Patrick's Day, with the original pins in the back still holding the fabric together. Mom's Sears sewing machine still works and is a valued part of Jeanne's furniture in her Albany home.

Dancing, Dating, New Friends, New Challenges

The changes in Mom weren't only physical or apparent. They were real and important. She had more energy, a new look and a new view. In addition to the dietary and vitamin guidelines Dr. Wilson prescribed, he also suggested that she'd benefit from some additional companionship. "Catherine, I think you should go out with friends more, find things to do outside the house, put time into hobbies and your own interests. Try to do things that will make you feel better." Mom agreed with Dr. Wilson's advice and began to follow it. She got out of the house more, took trips around Long Island in the car, and began doing something she enjoyed very much as a young woman, dancing. She'd learned from a friend of a place in New Hyde Park, half an hour west of Levittown, where men and women gathered to dance, mostly the old steps she'd mastered decades earlier. With little coaxing from us, Mom achieved something we never could have gotten her to do. Completely on her own, she ventured to New Hyde Park, found the dance place and gave it a try. She came home from her first visit elated, talking non-stop about the dancing, first with other women then, believe it or not, with some men, and the new friends she'd made. And she was happy. There was a small lounge below the dance place. A few weeks into her new hobby, she began joining her new friends for a drink and some conversation. She quickly became one of the more popular ladies in the group, with men wanting to dance with her, offering to buy her a drink, and even asking her out. One man, a 43-year-old detective, asked her out to dinner, and he thought Mom was younger than he. Mom was 55 years old, but didn't look it. This new social life was a lot for her to take on so quickly, as it had been more than two decades since she'd received any type of male attention. She confided in a few friends, Jill, Dennis and me, and often asked questions about what she should do when new situations arose. *Dennis, when you go skiing with friends, girls sometimes go along. What do you do?"* Dennis was a little uncomfortable answering so he just said, "Mom, I'm always looking for the right girl. That's all." With this new social life, Mom became concerned about certain things like how safe she'd be with men, what her behavior should be, what she should say yes to, and what she should say no to. But we considered these to be good problems. Rather than remaining at home alone as she'd done for so many years, she was now out with other people, smiling and enjoying her new life.

Jack

One of the men from the dance place that paid the most attention to Mom was named Jack. He smiled a lot, danced with her, made her laugh and feel good. Within a few months, Jack began taking Mom to dinner, stopping by the house, and bringing her gifts. At first, Dennis and I felt a bit awkward. It was a bit out of William Wordsworth's "My Heart Leaps," where the poet said, "The child is the father of the man." Dennis and I seemed to be assuming a different role, that of parenting our parent. We liked Jack, but were protective of Mom. She'd been through a lot in her life, and we were a little leery of "too much too soon." As young men, we didn't want to control her new life, and at the same time we didn't want to see her disappointed or hurt. Jack began to take her out regularly, mostly to lunch or dinner. Finally, in her mid 50's, Mom was socially confident and in charge of her own life. Previously, her life was governed by economic, personal and health struggles. Now she was at the helm. At last, we were witnessing a new Kay White, a woman rising from the basement of depression to the penthouse of long-awaited and well-deserved happiness. As with any relationship, there were ups and downs. On Christmas Eve 1974, Dennis stopped by to say Merry Christmas to Mom and to bring her a gift. He planned on making it a brief stop because he had moved into a new apartment with some friends and they were having their first party that night. When he arrived at

Mom's house, he found her teary eyed. The house was decorated nicely, the tree was up, and Christmas music was playing, but Mom was crying. She had expected Jack to come by, but he was 45 minutes late and hadn't called. Despite having so much to do in preparation for his party, Dennis decided to forbear it and stay with Mom. He always put Mom's needs ahead of his own. She looked at Dennis with sadness and said, *"You don't have to stay for me. Go out. Have a good time. I'll be fine."* Mom often had a way of saying one thing

Jack and Mom at Gatsby's Pub in late 1974

when she really meant another. Dennis stayed, more out of concern for her than from guilt, though both figured into his decision. They sat together for a while and he tried cheering her up with jokes and small talk. After about half an hour, there was a knock at the door. *"I'm not expecting anyone else. You answer it,"* she told Dennis. He opened the door and, … it was Jack, all dressed up and wearing a bigger-than-usual smile. In his hand he held a small, nicely wrapped package, which he handed to Mom. She opened it immediately and was surprised to see a brand new expensive watch. Mom's mood changed at once. Her tears of loneliness and sadness turned to tears of happiness and joy. "It was quite dramatic," Dennis said. "She went from being completely depressed to happy as could be."

Jack accompanied Mom on more than just dates, but to various family events, including my daughter Jennifer's christening in the fall of 1974. By keeping such regular company, joining in family activities, and surprising Mom with the costly watch, things between them began to take on a serious look, perhaps too quickly for Mom in such a short time. She was interested in friendship, companionship, and a little fun. Even though she was without a man for nearly 25 years and had begun the process of seeking an annulment, Mom was not shopping for a new husband just yet. She continued to see Jack, but decided on a slower, more deliberate course, which included seeing others as well.

In the summer of 1974, Jack asked Mom to go to a lake resort in Connecticut for a weekend vacation. This caused her a degree of anxiety. She knew and trusted Jack, who was very gentlemanly, but her knowledge of him was limited to mostly dinner and dancing dates. A resort in Connecticut, involving an overnight stay in a hotel, would be different. She didn't want to hurt his feelings, nor did she want to step into a life for which she wasn't ready. Excited and puzzled at the same time, she considered her options. Should she decline the offer? Should she go, but stay in separate rooms? Perhaps just go for the day, with no overnight complications? Or should she let go of her traditional values a little? Mom was 57 years old and, practically speaking, single. But she was from the "old school" and not part of the sexual revolution. Mom shared her concerns with us and we took our "parental" roles seriously, listening, advising and cautiously trying to be the best help we could. Mom went to Connecticut with Jack, and they stayed in separate rooms. After Connecticut, Mom continued to see Jack, however she did so in a broader, more open-minded way, affording herself opportunities to know and spend time with other friends, including men.

To this day, whenever any of us talk about the final two years of Mom's life, we speak of how great it was to see her revitalized, happy, relaxed, smiling and eagerly looking forward to this new stage of her life, one with less drudgery and uncertainty, fewer problems, and a new and exciting social life. Dr. Wilson and his treatment, her improved health and her newfound hobbies and friends were just what she seemed to need. Dennis, Jeanne, and I continued to drop by regularly to visit, do a few chores, and talk with her and were happy to see that she seemed to be out more than she was in. Sometimes our visits were cut short because Mom had places to go, things to do, and people to meet. After so many years of struggle, depression and loneliness, seeing her happy was a delight and a great relief. The fragile Kay White of the early 1970's became transformed into a new Kay White, a woman of newfound vitality, with an abundance of friends, leading an exhilarating new life.

THE LOSS

June 21, 1975

June 21, 1975, was sunny and warm, a perfect beach day. It was the day of the summer solstice, the longest day of the year. For a different, dreadful reason it turned out to be more than the longest day of the year. It became a never-ending day.

The Afternoon Before

Friday June 20, 1975, was the last day of classes at Holy Family School and Mom was looking forward to summer vacation for some well-deserved rest and relaxation. After work I stopped by her house to mow the lawn. She was busy getting ready for the Holy Family School graduation that evening. I planned on attending the graduation too and told her I'd pick her up if she wanted. Then I asked what she was planning to do the next day, her first day off. She said a man had asked her to go to Jones Beach. "Oh. That's nice. Who is he?" She said, *"A man I met at dancing. We're going to meet Dennis and his girlfriend there and have lunch."* Concerned but trying not to be nosy, I asked, " Do I know him? Is he a nice guy?" Her answer was a little lukewarm, *" As far as I can tell he's nice. He asked me to go out last New Year's Eve and I said no. I didn't want to disappoint him twice, so I said yes."* I didn't want to dampen her plans but I was concerned, so I said, "But Mom you don't really know this guy." She replied, *"Don't worry. I'll be all right. Besides, Dennis will be meeting me there."* I asked, "What's his name?" She said, *"Mel. I don't know his last name."* It seemed odd, Mom going out with someone for the first time, knowing so little of him, not even his last name. But Jones Beach was only 15 minutes away on the parkway, and Dennis would be joining her. I didn't pursue it any further and went back to mowing.

The Night Before

The Holy Family eighth grade graduating class of 1975 was composed of 150 students I'd taught two years earlier when they were sixth graders. Mom had many of them as first graders. On Friday night June 20, 1975, I was glowing inside. I had just finished my first year of teaching at Northport High School and received a positive end of the year evaluation from my chairperson, Dick Streb. I looked forward to being home more, and spending time with my 10-month-old daughter, Jennifer. It was going to be a good summer, or so I thought. I had taught at Holy Family School for three years, 1971-1974, and I was very close to the class of 1975. They were wonderful kids and I wanted the chance to see them one more time before they dispersed to different high schools. Mom and

**Sister Natalie, Mom and Peter,
Holy Family School graduation,**

I agreed to go to the ceremony and sit together. We arrived and joined the hundreds of parents, family members and faculty as they were entering the auditorium. I looked around for two seats together and noticed my favorite nun, Sister Natalie De Natale, sitting in the middle of the packed, sweltering gymnasium. There were two seats right next to her. Natalie smiled and pointed to the two seats, as if she'd been saving them for us. Natalie and I had been colleagues for three years. She taught sixth grade Reading and English, and I Social Studies and Science. We worked closely together, along with Mrs. Dot Corrigan, who taught Math and Religion, and had many good times together. The editor of Holy Family Life, the parish's monthly newsletter, took a photo of the three of us sitting together. Mom sported her usual broad smile. The photo appeared in the next issue. We enjoyed the ceremony and meeting many of the graduates afterwards. Two of my best students, Brian Colossuono and Brian Hughes came over to say their goodbyes. They were such wonderful young men that two years later I named my second child Brian, with them in mind. As I drove Mom home, I again asked about her beach plans for the next day, then said goodbye. It was the last time I'd see her.

The Next Morning

Jill, baby Jennifer, and I lived at 870 Carman Avenue, Westbury. We rented half of an old farmhouse from Dominic De Monaco. When I was a kid, I knew Dominic and his brother Freddy, owners of the 28-acre farm right across from Twig Lane. So I was now the tenant of my former neighbor. The De Monaco house on Carman Avenue was near the southbound entrance to the Wantagh State Parkway. Shortly before 9:00 a.m. on that warm and sunny Saturday, Dominic's daughter, Pat, left for Jones Beach. My bedroom was right above the driveway so I could hear all the comings and goings. At about 9:15 a.m., Pat returned disappointed. Her mom came out and asked, "What's the matter? I thought you were going to the beach." "The parkway is jammed," Pat said. "It's bumper-to-bumper as far as the eye can see. They're turning everyone back." I thought to myself, "Beach traffic can't be backed up all the way to Old Country Road. We're ten miles from the beach. Something must have happened." I went about my day, not knowing that at 8:50 a.m., unexpectedly, in a fraction of a second…BANG, a double fatality accident had taken place a mile south, in Levittown, where the Wantagh Parkway passes under Newbridge Road.

Dennis' Story

As planned, Dennis went to the beach with his girlfriend, Marie, to meet Mom. He described the events of that day in these words:

> It was a beautiful day with a bright blue sky, a perfect beach day. I picked up my girlfriend and headed to Jones Beach on my motorcycle. I entered the Wantagh Parkway at Hempstead Turnpike and was excited to be meeting Mom and her new friend. We were to meet at Field 9 at 2 p.m., but she wasn't there. I began walking the sand up and down and still could not find her. I got nervous

and kept going back and forth. This was before cell phones, so I used the pay phones to call her at home, thinking they had car trouble or had a change of plans. I kept getting no answer. At about 4 p.m. we headed back to Marie's home. I stayed there for only a few minutes and started to get a nervous tension in my gut. I drove to Mom's house and saw our neighbor Clem Randbeck outside. I asked Clem if he'd seen Mom and he said he hadn't. I went into the house and looked around and everything looked in order. There was no note. I called her name a few times and then went back outside to talk to Clem again. We chatted for a few minutes and I shared that Mom was going out with a new guy and I was worried because they were supposed to meet me at the beach but didn't show.

Just then a black car pulled up and the driver rolled down his window and asked, 'Do you know who lives in this house, 55 Twig Lane?' I got defensive, thinking it was someone nosing around for something. He didn't introduce himself so, not knowing why he was asking, I said, 'Who are you? Why do you want to know about who lives here? I'm her son.' The man then said he had an address found at an accident that had occurred on the Wantagh Parkway that morning. He introduced himself as a detective and said I should come with him immediately.

The detective didn't say what had happened, but I knew something had to be very wrong. I screamed. He seemed to be driving so slowly so I yelled at him to hurry. I said, 'What happened?' He tried to tell me, then I recall saying, 'It's her. Oh no! It's her. She never met me. Oh God! She's gone.' He told me to try and remain calm. He shared that there was a terrible accident and both persons were killed instantly. He said they could not identify them as there were no wallets or identification found at the scene.

I was taken to the Nassau County Medical Examiner's Office and saw the yellow tile walls and the small glass window by the door. They pulled a stretcher over to the window and pulled the sheet back and I knew it was she. I was in shock and broke down. I couldn't keep it together and I screamed and cried and there was nobody there but me. The cop then took me away from the area. I called my brother Peter and he answered.

Dennis' Call

Dennis' call to me was one of the shortest calls I ever received, and the most agonizing. Speaking slowly and pausing between words he said was, "Peter… This is Dennis… Mom was in an accident..." Then he paused a little longer. He didn't have to say any more. From the tone of his voice, I knew what his next three words would be, "…and she's dead." His words hit me like a piercing thunderbolt. I cried out loudly, upsetting Jill and ten-month-old, Jennifer, who both began crying as well. All I could focus on were the last three words "…and she's dead." Dennis and I didn't talk any further. It was not that kind of call. With no explanation of what happened, no other information, only grief and pain, I told him I'd be there as quickly as I could and got off the phone.

Although he said, "she's dead," I had a feint glimmer of hope that Dennis might be wrong. "What if it wasn't Mom? What if it was someone who only looked like Mom?" I lived at the north end of Carman Avenue and the Medical Examiner's Office was at Meadowbrook Hospital, about two miles south. Numb, I got into my car and began making my way on this incredibly sad journey. I wanted to get there as soon as possible because Dennis was alone, and because I needed the truth. At the same time I didn't want to get there. I didn't want the truth. As I drove I maintained my role of Doubting Thomas the best I could, leaving myself a thread of hope that it wasn't she. There were only two traffic lights between 870 Carman Avenue and Meadowbrook Hospital and I caught them both. As I sat impatiently and in shock for what seemed to be a never ending minute or two at the first red light, Stewart Avenue, one of my football coaches from ten years earlier, Mr. Tony De Sevo, pulled up next to me in his car, opened his window, smiled, and waved vigorously at me. I'm sure he thought I was being rude to him, but I could only look away. Under the circumstances, I couldn't say hello to my old coach, a friendly man whom I hadn't seen in years and who had given me so much. I couldn't exchange even normal pleasantries like "Good to see you, Coach," nor could I have answered him if he asked me how I was doing. So I just looked straight ahead and sped off when the light changed. On my way, I passed several familiar places I'd been to many times over the years, like the stores where so many football players and friends gathered after Clarke games, the drug store I worked at one year, the Carman Avenue swimming pool where I swam every summer, my high school friend Alice's house, my friend Ray Rottkamp's parents' farm, the East Meadow firehouse where Dennis was a volunteer, Eisenhower Park where I played golf for the very first time with Mom and Joan Fowkes, and the Nassau County Jail, where Jeanne's husband, Ernie Champagne, was a correction officer. These places meant nothing to me at that moment. I was on a different journey.

Right past the jail I noticed a sign saying "Medical Examiner's Office," pulled into the parking lot and immediately thought I was at the wrong place. There were no other cars, just an empty, abandon-looking parking lot. Then, at the far end, I saw Dennis standing alone. From about 75 feet away I put my arms out and yelled, "Is it true?" Dennis shouted, "Yes," and collapsed to his knees. We embraced, cried, and then went into the building. Though Dennis had said yes, it was she, I still had my scintilla of doubt. I had to. About such a thing there can be no mistake. Inside I saw the dirty yellow tiles of the wall, the ones Dennis had seen minutes before. I saw the grimy window by the door, the window through which thousands of shocked people have peered to identify their loved ones over the years. A morgue attendant repeated the same procedure with me as he had with Dennis, wheeling a sheet-covered stretcher close enough to the window for me to make a positive identification. As he pulled back the sheet revealing a woman's head and face, I tried to focus but couldn't. Tears and the fingerprints and smudges on the window from viewers-past clouded my ability to see clearly. The hair on this person was wet and straight back, as if it had been washed down. I continued to look carefully through the hazy glass thinking, "It looks like Mom, but there can be no mistake." I needed more certainty, to be able to view more closely, with my own two eyes, not through a dirty window. I asked the attendant if I could enter the room. He obliged. Even with this up-close inspection I was still unsure. There could be no mistake. I knew the location of a birthmark on her lower leg and asked if he could remove the sheet to reveal that portion.

Again he obliged. I hoped and prayed that I'd see no such mark, that this was not Mom but a different woman. These few seconds, waiting for the sheet to be lifted, knowing that if the birthmark was there all doubt would be removed, was an uneasy, angst-ridden point in time. But it was the moment of truth. With one gentle uncovering motion, the attendant drew the sheet back, revealing the mark, exactly where I remembered it to be when I sat on her lap as a child. Now there was no mistake. This was, in fact, Mom lying before me. At 6:00 p.m., June 21, 1975, the longest day of my life had just begun.

Natural versus Unnatural

I've lived through many blows in my life, had to face many tough situations and make a number of difficult decisions. But nothing prepared me for that moment in East Meadow, NY. Nothing could. It came so swiftly, abruptly and unexpectedly that even now I still find it hard to believe. Mom was there no more. Our rock, our strength, our root, our stability, gone. Our inextinguishable force had been extinguished, suddenly and inexplicably. Such a death, in my view, seemed so much tougher to accept than death that comes naturally. Sudden death leaves no one time to prepare, to discuss options with family and doctors, to say goodbye, to say, "I love you." All deaths are sad and leave survivors empty-hearted. This needs no explanation. But when death comes abruptly and violently, like a flash of lightning, leaving glass and steel parts strewn about the highway, then understanding and accepting it is so much more difficult, and the pain more intense and protracted.

The Collision

To this day, none of us has ever received any specific information about exactly what happened on the Wantagh State Parkway at 8:50 a.m. on Saturday, June 21, 1975. We know only that Mel Bostick, a Queens man Mom knew only briefly and not very well, picked her up that morning and they headed to Jones Beach together in his car as planned. Mel drove. Mom was the only passenger. The car was a mid-1960's Chevrolet without seat belts. They weren't required at that time. They entered the Wantagh Parkway at Old Country Road in Westbury and headed south. After traveling for about one mile, the car collided head-on into the solid stone center support where Newbridge Road crosses over the Wantagh Parkway. According to reliable sources like police, Medical Examiner personnel and a priest, both were killed instantly.

"A Levittown Woman," Newsday, June 22, 1975

There was a story the next day in Newsday, Long Island's largest newspaper. Beneath the headline "Two More Deaths In Accident On Wantagh State," the article stated:

> A Levittown woman and a Queens man died yesterday morning when the car they were driving in climbed onto the grass median of the Wantagh State Parkway and

smashed into the foot of a bridge support at Newbridge Road.

They were the fifth and sixth persons to be killed on a three-mile stretch of the parkway since February in accidents involving cars entering the median strip. The area where the accidents occurred has a 10-foot grass strip separating the northbound and southbound lanes.

Parkway police said Melvin G. Bostick, 62, of 114-77 224th St., Cambria Heights, Queens, and his passenger, Catherine White, 57, of 55 Twig Lane, Levittown, were going south at 8:50 AM when the accident occurred. Police have not determined the cause of the crash.

The president of the Long Island State Parkway Patrolmen's Benevolent Association charged … that the deaths would have been prevented by a guardrail. The PBA leader, Roland Russell, charged the Long Island State Park Commission with 'foot-dragging' in not installing the railing. He said that there had been three other fatalities near the crash site in 1972 and 1973. The commission has said that it plans to install a reinforced concrete median in the fall on the entire 13-mile stretch of the parkway between the Northern and Southern State Parkways.

Though we never learned why the car drove off the pavement, across the grass strip, and into the concrete bridge support, we did learn that most likely Mom died instantly as result of hitting her head on the dashboard of the car. At the very least, she was spared any suffering. While there is no way to make sure a road is crash-proof, the Newsday story points out that the parkway could have been made safer had the state responded to the previous collisions and taken certain steps sooner. Parkway police officer Russell's words remained with me, "These deaths would have been prevented by a guardrail." Such a simple, inexpensive step could have saved many lives, including Mom's. The Long Island parkway system was constructed in the 1930's at a time when there were far fewer cars using them, and they traveled at much lower rates of speed. As Long Island's population grew over the years, many more cars began using the parkways, mostly for commuting to and from work. As more and more cars came to use the parkways, more should have been done to make them safer. Today, in 2016, all the state parkways have guardrails, concrete medians, or other buffers that tend to prevent the kind of head-on collision that took Mom's life. Unfortunately, her collision took place prior to the state recognizing the wisdom of such preventative measures. Her accident served as a catalyst for the state to make its parkways safer, and consequently save lives in the future.

Questions, Inconsistencies and Crime

Shocked as we were at the ultimate fact of Mom's death, it wasn't until hours, even days later that several important questions and inconsistencies came to our attention, some involving foul play. We didn't know then and still don't know the reason for the collision. We knew that the car she was riding in had left the road and crashed into a granite overpass, but we didn't know why. We could only speculate. Did Mel, the driver, have a heart attack or some other medical emergency? Did an insect fly in the window and startle him? Was he suicidal? Was his car in poor condition? Did it have bald tires? Bad brakes? And what of foul play? Were others involved? Was the car sideswiped or cut off by another vehicle? These questions troubled us greatly then, and continue to this day. As he did so many times during her life, Mom's cousin Florence's son-in-law, Vin Nicolosi, Esq., handled many aspects of things, beginning with the accident itself. The car was towed away by Charlie's Auto of Bellmore, in accordance with a contract it had with the state parkway department. There were photos taken of the accident scene, the victims, and the car. Vinnie saw the photos, but wouldn't allow me to see them. Needing answers, I wanted to see the photos, but Vinnie was emphatic, "No, Peter. They won't bring your Mom back. Don't do it." With so much on my mind, I followed Vin's admonition and dropped the issue. To this day, neither I nor any other members of the family, with the exception of Vinnie, have seen the photos.

There were other questions and concerns that arose, some quite serious with criminal implications. The collision occurred shortly before 9 a.m., yet Dennis didn't learn about it until after 4:30 p.m., and only because he was concerned about why Mom didn't show up at the beach as planned. If he weren't standing with neighbor Clem Randbeck when the state police came to Mom's house, we might not have learned of the collision for days. Why did it take so long for the police to inform the family? We were angered to learn that no wallet or any other form of identification was found on either Mel or Mom, therefore the police had no way to quickly determine their identities. At first the parkway police assumed the victims were a husband-wife couple. Since Mel had no ID, the parkway police traced his address through the car's license plates, and learned that he lived in an apartment in Queens. This meant contacting the New York Police Department, which sent officers to Mel's empty apartment in Cambria Heights. It took the NYPD a while to determine that Mel had a brother who informed them that that he was a single man. This left the question, "Who then is the female victim?" The parkway police went to Charlie's Auto in Bellmore and inspected the car more thoroughly and discovered a slip of paper on the rear floor of the car which contained directions to 55 Twig Lane, Levittown. Still not knowing the identity of the female victim, they visited 55 Twig Lane where they met Dennis. Of course all this took hours and left us filled with more disturbing questions. Why was there no identification found on Mom or Mel? Since he was so anxious to take Mom to lunch at Jones Beach, he had to have some money on him, but he did not. Not even money for the park entrance fee. No license and no money. The obvious conclusion is that someone removed the personal property from both crash victims. But who? A motorist or passerby? A police officer? An ambulance attendant? A hospital staff member? Someone from Charlie's Auto? Again, even though these questions upset me greatly, as with the photos, they really didn't matter in the long run. If I learned who pilfered Mom's belongings, a criminal act, it wouldn't bring her back. I left the issue alone at the time, but it has gnawed at me ever since. Though the evidence of this criminal tampering was plain, no one from either the state parkway police or Nassau County Police Department ever mentioned or addressed it. For the record, there was no money found on Mel Bostick, and Mom had only a pair of reading glasses and a pocket sized change purse. It contained four single dollar bills and $1.02 in small change, not enough for them to have paid the park admission and have lunch, even if Mom were treating. There was no other property found on her. Someone in the Medical Examiner's Office gave me Mom's glasses and change purse. I brought them home and placed them in the green metal box in which Mom kept her important papers. Her glasses and change purse, with four one-dollar bills and $1.02 in coins still intact, have remained there untouched ever since.

The Next Few Days

Recalling the first few hours after Mom's death, Dennis said, "I remember how we both were in shock, screaming and crying. The rest was a blur for me. I became selfish and started thinking that she'd never see me marry, never see my kids. I was truly lost." We left the Medical Examiner's Office, Dennis on his motorcycle, the one I helped him buy – against Mom's wishes, and I in my car, and headed to my apartment at the other end of Carman Avenue. We needed to be together in the immediate moments of our grief. Amidst the jolt we suffered from the news of Mom's death and our visit to the Medical Examiner's Office, we were uncertain about what steps we had to take to move forward. Neither of us had ever planned a funeral and yet we found ourselves thrust into the position of being in charge, of communicating with others, of making arrangements. It overwhelmed us.

After about an hour Dennis left, not knowing where to go. He rode to what he thought was the scene of the collision and saw nothing. Puzzled by this he thought, "Shouldn't there be some debris? Some traces of a major collision?" It turned out that Dennis, in such a confused state, had stopped at the wrong overpass. Mel Bostick's car had collided into the Newbridge Road overpass a few hundred yards south of the one at which he stood alone. He left there and, not knowing where to go next, thought, "Where would Mom want me to go?" He proceeded to the place closest to Mom's heart, a place he thought he might find some solace, Holy Family Church. As he sat alone in the chapel praying and trying to compose himself, the pastor, Father McGrath, entered and began setting up for confessions to be heard. He approached Dennis and asked him if he'd like to go to confession. Thinking perhaps that receiving a sacrament would be helpful and something Mom would have done, he obliged. Unfortunately, Father McGrath proved to be less than helpful. Rather than provide comfort and support for a young man who had just lost his mother in such a tragic and sudden way, he probed Dennis about a variety of personal and other unrelated things, causing Dennis even more confusion and emotional pain. Offended at the inappropriateness of Father McGrath's manner and words, Dennis left abruptly and continued on his ride to nowhere in particular, trying to find some form or relief.

My wife Jill loved my Mom a great deal and was very upset. Jennifer, my only child at the time, was just ten months old and obviously unaware that she had just lost her grandmother. I remained in the house with them and I wept. I wept for Mom and how she must have felt in that flash of time, dying alone so violently. I wept for all the students and others who would never again be touched by the her. I wept for Jennifer who had just lost her strong and wonderful grandma. And I wept for myself.

The next morning, June 22, 1975, I found myself in a strange and scary emotional wasteland. Exhausted from not sleeping much, I didn't know what to do first. Actually, I didn't know what to do at all. The only thing I could think of was that Mom was laying on a gurney in Meadowbrook Hospital alone, with no one by her side. Who is prepared for such a moment? What steps must be taken? In what order? The only two things on my mind were the ultimate and permanent fact that Mom was gone, and that her body was alone, in a cold place with only strangers around. My mind raced at the finality and bleakness of the situation. I knew I'd have to contact Dennis and discuss the protocols we'd have to begin following, but that morning something compelled me to visit the scene of the accident. I felt I should see the last place Mom saw, the place where she spent her final seconds on earth. On that hot, sunny Sunday morning, I drove alone to where Newbridge Road passes over the Wantagh Parkway, parked my car and walked down to where the collision took place. Cars whizzed by as I looked over the area. A solid stone bridge support held up Newbridge Road above and divided southbound parkway traffic from northbound traffic. There was evidence of the crash on that gray stone support, a few scrapes and scars on the granite blocks. I stared at it helplessly, then looked around some more and noticed car engine parts strewn about on the grassy median and on the parkway itself. I touched nothing. I felt nothing. I was alone, weak and vulnerable. Fortunately, a bit of common sense came to me and I decided to get out of there. Standing alone on that grassy median, looking at that solid granite abutment, that fortress-like pile of heavy stone and concrete, was cathartic, but also very dangerous. What if I got hit by a passing car? I knew little about accident causation, so by continuing to stand there I was accomplishing nothing. I gave the place one final look around, just in case anything relevant came into view. It did not. I said a prayer, crossed the parkway to the grass, walked back to my car, and left. I've never gone back.

Jeanne and Robert

Jeanne and her 11-month-old daughter Michelle were upstate New York at the time. She'd learned only days before that her husband, Ernie Champagne, had decided to leave them. Greatly upset at this news, Jeanne wanted to get away, to have a break, so she went to the Albany area to visit friends. Though she planned to be away for several more days, we had to tell her this dreadful news. But there was a problem. Dennis and I believed it would be unsafe for her to drive that long distance all distraught, especially with baby Michelle on board. We thought her impending separation from Ernie, coupled with the added news of Mom's death would cause an emotional overload and create an unsafe situation for her. First we thought that one of us should drive upstate and tell Jeanne the news personally, spend some time with her, and we could follow one another home on the Thruway. But time was of the essence and that became impossible. Instead, we decided on the white lie approach, to tell her something, but not the whole story. The real bad news could wait until she got home safely. I called Jeanne and told her that Dennis was involved in an accident and that Mom thought it was best for her to come home right away, that she was needed. She hadn't been upstate too long at that point and was reluctant to return so soon. She questioned me on the phone, but I was able to convince her to get back to Long Island the next day. When Jeanne arrived at my apartment, Dennis and I greeted her with somber looks. Then, privately and as calmly as possible, we told Jeanne the brutal news. Our prediction was right; the jolt was awful. Soon to be a single parent, Jeanne had looked forward to the strength and wisdom Mom would have provided. But Mom was gone.

I phoned Robert and Charlotte in Hawaii the night Mom died and delivered the bad news. The next day they got on the first flight they could from Honolulu to JFK Airport where Dennis and I picked them up. I hadn't seen them since 1970, when they and their two-year-old daughter, Ann Marie, visited. Our reunion was bittersweet. Before the days of email and cell phones, communication between us was mostly by regular mail, or an occasional holiday phone call. Under normal circumstances, I liked catching up with Robert and Charlotte, finding out how Ann Marie was doing, sending my regards to Tony and Ida Gomes, who were so helpful to me when I lived in Hawaii eight years earlier, and how things in general were going in "paradise," as Charlotte and Mom so often referred to Hawaii. This was not a normal ride, but a quiet, nervous, nighttime ride from JFK back to Levittown on the Southern State Parkway. We spoke few words. There was little to say. I felt better that Robert, my older brother, was now on hand to help with decision-making. I felt the same with the arrival of Charlotte, a calm, wise, and organized woman who loved Mom very much. With Robert living so far away for 14 years, it was rare that the four of us got together. Now we were united.

Important Jobs

As everyone who has ever lost a loved one knows, there are many jobs that have to be done, and at a time when everyone involved is vulnerable and emotionally shattered. Jeanne and Dennis were out of sorts, emotionally topsy turvy, "truly lost," as Dennis stated. Most of the jobs that had to be done, like communicating with family and friends, funeral home, church and cemetery arrangements, selecting a casket, planning a post-funeral gathering, fell toward me. In one way this was good. I was so busy that I didn't have time to fall apart or concentrate on the reality of this dreadful time. Instead I was running all over the area doing jobs. The worst of these jobs was the meeting I had with the undertaker in the basement of the Dalton Funeral Home in Hicksville. I was shown about a dozen caskets and had to choose one. Mom was not a frivolous person, but quite practical, so I thought, "What would she do?" When shown a few inexpensive caskets, I thought they didn't look that bad and might suffice. Then the undertaker said, "They're not waterproof, and…this is your mom we're talking about." Needing no time to reflect further, I selected a middle priced casket that was nicer looking and waterproof, got out of that basement, and moved on with the many other jobs I had to do. Jill was a great help in organizing things on the home front, with people from out of town coming, phones constantly ringing, and planning a post-funeral gathering. Friends pitched in too. Gatsby's Pub former manager Artie Humbach and his wife, Anita, without being asked, worked for days facilitating so much, greeting people, picking up and dropping off people, ordering food, and hosting well-wishers who stopped by.

We selected the Dalton Funeral Home in Hicksville because it was near the Hicksville train station and just up the road from Holy Family Church where the mass would take place. While Mom had the deeds to two plots in Calvary Cemetery in Queens, NY, where Aunt Katherine and Aunt Nellie and many other McCoy relatives were buried, we decided to purchase a new plot in Holy Rood Cemetery in Westbury, NY. We believed that we'd be more likely to visit her grave if she were closer. On the south side of Holy Rood, near Old Country Road, we had a stone placed at plot 10-00-96. It reads:

WHITE
My Peace I Give To You
Catherine McCoy
1917-1975

Even though Mom's legal name was Catherine White and the cemetery required that the name White to be engraved on the stone, we wanted it to bear the name McCoy for several reasons. McCoy was her last name for 25 years, the name of her father and adopted parents Aunt Nellie and Aunt Katherine. It was also a name of which she was very proud, the name of her ancestors, and the name to which she promised to return if her application for an annulment were successful. We included the notion of peace since peace was a value she held dear.

I visit Mom's grave on holidays and whenever I'm in the Hicksville-Westbury area. Even though it is located near noisy Old Country Road, it is a peaceful place, a place to say a few prayers, reflect on things, and even have a chat with her, sometimes even aloud. Sounds crazy. It may or may not do anything for her after all these years, but it does make me feel better. While there I tidy up the plot, pluck a few weeds and cultivate a bit. Usually there are some very nice plants or flowers in bloom because Robert and Charlotte order something from a local florist to be placed on the grave every month. Sometimes there are a few leaves or twigs on the gravesite. I usually pick them up, bring them home and scatter them among the leaves and woods behind my house. It may sound corny, but I like knowing that a part of her presence on this earth is still somehow connected with mine. On a recent visit there I remembered that one of her favorite songs was "Danny Boy." I googled the words on my phone and sang it to her. I don't know if Mom could hear me, but it made me smile.

The Wake

With all the details that needed attention, I wasn't able to cry much. There was just no time to do so. The two day long wake was very crowded. People came from all over including neighbors, friends, relatives, former students of Mom's, and Holy Family parishioners. I have no idea how many people came, hundreds, maybe thousands. I sat with Dennis much of the time as people approached us. Tormented as we were, we sometimes felt badly for the many visitors. Each tried so hard to search for words of comfort that we weren't really able to hear anyway. Each tried to express his sorrow, often in a different way. Some would grab my hand and shake it really hard, as if the harder they squeezed the more sorry they were. Others said, "I'm sorry," or "I'm truly sorry," or "I'm very, very sorry," as if they were more sorry than others because they added a few "truly's" or "very's." Some embraced us and said they knew how we felt, which we didn't believe, because how could they? Dozens and dozens of young men and women came up to us, all dressed up, many in their early to mid-twenties and said things like, "I loved your mother very much. She was my first teacher," or "Your mom taught me how to read." Not that I needed proof, but this showed me the huge impact Mom had on so many little ones who grew up to become fine men and women, using the skills she had passed on to them. The wake lasted for two seemingly never ending days. Then we had a mass.

The Mass

I'm sure the funeral Mass was quite beautiful, but I honestly don't remember much about it. My head and heart were in a completely different place. I never liked funerals, for the same reason most people don't. But this was so much more intense than any other funeral I'd attended, so shocking, so final, so emptying. My dislike for funerals goes back to altar boy days. I didn't like serving them, the black vestments, the sobbing of the family members, the sight of the casket, knowing what it contained, the slow mournful music, the smell of the burning incense. Even the vocabulary – words like "final resting place," and "the souls of the faithful departed," made me shiver. Mom's funeral was no different for me. Mr. Lenahan, the church custodian, played the organ and sang "Ave Maria," a favorite of Mom's. Dennis, Robert and I served as pallbearers. The church and adjacent large auditorium were packed; a testament to how many people's lives Mom had touched during her life. Dennis was distraught during the mass and the youngest priest in the parish, Father Paul, noticed him struggling. Father left the altar, came over to Dennis and, in a very kind manner, said, "It's going to be fine." Dennis has never forgotten Father Paul's kindness. When it came time to read the gospel and make some remarks, Father Michael O'Leary said,

Gospel: Mark 10: 13-16

'People were bringing their little children to Jesus to have him touch them, but the disciples were scolding them for this. Jesus became indignant when he noticed it and said to them, 'Let the children come to me and do not hinder them. It is to just such as these that the kingdom of God belongs. I assure you that whoever does not accept the kingdom of God like a little child shall not enter into it.' Then he embraced them and blessed them, placing his hands on them.'

Every Christian who takes seriously the call of Jesus Christ to follow Him is drawn to a sacred but complex, challenging and often difficult openness to life. Each one must discover those unique and rich gifts which are his or hers to spend in the service of God and his people.

I feel that the Gospel story we have just heard describes an understanding of who

Jesus is, and a response to his invitation that marked the life of Catherine White. Obviously, Kay spent a great part of her life-energy in bringing children to Jesus and in removing and trying to break down those things which would hinder them. First, she gave completely of herself as mother to Bob, Peter, Dennis and Jeanne. No hardship or difficulty was ever allowed to dampen her determination to move ahead and to open the pathways of happiness and growth and education and faith to each one of her children. Their love and appreciation will always testify to her motherly gifts.

Then fifteen years ago, Kay began to bring that same dedication to the children of Holy Family School. Year after year she was able to touch a new group of God's little ones….working and teaching in the name of Christ, embracing them, blessing them, placing her hands and thoughts, her understanding, her affection and her example upon them. The countless visitors, Mass cards, flowers and tears during these last days bear witness to this.

But perhaps more key to the beauty and success of Kay's life was her acceptance of Jesus' words…'I assure you that whoever does not accept the kingdom of God like a little child shall not enter it.' I have not met a single person who has not spoken of and marveled at Kay's attitude toward life. She was always filled with hope, always pleasant, joyful and happy with each new morning. Kay was a woman who experienced creation as God's precious gift and saw it according to His plan. She saw all that God had made and she knew that it was very good. She believed that God created man in the image of himself and her own life helped others to believe it too. Surely, selfishness and sin had come into the world but Kay knew that God's goodness was still there…. That childlike acceptance of God's kingdom of which Jesus spoke was easily experienced by all who knew Kay; the openness, the concern, the gentle ways that told people she cared. Her appreciation of nature and beauty, her patience, her enthusiasm for the good things and people in life, her encouragement to family and friends, to students and faculty and parents alike, her strong faith and continuing oneness with God in prayer. In these and so many other ways, Kay White told the world that she was living the commandment of Jesus, 'that we love one another.'

Somehow then in the midst of this tragedy and all its sorrow and pain we can softly rejoice because we have shared in her life. We can give thanks and praise to God in this Eucharist, in this sacrament in which we celebrate and renew, the gift of Christ's own Body and Blood – given that we might have life in its fullness. Jesus has told us to take strength and example from one another. 'Let him who has eyes to see, see, let him who has ears to hear, hear.' The morning of Kay's new and eternal life has broken. We know that when it comes to light, for us, Kay shall be like Christ for now she sees Him as He is.

Father O'Leary's words speak for themselves. His portrayal of Mom working so hard with the little ones and having a childlike acceptance of Jesus' teachings presents a very accurate picture of her life as parent, teacher and Christian. Her life may have seemed simple, a local woman teaching first grade in a nearby school, but underneath that appearance, she was a complex woman, one who taught so many so much by her constant and unwavering example.

Letters and Cards

The number and quality of letters and cards that came pouring in after the funeral demonstrated how many lives Mom touched throughout her shortened lifetime. There were so many, including hundreds of mass cards, that they filled several large boxes. After the funeral, I called a few people, mostly friends and colleagues of Mom's, to let them know of her death. I was astounded to learn that they and so many more already knew and took the time to write beautiful expressions about her. One said,

> Holy Family School and the Parish are a little less 'whole' without the presence of Catherine White. She brought such joy to the little ones. She not only taught what was expected of her, Kay extended herself. She has left such beautiful memories to so many of us. Thanks be to God that we were blessed with her presence! I will miss her joyful smile and her kindness.

Another said,

> I was very sorry to hear of Mrs. White's death. She taught my son last year and I will always be grateful for her helpfulness with him. I will remember Mrs. White in my prayers.

In organizing and storing these many cards and letters, I came upon some of Mom's keepsakes. Among them I found a number of letters she saved, including one from 1963, written after she'd been teaching only three years. The handwritten letter was from the parent of one of Mom's first grade students and clearly shows the impact she had on children from the very beginning of her teaching career. The parent said,

> Just a little note to tell you how much we appreciated the efforts you've made on our son's behalf this year. We are so pleased with his progress and we are very aware that a great deal – in fact most – of the credit for his good record is due to your fine teaching and guidance.

> I am not speaking only of his scholastic achievement. The background in religion you have given him is so deeply gratifying to us that it is difficult to express our feelings in words. It is apparent in everything he does – his attitude, behavior, his every action. His love and knowledge of God is truly an inspiration to all of us. He has become a most loveable and loving son.

> I'm sure he will have many wonderful teachers over the years, but none will surpass you in our estimation. We will always consider his first year in school as the most important year in his life. You have given our son a gift he

will carry with him always – the gift of your wisdom, your fine example and your dedication to God and your work.

Aftermath

In the weeks and months following Mom's death, I felt anesthetized, numbed in the heart, unable to look at life the same way. Things once beautiful to me had lost their beauty, normal became abnormal, real became unreal. Before this heartbreaking catastrophe, I'd planned a trip across the country with Jill, our baby Jennifer, and Tim, a former student. No longer wanting to go, but needing to get out of town, away from all the surroundings of Levittown, Twig Lane, Holy Family, Newbridge Road, the noise of cars whizzing by on the Wantagh Parkway, all the reminders, I took the trip anyway, …but it was no use. I was tormented the whole way across the U.S.A. and back. On the way out west, I stopped at my former college, the University of Dayton, Ohio. I hadn't been back there since I finished in 1969 and thought it would be fun to see my old stomping grounds and how things may have changed. As I walked around the old campus, I felt awful. I saw Stuart Hall, the dorm I lived in during my freshman year. It was just a red brick structure to me now. I entered the lobby and saw the public phone, the one from which I called Mom once in a while. This sent a chill through me. I saw buildings in which I attended classes years earlier, but now swept away with grief, had no feeling whatsoever. I entered the Student Union, where I'd frequently held Dakota Street Project meetings and handed out literature to help starving Biafran children. Outside the union stood an unfinished statue of John F. Kennedy, the unfinished man. I thought of how Mom, who'd given so much to so many, was herself an unfinished woman, with so much life ahead of her that would now go unlived. I wondered how I would ever recover from this dreadful grief. As I walked the campus and drove around the surrounding neighborhoods, areas I once called home, I found I really didn't care about any of the changes and so I left Dayton and drove on to Chicago, the Windy City, the place of my birth. The same thing happened there. I passed by Highland Park Hospital where Mom gave birth to me 27 years earlier, and the house Mom, Robert A. White, my brother Robert and I lived for the first year of my life, took a picture, then drove on without sensation. I was stripped of all normal feelings, with no ability to see things as they were. My only vision was through the eyes of one absent normal emotion. I didn't care, I couldn't. And I'm sure it showed. I found myself driving, just driving on America's highways, hundreds of miles a day, every day. I was running away. But no matter how many miles I drove, any form of relief was elusive. I was empty, angry and alone in my own heart. Selfishly, I couldn't imagine how anyone else could ever feel the pain I was experiencing. I'd always believed that life was full of momentary ups and downs, but my life was now all downs. And, I hadn't cried, really cried. Not yet. With so much to do at the funeral, so many people around me, I hadn't cried. No matter how many miles I drove or how far away I traveled to change my surroundings, indescribable pain and anger remained. This pain and anger rode along with me everywhere I went. They had become part of me. I drove across the Great Plains states – through mile after mile of amber waves of grain in Minnesota and buffalo herds in South Dakota. I frolicked with the others high atop snow-covered mountains in Wyoming, visited a little gambling town in Nevada, and stood in awe of the mighty redwoods in California. Sadly, what would be an all-American road trip for most did little good for me. In Wyoming's Grand Teton's I took 11-month-old Jennifer for a walk down a trail and dipped her baby feet into Jenny Lake. Jen had a big smile as Jill photographed the moment. I wore a frown. I couldn't get the real joy that a dad should from such an experience. In Santa Monica, California I visited a close friend from high school days, Tony Acerra. We corresponded frequently during college days and were ushers in one another's weddings. Tony was a hard worker, a serious, scholarly law student and superb gentleman. Only a month before, he lost his dad, an FDNY battalion chief. Even though he was grieving himself, he expressed his sorrow at my loss. I admired his ability to go on. I hadn't yet found the way. I began to believe that I didn't have a life anymore. It's hard to have a life when you have a million-pound weight on your chest. That's what it felt like at all times for me, like I had a burdensome weight holding me down. We took Jennifer to Disneyland, where I tried to provide her with the happiness a little child deserves at such a place, a chance to smile and laugh. I rode the rides with her, sang "It's a Small World," waved at Mickey and Minnie, and did what all dads do. Jen smiled and was excited, but the visit did little for me. I'd sunken into an abyss and I didn't know how to get out or whether I'd ever get out.

Peter with 11 month old Jennifer, at Jenny Lake Wyoming July, 1975

We visited Jill's brother, Mickey, in southern California, stopped at a beach, spent a day at the San Diego Zoo, and had a few barbeques. Same result. Seeing family members didn't lighten my load, or bring me out of my emotional backwoods. I had become a different person, a very unhappy and unsure one. Was this new me going to be a permanent state, or something that would pass? Would I ever recover and feel normal again? It was all so colossal, so overwhelming.

After San Diego, we stopped briefly in Las Vegas, where it was a sweltering 99 degrees at midnight, and the Hoover Dam, then made a beeline for New York. This is when I stepped up the tempo, driving 900 miles in one day alone. I just drove and drove, perhaps trying to drive the pain out of my system. Once back in New York, it was time to prepare for Jennifer's first birthday, August 13, 1975. We had sent out invitations to a number of people before the cross-country trip and, despite my inability to feel, we went forward with the party anyway. Jen was innocent and knew nothing of pain, so I couldn't deny her the joy and excitement of a first birthday. I did my best when company came, but it was pleasure alloyed with pain. It was my first family gathering without Mom, who would have glowed on the occasion of her granddaughter's first birthday. Jen opened her gifts and pleased the crowd with her first steps and bright smile. People's joy and my emptiness filled the backyard of 870 Carman Avenue, the same place I received Dennis' ill-fated phone call just weeks earlier.

Back to Work

Two weeks after Jen's birthday, I began my second year as a social studies teacher at Northport High School, something I'd eagerly looked forward to only ten weeks before. I loved my chairperson, Dick Streb, who had given me a very positive end of year evaluation in June, the week before Mom died, and was anxious to see him. Actually, I needed to see him. Though Dick had never met Mom, he and one other teacher, Pat Driscoll, came to her funeral. I was glad to see them there. At least someone from my Northport life knew of my situation. I was also anxious to see my colleagues, meet my new students, and of course, get back to teaching, something normal. The first day back there were no students present, just teachers having meetings and readying their classrooms. Dick held a department meeting at which there were some 30 teachers present. He began with the usual go around with each teacher describing how he spent his summer. Some teachers had traveled; others took courses. One got married, another had a baby. All had good news. Then my turn came. It was my first time to speak to people in a formal setting about what I was experiencing. I spoke slowly and deliberately, trying to quickly describe to my fellow-teachers what had happened. The pain was obvious to them and unbearable for me. My colleagues were good people who tried to empathize. I got teary and stopped. One friend, Jim Eder, was very upset, partly at the fact that I had suffered such a loss, but also at the fact that there was no network in place for one like him to have known about Mom's death. This was the first he was hearing about it. Had he known, he'd have gone to the wake, or sent a card, or dropped by my house. He was upset at learning of my loss too late to be there for me.

More difficult than facing my colleagues, who genuinely cared, was the thought of facing my new students, 125 brand new kids who didn't know me yet. There is a marvelous energy among the student body in September. The kids are excited to see their old friends, make new ones, meet their teachers, and begin uncovering new things in the classroom. They want to get started with soccer and football and cheerleading, homecoming, parades and dances. It's always so exciting for them. I was their teacher, and I couldn't get up the energy required for the opening of school. I tried, but it was obvious to all that I was down in the dumps and struggling to find my way up. On the first day of classes, a 12th grade boy approached me angrily and said, "Hey, Mr. White. You gave me an 85 on my report card last June. That ruined my 90 average. Because of you I didn't get the boat this the summer." Frankly, he didn't even deserve an 85, but at grade-inflated Northport High School, he thought he deserved more. Little did he know that I wasn't able to hear his trivial tale of woe. His grumbling about five points on his report card and his loss of family boat privileges was not on my radar. I was an emotional basket case, and my basket was filled with gloom.

Students Bring Hope

Fortunately for me, a number of my new students were friendly, polite, hard-working, good people. Cindy and Judy, stand out. They were in my 11th grade American Studies class and members of the Northport Tigerettes, a group of about 20 talented kick line girls who won awards and trophies for their excellence and precision. Though I'd just met them, they immediately seemed to know and understand my heartache. Their smiles, energy and concern became important bright spots during those cloudy, dark days. They also embraced Jen, the one-year-old with the hurting dad. As a way of taking a break from enormous tension, I attended many school functions, band performances, ball games, and Tigerette competitions, and brought Jen with me. Jen lit up with the attention given to her by my students, and this was very important for me as well. At that time, when even a moment's happiness seemed so elusive, I was able to find little pieces here and there. When I first began teaching at Northport a year earlier, I thought many of the kids there represented the stereotypical, upper middle income, North Shore elite: selfish, self-absorbed and spoiled. But I was wrong. So many of them, like Cindy and Judy, were really wonderful, caring young men and women. Their bright smiles and positive attitudes shined an important light on the darkness in my heart.

Jeanne's Recollections

While we were all adrift, Jeanne experienced added suffering. In June 1975, only a week before Mom died, her husband of four years, Ernie Champagne, told her that he was leaving. Shocked and devastated, Jeanne recalled:

> After Ernie broke this news, I decided to go upstate to visit friends and get away. While there I called Mom and told her of my situation. She tried hard to comfort and reassure me. She said if I needed a place to go, I could come home and stay with her. I will never forget this. It was my very last conversation with her…. For me this was the absolute worst time in my life and there are no words to describe how I felt. Having Mom die and my husband leave in the same week was horrific.

After the funeral, Jeanne and Michelle moved into Mom's house with Dennis for the next year or so. It was a very tough time for both of them as they were dealing with their grief in different ways. Jeanne recalls:

> I was having a very hard time trying to take care of Michelle on my own with little finances and no job. I worked part time taking care of a woman who had MS while Michelle went to a babysitter. I received child support from Ernie for a short time, but then he stopped paying…. Living in Mom's house became difficult for me, surrounded by so many memories of Mom, and the sadness of her being gone. After living at Mom's for nearly a year, I moved with Michelle to upstate New York. This was May 1976 and Michelle was not yet two years old. I was hoping to change my life for the better, however the next few years were extremely hard.

Jeanne lost Mom at a time when she needed her most. With Ernie leaving, she needed Mom's strong shoulder to lean on, and of course, it was no longer there. Jeanne remembered how, in 1967, her best friend, Liz Schley, died in a car accident. Liz' parents, neighbors Charlie and Kitchie Schley, were driving her home from a school concert when another motorist collided with them only a short distance from their house. Jeanne recalled:

> Mom's help meant a great deal to me when my 15-year-old best friend, Liz, was killed. I knew her all my life. We were very close in many ways. Our birthdays were exactly one month apart. I was in shock when she was in a coma for five days, and then had a very hard time accepting her death. Mom helped me through the grieving process by listening to me, consoling and comforting me as much as she could. This helped me come to terms with the loss of Liz.

In addition to comforting and reassuring Jeanne, Mom also instilled a sense of confidence in her. In Jeanne's senior year of high school, 1968-69, she was enrolled in a nursing program to become a certified nursing assistant. As part of this study, she took courses and worked full time at Meadowbrook Hospital. Seeing how much Jeanne enjoyed this program, how maturely she handled it, and how it was guiding her toward becoming a registered nurse, Mom was extremely proud. Pleased with Mom's support, Jeanne said, "Mom often told me that I was good at helping people and that I would be a terrific nurse or social worker." As result of the sense of confidence Jeanne received from Mom, she went on to work for many years in the mental health and social work fields, helping others throughout her life.

While Mom did support and inspire us, she didn't always agree with everything we did, and she didn't always sugar coat her words when she disagreed. When Jeanne was 18 and working in the hospital, she met Nassau County correction officer Ernie Champagne. Ernie was eight years older than Jeanne, divorced and had a young daughter. Ernie seemed nice enough to Jeanne, and they began to date. In early 1971, Jeanne and Ernie decided to get married. Mom was not pleased to learn of this situation and was emphatic about her disapproval. Jeanne recalled:

> Mom felt that at 19 I was too young to marry and she was concerned that he was eight years older, same age as my brother Robert. She was a strong Catholic and believed divorce was unacceptable in the Church. She told me quite clearly that she could not approve of me marrying him, and was even fearful that such a marriage might have an adverse impact on her job at the parish school, that she could even lose her job. Mom's words were difficult and upsetting for me to hear. I felt she was being too strict and that I was old enough to make my own decisions. I told her, 'I'm going to marry him even if you don't approve.'

This disagreement caused quite a bit of stress between Mom and Jeanne. A few weeks later, Dennis and I spoke with Mom about putting Jeanne's needs ahead of the church's rules, about how Jesus stood for charity and that she might want to consider being more charitable towards Jeanne. After thinking things over, Mom told Jeanne that despite her underlying feelings, *"I'll give you my blessing."* Jeanne said,

> Mom obviously did not want to risk losing her relationship with me and wanted things between us to be good. She allowed us to have the wedding reception in the

backyard and to have it catered. I was so happy to have her blessing and for all that she did to make that day special. I didn't realize at the time how much Mom did to give me what I wanted.

In the years following Mom's death, Jeanne struggled. Her former husband, Ernie, lost his job and stopped paying child support. During the late 1970's, with pre-schooler Michelle to support on her own, Jeanne took several jobs and had to rely for some time on public assistance. Struggling to pay rent, she was forced to move several times as well. Of those difficult years, she said,

> It was then that I began to feel and understand the hardship Mom experienced after our father left the family. I remember saying, 'I'm reliving my mother's life.' This caused me to appreciate all Mom did for us so much more. I regret that I never told her this directly. I learned so much from her, and throughout the years following her death, as my life took different turns, I've applied the lessons she taught and been able to make my way through. Especially through those first few years, I felt I had God and Mom with me in spirit. Without them I might not have made it. When I was a single mother I often thought 'What would Mom do now, or what advice would she give me?' Though I made my share of mistakes I always tried to live my life to the best of my ability. I realized how much she really loved me throughout all the years. I'll never forget the last conversation I had with her, when I was so nervous and troubled. Mom comforted me saying, 'Jeanne, if you need to, come home and stay with me. You'll be fine.

In 1981, Jeanne married Norm Gregware and they had a daughter, Kathryn, whom they called Katie. A happy and healthy baby, Katie was named after Mom. When she was six months old, Katie developed a serious health problem, which caused her to stop breathing temporarily. Seeing Katie in the hospital with breathing tubes, a heart monitor and IV scared Jeanne and caused her to do a lot of praying. She recalled:

> As soon as I could I went to the hospital chapel and prayed my heart out to God that he would heal her and let her live. I was sobbing and never prayed so hard. Katie had surgery and soon began to improve. I consider her improvement to be truly a miracle, that God answered my prayers. This totally changed my life for the better as my faith in God became much stronger. I also believed that Mom was watching over Katie during this time…. Years later, I remember Mom words from the biographical sketch she prepared, 'I prayed that my children would find God in their own way.'…I feel that God brought me through many difficult times in life, and that Mom's faith in God was a strong inspiration for me. I strongly believe that Mom has always been with me in spirit and continues to watch over and guide me.

In 1989, Jeanne married Kevin Callahan whom she describes as

> …a wonderful husband for me and a wonderful father to Michelle and Katie. He

has been a blessing in our lives in many ways. I know Mom would not only approve of him but she would be so happy for me. Kevin gave me confidence and encouraged me to go back to school as a middle-aged woman, finish my bachelor's, then go on for a Masters in Social Work. I have put the lessons Mom taught me into my daily life, lessons like the importance of family and the values of honesty, kindness, respect for others, and the courage to move forward no matter what the obstacle. I thank God that He blessed me with my wonderful mother.

First Christmas

Mom always did her best to make Christmas special for us when we were kids. My greatest childhood memories are from those wonderful times. Christmas1975, our first Christmas without Mom, was different. I expected it to be difficult but I didn't know how difficult. I was still living in the De Monaco's house at 870 Carman Avenue. Jennifer was a year and a half old and just beginning to know Santa and what the many presents, decorations and lights were all about. Dennis came over and we had a nice meal, then tried to enjoy the rest of the evening the best we could, despite the glaring emptiness that surrounded us. We were all polite to one another, speaking mostly superficial words. Though it seemed a little forced, we did our best to get through this time positively. After dinner we sat around nervously, mentioning Mom a few times, and reflecting on the difference between this Christmas and previous ones Then something happened, an explosion of sorts for me, a catharsis that was long overdue. Dennis and I both liked Elvis Presley so we put his Christmas Album on the record player, thinking songs like "Santa Clause Is Back In Town," and "White Christmas" sung by "The King" would brighten up our quiet, reserved evening. Toward the end of the record, when all was quite peaceful and, quite literally, not a creature was stirring, the last song on the album, "Momma Liked the Roses," played. During this eerily silent moment, we listened to line after line of the very sad song. Then Elvis sang,

> "Oh, Mama liked the roses in such a special way.
> We bring them every Mother's Day and put them on her grave."

I burst into tears and cried uncontrollably. It was the first big cry I had since Mom's death, and while it put a damper on the holiday evening, it provided me with an important and quite necessary emotional release. Holidays, once fun, had changed.

Enlightenment from Dick Streb

In the weeks and months following Mom's death, I remained in a terrible emotional state. I frequented churches, seeking help through prayer. I was a prime candidate for psychological therapy, but I knew nothing about such things in those days. Fortunately there was one powerful, positive influence that brought me some much-needed help during that agonizing time: the honesty and wisdom of my chairperson at Northport High

School, Dick Streb. Dick was the father I never had. He was that and so much more to me; in so many ways he was my other tower of strength. He could see the torment I was dealing with and how it was beginning to show in my daily attitude and work. Rather than let me wallow in the depths of depression and despair, or sink further into the abyss, Dick took action. He called me into his office and, speaking more like a father than a boss, put his hand on my shoulder, looked directly into my eyes and said,

> I know you're dealing with a lot and I completely understand it. But you have to snap out of this. You have talent as a teacher and a great future ahead of you, so you have to find a way to deal with this and begin to concentrate again. As a World War II veteran, I've seen indescribable suffering. Your job is to pull yourself together, focus on what's important, and go on with your life.

My first thought was, "Easier said than done." I thanked him and left his office. His message to me contained no magic words that could bring me immediate relief. No such words existed. But at the very least I left knowing that I wasn't alone, that a strong man was on my side, one who truly cared about me. I've often referred to Dick as "The Great Dick Streb" for a number of reasons. Not only was Dick a master teacher, award-winning author and brilliant scholar, he was a human dynamo, an educational visionary, a generator of ideas, and a rock upon which so many others and I stood for support. In 1942, when he was just 17 years old, Dick left high school and joined the Navy to serve in the war. He spent three years in the Pacific as a radar operator aboard the U.S.S. Essex, the largest aircraft carrier in the fleet. On November 25, 1944, a kamikaze pilot hit the Essex critically wounding 44 of the ship's crew and killing 16 others. Memories of that attack remained with him throughout life, causing him to write a book 55 years later called Life and Death Aboard the U.S.S. Essex about that incident and the lives of the victims, eight of whom were white men and eight of whom were black. Picking up the remains of those dead men from the carrier's deck transformed him, a war hero with 13 battle stars, into a peace hero. He was a decorated veteran who provided an honest account of the horror of war as an effective plea for peace. In his mid 70's, for reasons of conscience, Dick willingly served six months in federal prison for having spoken out against the US Army School of the Americas at Ft. Benning, Georgia. Dick was no stranger to suffering, and he was asking me to put my suffering into perspective and go on. His outreach, patience and wisdom were important factors in helping me snap out of my sunken state.

The Aftermath Continues

It's been more than 41 years since that initial, excruciating pain seized hold of me. The jolt that stabbed my heart and felt like a million-pound weight lasted for at least six months, until Dick and others got hold of me and guided me out. There's a residual pain that continues to this day. While this left over pain endures, the passing of so many years has allowed it to spread out somewhat. The spreading out of pain is what makes life's difficulties bearable.

In early 1976, Jill and I learned we were going to have another child. This was good news to me, but there would be a difference between this birth and that of Jennifer two years earlier. Grandma White wouldn't be there to share the joy. In April 1976, when Jill was only two or three months pregnant, I chaperoned a group of Northport High School students on a five-day field trip to Boston. Jill came along as well, as did twenty-month-old Jennifer. One of the students got sick and by the end of the trip, so did I. With a high fever, swollen glands, and serious rash, I was sick as a dog. The doctor said I either had German measles, or something close to it, and he didn't want to take any chances with the pregnancy. He suggested terminating it. We were shocked. Abortion was only legalized a few years before and we'd never contemplated such a thought. The doctor's recommendation came as a complete surprise. While Jill never got the same symptoms as I, the doctor said she could have had a minor, undetectable, overnight version of German measles, enough to bring harm to a small fetus, and that staying pregnant contained the severe risk of multiple handicaps. We sought other opinions in the hope that we might find better news elsewhere. We even visited the rubella clinic at Manhattan's Roosevelt Hospital where we saw many children with the kind of handicaps the doctor described. Some were blind, some had missing limbs, some were retarded. This scared us. I wished I had the opportunity to consult with Mom. She'd have known what to tell me, she'd have given me the strength. Jill's parents, staunch Catholics, while generally opposed to abortion, confided that, under such extreme circumstances as these, where there was a strong chance that a child could be born with the inability to live a normal life, perhaps following the doctor's advice was best. We were quite confounded and really didn't know what to do. After the nightmare of Mom's death six months earlier, this turn of events was unbearable. Selfishly, I cried alone in church asking something Mom never asked, "Why me?" I was at a new low. After putting together all the information we possibly could, all the pros and cons, we decided against the doctor's advice and went forward with the pregnancy. For the next six months we patiently waited, praying and hoping for the best. On October 27, 1976, at North Shore Hospital in Manhasset, Brian Patrick White was born, intact, with all arms and legs, in overall perfect health. After leaving the hospital I visited Dennis at Gatsby's Pub and cried in his arms. I cried because the long wait of this ordeal was over. I cried because I once again saw how fragile life was and how I escaped with nothing bad happening. And I cried because I got a very much-needed and appreciated break. After more than a year of suffering the emotional downward spiral resulting from Mom's death and the troubled pregnancy, something good finally happened. Finally, my tears were tears of joy.

Childrens' Joy

I now had two cute, bright, terrific babies and, while they provided me great happiness and fun, I still felt the huge weight on me much of the time. Like a prisoner in one of those old movies with the iron ball chained to his leg, I was not free to live my life. Even though the children brought me great joy, I suffered still. Too much was missing. Each day, as these cheerful, cute, bright children would grow and learn, the sad side of me would rear up and show itself. There was no Grandma White to share that growth with. A few years later, Meredith and Brendan were born, each one healthy, alert, active and smart, wonderful pleasures in my life. The birth of my four children was a tremendous blessing that helped lift the weight from me and unchain the iron ball. In winter, there would be snowsuits to don and sleigh rides to take. In summer it was off to a beach or park. As they got older, it was soccer and baseball games, good report cards, the gifted and talented program, school concerts, birthday parties, trips to New York City, Thanksgiving Day parades, special kids' events at Gatsby's Pub, Northport High School ball games and events, gatherings with friends and family members, overnight visits to "Grandma and Popi's" as the kids called Jill's parents, and more. Outwardly, it looked like my kids were having a regular life with two regular parents guiding the way. Inwardly, despite the wonderful moments my children so often provided me, there was still pain.

Christmas 1983

At Christmastime 1983, we lived at 41 Burr Avenue, Northport. Jen was nine years old, Brian seven, Merry four and Brendan three, all perfect ages for an exciting holiday. On Christmas Eve, Jill woke the kids up and had them glance from the stairs at me in my Santa suit, placing gifts under the tree while giving them a wink and a smile. The real Santa was visiting and there was joy in the house. Christmas morning saw the usual merriment, with presents, mass, and a holiday meal. That night however, something different happened. Wanting to make sure the birth of Jesus was given proper attention, I took the children to church after dinner to see the nativity scene. We were the only ones in the church as I pointed out the Baby Jesus, Mary, Joseph, shepherds and wise men. I explained the Christmas story the best I could so each could understand. On the way back home I became quiet, pensive. Christmas is largely for kids, and my kids had a good Christmas. I began to think back to my own Christmases as a child, of how much they meant to me with Mom there, trying to give us all she could. At that moment I wanted and needed something more spiritual, for myself. At about 10 p.m., after the kids were all in bed, I took a ride. I didn't know where I was headed. I just took a ride to be alone and reflect. It had been seven and a half years since Mom's death but, for some reason, I missed her more than ever that particular Christmas. My holiday blues may have had something to do with Mom missing out on the joy her grandchildren provided, or the added joy they'd have had if she were present. With no thought given to where I was driving, I wound up at Asharoken Beach, about two miles from our house. The gate to the parking lot was open and I drove in. On this clear, cold, windy night, I got out of my car, and walked down to the same familiar beach where the kids took swimming lessons in summer. There I saw the narrow wooden jetty that protrudes out about 30 feet into the waters of Northport Bay. The jetty was wet and slick, and on that freezing four-degree night, with no planning aforethought, I climbed upon it and carefully tiptoed to the end until the frigid waters surrounded me on all sides. As I looked out on that Christmas night, I stared at the vast stretch of dark icy water, lit only by the glimmering of the stars above, and felt only the wind and the cold. I didn't know why I was there, but I felt compelled to there, alone, surrounded by sea and sky and nothing else. I struggled to maintain my balance on the slippery jetty, then managed to stand up straight and stare out at the dark water and up at the stars in the clear night sky. After a minute or more of silence, facing what appeared to be the entire universe, I spoke. "Mom…this is Peter. Merry Christmas." I went on speaking, aloud, with heartfelt words as if she were right there with me. I spoke honestly of how I was doing and feeling, and of her four wonderful grandchildren. I asked for her continued guidance as I marched on through life, especially as a young father with no fatherly role model to follow. I told her how sorry I was that her life had been cut short, and how it ended so suddenly and violently. I told her I missed her and that I would remain devoted to the values she taught me as a child. After talking to Mom for about ten minutes I began to cry out loud, hysterically, for several minutes more. Then I walked back to my car and drove home, feeling a lot better. That night I cried the tears that had been waiting seven years to come out.

In many ways, I'm a creature of habit. My talk with Mom on Christmas 1983 was so powerful and moving that the next Christmas I took the same late night drive, and did it again. And I have done so every Christmas since then, more than 30 years now. Whatever I'm doing on Christmas night, whether company is there, or I'm tired, or it's raining or snowing, no matter what the circumstances, I excuse myself for about half an hour and take my ride, to have my special Christmas moment with Mom. It's important to me, and I hope her.

A Reality Check: Putting Things in Perspective at Hofstra

Two years after Mom's death, during 1977-1978, I was living at 48 Twig Lane, right across the street from 55 Twig, our childhood home. Jill and I bought the former Schley house in 1976 to be closer to Dennis and Jeanne, and because we knew it to be a good house, well maintained by Charlie Schley. It was then that I began a master's degree program in Counselor Education at Hofstra University. I had mixed feelings about continuing on as a social studies teacher and thought a switch to counseling might be a better fit for me, giving me the opportunity to work with students and their problems rather than placing so much emphasis on skills, content and knowledge. About half way through the program I changed my mind once again, and switched to a master's in secondary education. Though I liked the counseling program very much, secondary education involved fewer very expensive college credits and I'd had enough of school at that point. I also had two young children and needed to work a second job rather than continue paying tuition to Hofstra. One course I took in the counseling program was called Peer Counseling. Some of the activities the professors led us through reminded me of how far I had to go to become myself again. One day, each student was asked to write a short message, something specific and personal, on a piece of paper, pin the paper on his or her shirt, then walk around the room in silence, reading each other's messages. Still depressed at the loss of Mom, I wrote, "I can't seem to make anything seem important anymore." As they read my message, though they remained silent, several reached out to me with facial expressions or a hand on the shoulder. I thought, "This is great. They care. I'm finally letting some feelings out and these folks may help me lighten my burden." As I browsed around the room, I read the messages written by the other students. While most seemed far less onerous than mine, some were actually on par or more serious. One student, a middle-aged man, had lost his parents as a young man and was left as caretaker of his severely retarded brother. It consumed his life. Another was a continuing victim of domestic violence, struggling with getting out of her situation. After about 15 minutes, we gathered and discussed each other's messages, and then the peer counseling fireworks began. I found it to be a great relief knowing that others, strangers for the most part, knew and understood my pain and helped ease it. More importantly, I realized that I wasn't alone. Others had problems too, and this helped me put mine into a new and different context. I was led to the conclusion that, while pain and emptiness from life's blows really never go away completely, the passage of time and the knowledge that others too have their own suffering has an ameliorating effect. Burdens become a little lighter with each passing year. Other events, whether joys or despairs, intervene into life's equation and balance things and sometimes even supersede them, allowing the initial pain to find its place. Over the years I've learned that the only thing that comes remotely close to healing this kind of wound is the passage of time.

Years later my close friend Drew Keenan lost his mom in a similar car accident. Doris Keenan was the innocent victim a young woman who ran a stop sign. Somehow Drew, his two sisters and brother were able to go on with their lives in a mostly normal fashion. I wondered how they were able to cope so much better than I. Maybe, with us having no father, Mom played twice the role, and our pain was doubled.

Four Decades Later – Things Missed

Though I continue to live on Long Island and am surrounded by constant reminders of that time, though the hole in my heart remains and the emptiness continues, I've tried to live a normal life to the extent possible. I've helped raise four children, had a 36 year teaching career, earned two master's degrees and a law degree, passing bar exams in two states on the first try, been honored as the 1999 New York State Teacher of the Year and 1999 National Teacher of the Year finalist, led thousands of students on more than 60 humanitarian trips to Central America and Africa, and authored more than 100 articles and chapters for educational books on service learning and related topics. These events, joyous as they have been, have come with a gigantic barrier attached: Mom missed them all. While she got to know and hold and love my oldest daughter, Jennifer, up until she

was ten months old, she missed the rest of Jen's life. She never got to see her tap dance on a big stage as a child, or play violin in her high school orchestra, or graduate from college and become a sterling school counselor. She never got to know and hold and love Brian, Meredith or Brendan, or see them play sports, become accomplished musicians, graduate high school and college, and become teachers. She never got to visit me in my own home, or share a holiday meal with my family.

Peter and Kathleen at National Teacher of the Year ceremony, Washington, D.C.

She wasn't present when I graduated near the top of my Law School class and was honored to make law review. She wasn't able to share my joy when I learned that I passed the New York and Massachusetts bar exams and was sworn in as an attorney in the beautiful Appellate Division courthouse in Brooklyn Heights in 1988, or when I received state Teacher of the Year honors from the Commissioner of Education in Albany. She died 12 years before I formed Students for 60000, the Northport High School community service club that continues to provide substantial aid, care and support for the needy, locally and internationally. She never knew of the hundreds of houses my students built in rural, impoverished Nicaragua, or the four schools they constructed, or the life-saving water systems and children's nutrition projects they funded, or of the $1.5 million they raised for these poverty projects. And sadly she never got to meet or know Kathleen, my loving partner for the past 18 years.

Mom was extremely happy that Robert and Charlotte married and made Hawaii, a land she loved dearly, their permanent home. She experienced the joy of visiting them several times, and of knowing and loving their youngest child, Ann. However, she never saw Ann grow up and become a mom herself, and she never met her Hawaiian grandson, Robbie, now a teacher in Korea. She was unable to congratulate Charlotte for being principal of a nationally recognized Blue Ribbon school in Honolulu, or take a tour aboard the U.S.S. Missouri in Pearl Harbor where Robert, now a retired hospital administrator, serves so proudly. She was not present for Dennis' wedding in 1977 or the birth of his two daughters, Lisa and Katelyn, nor did she get to know Dennis' five grandchildren. She wasn't here to know that Dennis followed through on his

Robert giving tour aboard U.S.S. Missouri, Pearl Harbor. 2006.

promise to honor her by officially changing his name to McCoy. She never got to meet Dennis' wife Beth and their two sons, Daniel or Matthew, a whole new family of McCoy's with the potential to keep the family name going. She never had the opportunity to visit them in their Arizona or Florida homes or witness their excellence in school and community service, or to be present when Daniel, now an officer in the Collier County, Florida Sheriff's Department, was honored by his Police Academy peers who voted him president of the class.

Dennis, Beth, and Matthew celebrate Dan's police academy graduation, 2015.

Mom was present for Jeanne's wedding to Ernie Champagne in 1971, but her time spent with Jeanne's first daughter, Michelle, was fleeting, just 11 months. Sadly, she wasn't alive for the birth of Jeanne's second daughter, her namesake, Katie. Mom undoubtedly would have provided much needed assistance to Jeanne when she was left alone to raise infant Michelle in 1975, and she would have been extremely proud of the way Jeanne raised her daughters, mostly alone until she met her dedicated husband Kevin Callahan. Mom would have marveled at Jeanne's perseverance as she worked as a typewriter repair women and school bus driver, accepting and working hard at any job she could find to provide for her children, just as she herself had done 20 years earlier. And she would have been in awe, as we all were, of Jeanne's determination and tenacity, seeing her work and struggle for many years, one course at a time, to receive her bachelor's and master's degrees in social work.

Jeanne's graduation with Master's Degree In Social Work, May 2005.

Dennis and I often have discussed the notion that, though we lost her early, Mom was spared the suffering so many senior citizens endure. She didn't live long enough to develop serious health problems like cancer or stroke or suffer the type of cognitive impairment that her adopted mother, Aunt Nellie, and so many older folks today must endure. She was independent all her life, relying mostly on herself. Had she lived, she'd be 99 years old as of this writing. Along the way, she might have gotten ill or required assisted living or nursing home care. So, while we lost so much so early, we were also spared the complications and dilemmas baby boomers with aging parents face today. I'm not suggesting that this is a blessing. I've always looked with a degree of envy at middle-aged and older adults who still have parents. I remember going to Jill's family events where dozens of people, many of them in their 80's and 90's, gathered for birthdays and holidays. There would be hugs and handshakes, food and drink, story-telling and laughter. I admit to having looked upon them with some jealousy, those lucky people who had so many years of life together. In recent years I've come to know Kathleen's family members well, including her mom, also named Catherine, age 93, her four sisters and brother, their spouses and their children and grandchildren. While Kathleen's dad passed away in September 2014, at the age of 93, her parents were able to tell stories of the old days, enjoy holidays, weddings, christenings and birthdays with their large, extended family, take vacations all over the country, and live in their own home well into old age. Most importantly, to this day, any time she wishes, Kathleen can pick up the phone and say "Hi Mom." Even better, she can get in her car, drive to Rockville Centre, walking distance from her childhood family home in Baldwin, drop in, give her mom a hug, have lunch and a nice parent-daughter chat. I'm sure that baby boomers who still have parents do value and cherish their good fortune, but I've often wondered if they cherish it enough. It's something they've always had, and something my brothers, sister and I have long missed. I've often said I'd give a million bucks if I could have just one day to be with Mom. In that sense, it makes those still with parents the richest folks in town.

Different Views

The first few years following Mom's death, Dennis and I called one another each June 21, just to check in, to see how the other was doing. We spoke of our recollections of June 21, 1975, how we felt, and how the passage of time was changing things. For me, the anniversary has a been permanent and unalterable reminder of a terrible time. Dennis felt the same way for the first few years, but then a shift took place, something that allowed him to turn the corner, at least part way. On June 21, 1978, his first child, Lisa, was born. While Dennis still reflects a great deal each June 21, and while we still call one another, he has tried very hard to make that date a happy anniversary for himself and his family, rather than a sad one. "I believe Mom had a hand in this, that she wanted something good for me on that day." I'm glad this transformation occurred for him. For me, it continues to be a day of personal reflection and remembrance. On June 21, 1976, the first anniversary of Mom's death, I was proctoring a Regent's exam in a hot gymnasium at Northport High School. Shortly before 9:00 a.m., very mindful of the date and time, I asked the head proctor if I could take a short break, which he allowed. I left the gym and walked away from the building, toward the railroad tracks a few hundred yards from the school. At 8:50 a.m., I stood among some trees, looked up, said a prayer, had my private moment with Mom, then went back into the gym. That June 21, 8:50 a.m. solitary walk has become a custom with me. Every year on that date and time I find a place to be alone and have a prayerful moment with Mom. One year, 2013, I slipped up, forgot about the date, and went to Bethpage State Park to play golf with a friend. While on the sixth hole of the Green Course, it dawned on me that I'd forgotten the date. At exactly 8:50 a.m., the air was still, not even a gentle breeze was blowing. As I walked up the left side of the fairway, I glanced at the sky and at the tops of four nearby maple trees, then stopped and said a brief prayer. At precisely that moment, out of nowhere, amidst the absolute stillness, a brisk, swirling gust of wind came by, a mini-squall. For about ten seconds, the leaves of just those four maples blew hard while the rest of the park remained still. Then, just as quickly, it was over. It was a remarkably unusual moment, provocative, inspiring, even jubilant in a way. Whether this was just a co-incidental phenomenon of nature, or some type of communication, I really don't know. But it seemed powerful to me.

Interestingly, three years later I played the same course with my son Brian. As we passed those same four red maples, I told Brian of the time they blew so hard on June 21, 2013. As Brian listened intently to my story, beneath those very same trees, he spotted something shiny, bent down and picked up a small heart-shaped charm. It was engraved with the word, "Forever." Coincidence? Communication? Brian gave me the charm and I placed it in Mom's old music box for save-keeping.

It has been very difficult for me to put aside the feelings I've described here, to say to myself, as many have urged, "Get over it." For one thing, unlike Robert, Dennis and Jeanne, who have lived live hundreds, even thousands of miles away for decades, I still live on Long Island and am surrounded by constant reminders. As the only Long Islander, I visit Mom's grave at Holy Rood Cemetery many times each year. I drive on the Northern State Parkway quite frequently. Whenever I'm in central Nassau, I pass the big green parkway sign that says "Exit 33, Wantagh Parkway, South, Jones Beach." That sign, or one like it may have been last thing Mom ever saw, the sign that guided her onto the last road she'd take in life. I normally turn my head as I pass that sign, not wanting to be reminded of the words "Wantagh Parkway, South, Jones Beach" again and again. And I *never,* take the Wantagh State Parkway, if I can help it, especially the section that crosses under Newbridge Road. These and other reminders are inescapable and a large part of why it's not so simple to just, "get over it."

AFTERMATH

Positive Reminders

Not all of my Long Island memories bring about such dark thoughts and feelings. Some of them cause the opposite; they provide me with a broad smile, and an important sense of peace and happiness. I go back to our old neighborhood at least twice each year to see what may have changed, take a swim in one of the Levittown pools, amble through the weeds, and see some visible reminders of the past. I walk by our old house at 55 Twig Lane slowly, trying to peer into the back yard. Our former simple house is now an unrecognizable McMansion, complete with a semi-circle driveway and a huge, gaudy stone wall in front, one that separates our old house and yard from the rest of the neighborhood and world. People felt welcome in our old Levittown. There are no signs on this wall, but to me it says, "Keep Out!" As I stand on the sidewalk beyond the wall, I look up to the second floor window and think of the many good times Dennis and I had sharing the cold

Corner of Twig and Branch.

room back in the 1950's. Eventually Mom had heat put in, but for years we loved that unfinished cold room with the rough wood floor and the partially sheet rocked walls. Though it lacked heat, it contained a special and wonderful human warmth. In that cold room we sat at our own window near the floor from which we could see Twig Lane below, the rooftops of our neighbors' houses, the weeds, the lights from the Wantagh Parkway, the stars of the night sky, our world. In that cold room we had our toys, our cowboy hats, our scout magazines, even an old 78 r.p.m. Victrola on which we listened over and over again to "Genie the Magic Record," a children's recording that gave us years of sing-a-long fun and transported our imaginations to far away places. I think of the fun we had playing on the front lawn, now paved over by the new owner, the games of hide and go seek and "johnny made a round hole" we played at the lamp post out front, the countless photographs Mom took of us with friends, the Larkin kids, and Aunt Katherine on birthdays and holidays. On these Levittown walks I see what I can of our old back yard, the place where we first played as kids while noisy Air Force planes from Michel Field circled overhead and we thought Robert A. White might be on one of them, where tomato plants were staked each summer and two apple trees, a pear and a peach tree once bore fruit, where on hot summer nights Mom hung a giant sheet and showed dozens of neighborhood kids black and white movies of "Abbot and Costello" and "Santa Claus" on her antiquated 8 mm movie projector, where Mom's dog Sugar once romped safely within the white picket fence I built while Dennis was in the Marines, where dozens of hula hoops swirled round and round the waists of dozens of neighborhood kids, where the shrill of Jeanne's bagpipes could be heard for blocks as she practiced, where Robert, dressed in full Boy Scout regalia, marched around in preparation for his two week stay at Camp Wauwepex, where I, scared stiff after watching "The Curse of Frankenstein," hid in the fort I built from "new section" scrap lumber, where we struggled to mow the high grass with a push mower until Mom was finally able to afford a power mower, where we played initial tag, stretch, running bases and every other game imaginable, where we decorated the tall blue spruce tree in front of the house with colorful lights, mostly red – Mom's favorite, each Christmas, weeded the lawn, shoveled the sidewalk, planted the flowers, and clipped and shaped the shrubs to please Mom. Such memories bring a smile, not a frown.

While some things look the same, like time has stood still for decades, there is evidence of change in the neighborhood. The house across the street, 48 Twig, formerly owned by the Schley Family, is unrecognizable, having been completely torn down by new owners who replaced it with a huge, unattractive structure, complete with stone lions guarding whatever is within. Some houses are well-kept while some others need more than a sprucing up. A few houses, like the Madden's house down the block at 35 Twig, look exactly the same now as they did in the 1950's, including the original carport with its small wooden shed. Most of our old neighbors are long gone. The Kaiser's house, the Joy's house and the Randbeck's house are all owned by others now, people who never knew our Levittown of the 1950's and 1960's. Some of these new owners were not born then, or moved to the U.S. only recently. Yes, our old neighborhood is now a bit more multi-national than it was in our time. I view that as a good thing, especially in light of the original 1940's Levittown plan requiring that houses be sold only to whites. As for former owners, only a handful remain. As of this writing, original Levittown homeowner Gerry Palumbo, now in her 90's, still lives at 17 Branch Lane. Ed Bennett lives in the home his parents purchased in 1950 at 20 Booth Lane. Next door to Ed on the left is original owner Clayton Edwards, who turned 101 years old in November 2015. And two houses away on the right, another original Levittowner, the other Mrs. White, lives with her daughter, Robin. Occasionally the old neighborhood visits provide me with a completely unexpected surprise, like the interesting encounter I had one summer day in 2013. I parked my car alongside the weeds in front of the Hoffman's house at 41 Twig, and took a bike ride through the neighborhoods of my Levittown, Hicksville and

Westbury youth. When I returned I noticed a woman walking her dog. We made eye contact and chatted. I asked her if she lived in the area or was just passing through. She said, "I've lived here all my life." She was easily younger than I, but it followed that if she'd been there all her life, at some point we had to have been neighbors. She said her name was Lisa, and her maiden name was Bottenus. I couldn't believe I was talking to the daughter of "Al Bottenus-Bath King," one of Levittown's first plumbers. Lisa married Mike, a new section boy and, since she liked the area, bought a house on Twig Lane. After chatting briefly, she invited me into her house and we talked further in her beautiful living room, which faces out onto our beloved weeds. It seemed like time had stood still as she filled me in on many things, including how she has remained in touch with Mary Madden, Joey's mom, and Mary's two daughters, Theresa and Paula. She also gave me a DVD of home movies of her family on Twig Lane from the 1950's, which was a delight to watch. Seeing Lisa was one of those very pleasant "small world" stories that occurs every now and then.

The Women and Men of Levittown

As I pass by each of the houses in the old neighborhood on these bi-annual visits, I mostly think of Mom and our family, and the kids I played with every day. I also think of the parents of those kids, adults whom I knew well as friend, paperboy, or borrower. Most of the women were stay-at-home moms who cooked, cleaned, shopped, gardened, ran errands, volunteered, visited schools, and formed the shuttle service that picked up and dropped off husbands and kids, and did everything else it took to run a busy household. A few of the women went to work, like nurses Grace Hoffman, Jeannette Bruschi and Edna Burger, but they were in the minority. The good thing about so many stay-at-home moms was that someone was almost always home at everyone's house. We weren't latchkey kids. Actual people parented us. After the war, these men and women moved with their new families out to Levittown, the "country" to them, from Queens, Bronx, Brooklyn and Manhattan. They were the first to give William Levitt's historic suburban experiment a try. They were the pioneers, Long Island's first commuters, the "Dashing Dan's" who spent hours each way on the old, steam powered Long Island Rail Road getting to and from their city jobs, and arrived home just in time to put their children to sleep. They were the do-it-yourselfers who lit the barbeques and grilled the burgers on the patios that they'd made themselves, after they finished planting the shrubs and mowing the lawn and trimming the hedges that surrounded their tiny basement-less suburban castles. These men were more than just weekend squires. Most were humble World War II veterans who rarely spoke of their combat service in Europe and the Pacific. Pete Kaiser was a pilot in Europe, Les Joy a Marine who fought through battles at Guadalcanal, Midway and Coral Sea. Frank Saladino, "The Sarge," was an Air Force mechanic who not only served in WW II, he remained in the reserves long after the war. We loved seeing him come home from his drills and meetings wearing his Air Force blues with the many stripes down the lower sleeve, a sign that he was a veteran of many years and many campaigns. Shortly after Frank Saladino got settled in Levittown, he returned to active duty in the Korean War. Fred Palumbo served four years aboard the USS San Juan, seeing more combat than any other in the neighborhood. Fred went on to become one of Long Island's first landscapers. Elio Bruschi, later Doctor Elio Bruschi, was a 16-year-old orderly at a Navy hospital in New Guinea. His superior officer was hospital director Lt. Commander Jeannette Guizot. After the war Elio married Jeannette, the only woman veteran in the neighborhood. As Lt. Commander, she also held the highest rank. Howard Kolbenheyer served in Germany and came home with a big Nazi flag. Les Joy a Japanese sword, bayonet and helmet. All the men served, all gave something, and all wanted to return to some type of normalcy upon their return. Happily and luckily for us, they chose Levittown to begin their new lives.

I admired these first men of Levittown. With no man in our house, Dennis and I were always intrigued when the muscular, well-tanned Mr. Joy took off his shirt and trimmed his hedges, or the knowledgeable Mr. Kaiser stooped down to help fix anything of Mom's that broke, or the scientific-minded Mr. Schley tended to his prize winning chrysanthemums and extraordinary, locally obtained, butterfly collection. Some of these Levittown men spoke what seemed to be a different language at times with words I didn't always understand. When someone's lawn mower wouldn't start, "Sarge" Saladino would take a look, give it a few pulls, then say, "She's shot." This meant the mower was broken beyond repair, time for a new one. As a young boy, this puzzled me because I didn't know mowers and other machines were female. If someone's car wouldn't start, Sarge could diagnose the problem just by listening, "She's not getting any juice." I learned from the Sarge that "juice" meant electricity from the battery.

I well remember some of the little idiosyncrasies demonstrated by these men and women. When playtime was over and dinner and homework beckoned, each had a special way of calling their kids in. Some whistled. We could tell which kid had to go in by the variety of different whistles. Others called their kids by name. When Stanley and Dinah Schwartz wanted Louise home they'd softly call, "Loooo-ise," and she'd scamper on in. There was no mistake about Joe Taormina who'd yell, "ROBERT, JAY, GET IN HERE!"

I looked up to many of these men. I was amazed that Bill Hoffman, who despite a childhood bout with polio, could swim across the 25-yard West Green pool taking only 16 strokes to do so! I envied my friend Gary, whose dad, Elio Bruschi, served as neighborhood mediator when kids quarreled. Elio always made sure we enjoyed fair play. When the sump froze over in winter he'd climb under the fence along with us and referee our hockey games even though he knew we were trespassing on town property. Fred Palumbo gave us rides in his landscaping truck and, when we were teenagers, paid us $10 a day to lay sod at the homes of the rich. Howard Kolbenheyer provided box seats to Yankee games more than a few times, and Bill Boeckelman drove us to the "House That Ruth Built" in the Bronx in his green 1957 Chevy.

Mr. Kolbenheyer once saved me from losing $40, no small sum back in 1959. At Christmastime, his son Jimmy and I sold Christmas trees at an outdoor lot on the corner of Newbridge Road and Stewart Avenue. The owner promised us a dollar an hour plus tips. We'd help customers pick out their trees, then tie them to the rooves of their cars. Most would give us a quarter tip. When the two-week tree season was finished, the owner, who did little all week except sit in his truck and drink, told us, "Sorry boys. You made more in tips than I thought you would, so that's your pay. I'm not giving you any more money." We tried to argue with him saying, "a promise is a promise," but we were kids and our case went nowhere. He just rolled up his window, pulled out his flask of whisky, took a drink and dismissed us. Jimmy and I told his dad how the tree guy swindled us. When he heard our story, Mr. Kolbenheyer, a tall, smart businessman, said, "Get in the car boys. We'll go see this guy right now." He drove us to the tree lot, banged on the truck window and confronted the guy saying, "These boys worked every night for the past two weeks out in the cold selling your trees. You better pay them what you owe them or I'll have the cops here in a minute." With that, the man forked over $40 to each of us. I was impressed with Mr. Kolbenheyer's strength and resolve. That was the first time a man had ever fought a battle for me.

These first Levittowners were honest, hardworking men and women who cared deeply for their families and their neighborhood. Without them, our family would have had a much tougher time getting by.

Holy Family Decades Later

Whenever I'm biking or walking in the old neighborhood I stop by Holy Family Church and School where I am surrounded by images of Mom. I've recently come to know the new principal there, Maryalice Doherty. She and I have met several times, mostly about the Catherine White Award that Robert, Dennis, Jeanne and I established in 2010. That first year, the award, which was created to provide families with assistance and to have Mom remembered in a special way, was $500. By 2015, it grew to

Dennis, Peter, Mrs. Maryalice Doherty, principal of Holy Family School, Robert and Jeanne, after discussing the Catherine White Award, a scholarship and gift to school we established in Mom's memory February 2013.

Holy Family graduate Caroline Jannace accepting the Catherine White Award, 2012.

$1,650, with $500 going to the community-service-minded recipient, and $1,150 to the school to assist needy families who struggle with tuition payments. Thirteen family members contributed towards this award. We're happy to do this each year, and we believe Mom would be happy about it. Maryalice has also invited me to visit 7th and 8th grade classes, to teach the school's law club and to share my experiences in Nicaragua, in hope that they'll be inspired and establish a project of their own. Without my visits back home, I may not have met Maryalice, and there might not be a Catherine White Award.

Lessons from Levittown

My "old neighborhood" visits allow me to reflect on my childhood and teen years in a unique and special way and to really appreciate Mom's efforts to make them safe, significant, worthwhile, and never to be forgotten years. They remind me of how her actions and dedication as a single parent made me who I am, one able to stand with confidence and speak his mind when necessary. Despite the losses we experienced as kids and the things of which we were deprived, Mom gave us a great deal, and I can see this much better now than when I was young. When I drive by our old shopping center on the corner of Newbridge Road and Levittown Parkway, I see how much I was allowed to learn from being a trusted, young family shopper. From that trust, I learned valuable lessons in honesty, good faith and respectability. By relying on me as she did, I developed the sense that I had to think and act like a man at an early age. Mom kept us together by doing any job she could, demonstrating, as Gandhi said, that all work is honorable. By the example she set, I was able to learn about responsibility and hard work from my many boyhood jobs, which she encouraged. With the money I earned, money she allowed me to keep, I remember her wisely suggesting that I save what I could by opening my own bank account at the Long Island Trust Company. As a ten-year-old, I became a charter member of that bank on the very first day it opened. I was the 26th person in the door that day. I know that because I'll never forget my very first bank account number: 12-26

When I walk or bike those neighborhood streets today, I remember how much Mom allowed us to learn about life and ourselves, by ourselves. She didn't micro-manage our activities like so many parents do today. By her example, she taught us important lessons, and then expected us to go out and apply those lessons in real life. Somehow she figured out ways, on very little money, to hang onto our basic little Levitt house for two and a half decades. By keeping that house and us safely in it, she provided us with many more opportunities to succeed than if we were forced to live in a shelter, housing project or an impoverished neighborhood somewhere else. Without 55 Twig Lane, that's where we'd have been brought up, in a shelter or project. We'd have gone to different schools, had a different peer group, and had fewer opportunities to succeed. This was Mom's plan: to provide not only a roof over our heads, heat, light, water, safety and health, but also a good community with plenty of playmates and a myriad of activities and opportunities. Fatherless and poor, we didn't really know of our deprivation because she protected us and gave us more than anyone similarly situated could possibly be expected to give. Looking back on it now, it's fair to say she accomplished the impossible.

The developers of Levittown built so many houses that they had to use a dictionary to come up with names for the all new streets. Our little enclave was named for things made of wood. For example, we lived on Twig Lane. Around the corner was Branch Lane. Off Branch was Booth, Block, Bench and Bud. The eastern border of our wooden section was Newbridge Road. East of Newbridge was the never-ending bird section with street names like Flamingo, Thrush, Blackbird and Swallow. You knew you were leaving the "bird section" and entering the "flower section" when you crossed the two-mile-long Orchid Road off which you'd find dozens of streets with names like Azalea, Violet, Gardenia and Hyacinth. When Levitt exhausted such themes as birds and flowers, he went alphabetically, as with the "G" section where Giant, Grace, Grange and Guild Lanes were all "belted" in by the lengthy curvaceous Greenbelt Lane. The Wantagh Parkway formed our western boundary. Hicksville was just to the north and the new section to the south. There, in our wonderful little suburban compound, we learned about fair play, trust, teamwork and concern for others. When neighborhood boys verbally or physically taunted or bullied another kid, we were taught to do something we'd always seen her do: the right thing. We were not to pile on and join in the bullying, but to stand with the victim and tell the others to back off. In the late 1950's a new boy named Neil moved onto the block. Since most of us had grown up together and were all quite close, Neil found acceptance difficult to achieve. A "momma's boy" fresh from the city, he was the newcomer who didn't easily fit in. His mother didn't make things easy for him either. She'd call him in for lunch or dinner, and to our shock, sometimes even for a bowel movement, right in front of the other kids, in a manner that embarrassed him and made him an easy target. A few unkind kids harassed him verbally; calling him names just to draw a laugh. One neighborhood kid bullied Neil physically, beating him up for no other reason than that he could. I remember standing on the lawn of a neighbor when the bully began taunting Neil, then shoving and punching him until he fell to the ground. Neil curled himself up in the fetal position for protection. A few kids laughed and cheered the bully on; others stood by and watched. Mom didn't teach me to be a bystander when things like that took place. By the example she set, I knew when some type of action was required. As the bully began kicking this defenseless boy when he was down, I yelled for him to stop it. I knew there was some risk involved in doing this. I might be next. Fortunately for me, several other kids stood with me. They didn't like what was happening to Neil any more than I did. My brothers, sister and I were not taught to be bystanders. Since those early days it's been easy, actually quite normal for me to stand up for others, despite the consequences. Thanks to Mom's example and ability to stand up and be counted when few, if any, others would, I'm happy to say I've most often done the same. Throughout my life, as a parent, teacher, attorney, union leader and advocate for the poor, I've been able to stand up for the rights of children, students, colleagues, plain citizens and the poor when they've become victimized. The foundation for my many poverty projects, a major part of my life's work, was laid a long time ago on the streets and lawns of Levittown thanks to vision and guidance of Kay White.

I didn't always possess the ability or willingness to intervene on behalf of others or myself. As a boy I was the victim of a few bullies myself and often accepted their taunts and physical abuse as just part of growing up. Throughout childhood I'd heard older kids and adults remind me not to be a tattletale, or to somehow figure out how to "fight my own battles." I thought I just had to accept being the victim until I got older. As a seventh grader, I was bullied regularly on the school bus ride to St. Ignatius. One boy, Jim, was at least two years older than I, but in the same grade because he'd been left back twice along the way. Older and bigger, Jim daily provided me with more than a few verbal taunts, and I was the regular recipient of several "noogies" a day, rather severe knuckle jabs to the head. While he was the primary wrongdoer, he had help. Other kids on the bus not only took on the bystander role as they sat back and watched, some were aiders and abettors, encouraging Jim with their derisive laughter and put downs. I accepted this verbal and physical abuse for a while, mainly because I didn't know how to fight back. Mom and the nuns had taught me that fighting was bad, even sinful. I was also afraid that if I fought back and won I'd get in trouble myself, and if I lost, things would just get worse for me. Being the victim of a bully annoyed me but it didn't consume me. Mom had long advised me not to listen to certain people. *"Peter, whenever you hear criticism, it's always wise to check the source."* I didn't think too much of Jim, in fact few did. So I let it all pass and, for that brief period in my life, I took my lumps. Around the same time, I became friends with Gary, a Branch Lane boy who was smaller than I. Gary and a few of his other Branch Lane buddies seemed to have no trouble standing up for themselves when they had to. When someone took advantage of them, they wouldn't sit back and take it, as I'd done. Once, when we were at the Meadowbrook Movies, a group of bigger kids cut ahead of us on line. Gary spoke up with authority, "Hey. Where do you think you're going? Get back in line." A larger boy stood face to face with Gary and retorted, "Who's going to make me?" Gary made a fist with his left hand and let go with a well-placed blow. The tall bully promptly became the recipient of a solid punch in the nose, causing uncontrollable tears and the letting of a little blood. I was amazed. Gary didn't take the crap that I did. Fortunately for me, this was only a temporary phase in my life. By the middle of ninth grade, after playing freshman football and working out quite a bit, I was no longer a punching bag for bullies but a more secure teenager. What I didn't learn from Mom about self-assurance and standing up for myself, I learned from Gary and my new friends on Branch Lane. It should be noted that Jim went to Clarke High School and never again bullied me. As I got stronger and more confident, Jim, corroded by cigarettes and alcohol, stayed the same size. While I could have sought retribution, I never really bothered with him, never returned the "knuckle sandwiches" and other punishments he meted out, and never made him the butt of jokes. I just went about my life as a high school student and athlete, even waving to him in the hallways once in a while as we passed one another. I learned back then that bullies are really cowards and I felt sorry for them.

Sunlit path in "The Weeds," our oasis while growing up.

The kids within our unique borders were luckier than other Levittown kids. Our isolation from other neighborhoods by geography and school boundary lines caused us to become an even more tight- knit group. Our houses were within the East Meadow School District even though East Meadow was miles to our south and we didn't know any kids from there. The northern end of Twig Lane bordered southern Hicksville, and the kids from those streets went to Hicksville schools. We didn't know any of them either. The kids east of us from "across Newbridge," went to Levittown schools and we knew nothing of them. To our immediate west was the Wantagh State Parkway, which we could not cross easily. This isolated us from hundreds of our elementary and high school classmates who lived west of the parkway. Separated and insulated as we were, we had each other, dozens of kids who got to know one other well, played ball together, rode bikes together, slept out in tents at night, made push-mobiles out of any set of spare wheels we could find, and experienced every aspect of life together. Directly across from Twig Lane was the unique nature preserve we called "the weeds." The weeds began as a nursery for the New York State parkway system, a few acres where young pine trees were grown for placement along Robert Moses' curvaceous new roadways. By the time Levittown came along, the weeds became more of a preserve, with tall weeds growing among the many remaining pine trees. State or town government rarely sent workers there, so the weeds grew wild and became a wonderful haven for us to play, hike, picnic, and get away from our houses, TV sets and parents. Any time a kid felt like running away from home, he usually fled to the weeds for an hour or so before returning home. The sanctuary provided us with daily opportunities to experience the beauty and wonderment of nature. Much of our childhood was spent playing with friends in the weeds, climbing trees, digging holes, building forts, discovering wildlife habitats, hiking trails we blazed ourselves, and hearing the sounds of the many species of birds and other wildlife, all right across the street from our houses. Playing in the weeds wasn't always bliss; there were dangers. We learned on our own, sometimes the hard way, about such things as poison ivy, ticks, snakes and other critters. All the kids in the neighborhood were mindful of these dangers and became savvy nature-goers, always on the lookout for poison ivy and regularly performing tick checks. There were other perils too, like the feared Kearney brothers, Hicksville boys from around the corner on Rim Lane. They were tall, fast and older than we. Actually, they turned out to be nice guys, some becoming doctors. But back then, we only knew that if you threw a pinecone at one of them, they'd run you down and make you wish you hadn't. That was a very important aspect of our play as children. Since we weren't directly supervised all the time, we were responsible for our own actions. If we got in trouble, it was our problem to deal with. Parents didn't set up play dates, or oversee every aspect of our day. We did. There were few "helicopter parents" in those days, hovering over all we did. We worked things out and learned about life in the process. By sitting on the sidelines of a stickball game until someone quit and went home, we learned patience, to wait our turn. By being "chucked" from a game of two hand touch as a ten-year-old because a 12-year-old came along, we learned that life wasn't always fair, that injustice was sometimes part of our existence. And we survived it all quite well.

Inventiveness and Making Do

Billy and Drew Keenan lived at 10 Twig and their backyard directly abutted the weeds. Both were talented athletes who worked hard to convert several hundred feet of the weeds behind their house into a homespun Olympic park, complete with a shot put area, a broad jump pit, a high jump, mini-track, and even a pole vault area. For months each year kids from our neighborhood, as well as many quality athletes from distant neighborhoods, developed their skills on that impromptu, kid-made park. Some of them went on to become star college athletes themselves, including Billy Keenan, an ocean beach lifeguard who swam competitively in college. In 2014, at the age of 71, Billy won four events in the Florida State Senior Swimming Championship. Drew excelled in all sports and went on to become a high school all-star and national collegiate championship shortstop. Of his homespun Olympic park, Drew said, "We improvised. Everything was homemade. We made it with whatever was lying around. That was part of the beauty of Levittown, we made do with what we had, and growing up that way provided us with a luxury kids don't have today, the luxury of being self-sufficient and more than satisfied."

In addition to the Keenan's Olympic park, neighborhood kids cleared a sufficient space of brush in the weeds and created a baseball field, complete with a backstop made of wood and chicken wire. No dads or moms helped. It was entirely the work product of kids. Even though it wasn't on our property, we felt an ownership of that field. We became caretakers and protectors of the field and all of the weeds, as if it was our very own. If kids from surrounding neighborhoods entered the weeds, or tried to play on our field, the war was on. Today, the Town of Hempstead Department of Parks manages the land we still call the weeds. They even put up a few signs saying "Keep Out." Occasional dog walkers frequent the space, but few could know of its importance to us growing up. When I take my semi-annual trip back to these roots, I become reinvigorated and realize how Mom did so much more than struggle to maintain a Levitt house on an eighth of an acre plot. She maintained a beautiful house and a well-kept yard situated right across the street from several acres of private woodlands, a beautiful oasis in which we all grew and learned so much.

Myths and Trust

By early adolescence, most of us spent a great deal of time out of the house, enjoying a tremendous sense of freedom. The 1950's and 1960's were mostly a safe time, and we didn't fear anyone or feel the need to look over our shoulders very much. Sure, some of the older kids teased the younger ones with tales of "The Hook Man" who roamed the weeds at night with his hook arms, or the "Nude Man" who could outrun any kid, or the feared coy dog, which was part coyote and part wild dog. Such accounts told by the older talebearers kept the young ones out of the weeds, especially at night. Despite such mythical legends, our neighborhood was safe. We didn't feel the need to lock our doors at night. People watched out for one another, and their kids. If a young one ventured out into the street and his parent wasn't watching, another parent would spot it, open her window and shout, "Get out of that street." As young kids, we were watched, but as we grew older, we were given the freedom to travel, explore, and become independent, self-directed learners. By fifth or sixth grade we were taking bike hikes to distant towns like

Wantagh, some ten miles away, where two ponds called Twin Lakes were located. We'd figure out how to get there, map things out, cross main roads by ourselves, bike our way there, investigate nature, and go fishing, by ourselves. What we didn't know, we learned by watching others, or by ourselves through trial and error. By age 12, Mom permitted me to go to New York City by myself. I'd pack a small bag of clothes, take the bus myself to Hicksville, the LIRR to Penn Station, then the Eighth Avenue A train uptown to 181st Street where I would visit Aunt Katherine for a few days. I didn't think too much of it at the time, but I do remember feeling proud of myself when I arrived there, from my Levittown door to Aunt Katherine's Washington Heights door, on my own. I'm not sure whether too many of today's 12-year-old children would be allowed the freedom to learn that we gained from such excursions, or whether they'd even want that freedom. I'm referring to the children who spend a great deal of their time each day locked into their games and social media machines, and whose mom's drive them to school in their oversized SUV's rather than let them take the school bus or walk. I don't envy today's shortchanged children at all.

As a boy in Levittown, I learned of the importance and the value of money from the way Mom let me earn it myself rather than giving it to me automatically as an allowance. My two friends, Freddy and Bobby Hoffman, received an allowance of 25 cents a week, which was eventually raised to the incredible sum of 50 cents a week. They always seemed to have money when the ice cream man came down the block, or it was time to buy a slice at the pizza place near the West Green Pool. I'm sure there were times as a child when I felt a little financially victimized, that others were the recipients of something, whether it was a new family car, or a vacation, or an allowance, that I didn't have. But when I look back, I realize the importance of the tenacity and fortitude Mom demonstrated, that if I was to have anything in this life, I had to be patient and self-reliant like she. She taught us self-control and how to separate what was important from what was not. I may not have gotten the same quarters or half dollars as my friends, but the advantage I received from the lessons Mom taught were worth their weight in gold.

Moreover, by watching my Mom do so much with so little I learned a great deal about thriftiness, the art of making sure economic ends were met, and the importance of not wasting anything. Mom was rarely given to splurging. Perhaps once a year, if Aunt Katherine or Mom's cousin Florence sent her a few dollars, she didn't buy anything for herself. Instead, she would take us to the circus or ice-skating. That was splurging enough, and those times, rare as they were, were the exceptions not the rule. No matter how tough things got for her financially, Mom never threw up her hands and said, "I quit." She always pointed herself in a forward direction. I can picture her sitting at the kitchen table with bills and other papers piled up, knuckling down several nights a week, with scrap paper and pen, checkbook in hand, bifocals balanced low on her nose, adding, subtracting, dividing, making sure every penny was accounted for, and bills were paid. When she absolutely couldn't pay, she'd call whomever she owed with an explanation to obtain a bit of breathing room. Mom was no deadbeat. She never fled from an obligation but faced economic dilemmas squarely and honestly. How she provided us with all she did, on the tiny amount she received, whether from welfare before she went to work, or from her undersized paycheck when she did go to work, bewilders imagination.

From her valiant efforts at scrimping and saving Mom somehow managed to hold onto our house and keep our family together. While we didn't know this fact until only recently through the miracle of www.ancestry.com, Mom had at least four half-brothers whom she didn't know. Due to extreme poverty, Mom's mom, Eugenia Paulson Timmerman McCoy, who died when Mom was only two in 1919, couldn't keep her four sons and had to give them up to the care of orphanages in the late 1800's and early 1900's. Mom had only partial knowledge of one of her half-brothers, and no awareness of the other three, and she didn't want that to happen to us. There'd be no splitting of the siblings if Mom could help it, and she was well aware of how important that little Levitt house was to our safety and wellbeing. Though she had to turn the deed over to Nassau County when forced to accept welfare, she devoted herself to the task of keeping us in it so we could live normal lives. Fifty-Five Twig Lane became more than just a roof over our heads. It became our salvation. It was largely responsible for our success as children. It kept us in society, like other kids, and not excluded or feeling like outcasts. It kept us in good schools. It kept us safe and healthy. It allowed us to avoid being split up, or raised in a shelter, or housing project, or slum. It also gave Mom great joy. She loved her gardens, and lawn, and the summer breezes she got in her very own back yard and open carport. She was proud of her accomplishment and it showed. She loved hanging her American flag out on holidays, decorating the windows and house with shamrocks for St. Patrick's Day, lighting a pumpkin for Halloween and placing lights on the outdoor tree for Christmas. While our house wasn't filled with fancy or expensive things, it was clean and orderly and never an embarrassment. Our yard and gardens looked as good or better than most others in the neighborhood. None would ever be able to pass by and say, "That must be the welfare family." And sadly, for the entire 25 years Mom toiled, gardened, painted and cleaned while she lived at 55 Twig, she did so without ever being in possession of the deed.

No Retirement

As much as she loved her house and feared the thought of losing it or having Robert A. White someday fall heir to it, Mom was somewhat trapped by it. By having to turn the deed over to the county, there was little equity in the house, but she always exuded confidence believing that things would get better if she just stayed the course. Long before Little Orphan Annie sang, "The sun will come out tomorrow," Mom knew and believed that.

Throughout the 1950's, the monthly mortgage was paid with funds that came from the county. Through the 1960's until her death in 1975, she was able to make mortgage payments herself, but housing prices didn't increase much during that time. In her mid-fifties, aware that old age was coming, Mom felt confined by the house and knew her choices were limited. If she sold it, welfare would take the proceeds and she'd be left with nothing. With no pension forthcoming, and perhaps only a meager amount from Social Security, Mom was not free to sell and retire elsewhere as many of her neighborhood peers planned to do. So while Levittown gave her and all of us so much, she was also very much stuck there, deedless. With no acceptable alternative, she faithfully stayed on, confident that things would work themselves out somehow. She never envisioned what took place in the 1980's, that housing prices on Long Island would skyrocket as they did. She owed welfare $19000, and the value of the house at the time of her death was only a little more than that sum. Had she lived into old age, she could have sold for more than $350,000, paid welfare back, and, like other retirees, used the proceeds well into her future.

At the age of 56, aware that she could not work as a teacher forever, Mom chose to do something by herself to secure her own future. In 1974, she took a bold, risky step. In the last year of her life she obtained a loan sufficient to have the upstairs of the house dormered into a small apartment in order to produce some rental income. While Mom was quite cautious throughout of her life, when big issues came along, and big decisions had to be made, she didn't hesitate to think and act big. At that juncture, with her financial future at stake, she believed there was no time for inaction. Dennis and I were surprised at her willingness to make this leap, but happy for her since her mind was made up and she was determined to make her idea work. She talked things over with us and we pointed out that she'd never been a landlord before, that she'd have strangers living in her house, that she'd have to deal with financial aspects like paying the loan back, collecting rent, record keeping, and tax consequences. She heard our concerns, then went forward. Within weeks, the familiar look of her charming, adorable, original 1950 Levitt house changed into a big, almost distorted-looking white box. But she gleamed, knowing that the newly dormered space, formerly called the cold room, would soon produce a small stream of income flowing her way and that some of her financial worries would be lifted. Almost immediately she found a young working couple to rent the upstairs and they began paying a modest rent. Gary and his wife turned out to be friendly and nice and Mom was very comfortable having them there. Gary was handy and at times lent his knowledge and skills to help Mom with repairs and other jobs around the house. Mom's courageous venture succeeded. She became less concerned about her financial future, and enjoyed a much greater sense of security. As she'd always done, she identified a potential problem, considered various options and solutions, assessed them thoroughly, made a decision, then made it work.

Without Levittown

These last few pages have been devoted to the wonderful miracle Mom performed, that somehow, despite the difficulties she faced, she found ways to keep her house and the four of us children safely in it. At the time she may not have been aware of just how miraculous her efforts were, nor how beneficial they were to our growth and development. Because of her wisdom and ability to stay focused on raising us in that house, because of her unfailing sense of duty to us, she succeeded admirably and magnificently. Though we often had to do Levittown on a shoestring and Mom was rarely able to give us a lot in the way of material things, by giving us Levittown she gave us a great and wonderful gift: golden childhoods. When I think of her now and of our days growing up in Levittown, I try not to think about what I missed, but of what I was given. At times, I've thought of what life might have been like had it not been for her miracle. By successfully keeping us in our historic little Levittown house, by requiring good citizenship of us, and by guiding us in the right direction, we were saved by our courageous mother. Were it not for her and the home she established for us, we might have been split up as a family, or brought up in a much less desirable, less safe place. We might not have had the good neighbors we had to rely on so many times, like the Kaisers, the Schleys and the Randbecks. We wouldn't have had our many friends, guys like Gary Bruschi, who throughout the years has helped me and several members of my family so much and remains one of my closest friends to this day. Without Levittown we wouldn't have had the institutions that reinforced the values Mom taught us, like Holy Family Church and its pastor Monsignor Martin O'Dea, who gave Mom such important counsel when she was first left abandoned, and who ten years later hired her as a teacher. We wouldn't have met the scholarly Father Buckley, who challenged us intellectually as young altar boys and with his brilliant homilies at mass, or Father Fagan who stopped frequently to check on Mom and made sure we had some toys at Christmastime. There'd have been no Holy Family School, where Mom was not only a charter member of the hard working faculty, but also a community leader and Hall of Fame teacher. Without Levittown there'd be no West Green Pool where Mom walked us on hot summer days to take swimming lessons from the patient and kind Mrs. Columbo, my first swimming teacher. I'll forever cherish her dedication and the effort she made to teach so many of us Levittown children that important life skill. Because of those Levittown pools, I was able to swim competitively as a teen and become a lifeguard as an adult. If I had to compare my summers at the Levittown pools with those of rich kids at their country clubs and yacht clubs, I'd take the Levittown pools any day. Without Levittown, I might never have been introduced to my favorite game, golf. I'd never have met my neighbor Sid Harris, the excellent home-spun golf instructor who taught other neighborhood boys and me the essentials of the game we love to this day, or my close friend Drew Keenan, with whom I still play regularly at Bethpage State Park or near his home in Ft. Myers, Florida. Several times each year, Drew, several boys from the block and I challenge one another to our now 55-year-old neighborhood golf championship. Without Levittown, I'd never have learned to ice skate or play hockey as I did whenever our local sump froze over in winter, or experienced rural Long Island life firsthand by riding the tractor with farmers Dominic and Freddy De Monaco and picking beets on their nearby 28 acre farm. Without Levittown, I'd never have gone to W.T. Clarke High School, where I met and became close friends with so many wonderful, talented classmates, young men and women who, even now into our senior citizen years, remain life-long friends. I'd never have been coached by dedicated professionals like Jack McDonald and Jack Boyle, the first men in my life, who did so much to help me achieve manhood; nor would I have been taught so well by so many devoted, hard-working educators like the brilliant and humorous science teacher Hugo DeCiutiis, the gentle, kind and scholarly social studies teacher Harry Healy, and my sharp-witted and demanding English teacher, Constance Green, dubbed "the commander" by her students. These men and women did far more then arouse my curiosity about learning, they inspired me to become a teacher myself. Without Levittown, I wouldn't have learned the importance of family teamwork. Throughout the 1950's, Mom washed clothes in the tiny Bendix washing machine that came with each Levitt house, then lugged the wet laundry outside and hung it to dry on the clumsy, ugly metal clothesline William Levitt provided each homeowner. After many years of hauling wet laundry, Mom wanted an electric dryer and we said we'd help. In the mid-1960's, after each of us had saved our pennies, nickels and dimes from whatever sources we could - paper routes, baby-sitting, snow shoveling and lawn mowing, we put together enough money to buy "the family dryer." No more lugging, no more clothesline. Such family teamwork was essential to help us survive. Without Levittown I don't know who or what I'd have become. For it was in Levittown, simple as that existence may have seemed, that I had everything. None of the things my brothers, sister and I had, new or old, big or small, tangible or intangible, would have been possible without Mom's ability to keep and maintain the eighth of an acre plot and simple dwelling we loved, 55 Twig Lane, Levittown, New York. Thanks to Mom's vision, wisdom, courage, tenacity and hard work we received the miracle of a safe and happy childhood.

Final Levittown Thoughts

I didn't know it at the time, but whenever I visited the West Village Green pool, which was located across Newbridge Road in Hicksville, not Levittown, I was swimming about two blocks from the boyhood home of Rock and Roll Hall of Fame legend Billy Joel. It's probable that he swam there too. Though he's two years younger than I and I didn't know him back then, I'm sure our paths crossed many times at the pool, the stores or even Holy Family School where his teenage band played at dances. In his 1977 song "Scenes from an Italian Restaurant," Joel made reference to our old neighborhood when he sang, "…then the King and the Queen went back to the Green, but you could never go back there again." I'm sure there are a number of interpretations that can be applied to the words of that hit song, and since life involves many struggles and passages, going back and trying to live life in the past can be difficult, maybe even counterproductive. However I believe going back on these semi-annual visits to the old neighborhood demonstrates, to me at least, that there can be a great benefit to doing so. Old, established roots can be re-traced, memories of good times recollected, and proper respect paid to those who made life possible. I consider my visits a wonderful, firsthand way of remembering my many friends and an paying an important tribute to Mom.

Rugged Individualism

I've never quoted President Herbert Hoover before, but I believe one quote of his can be applied to Mom. When the term "rugged individualism" comes up in history books, Hoover's name appears. Perhaps that's because he defined that phrase in a 1928 campaign speech when he said,

> While I can make no claim for having introduced the term 'rugged individualism,' I should be proud to have invented it. It has been used by American leaders for over a half-century in eulogy of those God-fearing men and women of honesty whose stamina and character and fearless assertion of rights led them to make their own way in life.

Whenever I thought of rugged individualism in the past, names like Daniel Boone, Abraham Lincoln and Theodore Roosevelt came to mind. They demonstrated the stamina, character and fearlessness of which Hoover spoke as they led this nation and the world, paving the way for so many. While Kay White wasn't a frontier folk hero like Boone, and she didn't make her way from a log cabin to the White House like Lincoln, and didn't carry a big stick around the globe or earn a Nobel Peace Prize like Roosevelt, few I know have demonstrated the characteristics of rugged individualism as well as she. In her own deliberate, private, moderate, respectful way, abandoned and penniless as she was at the outset of her journey, Mom was the sum and epitome of honesty, stamina, character and fearlessness and, in my view, a fine representative of the great American story.

As an individual, Mom followed her own path and wasn't much of a joiner. The only official group I remember her joining was the Cub Scouts, as a den mother. On Memorial Day or other holidays, when Pack 91 marched in a parade, she'd march alongside us wearing a blue skirt and a light yellow blouse with a scout insignia emblazoned on it like a uniform. Other than that, she donned no uniforms. Rather she stood alone, not following a path set by others, but leading by example, donning the uniforms of sacrifice, character and respect instead.

Did She Know?

When loved ones pass away, especially suddenly, survivors are left to wonder whether they actually knew how much they were loved. I've asked myself, "During her lifetime, did I say or do enough to let Mom know how I really felt about her? Did I do enough to show her what was in my heart?" Since she died suddenly none of us was given the chance to prepare or to plan any final moments with her. Despite this, I believe with substantial certainty that she knew she was really loved, and the essence of what was in our hearts. Whether we expressed our love directly enough with our words, I'm not sure. But I believe we expressed it sufficiently by our conduct. As an 18-year-old college freshman, I saved every cent I possibly could from my job at the Hotel Holden in Dayton, Ohio so I could send her $500 to make her first visit to Hawaii for Robert's graduation. In her emotional letter of thanks, Mom made it clear that she knew of my love for her. She knew of Robert's love by his hard work, dedication and success. That always pleased her. She also knew by the hospitality and kindness he and Charlotte showed whenever she visited. She knew by the many jobs that Dennis, Jeanne and I did for her around the house and yard. So very often we didn't know what we were doing, but by following her example of determination, trial and error, we figured out how to paint and panel, sheetrock and spackle, mow and plant, wash and dry. She knew by the direction our lives were beginning to take, how we began following her path of service to others the best way we could as parents, teachers, social workers and business persons in a classroom, a hospital, or the military, and by improving the lives of the poor, the mentally ill and veterans groups. And she knew because from time to time we did say it directly, orally and in writing. The best demonstration of this is a letter Dennis wrote to Mom November 28, 1969, from a hillside somewhere in Vietnam. It was his first Thanksgiving away from home.

Dear Mom,

Well, here it is Thanksgiving. I'm on radio watch. Time 0300. It's O.K.
though, I've already had my turkey – only I had mine in New York and it
sure was swell. This is my first Thanksgiving away from home and I guarantee
it will be my last.
I want to wish you all a Happy Thanksgiving, you know with the world crisis
the way it is today, we still have a lot to thank God for. For one, Mom, you have
raised a good family, one who loves you and respects you more than you will
probably ever realize. You have been great!! And I am thankful for that.
As kids the White Family had everything that everybody else had. Even though
things were harder for you, you always managed to make us happy. Mom, I only
hope that someday I can make you as happy as you have made me. I know I don't
always show how I love you when I'm home, but believe me Mom, I do. And I
don't want to sound like a momma's boy, but I miss you. I think I got my point
across. I am indeed thankful. Happy Thanksgiving to you all.

Love,

Dennis

Dennis' clear and concrete words convey very powerful feelings. I am very happy that he
wrote that letter and managed to keep it safe all these years. It was one of many that he
found among Mom's things after her death. At the time he wrote it, he had just arrived in
Vietnam for his one-year tour and felt far away from home for the holidays. At such
times, one has little to do but think and reflect. Rather than feel sad for himself, Dennis,
as was his style, chose to give Mom some happiness instead. Rather than sulk or do
nothing, he did something positive. And by putting his feelings down on paper and
mailing them off, he gave her a much-needed lift. From Dennis' letter Mom was able to
learn two important things, that her son was safe and that his heart was filled with peace
and love. Looking back now on those simple and eloquent words provides all of us with
the important knowledge that … she knew.

MOM'S OWN WORDS

Mom was a prolific writer, not of lengthy prose or poetry, mostly of letters. Unlike
today's abbreviated texting and Facebook communications, she took the time and
demonstrated the patience and discipline to write frequent, often lengthy, letters to
business and church people, her students' parents, friends, and us. Some of her letters to
us were newsy, bringing us up to date on what was going on back home. Others were
important and heartfelt expressions about things she wanted or needed to tell us. She'd sit
at the kitchen table, peer down through her bifocals at her nice but simple stationery,

sometimes just loose leaf, then thoughtfully and carefully craft her words. Fortunately, I saved 20 letters from Mom. Nineteen of them are handwritten in her beautiful penmanship. The other one was typed in 1965 on her old, manual, portable Royal typewriter. The keys on that time-honored black machine often stuck and blotched up almost every word she typed. A quick look at that 50-year-old letter reveals how hard she must have toiled, and how that aged Royal slowed her down. All her letters after that were composed in pen. There is no crossing-out and no sloppiness in any of the handwritten letters. All are neat and tidy and in beautiful handwriting. An example of her fine penmanship can be found on the back cover of this book. The word "Kay" is her actual signature scanned from a Christmas card she wrote in the late 1960's. Perfect pencraft in every way. Most of Mom's letters to me were written during 1965 – 1971 when I was away at college in Ohio and Hawaii, or stationed at the U.S. Army Infantry School at Fort Lewis, WA and Fort Benning, GA. Dennis saved more than 40 of Mom's letters, written from 1969 – 1970 when he attended boot camp at Parris Island, studied at the U.S.M.C. radio school in San Diego, and served in Vietnam. He furnished these precious letters for me to review for this writing. Each letter flows beautifully, is well organized, and provides important insights into her thoughts on what was going in the world, and of her concern for us. Important things were happening at home, in America, and throughout the world during those years - the first moon landing, the assassinations of Martin Luther King and Robert F. Kennedy, war, social and cultural change, and upheaval at home and abroad. Mom kept us abreast as well as she could of family and neighborhood matters, and sometimes offered a viewpoint or two on national and global affairs. Since letter writing has mostly gone out of style, these letters, some of which are more than five decades old, are dear treasures to us. When we were far away, receiving of a handwritten piece of hometown mail, especially from Mom, was a delight, the kind that people who use today's instant electronic media may never know. Not only was it a very personal way of communicating, it was also quite reasonable. U.S. postage stamps back then were six cents for first class mail and a mere eight cents for air mail. We'd post a letter to Mom from wherever we were, then wait a week or so for her reply. The topics contained in her letters ran the gamut and reveal quite a bit about her thinking at the time. When she had something important to say to us, she was often direct, pulling no punches and mincing no words. Her letters reveal her to be honest without being offensive, humorous without being trivial, and sensitive, encouraging and helpful without being corny.

An interesting pattern became apparent while reading Mom's letters, perhaps something of a flaw on her part. But for one year, Robert lived away since 1957. All references in Mom's letters about him are positive. He was more than 5000 miles away, working hard, making it on his own, doing well in school, and serving in the National Guard. He was a self-made man, and he could do no wrong in Mom's eyes. A few years later I lived away and Mom often wrote encouraging and supportive words to me, words like *"You and Robert are men now. I'm proud of you."* Yet she often let me know how difficult it was living with teenagers Dennis and Jeanne. In other words, Robert and I were away and were "good" in her eyes, while Dennis and Jeanne were home, doing whatever it was they did as teenagers, and in her eyes their conduct sometimes left something to be desired. After I finished college I lived home for a year and a half while Dennis was away in the Marines. An interesting flip took place. A few of Mom's letters to Dennis referred to me as moody and grumpy and of being a know-it-all because I'd finished college. Now Dennis was away and "good," while I lived home and my conduct left something to be desired. Dennis and I have concluded that, while we did our best to be good sons and to be there for her, they were trying times for Mom and for us as well. She wasn't always in good health, and her moods were ever changing. We were young men, often nervous about our own futures. Growing up, college, work, the war. So much uncertainty. So much apprehension. We also concluded that whoever lived home, no matter how many chores he did, ceilings he painted, sidewalks he shoveled, lawns he mowed, leaves he raked, errands he ran, stories he listened to or tears he dried, didn't always measure up to those who were away.

The following quotes are excerpts from Mom's letters, arranged somewhat topically, that show how she spoke and what she cared to write about. In pouring over and organizing these letters, actual first-hand thoughts of Kay White, reading and rereading each significant passage, I began to feel closer to her than at any other time during this writing. As I read her words, written in her own pen, there were times when I heard her voice in my head, a voice I've largely forgotten. Clear images came to mind and I could picture that about which she was writing as if it were yesterday and I was there. There were times when I felt so close I thought I could grab the phone, dial GE-3-5250 and have a chat with her. The letters are real, as are the thoughts they contain and the images they conjure up. Here is Mom in her own words:

On Being Alone

Dennis, Tuesday night I went alone to the Westbury Music Fair to see Mickey Rooney in "George M." It was wonderful. He can't sing too well but is very talented and a good dancer. He can play every instrument in the band. I love the songs from that show. When they played "You're a Grand Old Flag," everyone in the audience applauded loudly. They really feel that way. Of course most of crowd was older folks. Not too many young ones dig that era, the earlier 1900's. Just as I was writing this letter to you the radio played "Give My Regards to Broadway." It was one of the songs from the show, so I'll give your regards to that wonderful place. August 1969

Mom and Peter share a dance at friend Tony Acerra's wedding, August 1968

Peter, I just returned from the Westbury Music Fair. I went by myself to see the King of Jazz, Duke Ellington and Ella Fitzgerald. I thoroughly enjoyed it and am glad I went. October 1968

Peter, I sent off the card saying I would attend Tony and Jan's wedding reception. I wasn't sure if I should go, not knowing anyone, so I called Mrs. Patterson and she said I could go with her and her husband. Where I will be sitting I really don't know, but if I at least know someone it should be more enjoyable. July 1968

On Citizenship

Dennis, It was awful when a fellow who was sitting in front of me at Jeanne's high school graduation shouted out "boo" in a loud voice when Dr. McCleary said in his address to the graduates that he hopes "they all stay good American citizens." I spoke to the young man and asked him why at that particular part of his address did he boo. He said he knew he was out of order, but with the war in Vietnam and our foreign policy he could not agree with Dr. McCleary. August 1969

On Change in Attitudes

Dennis, When I went to New York City to see the show "Zorba" with Peter, I didn't like the dress I saw on "The Great White Way." I saw all types of people, hippies and others. I don't really care what people wear, but I guess I don't like it when no one bothers to dress for a Broadway show anymore. But this is the new way – everything is more relaxed. No more effort put into things. August 1969

Peter, We have two new teachers this year as two sisters left the order suddenly. Of course it probably wasn't sudden for them. That makes three who have left our school this year and are no longer nuns. It doesn't seem strange to me any longer, as when we went to the Mass of the Holy Spirit at the cathedral last week, there were thousands of nuns with short dresses and suits and some without veils. They looked lovely - very pretty. Now they are beginning to look like what they are – women. September 1968

Peter, I have a talk to give on a class I'm taking called "Parental Attitudes and Feelings." This was an easy topic for me, but of course I had to read up on it, so I was in the library quite a bit. I did find the books all stated what I had felt all along and my attitudes agreed with the author's. The only change is in the last year when the youth rebelled so much and some spoke out too violently. This is frightening to me and not natural. I think we all mature, but we still have to have a great respect for the people who put up with us as little ones. "Honor Thy Father and Thy Mother" still holds good for me. July 1968

Peter, I gave what I thought was going to be a short talk in the class I'm taking. The topic was "Parental Attitudes and Feelings." I did a lot of preparation for this, and then we had a question and answer period. This topic was the longest for discussion. We spent almost an hour following up on my talk. When I see the attitudes of my children in class, I can definitely say they inherit some of their traits from their ancestors. And of course I do from mine. We are going into the topic of personality this week. I have two more weeks, another term paper, then the final and it's all over. I will miss it. I want to continue on with my education in the fall. July 1968

On Finances and Other Struggles

Peter, We received your letter asking us to take your money out of the bank for next semester's tuition. So I am enclosing a few withdrawal slips just in case you make a mistake. We found your bankbook. Your account number is 12-26, so fill in this number on the green slip and don't forget to sign it. You have $400.74. So I don't know what you want to withdraw. You should get a few dollars in interest but how much I don't know. Dennis will lend you $100 which he will take out of his account and I will put your money plus his $100 in my checking. I will then send you a check for $525. I will put in the balance of $25 myself. Tell me how you want the check made out. To Peter White? To the University of Dayton? I think the school would be better as then you could hand it right in and not worry about trying to cash it. December 1966

Dennis, I sent your name and serial number to the American Legion, along with Robert's. They will send you some money from their Bingo games. When we were leaving your farewell party one of the vets told me to send them your address and # as they send something to their local service men. So you will maybe get $10 or so or maybe more. They make about $700 each week so I don't know how they work or share the money and if you get it just once or more often. August 1969

Peter, Mrs. Palumbo came over with your pay for the last week you worked for Fred, $12. September 1965

Peter, This morning when I went out to get going to the mass, I was all dressed up and going to pick up three nuns to drive them to the cathedral in Rockville Centre. The car wouldn't start. Bill Fowkes was at work and I was frantic. I had volunteered to drive the sisters and told the new principal I'd do so, and here I was stranded. I asked Mrs. Swearingen for help and she took me up to the convent. Luckily, the nurse saved the day by driving all of us to the cathedral. Now it is 5 o'clock and I have to pester Bill to help with the car. So you see, my problems are never ending. I'll have to take the school bus with the kids to school, but I'll manage. September 1965.

Peter, I am without a car since December 1 but we are managing fine. I get a ride to and from school and go to church with Joan and I will be going to the store with Mrs. Randbeck on Friday evening, so things do work out. In fact, I've been happy to stay home and not have to go out much. It is more restful and I am very tired. The rest will come in handy. December 1966

Dennis, *Your tax return from New York State came. It was for $10.* April 1969

Peter, *Christmas is in just another two weeks and I really don't feel Christmassy. I explained to Dennis and Jeanne that you, Robert and I haven't any money, and that is true, but I guess I can manage a few things. What it'll be I don't know.* December 1966

Peter, I received a nice letter from Charlotte and she is so happy to have Robert back

*again. He wrote me today and has been very busy with the Hawaii National Guard, drill
and physicals, and is finally a civilian again. He has been very lucky. He has been out
looking for a job and has a promise from G.E. for $500 a month and increases to come.
They will let him know next week. He found a nice cottage for one on Harding Avenue in
Honolulu, at $98.50 a month, furnished. He said it is nice and clean and comfortable
after what he saw for less. He feels he is lucky to get this.* December 1966

*Peter, I intend to mail this letter off to you Wednesday at 1 p.m. after I leave the bank and
take money from your account and put it in my checking account and I am sure it will
arrive on time. Your letter came today but Dennis could not get to the bank so I will do it
as I get off early on Wednesday. I didn't know how much to send you, so I hope I did the
right thing. You said only to send $400 but suppose you don't get the tuition reduction
and can't register. So just in case I made out a check for $425 to the college and one for
$100 payable to you. Your last letter said you needed $525 to register and I didn't want
you to be short and then have to rush back to register after Dennis was able to lend you
the money. If you don't need it be sure to keep it safe and not lose it. You could mark
"void" on it but I still need it back as I keep all my checks. If you have to cash it, it will
be OK as the money is in the bank, but only if necessary as we are getting along on a
shoestring with Christmas just a week away. Don't borrow any money as no one has any
money. Do what you want, but don't lose the check.* December 1966

*Peter, I received the phone bill for October and it came to $72. So only call on Sunday or
after 9 when it is cheaper. We will have to make it short because your calls have been
costing $4 each time you call. I'll tell Robert the same thing, as his calls run about $8
and $9. So these calls are out from now on.* November 1966

*Peter, Well payday finally rolled around. I never thought we would make it. I have just
made out all my bills and it is a good feeling. However, I owe you $272 and Jeanne's
doctor $175. I also owe $85 in X-rays, so I have a long way to go. There's also $300 to
Charlotte since last year. I hope no one asks any favors of me as I will be broke most
every payday from now on.... The regular bills were terrific too. The telephone bill was
$20, double what it should be. The month before it was $30. I just can't afford this to
happen again. So only call if you need to. The car was very costly last summer but now
since I have it to myself I can go two weeks for just $3 worth of gas.... Today I stocked up
on food. Our cupboard was really bare, so I went to Model's to try and save a few
pennies and I will continue to shop there for some items all the time.* October 1968

*Peter, Well things are fine. I am happy with my class this year, as they are very bright
and ever so good. What a change after last year. I feel that I had to get a break, and I
did. I got my raise but it was only $50 extra per month after taxes, I thought it was going
to be $70. At least that is something to be happy about.* October 1968

*Peter, I want to get this money right off to you now that I know your address. I'm sorry
you have to be so broke because of us. But things seem to be confusing for us financially.
Dennis owed you $267, minus this $40, so the balance is $227, just so you know. I am
keeping a record of it. Next month I can begin to pay off my debts. It seems I will be in*

debt forever. But on my small salary, what can I expect!!! The raise next month, plus Dennis' giving me $15 a week will help. September 1968

Peter, Dennis is working today and sends you the enclosed check for $27. As of last week he owed you $227, so now his balance is an even $200. September 1968

Peter, We have been so very broke – I just don't know how we ever survived until October 1. We just have to take things easy and not go overboard again. Too much company on no money, it just isn't wise.

P.S. Here's $20 from Dennis. His balance to you is now $180. October 1968

Peter, I'm sorry you had to be so broke. I thought you were OK or I would have gotten this off to you sooner. Please don't wait until the last minute. Dennis gets paid every Friday. His checks are small but next week he will make $100 as he and a friend are roofing a house alone. This is $20 more from Dennis, so his balance is $160 now. The other $80 is from me. I still owe you $200 more, so that is $360 still to be paid to you. October 1968

On Sharing

Dennis, Peter drove to the Bedford Stuyvesant section of Brooklyn to bring Cecilia here. She had two wonderful weeks with us. She is an 11-year-old black girl. We were supposed to have two girls but one's (Stephanie) mother decided not to allow her to go. Jeanne stayed home from work some days to keep her company. Jeanne is very good with children. Cecilia was exceptionally good. She is shy and very helpful. Dolores, Jeanne and Cecilia went to Salisbury Park and had a picnic and went on the boats. We had a cookout that night but Peter didn't get home until 10 p.m. Sunday we took Cecilia to mass and then we dropped Jeanne and her off at Jolly Rogers. Later Peter picked them up. He went on the bumper cars with them. We had a chicken cook out, then took her picture. At 3 p.m. she took a dip in the Pearlman's pool, then we had to rush off to have her back by 5 p.m. She fell asleep in the car. I was glad that Peter could see that the New Yorkers care for the underprivileged too as there were 50 or more families who took children from the ghetto. While she was here we took her to Great Eastern and she picked out some games and toys to take home. Also Dolores bought her a Snow White book and some bubble bath. June 1969

Peter, I volunteered to go to the Northport Veterans Hospital and do what I can for the elderly patients. Everyone discouraged me, but I went anyway and met the director. I stay two hours each time I go, playing games and checkers with the patients, some of whom fought in WWI. I go to the mental hospital building. I was frightened but after being there it wasn't so bad. July 1968

Sense of Humor

Dennis, Peter just washed our filthy car ... without me asking!

Peter, Is it possible for you to call every Sunday at 1:30 p.m.? I will be home. And talk for just three minutes please!

Dennis, Yesterday I bought three shelves for the den. Clem put them up and it really gives a nice look to the den now. All your mugs are up and our Hawaiian shells and my beautiful black coral, which Jeanne thinks looks like a branch from the weeds!

Peter, I went to the doctor last week and it cost me $45 to find out I'm fine!

Dennis, Peter hasn't cut his hair yet, but I won't say a word about what he does. This way we get along better!

Dennis, Jeanne took her road test Wednesday. She used Peter's car. The horn goes off when you signal to the right and that happened on Jeanne's test. She's waiting for the results.

Dennis, When you come home I want to surprise you with how lovely our house looks now with our newly painted walls, clean closets, and no junk around. And it had better stay that way!

Peter, Dennis was sick again today and had bad headaches and couldn't get out of bed. But of course he and Barbara had to go swimming at a picnic, so he paid the price!

Peter, Dennis is pestering me for permission to parachute out of a plane. I said no but I don't want to fight about it. It cost $40 for a three-hour lesson. Only one lesson then you jump. It is madness. Ed Reck did it a week ago. Can you imagine what they'll do next? $40 to jump into nowhere???

On Her Children

Dennis, With all the activity we've been having here to keep me busy, I still miss you very much and you will always be missed. Some of the things you said to me the day of your graduation still linger in my memory and I am not proud of you because you are a Marine, but because you are "you." You are a good son, very thoughtful and loving.
July 1969

Peter, Your gift gave me a wonderful feeling – it was not the amount that you sent me that made me feel like a queen, but the thought of your sacrificing and saving for me that made me feel your love and devotion to me. You know I never look for gifts and your traditional box of candy always made me happy because knowing you had no money it was the thought that counted. So when you, as a full time student, worked three jobs and unknown to anyone saved up this large sum how my heart puffed with pride…. I hope you really know what this means to me…. You gave me the surprise of my life. Especially when I had just been discussing wanting you to use your earnings on a car of your own,

you used this money for me. Thank you a million. God will bless you for your devotion.
April 1966

Peter, I have wonderful children and I thank God for them each night. April 1966

Peter, Life is so complicated these days that we must make use of every minute, and thank God for those minutes together. April 1966

Dennis, Let me thank you for my wonderful birthday. The dinner was so delicious. We had a wonderful evening. The painting is so lovely. I can't get over how you did all this without my knowing it. And the party – I had a grand time. July 1969

Dennis, Peter finally painted the two bathrooms and what an improvement. July 1969

Dennis, Jeanne's been very helpful with money and much more considerate since working at the hospital. She works long hours and is tired and not having any fun. You really learn of life when you mingle with the sick. They are so dependent on you for help. She said she loves her work and can't wait to go there. This is really amazing to me. I guess you never know what will appeal to people as a career. June 1969

Peter, You certainly deserve a lot of credit for your gigantic venture, taking four boys from inner city Dayton to New York and back and giving them a great time. I'm glad it was successful. They seem so appreciative. They'll always remember you. Their letters are cute. I wrote two of them, and will write the other two over the weekend.
September 1968

Peter, Thank you so much for your check which arrived Saturday. I was very grateful. I never expected you to send anything, as I owe you so much already. March 1969

Peter, Dennis did a beautiful job paneling the den. It looks so professional. After the den, he will start on the living room. It's hard work, but he does a good job. He is making use of every minute before he goes into the Marines. March 1969

Peter, Mrs. Gomes is in the hospital, in traction. She's had back pain for a long time and they may operate. Mr. Gomes is very upset. Charlotte and Robert are living there with him and he won't eat unless Charlotte sits him down and makes him do so. She is busy with school and taking care of two homes and cooking and washing for her father and running to the hospital every afternoon. Mr. Gomes goes in the morning and Robert tries to get there at night. They do a terrific job. March 1969

Peter, We have been besieged with letters from Mack, Charles and David Landers, and one from Ollie. We'll never be able to catch up on them. They really told us how much they enjoyed their visit. So it was a tremendous success. You should take a bow. You certainly did your part to promote integration. September 1968

Peter, It was just two years ago on the 12th that we lost Aunt Katherine. Dennis wants to go to the cemetery in Queens as a family next time you are home. September 1968

Getting Us to Think of Others

Peter, Don't forget to send Jeanne a birthday card. She will be 17 on November 6. October 1968

Peter, Dennis will be 19 on Thursday. Send him a card. November 1968

Peter, I got a letter from Dennis. Poor fellow. I hope you drop him a line. He is lonesome and not receiving much mail. We have to write to show him we care. April 1969

Peter, Please send the Gomes' a card. They really like you and should hear from you more. July 1968

Peter, Mrs. Gomes is in the hospital. Write her and cheer her up. March 1969

Peter, Please try to get an anniversary card off to Charlotte and Robert if possible. It is their 1st anniversary on July 22. I am sending a check from all of us. July 1968

On Sadness

Peter, On Tuesday we buried a little fellow from our school, ten years old. He was in my first grade. It just doesn't seem possible. I can't get him out of my mind. April 1966

Dennis, Kitchie Schley came over with a tiny gift for Jeanne's graduation. She said Jeanne had been so nice to Liz. Liz Schley would have graduated today with Jeanne. It's been two years since she's gone. Jeanne put some of her flowers on Liz' grave as a memento. June 1969

On Courage and Confidence

Dennis, I'm so glad you have the courage to try out for the USMC football team. It is very important in life to try things. You can easily make it, especially now that the Marines have you in good shape. I know you will be a success at whatever you set out to do. You proved it to yourself this year. Keep up your good work and courage. I am very proud of all your accomplishments. July 1969

Peter, I know you will get very good grades at college and I want you to have much more confidence in yourself. Look how nicely you did in Clarke High School and that was very strange after a Catholic school. So you will cultivate the same feeling for Dayton when you are settled and used to the place.... Aunt Katherine asks that you not be too serious. Get out and mingle with the fellows and girls and enjoy yourself. Don't bury yourself in the books. September 1965

Peter, Dennis is so happy about making the varsity team. Of course you gave him the confidence that he needed, and he can't believe he is now a varsity man. September 1965

Dennis, I knew Marine basic training would be hard, that is why I never really encouraged you to join up. But this being your choice I know you will get used to the routine and the training. It is all done for a purpose. Remember, when you get up against an enemy you will thank God you were well trained. April 1969

Peter, You're a man now. Make your own decisions. April 1969

On Her Future

Dennis, I've decided to not worry too much about the future. I saw the wife of the astronaut Neil Armstrong on TV. She was so calm and collected. She said she knew he would make it back from the moon ok. She never had any doubts. This is really the way we should be, but fear sometimes comes and destroys our courage.... So I will just patiently wait and see what happens with me and not plan it all out in my mind just now. July 1969

On Current Events

Dennis, It rained all week except yesterday, and it is raining now. So it is a bit depressing but I have been glued to the TV set watching the astronauts splash down after being on the moon. It was so beautiful. Then of course the Ted Kennedy scandal, or accident saddened everyone. We listened to him on TV. He spoke for half an hour to the nation but mainly to the people of Massachusetts. I guess Barbara's parents weren't too far from the accident. So you see everyone has troubles. No one is without them. July 1969

Peter, Well, the election is over. I'm pleased. I have a feeling things may be better with Dick (Nixon) *than with Hubert* (Humphrey). *We can only wait and see.* November 1968

On Religion

Peter, I'm very glad to hear you turned to prayer for help and guidance because God will hear and answer our prayers. September 1965

Dennis, Last Sunday night, Bill Fowkes' dad, Mr. Fowkes, died. He was in the hospital for only a week, but his illness was coming on him for a long time. Bill said his dad was not in pain and he joked right to the end. When his doctor told him there was nothing more that could be done for him, Mr. Fowkes said, "I'm been a good Christian all my life. I'm ready." June 1969

On Military Concerns

Dennis, The enclosed letter came today from Jimmy Kolbenheyer. It is from a hospital in Japan. I didn't want to tell you this, but he was wounded. He has seen much action at the Cambodian border. I met his mother Vera last Thursday at the school board meeting and she told me she was so relieved that he was removed with his outfit to the hills to rest. It was there in a truck that they were hit. He was lucky as two were killed. I just spoke with his mother on the phone telling her he had written to you. She said he just telephoned her from Japan and was doing very well and is in good spirits. He is coming home in May for a 30-day furlough and rest. She feels he is very lucky to have only been wounded in the hand. He will have his nose fixed while he is in the states as he broke it while in basic training and it never was fixed. Last Monday an envelope with the Purple Heart arrived saying he was wounded, but contained no other information. Vera contacted the Red Cross who gave her all the information about him being in Japan in a hospital. She also said that when Les Joy heard about this he came to visit her and told her of his injuries and how well healed he is and that everything would be ok.... Please take care of yourself. April 1969

Dennis, I just got home, had dinner, and Bill Fowkes came over. We talked for a while and I still haven't done the dishes yet. But they can wait because I want to get this letter out to you. You're 12,000 miles away and are more important. April 1969

Dennis, I am worried about your hand. Not just for now, but you do not know the long range seriousness of this. Why did I spend $10 on the doctor and two tubes of salve at $6 each to fix you up so the Marine Corps would accept you? They should have delayed your induction until your hand was better. Now after nine months it has not healed. This is serious and I can tell you right now I am doing something about your hand, whether you or the Marines like it or not. Not because I am your doting mother but because of your future health. This is my main concern. I don't place too much concern in these military doctors and you only have two hands. However what I am referring to is this infection could spread to your blood. Don't be a fool. When they threw away your prescription it just wasn't right. I don't think they have any right to fool around with something they don't know about. ...I feel that you will be angry with me for being so frank about my feelings – but this is my duty – just as you would feel about your son's health. Other than this you are in perfect health – thank God. Well, I've said enough – and I do hope that you will realize that my interest in you comes before my own interests. ...You are doing splendidly in radio school. You should feel and have more confidence in yourself. Please take care of yourself. I love you and want you home again – remember that always. Keep up the good work! I'm proud of you. September 1969

Dennis, Jeanne wrote for tickets to see the Johnny Carson Show. Bruce asked her to as he watches him in Vietnam and requested that he would like to see a live show. Today a card came saying they were sorry, as they were booked into 1970. I am so annoyed at this and plan to write and tell him so. It seems that if you spend a year of your life in

Vietnam and enjoy a program they should accommodate a returning veteran. Joey Bishop is always proud when he calls on the servicemen and asks the camera to be put on them so their families can see them. This makes me dislike Johnny now. As if they couldn't keep a few extra tickets out and if no one uses them let the people who come that night use them. Well it's a fine world when no special privileges are given to returning veterans. September 1969

Peter, Well it won't be long now before you'll be home. Someday I'm sure you will be glad you had this training. July 1968

On Being Frank

Dennis, This is my second letter to you from Hawaii and I've been here a week and a half. I have received two letters each from Jeanne and Peter, so I hope your letter is enroute to me by now. I know you are busy but some part of the time you could find a minute to write me. I know Sugar would if she could.... Get busy and write to me! June 1966

Dennis, Peter and I got talking last night, but we didn't get too involved. I've come to the conclusion that we both think the same thing except that he is too idealistic and I am not. So let him lead his own life and I'll lead mine. June 1969

Peter, Jeanne wanted permission to smoke. I denied it. November 1968

Dennis, Peter said you didn't have to go into the service, that you could have pleaded hardship. I have news for him. I intend to work until I no longer can, and if hardship echoes from our home, I can't find it. We eat well and have a comfortable home, exactly what I want. I'm also happy with my children in class and with my colleagues. I thank God He sent me here and helped and encouraged me to maintain my house and not be ashamed of it. September 1969

Dennis, I heard that you wrote someone and said you volunteered for Vietnam. Is this true? Why did you not tell me? I did not hold you back from enlisting in the Marines nor will I interfere if you do volunteer for the battlefield, but are your friends the first to know it and I the last? Am I not the one who is more interested in you than anyone? You can't tell me your plans? I never stopped any of you from living your own lives – I never wanted any of you to look back and blame me. I had enough difficulty in managing my own life alone without advice. But I do want to know what your decisions are. Is this asking too much? Perhaps the information is incorrect. September 1969

Dennis, A lawn man told me that the fall was the best time to get the best results for lawn repair. Even though he said this, I had to argue with Peter on that point. Clem had to tell him because mother can't be right. I've kept a lawn before he was born and he is even working with Fred Palumbo on lawns, but he still insists spring is the best time. How can you be so stubborn? September 1969.

On Simple Pleasures

Dennis, I am now on my vacation. It is really unbelievable. Today at 10:30 all were out of the school. Then the faculty including all the nuns had a swinging party. Tons of food and screwdrivers galore. We all danced and sang. Nuns dancing with the men on the faculty. Four of the teachers were leaving so we gave them gifts. We all had a grand time. It was so hot but we sang as one of our teachers plays a mean guitar.... Tonight I went to Holy Family's graduation. I saw my second class graduate. One of my favorite boys won the General Excellence medal. I felt proud that I had him to start his young life with me.
June 1969

Peter, Sunday I went along with 17 others to the Harbor Golf Club in Port Jefferson where Bill Fowkes had a private dinner party for Joan. We had a lovely time. Lois and Vin and Joan and Bill were there. We sat facing the Long Island Sound and enjoyed a cocktail, then champagne and a toast, and then a delicious steak, individual!
October 1968

Peter, Well summer is over and another year is upon us. I hope it is a good one for all of us. Tomorrow I meet my little cherubs in 1st grade. I hope they are good.
September 1968

Peter, I have a darling class this year, only 37 children, which is just great. I used to have 50 every year. All are good, cute, intelligent and obedient. What a blessing! It makes things so much easier. They love school and I know I will have a happy year. Also there are no neighbors' or friends' children in my class to complicate matters.
September 1968

Peter, I am trying to do all things orderly so that I can have a relaxed year. After last year anything would be relaxing. The nun who has about ten of my problem children from last year is going out of her mind. But no one cared when they were problems for me last year. September 1968

Dennis and Peter, This trip (Mom's only cruise ship experience) *was the greatest idea of them all. So many wonderful people, so very friendly. We have an elegant room, air-conditioned, a shower, and maid service. We can even be served in our room if we wish to be. The food is the best I've ever had. All you want to eat and the Norwegian deserts are out of this world. I forgot all about my worries, but I have been thinking about you boys. I miss you all. We all talk of our families and where we come from. They have three bands that play all types of music. Tonight was "Roaring 20's." Jeanne dressed up and looked wonderful. Today I swam again in the Caribbean Sea and tried to keep out of the hot sun because we got a burn yesterday. Jeanne is having the time of her life. This is the ideal vacation. April 1969*

Peter, The island Jeanne and I visited reminded me of Hawaii. Their streets are tiny and narrow. They have no TV, but are very happy people who work hard and laugh a lot. It was so easy to notice this. We have lost all the beauty they possess. April 1969

Peter, Today I am invited over to the Randbeck's for Irene's birthday party. They have their family over for a delicious meal and drinks every year at this time and I am always included. July 1968

Peter, I finally finished a long letter to the Gomes' last week. With running out early every morning to work and trying to get things done in the house, I just found it hard to finish. They extended themselves to me and all of us more than anyone I know of, so at the very least a letter like this was due them. I just wish they weren't so far away as I enjoy their company. I feel this way about the Randbeck's too. I am very lucky to have such nice neighbors. July 1968

Peter, I love my course in Child Psychology. If you haven't taken such a course, you must be sure to do so. We have equally as many fellows as girls in the class, and a rehabilitated alcoholic. He is about 40 and he lectures in the high schools. He has many things of interest to offer and it was well worth the $41 I invested. I hope to continue at least one course in the fall. I enjoy the teacher. He makes it simple and I feel I have learned a lot in just the first two weeks. Young people should take Child Psychology as in brings a greater understanding of children and ourselves. When you marry you will then be equipped to more easily take on the tremendous job of parenthood. It will help me in my future dealings with my class. July 1968

GOING FORWARD

Ultimate Triumph

In October 2013, I visited my daughter, Jennifer, in Hawaii where she'd been a guidance counselor at a very large elementary school on the poor side of Oahu since 2006. While there we had lunch one afternoon at an outdoor café near Pearl Harbor. Jen was only ten months old when Mom passed away suddenly in June 1975 and has no recollection of her. As we ate, I mentioned how I'd begun writing about Mom, and of my desire to have as many family members as possible share their stories and reflections so the life of Kay White could be described accurately. We spoke of how, though some events in Mom's life involved sadness, struggle and other things that might be characterized as negative, being aware of and understanding the many positive aspects of her life were of the utmost importance and the essential reason for writing. The Kay White story does contain more than a few struggles, and discussing them and showing how she overcame them are necessary to demonstrate the very real triumph of her life. Orphaned before the age of five, with no mother and father to provide a parental role model, she triumphed by becoming a sterling parent herself. The daughter of uneducated immigrants, a bricklayer and a laundress, she triumphed by starring in high school and excelling in college at a time when some women didn't go past eighth grade. Left penniless and without any resources as a young mother of four, she triumphed again and again, always going forward, always advancing herself, always growing. By being a dedicated parent and a hardworking teacher, by constantly taking courses to improve herself and her skills, by serving her family, her community, her church, and her God, she triumphed, overcoming the impossible to become an outstanding role model for so many. In her many letters to us, Mom frequently brought up things that may be considered negative; she didn't shy away from or avoid mentioning her struggles. Perhaps she did so because she was honest and wanted to keep us abreast of what was happening on the home front, strife and all. Perhaps she viewed struggle as part of life, something not to be ignored. A careful reading of her letters shows not an iota of woe, not a speck of self-pity, and not a trace of bitterness. When life's events took their toll on her and she found herself sinking from loneliness, depression and financial hardship, she trusted in herself and God, always redirecting herself, always becoming more and more focused. Mom never sought a scapegoat; never blamed others for her problems; and was never heard to say that a particular problem of hers was someone else's fault. She faced things head on, methodically, confidently, bravely and patiently. She never allowed herself to become consumed by problems; rather she fended them off or embraced them as they came, and became strengthened by them. Annoyed, irritated, worried, bothered, even plagued by many of life's hardships, yes; however she chose not to allow life's misfortunes and uphill battles to control or define her. She knew enough about Christ's suffering to follow His example, to take up her own cross when necessary, and find ways to continue going forward, to become a great mother and teacher, and to lead an exceptionally productive and worthwhile life.

It is hoped that the stories and lessons described herein, including some told directly by Mom, in her own words from her many letters, the goal of this writing has been realized: that one can achieve great things in life despite the playing field being uneven; that one can not only survive but inspire and lead the way for others despite constant slings and arrows being hurled their way; and that one can rise from the ashes of poverty, depression and a sense of hopelessness and, through honesty, hard work, perseverance, devotion to God, family and community, triumph over all and become a model parent and citizen and enter life's Hall of Fame. The great philosopher Father Pierre Teilhard de Chardin wrote, "The most satisfying thing in life is to have been able to give a large part of oneself to others." With this notion in mind, it is my belief that Mom, who gave such a large part of herself to others, is looking from her special place in heaven, feeling more than satisfied.

"We Can Go On"

In August 1975, William P. Bennett, the editor of Holy Family Church's monthly newsletter "Holy Family Life," said the following about Mom:

> Our summer here at Holy Family certainly has started with extremely sad news. Our parish and school suffered a tragic loss with the passing of Mrs. Catherine White, a first grade teacher at Holy Family School. Mrs. White was killed in an automobile accident on Wantagh State Parkway the very next morning after her attendance at Awards Night at our school. It was extremely shocking to hear the

news after experiencing such joy and satisfaction in seeing our children graduate that same day; the very students that were under her care and guidance some years before. We must turn away from the thoughts of loss and loneliness and think of the accomplishments Mrs. White achieved while a teacher here at Holy Family. They are a part of those she taught during their impressionable years of learning. To love Christ, the Blessed Mother, lead a true Christian life, and be forgiving, we can go on. Mrs. White lives in the minds and hearts of all her children, her family, her colleagues at the school, and all those she came in contact with.

For decades now I've tried to do what William Bennett suggested so long ago: "go on," … even with the knowledge that Mom lives in my mind and heart. While I'm proud and honored to be her son, I sometimes find "going on" to be a difficult thing. I'm a senior citizen now, twelve years older than Mom was when she passed away. When troubles come my way, I find myself speaking to her, aloud at times. When good things happen, I sometimes look up, with the hope that she's there somewhere, smiling and witnessing it. When I decorate my Christmas tree each year, I pause and reflect as I touch one small, wooden, hand-painted ornament and place it on the tree. This Christmas tree ornament, of two small children holding hands, is my favorite. It was made and painted by Mom in the early 1970's. I'm well aware that it's only an inanimate object, a piece of painted balsa wood. But it is so meaningful to me because it's an actual, physical extension of Mom, a part of her. It's her art; a priceless masterpiece to me. The values she taught by her conduct and the life she led will stand forever as major influences for me. Gone as she has been for the past four decades, I continue to lean on her for strength and I believe I always will. It's how I go on.

Legacy

I've been thinking quite a bit about how to suitably conclude this journey. Writing it has been a bittersweet activity for me. It has caused me to think hard for many months now about some rather difficult times in her life and my own, and to miss her even more than I did before, if that's possible. It also has caused me to speak with family members, mostly Dennis, and Kevin, about her on a frequent basis. They helped me to honor Mom by preparing this memoir; a document that I hope will serve future generations well.

There is no surprise ending or major revelation coming here. The story of Kay White is what it is, that of a good woman who lived a relatively ordinary life doing the ordinary work of teaching and parenting. If she were able to read this, she'd probably say, *"Peter, why make my life sound so extraordinary? The things I did were ordinary things, things I was supposed to do."* But I'd argue and say, "Mom, you had many obstacles to overcome and situations to adapt to, and despite the circumstances, you did those ordinary things in an extraordinary way." Mom's legacy lies in the lessons she taught her children and her students, the obstacles she had to overcome to teach them, and in what they and we did with those lessons throughout our lives. In reflecting on what Mom wanted to pass on to us, what she wanted us to inherit from her, remember most about her, and be able to pass on to our own children and future generations, I didn't need to search far. In 1972 Mom wrote, *"My life goal was to be a good Christian, have a large family and teach them to love and serve God in their own way."* She spoke simply and forthrightly, not of achieving great wealth or fame, not of owning a big home or an abundance of material things, but of goodness, family, religion, service and love. By her day to day ability to focus on her family and her work serving others, by her manner of being at ease with everyone, especially young children, by her willingness and commitment to follow the right path, despite the consequences, it is evident that she built a powerful and wonderful life for herself and others and succeeded in achieving her life goal.

As a son of Kay White and a direct beneficiary of the example she set, I received many gifts from Mom. It would be difficult for me to name that which I consider her greatest gift, for they were all important. Mom was a very respected and respectful woman, genuine, the real thing, the best example I ever saw of elegance and grace, a non-pretentious, non-ostentatious, down-to-earth person. She worked hard to accomplish important things. Some have referred to what she did with her life as "God's work." Mom was no expert, and she knew it. When she was uncertain about things or felt she was in over her head, she either sought the wisdom and experience of others or relied on her deep faith for inspiration. Selfless to the core, I never remember her seeking any reward, acclaim, or even a pat on the back for herself. All who knew her admired her. In her community, the very words "Kay White" were powerful words, words that conjured up only the most positive notions, notions of character, strength, and stick-to-itiveness.

As to her legacy, if Mom were to come back today for a brief visit, I believe she would very much like what she'd see. She'd see how all her four of her children, on their own, went to college, earning associates, bachelors and master's degrees, as well as an MBA and a law degree. She'd see how they became hardworking professionals and leaders in such fields as hospital administration, education, law, business, nursing and social work, and how they used their educations to give to their families, their communities and the poor. She'd see Robert's life-long dedication and devotion to his family, his church, his profession, and the thousands of people he guides on tours at Pearl Harbor. She'd see how I devoted a great portion of my teaching career and volunteer time to organizing and leading students and adults to become better citizens, citizens more concerned with the needs of others than their own. She'd see how those students and adults raised more than a million and a half dollars the old-fashioned way, one dollar at a time, for their local and international poverty projects, providing clean water projects for hundreds of families who'd known only contaminated water, building several schools and hundreds of houses, and establishing a nutrition project that feeds 1800 hungry children every day. She'd applaud how Dennis, owner of a tavern and restaurant in Westbury for 20 years, regularly used his establishment to provide the community with opportunities to raise both awareness and funds for the families of wounded police officers, sick children, and struggling veterans. She'd be more than pleased with Dennis' and my efforts to organize hundreds of individuals, from among his patrons at Gatsby's to the Nassau County Executive himself, to raise $35000 for the family of a friend who succumbed to the most agonizing form of cancer resulting from his exposure to Agent Orange. And she would be greatly moved by the tenacious and enduring manner in which Jeanne cared for the sick and those with disabilities throughout her life, including taking severely handicapped children into her home to raise as her own.

Not only would Mom be proud of what we, her four children, have done with the proper role model, good character and solid values she provided for us, she'd be honored to see the splendid accomplishments achieved by so many of her grandchildren. Like Mom, several of her grandchildren have adopted her ultimate life goal and become dedicated, caring parents themselves. Like Mom, a number of her grandchildren have become teachers, from pre-school to high school, opening the minds of kids in programs from special education to advanced placement. They've taught not only in suburban communities like Mom did, but in schools that serve the disadvantaged children of inner-city Brooklyn and the South Bronx. One grandson is in his 17th year and another in his ninth year of teaching in the impoverished Mott Haven section of the Bronx. A granddaughter served eight years as a counselor in a poor neighborhood in Hawaii, and a grandson, after teaching high school science in Los Angeles for 15 years, recently began a teaching assignment in a remote region of South Korea. Mom's remaining grandchildren have all demonstrated a similar willingness to serve others in fields such as special education, hospital administration, insurance, hospitality, tourism, and law enforcement. From the paths her grandchildren have taken so far in life, it's clear that Mom's exemplary role model and character have spilled over to future generations.

An old Twig Lane friend recently wrote, "My mom and your mom were good friends. She was a good person, one who persevered with dignity through so many obstacles." In large part, I believe this expression represents and summarizes the thrust of this book. Given the hand she was dealt in life, Mom charted a certain course, stayed that course, rarely strayed, and, though her life ended abruptly and prematurely, reached the finish line she set for herself. And in so doing, she was able to pass on valuable knowledge and skills to us and so many others. As an orphan, she overcame the loneliness and uncertainty of a solitary childhood into one of love and joy by being a good daughter to her adopted parents, and by being a hard-working, successful student. As young wife and mother, she turned abandonment by her husband into dedication to her children and community, and the trials and tribulations of a welfare existence into fundamental life lessons for us. Entirely on her own, she rose from being a jobless middle-aged woman to become a respected Hall of Fame teacher. She never won any awards or prizes during her life, nor did anyone ever suggest building a statue of her in the park or dedicating a street or boulevard in her name. But by her many accomplishments, the example she set, and her unwavering dedication to a value system that worked, she inspired and substantially changed the lives of many people. Considering the uphill nature of the many difficulties she faced, and the dignified manner in which she faced them, Mom's untarnished journey through life was nothing short of triumphant.

APPENDIX A

A Message to Future Generations and Others

Kay's Triumph describes only part of Kay White's life journey. Largely based on recollections from many years ago, valuable contributions from my brother, Dennis, and sister, Jeanne, some of Mom's own letters, and a vivid autobiographical sketch she wrote two years before her death, this memoir should include much more. Certainly, there are many stories from her early childhood, teen years and young adult life of which we know little. I regret not asking her more questions when I was young so there would be more to share now. You younger generation folks still have that opportunity in your families.

Of the many stories contained in this memoir, I have a few favorites. One is called "Loyalty and Perseverance – The Uniform Store" because it seems to sum up what kind of person Mom really was. A week after she willingly gave up her job as a teacher at Holy Family School to take care of her sick and aging aunt, Aunt Katherine passed away, leaving her jobless. Rather than sulk or fall apart, she understood and calmly accepted the facts as they were and took a menial job for less than half the pay. Armed with patience and determination, she didn't complain about her plight, but carried on with dignity, knowing that she was doing her best. She wasn't embarrassed or troubled by this economic step downward. On the contrary, she saw such problems as opportunities to overcome life's difficulties, opportunities to rebuild, to grow and to go forward. This is who she was.

So my message to future generations comes in the form of a few questions. How will Kay White's journey affect your life? What parts of her story captured your attention the most, caused you to look at things differently, or altered your thinking in some way? Why? How did anything you uncovered from her story make your life or the lives of others better? Now that you know the story of Kay White, what will you do with it?

Additional Photos

Grandchildren Michelle and Katie Dorsey
with Jeanne and Uncle Robert.

Grandson Rob White

Granddaughter
Ann Marie White Medeiros

Daughter
Jeanne White Callahan & her husband Kevin
at 9-11 Memorial

Granddaughters
Katelyn Peterson & Lisa McCoy

Grandchildren
Brendan, Merry, Brian and Jen White

Appendix B - Reasons

When I first contemplated writing these stories, a friendly critic who knew Mom a long time said to me, "She's been gone many years now. Why do you want to do this? Why not leave the past alone?" I felt differently and decided to go forward for a number of reasons. First, I wrote this for me. Before it became too late to do so, I felt compelled to go back in time, reflect, analyze, and articulate certain parts of the past. This is something I've wanted to do for years – share Mom's journey so others may benefit from it. As a student and teacher of history I've always believed that it is important to look at the past and use it to help shape the present and the future. At age 69, these stories are still within me. If I remained silent about that which I know of her, then these stories will disappear with me someday, and become extinct. Second, I wrote this for others, whether they are family members like my brothers and sister, our children, grand-children, or total strangers. All, especially parents, may benefit from the life and the lessons taught by Kay White. Robert, Dennis, Jeanne and I knew Mom well, but our offspring did not. Of her 12 grandchildren and currently nine great grandchildren, only three were alive at the time of her death, and they were infants or toddlers at the time. The members of these subsequent generations, who refer to her as Grandma White or Granny White, know her only through stories, photos or an occasional visit to Holy Rood Cemetery in Westbury, NY where she is buried. Kay White's journey contains messages of struggle, hope and triumph that others should hear, messages that arise from vivid memories of her life. Finally, and most importantly, I wrote this for Mom. She lived an exceedingly worthwhile life. From 1951-1957, Bishop Fulton J. Sheen starred in a religious TV show called, "Life is Worth Living." Mom was a big fan of Bishop Sheen and his show. She watched him every Sunday night and made sure we were quiet so she didn't miss a word he said. I believe she carried out the true meaning of Sheen's message. Despite many hardships, hers was an exemplary life, one very much worth living. She was a model teacher who taught well by the example she set. She was not thin-skinned. She never whined or blamed others for her plight. Instead she accepted and embraced difficulty and hardship with amazing humility and strength. Such a life should not be forgotten but cherished; it shouldn't wilt, lapse or become lost to history. It should flourish and be celebrated, available to guide and serve others.

Appendix C

The First Time I Realized We Were Poor II

T'was the week before Christmas, 1954, when our priest, Father Fagan, knocked on our door.
It was nearly bedtime when we heard his knock, Mom rushed to the door and opened the lock.
Father had a thick Irish brogue when he spoke, and a round looking face, a right happy bloke.
 "Come in Father," Mom said with a smile. "Nice to see you, Kay. It's been a while."
We peeked as much as we were able, as Father laid a big box on our table.
It was decorated like a chimney, white and brick red. *"Stop looking,"* Mom said.
"Now scoot off to bed."
This chimney crepe paper was a Christmas disguise. But what was inside? Maybe a surprise?
A man in our house, especially at night, was something quite rare, an uncommon sight.
As I climbed into bed I thought, "What's in that box?" Was it clothing, or toys, or shoes and sox?
Through a tear in the side I thought I could see, the wing of an airplane, a toy for me?
But why would a priest bring this to us, by himself, at night, with all this fuss?
I slept not a wink; it was so hard to settle. That wing looked blue and was made out of metal.
Wasn't it Santa who brought the toys, to all who'd been good girls and boys?
Days later, on Christmas I'd learn, the answers to these questions that caused me concern.
As we inched down the stairs we were able to see, that a giant white sheet hid gifts by the tree.
Santa had come, but we'd have to wait. *"After mass children, get moving, it's late."*
It was Jesus' birthday so mass came first, our curiosity causing us to burst.
Once we got home Mom took off the sheet. *"We'll go in order, so each take a seat."*
Jeanne got a doll as part of her treasure. Our excitement ran higher than we could measure.
What happened next I'll always remember, especially at Christmastime each late December.
My eyes spotted something shiny and blue. It was the plane from Father Fagan,
slightly broken, not new.
"From Santa To Peter," said the card. The reality hit me, but not very hard.
The plane wasn't from Old St. Nick, but from Father's box, with crepe paper of brick.
The truth didn't matter to me at the time. I'd gotten something. I smiled. I was fine.
It didn't fly but like many toys; the wheels turned fast and made some noise.
As I pushed it faster, out flew some sparks. "This will be neat. It'll glow in the dark."
With the things we'd received, we were always amused. Some were brand new, not all were used.
New things were special, to us something great. They came from the kindness of
our great Aunt Kate.
Mom's cousin Florence also helped out, so there'd be a Christmas without a doubt.
With gift giving over we went out to play, to see the things our friends got that day.
Most received much more than we, that's how things were with our family.
We knew our simple toys were no match, for the kids with new ball
gloves having a catch.
Some got bikes, Sandra Chiffer a car, a gas powered go-kart that went fast and far.
Sometimes I'd wonder if Santa was fair, so much for some, didn't he care?
I never asked Mom about toys new and old, I knew the answer and needn't be told.
Nor did I ask, it wouldn't be right, about Father Fagan's visit that night.
I never let on that I'd seen the wing, of that broken little plane that Father did bring.
I chose not to put Mom to the test, she did all she could to make Christmas the best.
I was at an age when I knew, that the Santa Claus myth was not really true.
How could a fat jolly old elf, go all around the world in one night by himself?
More than this, I saw our plight, so pressuring Mom just wouldn't be right.
Unlike the rest of the neighborhood mothers, Mom had to accept the kindness of others.
For her, Christmas toys were not a hard search, help came from relatives and

the good folks at church.

Back then as a young boy I began to see, that we were a needy family.

The kind that sometimes needed a break, so into our hearts there'd be less ache.

I wasn't upset to learn we were poor, having so little I'd have to do more.

No matter the problems, the struggle and strife, I knew I'd be asked to work harder through life.

Understanding the truth made me tougher instead, confident, self-reliant, no
matter what was said.

Having less never caused me to hide, rather I felt a great sense of pride,

At having a Mom who chose not to perish, who taught us instead that we should cherish,

That which we had though never a lot, *"It's best to be happy with what you've got."*

Christmas 1954 opened my mind, to see things more clearly and to be less blind.

To be proud of my Mom who gave all she could, so we could have Christmas and
enjoy something good.

Now sixty years later I'd give anything, to still have that toy with the broken wing.

I'll never forget that little blue plane, and the great Christmases we had on Twig Lane.

Appendix D

Pedaling through the Past

Sunday, September 6, 2015

Doris Day's postwar hit song "Sentimental Journey" describes someone about to visit a place for which they have a great emotional attachment, home. The opening verse is:

> Gonna take a sentimental journey
> Gonna set my heart at ease
> Gonna make a sentimental journey
> To renew old memories.

I feel that same attachment for my old neighborhood in Levittown. Visiting brings me peace. So I go back home, once, sometimes twice each year, to see what's new, what's stayed the same, and to renew old memories.

It's a hot day in early September, the day before Labor Day 2015. I drive from my home in Centerport to Levittown, park my car on Twig Lane under the shade of a tree alongside "the weeds," and recall that on this very spot, Bobby Hoffman, his brother Freddy and I pushed one another in the homemade push-mobile their dad, Bill Hoffman, helped us build from scrap lumber and old baby carriage wheels. I remove my bike from the carrier and ready myself for my annual ride through parts of Levittown, Hicksville and Westbury – the neighborhoods of my childhood. Memories of Mom and the joy of my youth await. Before I mount my sturdy new "Urbanite," I take a quick look around, first at the well-kept, expanded house once owned by Levittown pioneer Al Bottenus, "Bath King," one of Long Island's first plumbers, then at # 35 Twig, the former house of Mary, Joe, Joey, Theresa and Paula Madden. It's still a basic 1950 Levitt, with its open carport and original wooden shed, a rare visible reminder of the past. My eyes scan right, past #37, the Swearingen's, and #41, the Hoffman's. Both look the same as they have for years, neat and orderly. There's the driveway where Bobby and Freddy Hoffman, Les Joy and I first dribbled a basketball and played H-O-R-S-E. It's also where, on the afternoon of May 12, 1958, Bill Hoffman sat us down and gently told us the sad news, that Joey Madden had just been killed crossing the nearby Wantagh State Parkway. Against his parents' instructions, Joey had taken that dangerous shortcut home from school. To the right is the former home of "The Indestructible Ken Canning," the name we gave to the boastful New York City kid who moved in during the early 1960's, thinking he knew everything. It's boarded up now. A zombie house. As I look down Twig, to my right is "the weeds," the name we gave to the few acres of town land that was our playground, nature preserve, hideout, hiking trail, bird watching area, baseball field, Olympic park, campground and our adult-free childhood oasis.

I climb on my bike and decide to take a spin around the blocks of Twig and Branch first, out of respect. As the wheels of my bike begin to go around on the pavement, thoughts of Mom and my youth go around within me. The first house on the right is #48. The Schley's were the first owners, and I was the third owner of that once-bright yellow beauty. My son Brian was born when we lived there in 1976, the year of our nation's bicentennial. Subsequent owners tore it down completely and built a gigantic pseudo-palace, complete with stone lions from Afghanistan standing guard. This non-Levitt-like structure is an anomaly, completely out of whack with the rest of the neighborhood. On a previous ride, the new family told me they found a large coin collection within the walls when they tore the neat and tidy original house down. That collection was one of Charlie Schley's most valuable possessions, the product of a lifetime of gathering coins from all over the world. Apparently he'd forgotten about it when he moved to Tucson years earlier. I said, "That's great. It just so happens that I know the true owner, Charlie Schley. He was the first owner of this house. He'd be ecstatic to get his collection back." The new people weren't interested at all. "We bought this house and everything in it. They're our coins now." Legally, they are right. They did buy the property and all of its contents. But their callous disregard for Charlie's feelings upset me. I look carefully at the back yard, where Charlie Schley once cultivated his award-winning Chrysanthemums, where my son Brian, still in diapers, took his first swing with a baseball bat and a golf club and Jen played so creatively in the blue wooden sandbox I built for her.

I ride past the former house of Ken Foster, later Ann Legg's house. Ann, who befriended Jeanne when she was a teenager, passed away a couple of years ago. Next door was the Polansky's, whom we thought were rich because they vacationed in Cuba during the 50's, before Castro's revolution, then the house next door to ours, formerly owned by the Bowen's, the Pearlman's and the Miller's. Now someone else lives there. I can barely make out the pool in the back yard, where my young friends, the four Landers kids from Dayton, Ohio, swam back in the summer of '68. Then the most important stop of all, 55 Twig Lane, the home of my youth. It's different now. The charm and dignity has vanished. What was once a bright, white shining example of how nice a Levitt house could be has been expanded in every direction imaginable into a grotesque-looking McMansion, complete with pre-fabricated pavers which have replaced our curvacious front lawn. Gone is the grass, so immaculately kept by Mom and mowed so many times by Dennis and me, green turf where Mom took so many family photos, and onto which she so dutifully marched us for holiday flag-raising ceremonies. Gone are all the original plantings, some by Levitt, others by Mom. Not one original bush or tree remains. Gone is the backyard fence I built in 1970 for Mom's dog, Sugar, while Dennis was in the Marines. Gone is the openness that once emanated from that house. There's an ugly wall surrounding the entire front now. What used to be a welcoming place that said, "Come in," is now an unattractive, sterile place that shouts "Keep Out!" All that's missing is a moat with crocodiles. I am saddened by this, so I bike on, past 54 Twig, the Chiffer's, remembering when Floyd Sr. tried to dig a well in his backyard to lower his water bill, and where he first played catch with his son, Floyd Jr. "Floydie Boy," as his parents called him, went on to pitch several seasons for the San Diego Padres. Next door is 56 Twig, home of the Kaisers. Pete Kaiser, our "Bob Vila," was the neighbor who helped Mom many times with his handyman advice and know-how. Beyond Kaiser's is the Kozluck's, later the Ahearn's house, where Dennis so often shoveled snow to help out the aging Mrs. Ahearn after she'd lost her husband. To my left is 61 Twig, former home of kind and thoughtful Clem and Maude Randbeck, Mom's best friends on the block. On the right, the former homes of Louise Schwartz and Franklin Berger, kids I played with 65 years ago. As far as small-world stories go, Louise and I remain neighbors to this day. She has lived in nearby East Northport for many years, and as a teacher I knew her very musically talented sons when they achieved so much at Northport High School. She's now a retired teacher, same as I. As I near the left turn onto Branch Lane, I navigate past # 65 Twig, the home of the Joy's. Les Joy, a fairly apt name in a way, was my first friend in life, the first kid whose house I slept over at. He was also the young Marine whom I visited in St. Alban's Naval Hospital after the hellish year he spent in some of Vietnam's hottest spots in 1967 and 1968. Les died young and is buried in the National Cemetery of the Pacific, Honolulu, Hawaii. The Joy's house looks simple and open now. The hedge that surrounded their large corner lot, the hedge that Les Joy Sr. planted and so proudly maintained, has been ripped out. As I pedal by I can almost hear the sharp words of Mrs. Deannie Joy ring out when any of us would attempt to cut through their property or fetch a baseball. "Get out of that hedge!" She was always vigilant, always watching. Biking past the Joy's house used to be a fearful time for me because I was chased daily by their fast-running, hostile dog, Peppy. I never trusted that mutt. The extension Mr. Joy added on for his elderly mother remains. When she moved in from South Carolina in the late 1950's, Grandma Joy wore a fringed leather jacket, causing us to think she was part Indian. Maybe she was.

Next on Branch Lane is the Saladino's house, home of Frank "Sarge" Saladino, his wife Anne, and their kids, Frankie Jr. and little John. Neighbors referred to Frank Saladino as "Sarge" because after WW II, he remained in the Air Force reserves and often came home in uniform. Like Frank, most of the men in the neighborhood were WW II veterans. Frankie Jr. was the mechanic of the neighborhood, the first to attach an old lawn mower engine to a bicycle and make himself a homespun motorcycle. Zooming at high speed around the neighborhood for years paid off for Frankie. He became a successful Industrial Arts teacher, making his living teaching high school kids about engines. Across the street from Saladino's is the Woolard's house. They were one of three families that built fallout shelters in their back yards in the late 1950's, places where they thought they'd be safe if the Russians dropped an atomic bomb on Long Island. I stop on my bike and say a prayer for their daughter, Diane, who died of leukemia during the mid-1960's, only a few years after finishing high school. I pray also for the other neighborhood kids who passed away young and missed so much of life. Some, like Joey Madden, died as young as age 12. Liz Schley died in an accident at the age of 16. Les Joy was 36, and his brother, John only in his 20's. Both died of illness. Tommy Boeckelman, Skippy Pavlakis, Kathleen Noon, Kenny Swearingen and Jeannette "Baby" Harris all died too young as well, also of illness. There are others. I split for a moment from Branch and go halfway down Booth Lane to see if soon-to-be 101-year-old Clayton Edwards is sitting out front. He is not. Last year, Dennis accompanied me on a similar bike ride and we stopped at Mr. Edwards' house, chatted, and took some photos with him. He's an original owner, a retired member of the FDNY, and the father of the Denise and Judy Edwards, who went to St. Ignatius with us.

Back on Branch, I bike past the house of the girl every boy had a crush on, Joy Gillen. She was an only child and lived with her mom. I never remember Joy having a dad, so I guess we weren't the only family in the neighborhood to be raised by a single mom. Joy moved out west and became a Las Vegas card dealer and big casino manager. I heard she retired and now lives in Panama. Next door was the home of Sid Harris, businessman and golf expert. Sid spent many hours teaching me and other neighborhood kids the basics of a good golf swing, something we benefited from throughout our lives. Across the street is Taormina's house. I co-owned a 7' X 9' wall tent with Robert Taormina, who's now pastor of a Uniondale church, and his brother Jay, a CPA in Suffolk County. Recalling the many nights we slept out in that tent, telling scary stories and going on nighttime raids to the yards of other kids who were also sleeping out, causes a big smile to come across my face. I pass #17 Branch, where one of my then-closest friends, Bob Palumbo, now Doctor Palumbo, grew up. Actually, like Clayton Edwards, Robert's mom, Gerry, still lives there. In her mid-90's, she's one of very few remaining Levittown first-owners, a true suburban pioneer. Bob's dad, Fred Palumbo, was one of Long Island's first landscapers. When we were teenagers, Fred hired many of us for ten bucks a day to lay sod at the big estates of his jockey friends and other wealthy clients in Kings Point and Great Neck. Fred liked playing the horses. Next door at #15 Branch is the boyhood home of Gary Bruschi, one of my oldest and best friends to this day. Gary, now Doctor Bruschi, wasn't the biggest guy on the block, but he was fearless, the least afraid to take risks, the first to date girls, and last to back down to anyone, no matter his size. His dad and mom, Dr. Elio and Jeannette, were special people, always welcoming me into their home, offering me a snack, and including me in their camping trip to a beautiful place I've returned many times over the years, upstate Bash Bish Falls. Elio was a "kid person," one who peacefully settled disputes when our games of stickball and two-hand touch got out of hand. On a few occasions, he even climbed under the fence of the sump behind Branch Lane when the water froze over, donned a whistle, skates and his black and white striped shirt, and refereed our hockey games. Jeannette was a nurse during WW II. As a Lt. Commander in the U.S. Navy, she ran a hospital in the Philippines and was the highest-ranking war veteran in the neighborhood.

Finishing on Branch Lane I re-enter lower Twig Lane and spot #10, the home of Drew Keenan, my other life-long best friend. Drew and his brother Billy were natural athletes. Drew was selected the All County shortstop back in 1965, at a time when only nine players were given that honor, not the hundred or more you see today. And Jones Beach lifeguard/college swimming champ Billy is still winning statewide swim meets in Florida at the age of 72! I pass by #16 Twig, former home of my second cousin Joan Larkin Fowkes and her husband Bill. They bought it from the elderly European immigrant couple, Pop and Penny, in 1960, lived there for 12 years, and provided Mom with great help and companionship while they were there. I figure I'll head all the way up Twig Lane, to the stores, where Mom so frequently had us do the family shopping. As I pass by 55 Twig for the second time, something causes me to slow down. Despite the fact that everything good about that once-wonderful dwelling seems to have been replaced by something gaudy and artificial, one thing seems to be the same but it takes me a few moments to figure out what it is. Finally, my eyes gaze upward and I notice the only thing that remains from our old house. The chimney. It's white. When Dennis and I painted Mom's house in the early 1960's, she wanted the chimney to match the rest of the house, but at that time we were too young to get up on the roof and paint it. Several years later, when I was away at college and Dennis was a high school teenager, he and a few friends replaced the entire roof with white shingles, and painted the chimney to match. I'm happy that, though some of the white paint is chipped and flaking off, it's still the original white paint applied by Dennis so long ago. At least something from Mom's 25 years at 55 Twig has lasted. This makes me smile.

I pick up a little speed as I bike the four tenths of a mile up Twig toward the stores on Newbridge Road. I pass by the Kolbenheyer's, former home of Vietnam vet and Purple Heart recipient, Jimmy, the Boeckelman's, the one-time home of Billy Boeckelman, a.k.a. "The Squid," the neighborhood wrestling champ, the Maslak's, the Fisher's, the Volante's, former home of Meyer, now a doctor in St. Louis, MO, the Elefante's, former home of John, ontime lead singer of the rock group Kansas, the Brown's, and the Hutchins.' All these houses look pretty good. They always have. Sadly, toward the end of the block, there are two that seem to be neglected, maybe ready for the iron ball. More Zombie houses. I pass #110 Twig, former home of Bobby, Mike and Kathy Snowden. We called Bobby "Snowpile." The Snowdens were pretty wonderful kids, having to almost raise themselves after their mother divorced and left and their dad died. Their dad's elderly Aunt Mamie stayed with them, requiring them to pitch in and grow up quickly to make the household work. There's the Frazetta's house. Mrs. Diane Frazetta was the crackerjack checkout clerk at the Grand Union supermarket long before the days of bar coding and conveyor belts. Everything she did, she did manually and with great efficiency, the most capable worker I've ever seen. Her sons Steve and Joe were top athletes. Across the street, only one or two houses from the end of Twig, is the house of Gerry "Tabby" Angus. He graduated from Clarke High School in 1959 and was one of the premier athletes of his day, setting records in football and other sports. Each summer, when other neighborhood kids and I went to the West Village Green pool, we'd stand in awe at Tabby's self-taught, Olympic caliber diving ability. None was better. Tabby continues to live on Twig.

I turn left, toward the stores, our shopping center. On the corner is the Harmony Bar, still there after more than 60 years, quite an accomplishment. Even now I can hear Gary's wise-guy voice as he'd bike by the Harmony yelling to the customers inside, "Hey. Go home you drunks." Next door, now a card store, was Teddy & Paul's Luncheonette. Many neighborhood kids, like Dennis and Jay Taormina, got jobs there as soda jerks and short order cooks, or just folding newspapers, their first employment opportunities. Mom didn't like us going in there because, in addition to candy and soda, Teddy and Paul peddled what she called "dirty magazines." Lots of young boys got their first look at the female anatomy by peering over the shoulders of the men who flipped through the colorful pages. I bike on, past the old bakery where we bought hard rolls after mass most Sundays, the bank, where I opened my first account as an eighth grader, Mr. B's Five and Ten, where many a time we bought Mom a Christmas or Mother's Day gift with the few pennies we had, Shultz' Deli, which made the best potato salad any of ever tasted, the liquor store, and Lou's Barber Shop, where Lou or his toothless dad, Tony, cut our hair for fifty cents. When the haircut was done, Lou or Tony would apply a heavy dose of a green, slimy substance called "Hair Slick," which made our newly-cut hair temporarily harden up and stay in place. Rather than maintain a hairdo with a wave and deal with the Hair Slick, most neighborhood boys preferred crew cuts, flat tops being the most popular choice. The last store of the small shopping center is now a pizza place, but for nearly 50 years it was Economy Drugs. They charged high prices and were anything but good for Mom's economy. On the side of the drug store there's a large brick wall to which some applied graffiti during the 60's. This is where the Corner Boys, a group of black leather-jacket clad teens crooned their doo-wop songs. One such young Corner Boy was rumored to be junior high-age Billy Joel, who lived about half a mile away, in Hicksville.

I cycle my way across Newbridge carefully. It used to be a manageable, two-lane road. Now it's a four-lane highway with cars whizzing by at top speeds. I pass the old Sunrise stores, our shopping center in the early 1950's, before the Grand Union was built, and the West Village Green pool. It's a sunny day and I have my bathing suit and towel with me, just in case. I decide to wait and swim at another pool later. William Levitt built nine large pools and I'll be passing three of them on my ride. Crossing Newbridge Road brings me to Hicksville. Not downtown Hicksville, but the southernmost part where there are Levitt houses. As I pass the West Green pool, I remember back to 1952 when, as I five-year-old, I was taught to swim by the smiling and friendly Mrs. Columbo. I cut up Cherry Lane, heading north, past Holy Trinity High School, built in the late 1960's. Prior to that, the dozen or so acres upon which the school and its athletic fields now sit were farmland. We'd pass it on the school bus on our way to St. Ignatius every day and watch the migrant workers clearing the land and planting each spring, and harvesting the potatoes each fall. Much of Nassau was potato fields before the coming of suburbia, much like the north fork of Long Island is today. At the northern end of Cherry, I see the gas station on Newbridge where, in the early 1970's, Mom would sometimes have her car looked at while she worked at Holy Family School, right around the corner. In between the gas station and Holy Family there are some large houses that were built in the early 1960's. In the 1950's, when I was an altar boy and Tablet boy, I'd ride by on my bike and see a small herd of cows standing quietly there, chomping away at the tall grass. That pasture was replaced by several houses. Gone are most of those reminders of Long Island's rural past.

I cut down Elwood Avenue, then Cornell Avenue, where so many of my Holy Family sixth graders lived, and stop at Holy Family School where I fix my eyes on two classrooms on the east side of the building. The first is Mom's, on the ground floor, then mine, directly above hers. I take out my cell phone for a few photos and notice the cornerstone of the building, laid in 1960 by Bishop Walter P. Kellenberg. Mom brought us all to the ceremony. We walked there together, as a family, on a scorching hot day. I'm standing in the parking lot where, for the three years as sixth grade teacher, I served on playground duty during lunchtime. Visions of hundreds of kids playing keep-away and jumping rope swirl through my head and I smile. Many of my former Holy Family 11 and 12-year-olds are now retired cops, firefighters, doctors, businesspeople, moms, dads and even grandparents. I decide to spend a minute at the far northeast corner of the school grounds, where a special garden once was. After Mom died in June 1975, several Holy Family seventh graders cleaned up that corner area and created the Catherine White Memorial Garden. They raked the spot thoroughly, cultivated the soil, and planted nice flowers creating a garden to be proud of. Two years later those kids graduated and the garden withered. It was a nice gesture on their part. I bike toward the church, past a few women chatting in the parking lot. Different people run the church and school now. Except for the new principal, Mrs. Maryalice Doherty, and the new pastor, Father Gerard Gentleman, I no longer know anyone there. After a brief visit to the altar and a few glances around, I bike around the back of the rectory. No one is there. I notice the rear sacristy door, where I entered so many times to don my altar boy cassock and prepare the cruets and other things necessary to serve mass. I see the small room between the sacristy and the rectory where we biked to every Saturday morning to pick up our Brooklyn Tablet newspapers. After rounding the corner of the rectory the image of Father Martin O'Dea relaxing on the rooftop patio he made for himself and the other priests comes to mind. Then I spy the front church doors and stop for another prayer. Those are the doors where the casket bearing Mom's body was wheeled through on the day of her funeral.

After crossing Newbridge Road at Fordham Avenue, the road changes names to Elmira Street. I remember each house on Elmira because Mom sometimes made me go "the long way" when I biked to Holy Family in bad weather in order to avoid busy Newbridge. Elmira ends at Blueberry Lane and I turn right, then left on Beech Lane, right again on Boxwood, left on Bobwhite and right on Bamboo Lane. On Boxwood a smile comes across my face once again as I recall going to an 8th grade graduation party at the home of St. Ignatius classmate Kathleen Corcoran. Kathleen was a cute girl, liked by all. I was happy to be invited. I walked the mile or so from our house to her house on Boxwood and saw that there were about 20 others there already, all dancing "The Twist," the 1961 dance sensation created by rock and roll's Chubby Checker. The party took place in Kathleen's garage, which she'd decorated with colorful lights and graduation symbols. There were a few folding chairs and her parent's picnic table benches for seating, but few sat. Most, including me, "twisted" for several hours. I walked home that night a tired and very happy thirteen-year-old. Kathleen developed leukemia a year later and passed away at the age of fourteen. I say another prayer.

The large corner house on Bamboo Lane is that of the cute and smiley Pamela Edginton, Gary Bruschi's first girlfriend. Pam was great fun to be with and every boy who swam at Levittown Parkway pool had a crush on her. In 11th grade, Gary took Pam, a Hicksville High School girl, to our junior prom. Around the corner, where Blueberry Lane meets Levittown Parkway, I slow down as I pass the former office of the friendly, painless dentist, Dr. Seymour Weinstein. I remember going to his office by myself and asking him if he'd take me as a patient. He agreed and, since Mom didn't have dental coverage, charged only what we could afford. Billy Boeckelman went to him too and we always laughed at how, whenever we sat helplessly in his chair, all we saw was his many nasal hairs and all we heard was his constant singing of the same song, over and over again, "Sweetheart, sweetheart, sweetheart…."

A left onto Levittown Parkway and I'm heading south, toward the Levittown Parkway pool. I've been biking for a while and it's hot, so I decide that's where I'll be taking my swim. The Levittown Parkway pool is adjacent to Levittown Hall, which happens to be situated in Hicksville. None of us could ever figure that out. As the pool comes into sight, I see the bright blue water of the pool, but notice that there ae no swimmers. There's the bright blue water of the pool, but there are no swimmers. "Good," I think, "I'll have the whole pool to myself." But I'm wrong. The gates are locked. The pool is closed. And it's not even Labor Day yet. Historically, all nine Levittown pools remained open until Labor Day. I guess there aren't enough lifeguards and they had to close some pools early. Disappointed, I bike on, passing the large ball fields behind Dutch Lane School where I coached Holy Family football for three years. I stop briefly and smile, remembering August 13, 1974, the day my first child, Jennifer, was born. Back then, before the advent of cell phones, news traveled more slowly. After a 17 hour, overnight labor, Jen was finally born. It was a natural childbirth and I was present. I knew Mom was anxious to hear the news, and Jill's parents, Mike and Lucy Papa, were eager to have neighbors over for a celebration. After Jen was born, I drove from Plainview Central General Hospital to Mom's, passing the Dutch Lane fields and saw my two fellow coaches, Dick Patwell and Al Sapperstein, and our entire 7th and 8th grade football team practicing. I stopped my car, ran over, gathered the team together and told them the news, "It's a girl!" They smiled and clapped loudly, then I left, dashing home to tell Mom the good news. It's interesting to me now, 42 years later, that my football players were actually the very first to learn of the existence of Jennifer White, and of my first moment being a brand new dad. I wore a large smile as I pedaled by that field, made a right onto Stewart Avenue and headed toward Westbury.

As I turn, on my immediate left is the Parkway Community Church, the Protestant church where, in August 1966, along with hundreds of others, I attended the memorial service for former classmate U.S.M.C. Pfc. Weston D. McLean, who died two weeks earlier in Vietnam of multiple gunshot wounds. Another prayer. I bike past the former site of Boos Brothers Nursery, over the Wantagh Parkway, careful not to look south, toward the overpass where Mom lost her life, cross Carman Avenue and pedal a half a mile or so to my first school, Bowling Green. I remember back in 1952, when I was a kindergartener, there was only one building, and it was crammed with young kids, all new to the growing suburban communities of Levittown and Westbury. Now there are two buildings. I circumnavigate them and I see the grassy area where, 62 years ago, I stood with my young classmates on kindergarten graduation day wearing the red felt caps we made ourselves. It was a very hot day and many of us had beads of bright red sweat pouring down our faces and necks from the mixture of our perspiration with the red felt. Around the back of the school I spot where I once met Clarke classmate and good friend Nancy Ligouri for an impromptu date. I leave the school grounds and cycle through the "P" section, with streets named Prince, Pride, Patience and Pilgrim. I spent many days there, visiting the homes of Richard Walsh and one-time girlfriend and prom date, Sharon Patterson. Though I'm technically in Westbury, these are still Levitt houses. TV host Bill O'Reilly, who says he hails from Levittown, was really brought up on Pilgrim Lane, Westbury. I didn't know him, but Dennis did. They were kindergarten classmates at Bowling Green School.

I cross Stewart Avenue again and head down Elda Lane, toward Clarke High School, the place I entered a boy in 1961 and came out a young man in 1965. I recall the exciting times I had on the team bus with my fellow Clarke Rams after returning from an away football game. Whether we won or lost, we knew that there'd be some type of greeting from friends, cheerleaders and parents when we arrived, so there was always a lot of noise going down Elda. I gaze at the back of the school, built in 1958 to accommodate the growing East Meadow secondary school population, and think of the many gym classes, football practices and games from the days of my youth. The most prominent feature of the school is the large gymnasium, recently named the Frank Saracino Sports Complex. Frank was a social studies teacher who later became a principal and superintendent of schools. I reflect on how he was always good to Dennis, Jeanne and me, and, as a member of the Holy Family School Board of Education, especially important to Mom. I pedal around the streets along the west side of the school grounds, past the temple, which abutted our practice field, and enter the school's west parking lot. Gazing at the building, the first thing I spot is the corner classroom, my homeroom for four years. From the window of that room I used to envy the family in the house closest to the parking lot. They had an outdoor pool. On so many hot September and June days, I wanted so badly to leave that sweltering room, hop the fence and take a dip. Around to the front of the school, the north side of the building, I see my second floor classroom where Ms. Dorothy Fronefield so patiently taught me Latin for three years. I recall her saying, "Agricola malum est," or something like that, "The farmer is wicked." I peer through the front door of the building and notice the fairly new Clarke Hall of Achievement. There are not many plaques are on the wall. Hopefully that'll change because many Clarke alumni have made significant achievements over the years. (Note: Interestingly, a week later, I received a letter from Clarke's principal informing me that, based on my work with students in Nicaragua and other poor places throughout the world, I am to be the tenth inductee into the Clarke Hall of Achievement on October 17, 2015). I glance to the right and see the main office and recall the hot August day in 1961 when Mom and I walked all the way there to get me enrolled. Mrs. Gray was the principal's secretary back then. She gave us all the papers we had to fill out. Mom was the one who suggested that I sign up for Latin. *"It'll be a big help to you throughout life, Peter. You'll see."* I think she was right. The roots of English words intrigued me, and years later I had a much easier time than most law students mastering the Latin phrases commonly used by attorneys in legal briefs. I have a few favorites: "Res ipsa loquitur," "the thing speaks for itself;" "Res judicata," "a thing decided;" "Nunc pro tunc," "Now for then." After registering, Mom and I made the long, 1.8-mile, hot trek back home the usual way, on foot. I remember arriving back home relieved that I was now a Clarke Ram, and registering was "res judicata" for me.

My bike ride continues through the section of small houses just east of Clarke called Post Acres. I notice that many of those tiny dwellings, like so many Levitt houses, have been expanded and dormered in every direction, making them quite different from the Post Acres houses of half a century ago. I remember how there was an economic division among some of us back then. The Post Acres families were mostly blue-collar families, with fathers who often worked two jobs just to earn the family's daily bread. Same with many of us who hailed from the Levitt neighborhoods. East of Clarke was the neighborhood called Birchwood, with its bigger homes, larger properties, and greater family incomes. Those households included CPA's, dentists, stockbrokers, people with more education, newer, more expensive cars, and more political clout. Birchwood kids wore nicer clothes, rode better bikes and took family vacations to far-away places.

Though I had some good friends from Birchwood back then, I was quite happy to be from good old Levittown.

I begin noticing that my time is growing short. I told Kathleen that I'd meet her at her mom's in Rockville Centre by 4 p.m. and it was already 2:30. So I make my way through the "C" section, with streets named Cameo, Crown, Crystal and Choir, passing #33 Choir, where my good friend Tony Acerra's mom, age 94, still lives. I speed down Carman Avenue and check to see if the Carman Avenue pool is open and am pleased to see that it is. I lock my faithful Urbanite to the fence and conjure up a small fib. In order to enter the pool, I need a pool tag, and since I haven't lived in Levittown for many years, I don't have one to show to the teenage gatekeeper. "Hi. I'm from Twig Lane (Actually, not a lie. I used to live there) and I don't have a pool tag with me (Also not a lie. I don't have one). Any chance I could take a swim anyway?" The teenage gatekeeper is in charge and says, "Well, I really shouldn't. But since tomorrow is the last day for the pool to be open, I'll let you in. But just this one time, understand." I thank him, proceed to the men's room, change into my suit and crank out 50 laps, 1250 yards, something I do every day either in the L.I. Sound, the ocean, or at the Suffolk Community College pool in Brentwood. I really enjoy swimming in the Levittown pools on these annual visits. It brings back important reminders of the old days, of diving off the 10' high board, the smell of the chlorine, and the bronzed bodies we all sported back then.

I thank the young gatekeeper on the way out and notice 754 Carman Avenue directly across the street. It's the childhood home of Alice McPartland, a special friend from high school. I beam as I remember telling her how much she looked like Natalie Wood back then, and how happy I was to skate with her a few times around the Roosevelt Field ice rink one night. I didn't bring a lunch so, hungry from the miles I've cycled, I stop at Venere's, a nice looking Italian restaurant at the nearby Carman Avenue stores and see if I can get a slice. Venere's was formerly a simple pizza place, known then as the Pizza Oven. Many Clarke kids, like Kevin Buckley, worked there as pie men and slices were fifteen cents. It's now an upscale place so I'm not sure if they'll sell me just one slice. "Can I get one slice please?" "Sure," the young man says. I offer three dollars, thinking that a slice is two-something. He takes two dollars, hands me back one dollar, then gives me my slice and fifteen cents change. A slice is only $1.85. Not bad. I finish quickly and then decide to make no further stops. Time is getting to be of the essence so I have to wrap up this trip. I continue down Carman, past a few more streets where I once knew so many. Whizzing by the Rottkamp's farm on Carman Avenue, I stop at Salisbury Park Drive, where to the left I notice hundreds of new condos that sit upon land that was once the Nassau County Jail's honor farm. Inmates were allowed to till the fields and work the farm, planting, tending to and harvesting cabbage, cauliflower and other vegetables, without being fenced in. They never ran away, though they could have. They probably were getting out soon and didn't want to jeopardize their release. So the old jail farm is now condos. I circle back through the "M" section, Jim Kahrs' house on Melody Lane, then by Martin, Mist and Merry lanes, winding my way back to Stewart Avenue and head east, toward the Wantagh Parkway. I pause briefly at the solid granite wall that protects passersby from the parkway 20 feet below, recalling that it didn't stop Les Joy from tightrope- walking across it as a kid. He was always the neighborhood daredevil. On the east side of the overpass, I stop and look at what we used to call "Boos Brothers Hill," a tiny hill down which we used to sled. I bike down the hill, across the bumpy grassy area, and follow a short trail out to Rim Lane where I see the former house of Jimmy Montalto. Jimmy went to St. Ignatius with Robert, Dennis and me, and then to Chaminade HS with Robert. The Montalto family was a stop on my paper route. I remember the good smells emanating from their kitchen. Mrs. Montalto was always cooking something. Next door is the former home of an elderly woman Mom and I called "the Irish lady." We didn't know her name, but she had a thick brogue and was very generous. The Tablet, a Catholic weekly newspaper was ten cents, and this nice woman gave me $.35 a week, ten cents for the paper, and a whole quarter for a tip. She had an electric mower, the kind that had a long cord attached and was plugged into the house. She was too old to mow so I decided to apply the values Mom taught me and volunteered to help her out. I wanted to return the kindness she showed me for so long with her generous tips. She agreed to my mowing her lawn, "but only if I can pay you, laddie." I mowed her lawn whenever it needed it, and, since it was a small lawn, was usually done in the blink of an eye. Though I didn't ask for money, I was surprised when she paid me $5! I'd mowed much larger lawns for less money, and Mom and I agreed this was far too much. I was directed not to accept it. The Irish lady would have none of that, and said I could no longer mow her lawn unless I accepted her terms. So I mowed. I always wondered what happened to that nice Irish lady, and surprisingly, I was about to find out. As I pass by the Irish lady's house, an elderly man appears and begins to do a little weeding. I stop and ask, "How are you, sir? How's the neighborhood?" He answers in an Irish brogue saying, "I'm fine here son. I've been here for many years. Things are mostly the same." I wonder, "It's been more than 50 years since I've mowed this lawn. Could this man and the Irish lady be related?" I mention that I used to be a paperboy and mow the lawn here and of my relationship more than half a century ago with the kind Irish lady. He said, "Oh. You mean Mrs. Gallagher." I learn from this Irishman that the Irish lady's sons live next door. "They lived in her house after she passed away, but they sold to me and moved next door, to a bigger house." I didn't catch the relationship, but I believe this gentleman with the brogue may have been a relative also. This whole story puts my mind at ease about what happened to my good friend, the Irish lady, from so many years ago. I thank him for the chat and bike on, down Rim Lane, make my right on Twig and in a matter of seconds I'm back to where this grand tour began. I'm happy to see that my car, parked near "the weeds," is still there, untouched. No problems. Still the same safe neighborhood I remember.

Mission accomplished. While getting a little exercise, I'm able to enjoy the very special places of my youth, the places where I first felt comfortable, where I formed so many relationships and learned so much. For that, I thank Mom. By her hard work and determination, she made all that possible for my brothers, my sister and me. It's been a great day. I drive away, eagerly looking forward to my next sentimental journey.

ABOUT THE AUTHOR

Peter White, the second son of Kay White, is a retired teacher and attorney currently living in Centerport, NY. Due in large part to his many years of volunteer work with students in Nicaragua and other poor regions, he was honored to be named 1999 New York State Teacher of the Year and 1999 National Teacher of the Year Finalist. Since his retirement in 2008, he spends much of his time writing, speaking, and working on sustainable projects for the poor and needy with the charitable, not-for-profit organization he formed in 2006 called Friends of Students for 60000, Inc. For more information about his group's poverty initiatives, see www.fsf60k.org, or contact pedro831@optonline.net.

Peter at the White House with President Clinton at the 1999 National Teacher of the Year ceremony.